STUDIES IN MAJOR LITERARY AUTHORS

Edited by

William E. Cain
Professor of English
Wellesley College

A ROUTLEDGE SERIES

Studies in Major Literary Authors

William E. Cain, *General Editor*

No Place for Home

Spatial Constraint and Character Flight in the Novels of Cormac McCarthy

Jay Ellis

Routledge
Taylor & Francis Group
New York London

Routledge
Taylor & Francis Group
605 Third Avenue,
New York, NY 10017

Routledge
Taylor & Francis Group
2 Park Square,
Milton Park, Abingdon,
Oxon, OX14 4RN

© 2006 by Taylor & Francis Group, LLC
Routledge is an imprint of the Taylor & Francis Group, an informa business

ISBN13: 978-0-415-97734-0 (hbk)
ISBN13: 978-0-415-80293-2 (pbk)

Library of Congress Cataloging-in-Publication Data

Ellis, Jay.
    No place for home : spatial constraint and character flight in the novels of Cormac McCarthy / by Jay Ellis.
        p. cm. -- (Studies in major literary authors)
    Includes bibliographical references and index.
    ISBN 0-415-97734-7 (acid-free paper)
      1. McCarthy, Cormac, 1933---Criticism and interpretation. 2. McCarthy, Cormac, 1933---Settings. 3. Personal space in literature. 4. Home in literature. 5. Family in literature. 6. Men in literature. 7. Setting (Literature) I. Title. II. Studies in major literary authors (Unnumbered)

PS3563.C337Z65 2006
813'.54--dc22
                                          2006008045

Visit the Taylor & Francis Web site at
http://www.taylorandfrancis.com

and the Routledge Web site at
http://www.routledge-ny.com

For Suzanne and Henry.
And for my mother and father.

Contents

Acknowledgments

I am deeply indebted to Rick Wallach, Edwin Arnold, Dianne Luce, John Wegner, Nell Sullivan, David Holloway, Robert Jarrett, Georg Guillemin, and the many others whose dedication to McCarthy scholarship makes it possible to see farther into the work of a living author. The volume of serious scholarship on this author creates frequent situations where critics arrive independently at similar interpretations; I hope to have credited them all as often as reflects their influence on my reading of McCarthy, and as fairly as possible where several sources provide similar, if independent, ideas.

I am grateful to Josephine Hendin and Pat Hoy for advice in the early stages of this project—especially to Pat for the encouragement leading to major revisions in this book. I owe particular thanks to Natalka Palczynski for an enlivening collaboration amidst a heavy load of teaching. In revision, Peter Josyph, Piper Murray, Dieter Boxmann, and Damian Doyle provided invaluable advice. David Holloway's example proved to be priceless.

Without the ability of my parents to see beyond the constraints they left behind, I would never have begun this project. Without the patience and understanding of my wife, Suzanne Blossfeld Ellis, I might never have finished. Finally, it is my young son Henry to whom I owe the constant renewal of my sense of humor, and the knowledge that work and play go together.

Chapter One

Spatial Constraint and Character Flight in McCarthy

> [O]ur "Lexicon" would look upon literature as the thing added
> —the little white houses in a valley that was once a wilderness.
>
> (Kenneth Burke)[1]

GROUNDING

Blood Meridian led me to my first work on the writing of Cormac McCarthy, in simple admiration for the aesthetic achievement reached by his language. There, the counterpoint between speech and action, between the judge's high oratory and bloody war written over a landscape of "neuter austerity" (*BM* 247), suggested some correspondence between Holden's philosophy and McCarthy's descriptive technique. Then I noticed that, beyond the judge's oratory, this author's powers of description, the unusual word that turns out to be the perfect choice, his control of language at the level of sentences and paragraphs—these attributes of McCarthy's remarkable style appeared more often than not, and most powerfully, in his descriptions of setting. In McCarthy settings, language spreads a surface of dry lakebed description, or by contrast, rolls in waves of words laden with narrative import. This led me to begin a book reading the settings, particularly houses, graves, and fences, in the novels.

How could one narrator so regularly veer back and forth in descriptive habits, first refusing any human terms of perception and comprehension, but then claiming mythic consequence and alluding to layers of significance? In reading the other novels, it became obvious that McCarthy relies more on setting than on plot, or even character. Beyond the length and frequency of passages describing woods, hillsides, deserts, and broken-down houses, the style lavished on these descriptions highlights their importance. Even the title of McCarthy's latest book, *No Country for Old Men*, points to setting.

McCarthy presents his settings through language not usually allowed the characters, in neither their speech nor their thoughts and feelings. He instead lavishes words on space and place, reaching in those descriptions what Denis Donoghue calls his "high passages." These high passages must "speak up for values the characters could not express; for regions, places, landscapes, vistas, movements of the seasons, trees, rain, snow, dawn, sunset, outer and inner weather; and for times not our time" ("Dream Work" 8). One of Donoghue's metaphors, however, has much to do with characters: "inner weather" is a subjective condition. McCarthy characters do experience inner weather, even if we seldom receive any direct sense of that weather. Rather, it is in the "high passages" of McCarthy's style, especially in descriptions of outer weather—of setting—that we may extrapolate from the style some sense of a character's interiority.

McCarthy's descriptive modes therefore enable the inference of psychology in a style that refuses (usually) to indulge in standard psychological techniques, such as first person, interior monologue, free indirect discourse, or even direct indications of psychology by a narrator. (The sudden frequency of "He thought about that" (*NCFOM* 172) and similar indications of character thought in *No Country for Old Men* generally stop short of indicating what, exactly, the character is thinking; Bell's extended confession complicates this assessment and must be dealt with later.) If not psychology itself, the limits of human epistemology, can then be inferred even from settings that indicate a mere surface landscape oblivious to human existence, occurring at the farthest possible remove from the interiority of characters.

Those descriptions of a world oblivious to human movement, let alone feeling, simply indicate the human condition from a distant view—a Hitchcockian God's eye (that in Hitchcock's strongest terms, is simply the uncaring eye of a hovering bird, and thus an eye of nature unassuaged by anthropocentrism). The famous "neuter austerity" of *Blood Meridian* does not necessarily negate the kid's moral dilemma, but it does remind us that such a dilemma can only be felt at an intermediate level of existence, above that level of geological time and "optical democracy" (*BM* 247) in the desert, but below the higher orders of reasoning at which the judge refuses human morality. Then such a setting reinforces the fact that the kid's moral dilemma cannot be reconciled with a judge of the false coins of human meaning, who claims access to higher knowledge. The judge's knowledge reaches so far beyond good and evil that it demands that the reader either condemn him as a moral outlaw—a devil—or find some other solution, such as an Eastern conception of a universe in which good and evil prove illusory. That landscape of "neuter austerity" makes it difficult (impossible for some readers) to keep hold of the kid's dilemma as anything real and powerful in the book.

Conversely, those passages of descriptive setting that ring with human meanings amount to more than perceptive feints on the part of a wholly disinterested narration, and instead simply obtain their validity only at the level of human experience below that allowed the narration and some vatic secondary characters.[2] These settings can nonetheless grant our limits of perception some meaningful connection with nature. (This can be true even as some such descriptions serve to distance us from such a connection, or lead us to question the validity of that connection experienced by a character.) They simply reserve for that connection a relatively local space—if we can remember that human mythology remains, in geological, let alone universal time, an enormously recent phenomenon. *The Orchard Keeper* provides an early example of this.

A chestnut tree hit by lightening is described as having "erupted to the heart" before it fells Arthur Ownby with part of its split trunk. "A slab fell away with a long hiss like a burning mast tilting seaward. He is down. A clash of shields rings and Valkyrie descend with cat's cries to bear him away" (*TOK* 172). The cat's cries are those of a real cat, yet we are allowed to listen in on how they are heard in mythic terms. Are those terms Ownby's or the narrators? The passage remains unclear on this. But McCarthy does not include here any description of setting to undermine the validity of the allusion—even if it reads as a bit of a stretch.

Ownby lives, lying unconscious for days in the rain-soaked woods, while the narrative moves off with other characters, so it is unclear how much time passes before Ownby comes to. But a flooding rain described in the meantime lasts seven days. Still, the narrative refuses to describe Ownby's surroundings as indifferent to his fall. Instead, the italicized return to him suggests that some magical connection, between the woods and this old man described in the terms of Norse myth, remains:

> *The wind had died and the night woods* in their faintly breathing quietude *held no sound but the* kind *rainfall [. . .] With grass in his mouth the old man sat up and peered about him, heard the rain* mendicant-voiced, soft chanting *in that dark* gramarye *that summons the earth to bridehood.* (*TOK* 184, my emphasis)

The personification of nature here remains rare in McCarthy. But it does not disappear in the later books. And in this scene, not only is the rain-fall "*kind*" and "*soft chanting*" in the voice of a beggar—a metaphor revers-ing the usual differential between setting and character in McCarthy—but it speaks also in "*that dark gramarye*" that *The American Heritage Dictionary* tells us is the language of "[o]ccult learning; magic." This space, then, is the space of Frazer's *Golden Bough*, where humans make sense of their surround-ings through magical belief in correspondences between themselves and the dark world surrounding them. In *The Orchard Keeper*, at least, McCarthy says nothing to suggest that such beliefs are false within the biological space of humans and flora, though we may assume that Ownby possesses some vatic knowledge uncommon among most of McCarthy's major characters.

Such correspondences remain limited in McCarthy, and they rarely appear through the pathetic fallacy. As I reread the novels, the natural world depicted in them most often seemed oblivious to the activities of human beings. Nevertheless, McCarthy's settings indirectly suggested the interiority of characters, by presenting us with a regular conflict between character and setting. After narrowing my focus to the setting in the other novels, I began to discern underlying rules governing McCarthy's descriptions of space.

Describe few houses of reliable construction; where the house would stand, reveal nothing of a full family inside. Describe regular problems around graves and burial. Have the characters cut, mend, place, and burn for fuel the very fences that would constrain their movements. The ease of iden-tifying three particularly common types of spatial constraint—houses, graves, and fences—lent the early versions of this study a much-needed focus.

In reaction to those failed constraints, characters must take flight, or they must circle around within a larger constraint of space that usually can-not contain them. All protagonists (through eight of nine novels, at least) are young men. Fathers are gone, incinerated, hanged, corrupt, or emascu-lated—unless we count the judge. *No Country for Old Men* might seem to ignore these last two rules as it begins with a lone male protagonist who proves to be thirty-six, and who then gives way to the true protagonist, an older man. But Sheriff Bell (surprisingly, only fifty-seven) has lost his child and thus his role of a father (which he loses again in retirement). The novel's final vision of his long-dead father only reinforces his role as a son, if not indeed an orphan.

Protagonists, therefore, must be orphans, in one way or several ways. Finally, let characters die in the open, or oddly contained in death, discarded in pits, bags, trees, outhouses, and boxes. Noting the regularity of these turns in the novel's plots, of these character conditions, and of descriptions of setting, the novels all seemed to be about constraints of space—ineffectual or otherwise—about the flight of characters, when they could fly—and about some problem with families behind them.

This last interpretation, however, came with difficulty, though it extended from complications in interpreting the many broken houses in the books. Because of McCarthy's general rule against direct psychology (at that time broken regularly only in *Suttree*), it was still the case that one had to make reasonable inferences of character motivation by close reading descriptions of space—unless one wanted to interpret character dreams. But because the salient feature in McCarthy's style still seemed to me to be his descriptions of space and place, along with the absence of regular psychologizing, dreams seemed better to read for only one part of a character's motivations. Dreams in McCarthy point more to delusions, beliefs, and provisional truths, more than to larger truths; they indicate a key part of character motivation, but not all of that motivation, much of which McCarthy places beyond even the unconscious knowledge of his characters.[3]

Dreams usually place protagonists out in the open, for instance, and in this mode, they certainly indicate the need for flight in the characters. Yet, John Grady's dreams of horses do not tell us everything about his first quest to Mexico; for an understanding deeper than John Grady's dreams, we need only observe him (as we will in Chapter Six) in his grandfather's study. I began to think that son and father trouble lay behind much of the flight of McCarthy's protagonists. In returning to *Blood Meridian*, and then attempting to make some sense out of the aesthetic problems posed by *No Country for Old Men*, I felt compelled to examine possibilities of spatial constraint and character flight at a further remove than the psychological tensions of literal fathers and sons. The resulting book remains an attempt to account for space and place in McCarthy, and an attempt to account for the similarity of character flight in his novels, even as the types of spatial constraint I examine grew beyond those of houses, graves, and fences.

This book therefore enacts a critical progression, from something relatively simple to something more complex. Beginning with the more manageable project of close reading a relatively small set of McCarthy's descriptive habits, I move to unavoidable inferences concerning the character motivation behind flight in these novels. Eventually, *Blood Meridian* then demands a wider view: attention to space at several levels allows us to see how these novels address a variety of problems, from psychology, through history, and beyond history to problems of philosophy that stand outside human history (as McCarthy's work at the Santa Fe Institute, his few interviews, but more importantly his judge, all claim).

This movement is not, of course, linear and non-recursive. Looking back on the earlier close reading that began the project, I see more clearly how inferences of son and father trouble, for instance, unavoidably arise in reading *The Orchard Keeper*, and indeed, all the novels. And of course, the invaluable wealth of criticism quickly growing alongside McCarthy's continuing work has necessarily added to, and complicated, my views here.

If the results risk the fault of not laying out in immediately clear terms a nested set of theses regarding space in McCarthy, that is at least intentional: his novels continue to hold interest for me in their polyphonic and polysemantic quality. With a novelist whose obsessions run parallel with one another but at varying degrees of conscious intention, perhaps it is most suitable to follow an approach that itself develops alongside the progression of the novels themselves. My hope, then, is that the interpretive work here builds throughout the chapters.

It also made sense to me to add my interpretations only where they might be most useful. Excellent work on McCarthy's settings has already made my job easier here, as understandings of those settings under other theoretical lights has already been done elsewhere. If this book can contribute anything to that work, and to criticism focusing on the characters in the novels, it is perhaps in making the link between setting and character motivation. For this reason, for instance, I keep my remarks on McCarthy's famous "optical democracy" (*BM* 247), and on the more regularly ecocritical treatments of his settings, brief.[4]

Eventually, I will make some inferences toward biographical criticism. This too has been done with McCarthy's work, but with research on his life (and sometimes with access) that is beyond my expertise or reach. Dianne Luce, Edwin Arnold, and Wesley Morgan continue to trace connections between McCarthy's works and their likely correspondences—in both the books of other authors and the life of McCarthy.[5] Arnold has also shown an intriguing shift in McCarthy's image that corresponds to changes in his writing and in his reception. In a provocative study of the jacket photographs for the books, especially the series of photographs provided the press with the release of *All the Pretty Horses*, Arnold argues persuasively that McCarthy has tailored his image as much as his fiction ("Creating McCarthy").

I can only add to this burgeoning biographical criticism through my readings of the texts, only daring to suggest correspondences between the life and the art where textual evidence simply overwhelms an avoidance of what can otherwise become a critical fallacy. McCarthy's reputation for reclusivity apparently proves to be a mask; more accurately, he simply avoids the particular culture around literature, including interviews (beyond two exceptions in over forty years of publishing), panels and awards ceremonies, and even casual conversation about his work. Particularly as I lack any inside information on the life of this writer, whatever hints of anxiety I find in the novels and then might imagine originate in the author's life are of limited use to a fair understanding of the work. Instead, I hope to add to the trend in biographical criticism only an understanding of how descriptions of character flight from domesticity (in particular) and ineffectual spatial constraints of a domestic nature haunt these books, and how some of these anxieties might be creative extensions of something in life.

Even if relatively scant biographical information might tempt us to connect the son and father trouble I read in these novels to a similar level of tension in McCarthy's life, for instance, that seems to me a reductive enterprise for serious criticism. To wonder, for instance, if McCarthy Senior's employment with the TVA, or the author's naming of his first son, might rather express themselves in the novels in ways that exhibit much anxiety about fatherhood, simply assumes that life informs the work. It does not follow that the level of son and father anxiety present in that work accurately represents the author's life. True artists know how to make something more interesting and complex out of things that, in life, are all too often simple to the point of boredom.

The point here is rather to answer questions that arise within the work. I will therefore explore, and then attempt to connect, all the various iterations of constraint and flight that create a fundamental tension through these novels. Furthermore, the power of language in McCarthy persists, thankfully, such that the complexity of his ideas cannot be simplified to fit a single interpretive approach. Here this means that there are simply too many interesting types of spatial constraint to warrant limiting our view to the merely psychological, let alone the merely biographical. Ultimately, a progression of studies of space at various levels of interpretation will require a combined interpretive approach.

OVERVIEW

After outlining the chapters to follow, I will introduce the various types of spatial constraint that each chapter will then examine at greater length. Along the way, I will discuss some of the writers whose ideas on space regularly informed this study. Teri Witek's "Reeds and Hides: Cormac McCarthy's Domestic Spaces" remains indispensable as an early and incisive, if brief, study of houses in McCarthy; where my interpretation runs differently than Witek's is important to make clear. Closer to the intent of this study is

Richard Poirier's *A World Elsewhere: The Place of Style in American Literature*, which, without including McCarthy, provides a model of reading for intersections of style and spatial anxieties in a novel. Several McCarthy scholars have already led the way in reading spaces in the novels, particularly in historical terms. Finally, Patricia Nelson Limerick's reading of the perennial power of Frederick Jackson Turner's mythic geographical thesis on the "closing" of the American Frontier provides my work with *Blood Meridian* and *The Border Trilogy* necessary historical context.

Chapter Two then performs a close reading of *The Orchard Keeper*, thus beginning the larger argument with a focus on the specific constraints of houses, graves (improvised and otherwise), and a cemetery fence. From that reading, however, the interpretation toward some structural explanation for why McCarthy characters take flight begins to emerge. So, too, does the orphanage of John Wesley Rattner indicate early on that son and father trouble lies beneath much of the impetus to character flight in McCarthy's work.

In Chapter Three, a similar problem for Lester Ballard leads to a larger spatial conflict. *Child of God* describes a man's descent into hellish perversions of domesticity, but follows not so much his flight from his family as it does his desperate attempts to reclaim his family home—even as he can only repopulate an underground substitution for that home with the dead. The transgressions of Ballard become ironic, however, when we see the degree to which he is outcast from the community, further deprived of his senses, and forced outside even his paltry simulations of home life after these have been driven underground.

Chapter Four combines readings of son and father trouble in *Outer Dark*, *Suttree*, and *Blood Meridian*. Originally, I had found that *Blood Meridian* seemed to have nothing to do with the home, let alone with sons and fathers. And what had also struck me in that book—in both the judge's speeches and the narrative description—similarly stood out from the other novels: its astonishing scale. *Blood Meridian*'s literal and figurative spaces overwhelmed my method of reading for descriptions of attempted civilized spatial constraints. The judge spoke of nothing less than the order of the universe, even as he warned that no human mind could comprehend that order. The judge delivered these speeches alongside enjoinments to war as the ultimate game, and furthermore, McCarthy interleaved the judge's philosophy with descriptions of horrible deeds whose understatement only added to the reader's horror. These matters seemed beyond the scope of my original thesis.

The judge's philosophy simply demanded a different order of understanding spatial constraint—and resistance to that constraint—on a higher level than the bloody history the book also took as its partial source of origin. Even though the book detailed horrible deeds that can be found in history, its epigraphs and narrative warnings compel readers to go beyond a mere historical reading, let alone the psychological one which, at that time, never even occurred to me. But *Blood Meridian* certainly was about space. Its title pointed to it, its Epilogue described it, and the judge's many lectures regularly employed spatial tropes.

Meanwhile, it seemed impossible to reconcile the judge with any human value. (There still may not be such a way.) Yet, he obviously served some purpose beyond that of a negation, a devil, a darker precursor to Nietzsche. Of course, the first way to read that book had nothing to do with family, with home, and everything to do with questions far outside the home fires that in Freud (and in *Blood Meridian*), are the business of women.

But that is of course another way of noticing that the insistence with which *Blood Meridian* usually refuses to describe women in any but three ways—head-shot victims, vatic soothsayers, or prostitutes—actually demands that we consider the novel's uneasy relationship to home and hearth. The shortest chapter in *Blood Meridian* actually describes women in a different role, as it follows the attempt by Sarah Borginnis and "the women at the crossing" to civilize James Robert (*BM* 256–259). Including its space break, the chapter barely runs two and a half pages, and the work of "The Borginnis"—so noted with an article as to suggest that she alone carries the entire burden of civilizing female influence—fails. James Robert wriggles out of his clothes and heads to the river to nearly drown and, rescued by the judge, return to the world of this most masculine of books baptized back into naked depravity, a probable sex slave for Holden. So much for home life in *Blood Meridian*.

Nevertheless, it was easy to see that the kid left his home on the run from another vitiated family: "The mother dead these fourteen years did incubate in her own bosom the creature who would carry her off. The father never speaks her name, the child does not know it. He has a sister in this world that he will not see again" (*BM* 3). The odd syntax positions the infant kid in the guilty position of a matricide so ignorant as to recall Oedipus with a twist on the gender of the doomed parent. The kid did seem like an early, if rougher, John Grady Cole (combined with Jimmy Blevins, perhaps). And the judge does say to the kid, "Dont you know that I'd have loved you like a son?" (*BM* 306)—about twenty-seven pages before he loves him to death in the jakes.

In other words, I began to see through rereading that not only in the technique (avoiding diacritical marks, avoiding direct psychology, avoiding names), but in the subject matter, *Blood Meridian* shared all of the concerns that arise in the other novels, even if many of them arise less frequently, or with less emphasis, in this singular book in the McCarthy oeuvre. McCarthy's characters bore a remarkably common anxiety that, although it led to various goals, arose from similar circumstances and expressed overlapping origins. The novels therefore expressed repeated concerns around space, even as some focused more on the concrete domestic constraints (and security) of the home, and some focused more on the wider spaces that promised freedom (whether allowing it or not) to a young man on a horse. All the novels address tensions between freedom and security, lawless space and confining place. They simply do so in different ways, and at different levels. And in many cases, various spatial conflicts not only coexist, but also connect with one another.

Even *Blood Meridian*, with its focus on larger questions of history and philosophy, continued to revolve around the kid's moral dilemma, and that in turn presented itself in the odd son and father relationship between the kid and the judge. This fit the loose pattern of the other novels even as it stretched that pattern to allow for larger themes. In all the novels, problems of home life, jettisoning sons off into wandering adventures, connect to disputes over national borders and moral boundaries, which in turn can only be fully understood as provisional historical and moral disputes (even if they reach far back), and these disputes are themselves swallowed up in a universe that cares nothing for human concerns at all.

So, too, in *Blood Meridian*. The kid sits at the fire where the judge sketches the rusting "footpiece from a suit of armor hammered out in a shop in Toledo three centuries before," only to squash "it into a ball of foil and [pitch] it into the fire" (*BM* 140). The moment first points to Holden as a parodic agent of the Enlightenment, recording things in his book only to destroy them. And not only nature, but also history, comes under his study and destructive control.[6] But the scene that follows this immediately takes another step beyond Melville, as the men of the gang, represented by Webster, come under the judge's figurative heel. This in turn leads to the judge's dismissal of any fundamental difference between the "old Hueco" Indian whose likeness became "unwittingly chained" to him by the judge's portrait (*BM* 141).

I read this as a warning against fitting the judge too tightly to one historical moment, and even to the constraints of a movement so large as European Enlightenment. This difficulty, of fitting *Blood Meridian* to one mold, becomes even more evident as this scene continues with the judge's parable of the harnessmaker in the Alleghenies. (Indeed, this parable, in which the man's trick of dressing as an Indian to beg from travelers, follows one of the gang's questions as to the identity of the Indians that once lived in the area of their encampment.) Holden's parable revolves around identity and race, and a biblical sense of morality, but also ultimately leads to a problem between a man and his son. After the harnessmaker's crime of killing a traveler (despite the man's apparent conversion of him), he lies dying and calls to his son, confesses, and asks the son to forgive him.

> And the son said that he forgave him if it was his to do so and the old man said that it was his to do so and then he died.
>
> But the boy was not sorry for he was jealous of the dead man and before he went away he visited that place and cast away the rocks and dug up the bones and scattered them in the forest and then he went away. He went away to the west and he himself became a killer of men. (*BM* 144–145)

This parable cannot be treated fully without noting its context: its context in the novel as a whole (at least as an "answer" to the question regarding the identity of the Indians), and its context as a parable of a white man assuming a "savage" identity. That the story ends with a son's disinterment of the traveler's bones echoes through this novel to *Suttree*, where the father is too easy to connect to McCarthy Senior, in his role as the lead attorney for the Tennessee Valley Authority. And indeed, the last we hear of the son, that "[h]e went away to the west and he himself became a killer of men" fits the kid too well.

Thus, in the brief span of six pages, the concerns of *Blood Meridian* sweep down from history, up to philosophy, and back down to history, only to rise up to the opacity of a parable that itself drops down to the psychological tensions that power not only the relationship between the son and the harnessmaker father, but also the kid and the judge, Suttree and his father, John Wesley Rattner and his father—indeed, all the sons and fathers of all nine novels, if not Cormac McCarthy and his father as well. In my final chapter, I address some possibilities for fitting studies of various levels of space (such as the domestic, as well as the historical, etc.) into a comprehensive view. But in the meantime, it became apparent that I needed to address more than one type of spatial conflict in some of the books. In the case of *Blood Meridian*, this required some treatment in two different chapters.

Rereading *Outer Dark*, of course, raised the question of son and father trouble so prominently—particularly through the wordplay around names that I will explore—that I could no longer avoid this path in attempting to answer questions about the plots of the novels that themselves would not go away. Why tell the story of a father watching his own child throat-cut? Why is it worse to be a baby in a McCarthy novel even than to be an animal? Lost children haunt more than one of these novels. Fathers are often missing, and mothers too; it is the father, however, that seems most to haunt these protagonists. After my initial interest first in the sheer aesthetic power of these novels, then in the structural reading of space and character tensions, more quotidian questions began to nag me.

As I will argue in Chapter Four, the son and father tension most obvious in *Outer Dark* continues notably through *Suttree*, and on into *Blood Meridian*. There I hope to clarify that at least one thread of anxiety has powered the anxieties around more domestic constraints of space. Certainly, son and father trouble similarly haunt *The Border Trilogy* and the other novels as well. But in these three novels, we can follow a striking progression of this tension far enough to set up my later reading of the structural shift to myth that ends *No Country for Old Men*.

Chapter Five attempts to interpret those larger orders of magnitude in *Blood Meridian*. Even though, as the judge warns, "the order within [the universe] is not constrained by any latitude in its conception to repeat what exists in one part in any other part," there remains the work of understanding the larger spatial tensions in that book. That McCarthy actually connects problems of orphanage and character flight to larger historical and philosophical problems gives his novels greater depth. Because *Blood Meridian* is also about myth, and about history, I examine these types of demarcations in Chapter Five by inquiring into the various meanings of "meridian" in the book, ultimately by moving from a philosophical reading of the novel to a historical reading of its Epilogue.

In Chapter Six, I examine what begins to appear in more genre-directed terms: the various roles played by the young men McCarthy follows across the American Southwest and Mexican North after its transformation by the action and then Epilogue of *Blood Meridian*. John Grady Cole, and Billy and Boyd Parham, can be read in genre terms that have always influenced the myth of the cowboy but that derive from older myths. In fact, these characters may be better understood apart from those aspects of American Western genre that have made *The Border Trilogy* more popular than previous McCarthy novels. Particularly by examining the struggle for intermediary domestic spaces, the continuing preoccupation with fences, and the problems of burial in these books, it is possible to see the trilogy's protagonists as knights, squires, courtiers, and ultimately a would-be husband.

Chapter Seven continues this combination of spatial reading and genre study in *No Country for Old Men*. As we read through this remarkably structured novel, the tension increases between the fetishism of its Western noir beginning and its structural collapse into jeremiad. *No Country for Old Men* again reveals the fractured and disappointed domesticity behind its main character's actions. Along the way, the domestic spaces abandoned by its apparent, and then its real, protagonists again point to problems between the son and the father, and heighten our sense that one of the many ironies in the hearts of McCarthy characters is their ignorance of what constitutes the plausible domestic responsibility required to find a home in the world. The structural analysis in this chapter follows the unusual shift from one genre to another, until we follow the novel into another instance of a McCarthy dream world.

Chapter Eight will serve as an extension and summary addressing all the novels. *No Country for Old Men* also poses questions about the relation of free will to fate, in a boiled-flat novel that rewards deeper reading for philosophical content, if on an aesthetic level it continues to disappoint. Ironically, the questions deepen even as the structure fails, when Bell's unease about his own behavior is answered only by a nostalgic dream of his father. It is in this structural collapse, surprisingly enough, that connections between son and father anxiety and larger spatial constraints on free will become more apparent. This leads into my concluding chapter, where I will review such connections in the other books, and argue for a structure of critical approaches to McCarthy allowing fuller attention to problems of space as they occur at various orders of magnitude.

BROKEN HOUSES AND UNBURIED CHARACTERS

Types of architectural spatial constraint in McCarthy are not limited to those of domesticity. The house—its spatial configurations, both its promise of safety and its limits on freedom—is the most common type. There are, however, also prisons, cemeteries, hospitals, and insane asylums with which the characters contend. But houses create the most recognizable constraint on space in relation to character flight in these novels. Lester Ballard's flight from the hospital has more to do with his homelessness, and his desire to recreate a home, than it does with the confines of the hospital itself, even as his flight toward a desired home stands as an exception in the novels. In McCarthy novels generally, houses do not generally establish civilized places as much as they simply constrain character movement—or in some cases would do so, if they were stable enough. Character movement therefore reveals itself most obviously in flight from this particular form of constraint.

Because the varieties of houses and house-like structures that serve both to shelter and repel McCarthy characters are rich and strange, I will use the word generally for any human construction of interior space, and be more specific when McCarthy is. From the dictionary, "[a] structure serving as a dwelling for one or more persons, especially for a family" is optimistic as a definition of a McCarthy house. "Something, such as a burrow or shell, that serves as a shelter or habitation for a wild animal" better suits many McCarthy abodes.

"A dwelling for a group of people, such as students or members of a religious community" makes a good, if ironic, description of many of Cornelius Suttree's haunts. After a priest wakes the sleeping Suttree from his rest on a church pew, this house's implicit claims for special designation are dismissed. The priest tells him, "God's house is not exactly the place to take a nap." "It's not God's house," is Suttree's reply (*S* 255). This from a man who, having shunned his family's fallen mansion, lives in a house*boat*. Suttree's complaint rings true, however, as this house (church) that claims to harbor the homeless actually charges spiritual rent, asking Suttree for more than he is willing to give: confession.

In notable instances, however, spatial constraints on characters take a very different form, without being so obvious to them or to the reader: the earth itself. I follow the preoccupation with improper burial in *The Orchard Keeper* with a study of both houses and caves in *Child of God*. Graves present an odd example of spatial constraint. It might seem ridiculous to suggest that a grave functions as a constraint on a character's movement, but in McCarthy a grave does not always do so successfully, such as when the harnessmaker's son disinters the murdered traveler (*BM* 141). What would seem to be the final resting place for characters becomes as ambiguous in its reliability as do McCarthy houses. There is also a regular problem with burial in McCarthy novels. One character with a particularly close relationship to the dead nearly finds himself constrained forever in the earth, in a natural enclosure that is both a kind of house and premature grave.

Lester Ballard, McCarthy's necrophilic murdering *Child of God*, temporarily escapes the law by hiding in a cave. He then becomes stuck in what is described as "a small room with a thin shaft of actual daylight leaning in from the ceiling. It occurred to him only now that he might have passed other apertures to the upper world in the nighttime and not known it" (*COG* 188). Ballard, McCarthy's darkest character, has reached in this passage a lower world opposite that "upper" one evidenced by the "thin shaft of actual daylight." In this lower world, what would be a house is also a grave:

> In the night he heard hounds and called to them but the enormous echo of his voice in the cavern filled him with fear and he would not call again. He heard the mice scurry in the dark. Perhaps they'd nest in his skull, spawn their tiny bald and mewling whelps in the lobed caverns where his brain had been. His bones polished clean as eggshells, centipedes sleeping in their marrowed flutes, his ribs curling slender and whitely like a bone flower in the dark stone bowl. (*COG* 189)

This well illustrates the fundamental ambivalence of McCarthy's characters toward spatial constraint; Ballard's is a recurrent attitude (conscious and unconscious) in the novels. They fear and yet desire containment. In most of the characters, the fear is stronger than the desire; therefore, they most regularly try to evade constraint. Ballard, however, has a particularly strong desire to create some form of home to replace the one he loses at the beginning of the book. The cave provides an ironic means of escape for him, an unwitting movement to burial before death, rather than to the home he has tried to reclaim.

What Ballard chooses and endures in his ambivalent search for a new home takes him farther astray in behavior than other McCarthy characters. But a study of the settings from which they regularly flee suggests a recurring fear: a fear of becoming one with what contains one's body. The cave that traps Ballard is at first promising, a "small room" substitute for the barn and house he loses in the novel's beginning. This "small room," however, then threatens to become a grave, in which Ballard's body itself becomes both house-like and cave-like. Both whelping pen and "lobed caverns," his brain as home is similarly unhomelike, being at once a domestic residence for rodents, and a cave. His ribs are then "a bone flower" in an oddly domestic decoration, set as they are in "the dark stone bowl" of that cave (*COG* 188–189).

In this extreme example, variations in McCarthy's set of spatial constraints become conflated. Cave is grave is house, and, finally, something else. After the description is decorated by the ironic feminine touch of Ballard's ribs contained as a flower, his only hope is to be rescued by some fecund power in this dark earth. To be birthed from this dark cave seems to require an external assistance—a feminine one: "He'd cause to wish and he did wish for some brute midwife to spald him from his rocky keep"

(*COG* 189). The conflation now includes the earth as womb, and the origin
of ambivalence is as palpable here as is Ballard's "rocky keep." His place of
rebirth is already the type of place he is destined to die in, a "keep;" Ballard
eventually dies in a mental institution that, in McCarthy's brief description,
resembles a medieval prison.

In *Child of God*'s cave passage, McCarthy's rendering of contrasting
images of shelter and constraint allows us to infer the extreme ambivalence Ballard feels toward his most unhomelike home. Both the desire for a
home and the fear of a grave pass through this alembic of setting, and the
distilled ambivalence is simply a purer form of what is suggested throughout McCarthy's work. Most of his major characters are deeply ambivalent
toward any form of spatial constraint, so the fact that our recognition of
this depends on reading the settings in which we find them adds irony
to their predicaments. Houses regularly entrap them, in the few scenes in
which they are even housed. Problems the characters have with both houses
and graves suggest commingled anxieties about domesticity, entrapment,
and death, and thus houses and graves are regularly conflated.

Failures of the ultimate constraint on the human body in death haunt
these novels nearly as much as do insufficient houses. In *The Orchard
Keeper*, we see a dead man put away in an insecticide pit; later, upon discovery, his bones are handed over in a small bag. *Outer Dark* disinters the
dead from a churchyard, hangs a man in a tree, and leaves a baby's bones
in the cold ashes of a campfire. *Child of God* entombs several victims, wax-
museum style, in a secret cave; the killer is dissected and then scraped into
another bag. *Suttree* includes a midnight unauthorized burial at sea (as it
were), the body weighed down with chains. *Blood Meridian* hangs babies
on tree limbs, and follows the protagonist to his rape, murder, mutilation,
and abandonment in an outhouse. *All the Pretty Horses* suggests that a murdered boy's body is merely left in the desert. *The Crossing* expends significant time on the unsuccessful repatriation of a brother's bones. *Cities of the
Plain* softens, its hero dying in a packing crate but retrieved by a friend. *No
Country for Old Men* begins with the discovery of drug dealers dead in the
desert, slumped over in their trucks and lying out in the open, and then
discovers a murdered salesman in the trunk of his recovered stolen car.

The ultimate spatial constraint for the body is a coffin, yet most of
the many dead we encounter in McCarthy novels never enter that container. Improperly buried people create problems in several of the novels,
as people without homes are unlikely to receive proper burial: the body
on the move in life becomes the body that is refused a proper container

in death. The movement that puts so many McCarthy characters abroad often begins with a domestic failure, but it also regularly depends on a significant break in a fence.

UNFENCED AND ON THE ROAD

The failure of domesticity spurs characters to the road in McCarthy's novels, reinforcing a second order of conflict between inner and outer constructions of space that are larger, even social and historical. This conflict often presents itself through larger spaces created by fences and escaped by roads. That second order is evident in tensions between putative outdoor freedom (whether on the supposedly open range of the American Southwest or within a more vertiginous wilderness of Appalachia), and the historical reality of landscape.

Land is, in my use of the term, only land without human interaction. As soon as humans set foot on a particular piece of land, they render it into landscape. Maps only enact this transformation in theory, often allowing the realization of demarcations across land at some future moment. Or, as in the case of John Grady Cole, a map's apparent lack of feature suggests a consequent freedom of movement within a space not already encountered.[7] I will employ the terms *place* in opposition to *space* to distinguish between constraints on character movement (both indoor and outdoor) and the void of the natural world without human construction. Briefly, a *place* is a construction of the possibilities of *space* into a fixed set of circumstances. Place is ontological, space existential. Fences, however, both literal and figurative, constrain larger movements once a character has escaped the gravity of houses and forestalled the pull of unnatural graves. They turn space into place.

McCarthy's awareness of this becomes most obvious in his regular depiction of landscapes that circumscribe space into place by fencing. But scenes of road building, bridges, and border crossings similarly point to demarcation across the natural environment by humans. Beyond his descriptions of setting that circumscribe land into landscape, McCarthy also employs more extended metaphors for human demarcations, such as the deeply layered title and subtitle of *Blood Meridian: Or, The Evening Redness in the West*, or *The Crossing's* "matrix." Nowhere are his transformation of land into landscapes more acutely depicted, however, than in his descriptions of fencing.

Fences, as demarcations of the dimensional space of landscape of McCarthy wildernesses and McCarthy deserts, serve multiple functions. In the first novel, they serve as boundaries between the spaces of the living and the place of the dead. In the novels of *The Border Trilogy*, they create unnatural limitations on an otherwise supposedly natural land. When the Glanton gang of *Blood Meridian* rides on its murderous rampages, they encounter no fences. A hundred years later, the protagonists of *All the Pretty Horses* and *The Crossing* can hardly ride through the same countryside without cutting their way through fences of barbed wire. Ironically, *Cities of the Plain* reveals that these protagonists only ride horses now as part of their job—which includes mending fences.

Character flight so regularly propels the plots of these novels that we might conclude that in the McCarthy worldview there are no good houses, proper burials, and justifiable fences—nowhere to rest and no means of settling down and making reasonable distinctions between one part of the landscape and another. As this lack of positive enclosures allows a positive scheme for character flight, Billy Parham encounters a plethora of road-as-narrative-as-life parables and aphorisms in *The Crossing*. Yet there are glimpses in these novels of reasonably good places to remain, hints of life lived in terms other than those of these characters—who are all in one sense or another orphans, homeless.

The variety of constraints from which characters take flight merely mitigates what is a standard preoccupation in McCarthy's work. Forces of history, as well as the smaller forces of son and father conflict, account for the particular difficulties encountered by particular McCarthy characters on the road, such that none simply lives in a house and dies and is buried in a proper grave. But the prevalence of road narratives reminds us to keep some attention to the pure conflict between constraint and flight. To avoid a reductive interpretation, we might remember that this conflict can also be understood through theoretical terms—suggesting more the laws of physics than those of culture.

This possibility is bolstered by the lack of not only direct psychology, but also the lack of any discernible change in psychology, even when we can infer that psychology through setting. The settings shift, yet the characters, for all their external movement, experience few internal shifts at all. His novels do not, with the possible exception of *Suttree*, describe characters that change.[8] Another potential exception to this could be *Child of God*. Lester Ballard seems to become a necrophile, and then a murderer, in no small part as an unconscious reaction against his ostracism from healthy social connection. Yet, even here we must guess at whatever normalcy might have been found in Lester before the novel begins. So many dark doings oppress McCarthy's first two books that the claim in the opening of his third novel is conditioned by our expectations. That McCarthy's main narrator describes Lester as "[a] child of God much like yourself perhaps" says more, perhaps, about our own normalcy than about Ballard's deviance. Although Lester's behavior indeed worsens through the course of *Child of*

God, it is not clear that he experiences any significant internal change of character.

Rather, they change their skies, by taking to the road. It is ironic then that several of McCarthy's novels nonetheless employ elements of a genre that usually depends on character change. He regularly writes in the form of the Bildungsroman.[9] There is less evidence, however, that a character such as *The Orchard Keeper*'s John Wesley Rattner reaches any kind of epiphanic moment that allows him to leave home, than that the already present force in him to leave is simply allowed its course through the opening up of the boundaries containing that force. It may be that John Wesley leaves Red Branch because of some understanding he reaches; we cannot know with any certainty. I argue from the available evidence that John Wesley's character flight, and the flight of characters like him, is rather enabled by the failure of the constraints on space that previously prevented it.

Human demarcations of the natural landscape provide ambiguous limitations on protagonists bent on escape, engaged in what Gilles Deleuze and Claire Parnet termed a "line of flight" that is characteristic of Anglo-American literature: "To leave, to escape, is to trace a line. The highest aim of literature, according to Lawrence, is 'To leave, to leave, to escape . . . to cross the horizon, enter into another life . . . It is thus that Melville finds himself in the middle of the Pacific. He had really crossed the line of the horizon.' The line of flight is a deterritorialization" (*Dialogues* 36). For Deleuze, this is a good thing: his title for the chapter begun by the passage above is "On the Superiority of Anglo-American Literature." In Deleuze's terms, escape is possible. Certainly, in fiction that raises the road narrative to mythic levels, escape can be imagined. Yet, even in *The Crossing*, where so many references to the road as a way of life abound, our protagonist finds anything but a home there.

Even in the absence of actual roads, road narrative exerts a force over character flight. McCarthy characters do sometimes move over unmodified natural terrain. In *Blood Meridian*, there are hardly any roads; sometimes the gang even travels without trails. *All the Pretty Horses* is often a story of boys avoiding roads, as they seek to leave one lost paradise for a second one that will not allow them permanent residence. There is the temptation, in the later novels, to imagine the characters riding with a freedom of range befitting the mythology of the American West, or suggesting the equally problematic North American imagination of a lawless and mysterious Mexico as an undemarcated playground—if not proving ground—for young North American men. Yet, travel without roads is difficult for McCarthy's twentieth-century characters. It is really only the Glanton gang that travels without roads or trails,[10] and they do so in a manner that erases their own history:

For the next two weeks they would ride by night, they would make no fire. They had struck the shoes from their horses and filled the nailholes in with clay and those who still had tobacco used their pouches to spit in and they slept in caves and on bare stone. They rode their horses through the tracks of their dismounting and they buried their stool like cats and they barely spoke at all. Crossing those barren gravel reefs in the night they seemed remote and without substance. (*BM* 151)

The antinomian quality of the Glanton gang is achieved, ironically, through the dissolution of each member of the gang into the collective of outlaws without much particularity: "For although each man among them was discrete unto himself, conjoined they made a thing that had not been before and in that communal soul were wastes hardly reckonable more than those whited regions on old maps where monsters do live and where there is nothing other of the known world save conjectural winds" (*BM* 152). Here McCarthy uses a landscape analogy, that the "communal soul" of the gang has within it "wastes" of land, to make clear the deracinating effects of crossing trackless landscape and of doing so incorporated into a group effort. The degree to which the gang moves in this way depends on an absence of roads.

The judge will admonish the kid for exempting himself from full incorporation into the group, and this is why we suspect—on little other evidence— that the kid may share some similarity with his twentieth-century counterparts in *The Border Trilogy*: he too is homeless and does not quite find a place among others. The absence of fences and roads in much of *Blood Meridian* suits this theme of the individual dissolved into the murder of his own history: where all movement is possible, no movement is discreet; where landscape is still a space governed by optical democracy, no place is safe. Only the judge, who seems to be everywhere, is safe; he is perhaps the only McCarthy character unconstrained by any particular place and so free that he is never truly in flight from anything. The plot simply pushes the rest of the gang through trackless wastes, until they "run plumb out of country" (*BM* 285).

The recurring means of escape for McCarthy's more "discrete" nomads is the road. The hundred years between the birth of *Blood Meridian*'s kid and the teenage boys of *The Border Trilogy* witnessed an unprecedented change in how Americans traveled. In *Country of Exiles: The Destruction of Place in American Life*, William Leach describes how America's system of roads underwent new development after 1920:

> Americans much extended a distinct set of parallel roads—one national, the other local. [. . .] [T]he landscape writer J. B. Jackson distinguished

between these two road systems. The national one he called "centrifugal," or "palace," because it reflected the interests of the ruling elites, surged outward, and ignored boundaries. The local system, on the other hand, was "centripetal," or "vernacular," formed for ordinary people and to draw them into their neighborhoods [. . .] (34)

When Marion Sylder drives the back roads of rural Tennessee running moonshine in *The Orchard Keeper*, he is running the "vernacular" roads with liquor that is illegal because it has not been taxed by the state—not by the local community. Sylder calls his arrest at the end of the book

> a little disagreement [. . .] as to whether a man can haul untaxed whiskey over tax-kept roads or whether by not payin the whiskey tax he forfeits the privilege of drivin over the roads the whiskey don't keep up that ain't taxed or it if was would be illegal anyway. I think what they do is deeport you. (*TOK* 210)

If we translate Sylder's diction, we find this antinomian motivation: what rankles him is the irony of relationships between personal, local, and state authority. Sylder's roads are not the ones he did not ask for—as if he might have the freedom to drive where he pleases without roads at all. At the end of the last novel, *Cities of the Plain*, Billy Parham is wandering the highways of the American Southwest as they see new use as conduits of a new level of trade into and out of Mexico. Here too, the feature of roads in the novels reinforces the common condition of McCarthy characters as outcasts, or nomads.

DOMESTIC CONSTRAINTS

Whatever the path they take from home, McCarthy characters do not get far in the end. This isn't surprising, coming from a novelist devoted to subject matter beyond the broken teacup, and indeed we see many of these nomadic characters die and none of them marry within their novels. The introduction of married characters in *No Country for Old Men* only highlights their absence in the earlier works. Marion Sylder is already married when we meet him in *The Orchard Keeper*. But he may as well not be. The death of Wanda Reese, pregnant with Suttree's child, reads more as yet another loss suffered by Suttree, than as an escape from marriage, and yet she dies when the wall above the camp falls on her: she is literally crushed by the failing wall of a makeshift home. This wall of stone, constructed only through the happenstances of geology and unsuited to protect anyone after days of rain, does not even complete any real enclosure. What rude form of parodic house it suggests does not even threaten Suttree, of course, who sleeps well away from this family and its one wall, and therefore lives to suffer someone else's death. Meanwhile, it remains unclear as to whether he had any intention of remaining with the mother of his second child (*S* 361–363).

Suttree seems rather to extend the line of Culla Holme in avoiding the consequences of sex, or at least in avoiding the encumbrance of a regular connection to a woman. When we next see this subject come up, we have crossed the meridian of McCarthy's great fifth novel, and marriage—at least as it presents itself as a dream of John Grady Cole's—has become inextricably connected with larger issues of spatial tension. John Grady's imagination of Alejandra as someone he might actually make a life with runs counter to every constraint of class, gender, national identity (through the revolution), and social convention. Rather than finding that Mexico provides an open space in which to realize his dreams, John Grady finds a surprising number of entanglements that prevents him, in part, from marrying Alejandra. As David Holloway points out, John Grady's delusions of freedom from economic realities only further entangle him in exchanges he can ill afford. If the class differential between him and Alejandra prevent his first attempt at marriage, the literal commodification of Magdalena prevents his second attempt; she is only for sale within the system in which Eduardo markets her—not for John Grady to remove her from it (20, 39, 61). The one character that seems most headed for marriage, rather than death, cannot afford any marriage he seeks—and so ends up dead.

No Country for Old Men introduces the first claims by a main character that marriage provides the ultimate improvement of a man's circumstances, even throwing into negative relief his own worth. But its one scene of marital intimacy fails to convince us, as does the book's closing imagery, that son and father trouble has ceased to be the salient tension in the home of a McCarthy character. Sheriff Bell may keep his wife, but he leaves his figurative position of patriarchal authority by resigning as the Sheriff of people he no longer feels he can protect. And Llewelyn Moss's quick trip to the back of the trailer he shares with Carla Jean does not alter the behavior through which he ensures the murder of his own wife. This he does not only when he chooses to return to the scene of the drug rip off, but earlier, when he first takes the money. At his unusually advanced age of thirty-six, this McCarthy character cannot imagine he can do this without the next part: run. When he finds himself cut off from returning to his vehicle, his thought is not that he will never see his wife again, but that he will never again see his truck.

Domestic constraints at the adult level—of marriage—rarely threaten McCarthy men at all. When they do, other spatial complications intervene. The invisible dividing lines between nations, social classes, and even the philosophical line between determinism and free will all prove more interesting in these novels than those between the sexes. While I cannot agree with Nell Sullivan's general thesis that the regular depiction of women as abject, threatening, and wholly other to the male protagonists explains this and the general lack of attention to women characters, I can agree that the emphasis on both familial and social relationships in the novels remains homosocial. The depictions of women in the novels may continue to be disturbing, but the relatively rare attention given to the subject of sex at all evinces a compartmentalizing ability in the narratives. The son and father trouble simply eclipses other psychological tensions, and the focus on traditionally male subjects displaces—as in much less complex narratives aimed at pre-adolescent males—any focus on women at all.

In "Emasculating Papa: Hemingway at Bay," James Tuttleton attempts to reconcile a variety of feminist critiques of Hemingway (such as Nancy Comley and Robert Scholes's *Hemingway's Genders*) with more traditional values granted masculinist fiction. Tuttleton wanted to rescue "Papa," yet his own work, which specialized as much or more in the domesticity of Wharton and James as in the outdoor vigor of Hemingway, or the tough trails of Naturalism, kept Tuttleton's strained name-calling from dismissing their critiques as much as his intentions announced. Ultimately, this interesting essay arrives at a richly mediated view—helpfully situated between "canon-busters" (241) and what might have been another conservative diatribe against them. Tuttleton's sensibilities included not only his appreciation for Hemingway's masculine values (which, it must be noted, can only be assumed necessarily to entail conservative political values, through a process of reasoning that remains spuriously contrived), but also the complexity of the "genders" of Hemingway, his male and female companions, and all his characters.

The resulting essay leads to an appreciation of the androgynous ideals embedded in Hemingway's work, where women are allowed a position for the crucial act of sex (however positioned) but must in other matters act essentially as masculine friends. But the women are there, very much so. The problem with Papa, as Tuttleton sees it, is that women provide the Hemingway male something essentially beyond pleasure in the act of sex:

> Good sex with a woman is a Hemingway necessity: the moment of ecstasy eclipses, however momentarily, one's consciousness of the *nada* at the heart of existence. But sex enmeshes the man, as well as the woman,

in the biological trap. There are always complications, circumscribing consequences, in human relationships: Nick's wife if going to have a baby. (259)

This points to the fault in the Hemingway man's ability to become a father. Yet far from undermining the value of what Tuttleton calls "the virtues of courage, fortitude, cunning, strength, leadership, and persistence" (241), Hemingway's apparent need (and certainly that of his characters) of women accommodates their night time use for escape from that *nada* by enlisting them in traditionally homosocial activities during the daytime. An androgynous woman (hair bobbed short) who could join him in outdoor adventures "of direct engagement with nonhuman nature" (260) proves to be the ideal woman in Hemingway—as long as she does not become pregnant.

Of course, McCarthy's characters are, as far as we know and ought to assume, merely reflections of male anxieties that may not have any of the origins in biography that we now know existed in Hemingway's life. But if both Hemingway and McCarthy continue to reveal domestic anxieties in their characters through a lack of families on the page, their work differs in this area in the near total absence (comparatively) of that focus on "[g]ood sex with a woman." Indeed, John Grady's scene with Alejandra in the water seems to connect him with nonhuman nature as much as it does with her, the woman called Alejandra. In this sense, the scene reads like a dream of sex conflated with his dreams of horses, or with his feeling of the earth turning beneath him. Domestic constraints of the marital and sexual variety prove therefore to give way to other spatial anxieties, or at least always to link to them.

Sex in McCarthy, wherever we find it, seems to supply a deep human need for intimate companionship—as, surprisingly, it does for Lester Ballard as much as Cornelius Suttree. But the rest of the relationship hardly exists at all. When Billy and other male friends help prepare an old house for John Grady to live in with his future wife, the yet-to-be-rescued prostitute Magdalena, that activity remains homosocial. Even though the house's domestic space commands more respect for its future female inhabitant than the brothel keeping her as a commodified captive, it remains anterior to her. In this respect, this house—which she never sees—echoes the bar in which the ranch hands joke around and drink, before going to the back with prostitutes. What would provide a space of domesticity instead parallels that homosociality that Nell Sullivan finds in all the bar and tavern scenes throughout McCarthy; it remains a "masculine space" ("In the Barroom" 1).

Given what John Grady risks (for a best friend whom he leaves behind when he moves up to the barn), the desperation of Ballard's desires, and even the vicious disregard for himself that matches Suttree's treatment of women, it would be a mistake to write off the absence, and problematic representation, of women in McCarthy as simple misogyny. The rare relations between men and women in these books rather suggests a value so far from attainability, and perhaps carrying with its possibility that much more of a threat of constraint, that it echoes the need for sex in Hemingway at an even further remove from reality. Two people can lose themselves in one another, even as Hemingway needed to imagine. In McCarthy, however, the closest the men come to any real domestic relationship usually comes at the remove of delusional projections—if they even come that close.

This matches the fact that what Tuttleton valued as a masculine "direct engagement with nonhuman nature" (260) never reveals itself with the joy one sometimes finds in Hemingway. Rather than the exhilaration of the hunt performed with honor, we see Llewelyn Moss take a ridiculously long shot at an antelope, wounding it so that it will die slowly, alone, and wasted. As Edwin Arnold notes, John Grady watches a well-shot deer doe expire and, rather than witnessing the "secret" "in the beauty of the world," he realizes that "the world's pain and its beauty moved in a relationship of diverging equity and that in this headlong deficit the blood of multitudes might ultimately be exacted for the vision of a single flower" ("Go to sleep" 57, *ATPH* 282). When Hemingway's adventures, whether in war and lesser contests with other men, or in hunting and fishing, leave his characters feeling lost in a meaningless world, they can find solace (at least for a moment) with a woman, or in drink. In McCarthy, the male protagonists have nothing to fall back on but the booze, and after *Suttree*, even that escape disappears. The resulting worldview is darker than anything one can find in Hemingway's proud disappointed male idealism, which continually reasserts courage as a saving grace (until that routine becomes exhausted and self-parodic). The lack of domestic spaces, indeed, of real relationships with women in these novels, may be part of the problem; in any case, this lack certainly leaves the characters on bleaker rocks than any seen by Nick Adams.

BORDERS, WARS, AND HISTORICAL CONSTRAINTS

In the Jack London short story "Make Westing," the captain of a ship attempting to sail around Cape Horn murders a man rather than risk failing his course. London's story depicts a lesser Ahab; his Dan Cullen is determined to round the cape after seven weeks of failing to do so. Captain

Cullen blames God, and when one of London's misplaced effetes gets in the way, Cullen murders the man and calls it an accident. Whatever the price, the way west must be made, as London quotes *"Sailing directions for Cape Horn:"* "Whatever you do, make westing! make westing!"

Blood Meridian is the only McCarthy novel so far set before the twentieth century,[11] and it is the first to take place primarily in the American Southwest and Mexican North. Yet, as many critics have pointed out, the preceding novels (with the exception of *Child of God*) also end with westward movement. In the regular trespass of its characters across the barely-created new border between the United States and Mexico, *Blood Meridian* similarly prefigures *The Border Trilogy*. For some readers, such as Rick Wallach, this makes *Blood Meridian* part of a tetralogy that simply continues through *The Border Trilogy* ("Introduction: The McCarthy Canon Reconsidered" vi).

If we follow Wallach's lead, it is easy to see that chronologically the movement begins with the establishment of the Mexican-American border after a war, and ends with the building of highways to effect—through the North American Free Trade Agreement—a significant erasure of that border. Looking back to John Wesley Rattner and Cornelius Suttree's departures for points West, we see that their territory reaches limits. The frontier crossed by the Glanton gang becomes the border crossed by John Grady Cole and Billy Parham. Thus, it is tempting to read the Western shift in McCarthy's settings from the four Southern novels to the border "tetralogy" in political terms.

In "Overcoming the Regional Burden: History, Tradition, and Myth in the Novels of Cormac McCarthy," John Wegner does just this, while also outlining how "McCarthy's literary aesthetic develops and changes as he moves from Tennessee to Texas" (3). By the move to Texas, "*Blood Meridian* is not merely a historical chronicle of Western expansion. Instead, McCarthy focuses on the Edenic myth of the frontier, and how we created the myth not just of Adam in the new Garden, but of America as the New Adam rightfully inhabiting the new Paradise of the West" (117). But although he argues that in the West, McCarthy finds a space that is less circumscribed by history than the South, Wegner's reading of *All the Pretty Horses* points to the historical constraints on its protagonist. McCarthy's story of a young man headed into Mexico to find a better life,

> complicates the boundaries between fiction and non-fiction [. . . and] points to a universal class system designed to defeat progress and oppress the individual. Cole, unwittingly and unconsciously, stumbles into the

realization that his plight differs only in nationality from the plight of
the Mexicans his "family's been practicin medicine on" for a hundred
years. (170, *ATPH* 278)

Wegner sees a history lesson embedded in this novel, where "the failed presi-
dency of Francisco Madero" and "the poverty and powerlessness of the Mexican people"—and apart from his different nationality, the powerlessness of
John Grady himself—are best understood in a causal relationship.

In this sense, Wegner has already provided the guide to John Grady
Cole's problems with constraints of a larger nature than those of domesticity.
In "'Wars and rumors of wars' in Cormac McCarthy's Border Trilogy," Wegner provides an extended examination of the conflicts encountered by all the
protagonists of the Western works in terms of border constraints and international conflicts larger than these characters can imagine. Given this work,
the most I might add to an understanding of historical constraints of space is
the historical background informing the Epilogue in *Blood Meridian*.

INTERPRETING SPATIAL CONSTRAINT

If one were to fly over the actual countryside that corresponds (roughly) to
the fictional landscapes of these novels, one would see a general movement
westward and a marked shift at the line of aridity (around the middle of
Texas), from shades of green forest, to shades of brown desert. Generally, that
is, there is a movement through all of McCarthy's books from one part of
North America to another, contrasting, part. Of course, this movement has
its precedent in American literature, as well as a more complicated precedent
in history. Again, John Wegner notes this movement in aesthetic concerns
that match the movement in settings. But *Blood Meridian* and the books that
follow it suggest even larger movements.

Most of McCarthy's characters flee spatial constraints less obviously
dark and unnatural than those sheathing Ballard in his "rocky keep," but all
the major characters, in one sense or another, are in tension with interiority;
those in the Western novels run afoul of the larger constraints demarcated by
borders. This has left some readers to assume that the latter characters inhabit
rather naive novels embracing worn notions about wilderness, masculinity,
and a picaresque life. The shooting script for Billy Bob Thornton's failed film
version of *All the Pretty Horses* indulges in this type of misreading, most notably when it moves from John Grady's laconic speech at the end of the novel
to the kind of wrap-up that one suspects would be accompanied by a slow
swell of music. The book does risk a couple of stoic cowboy clichés about

the loss of the boy's father, and about "what happens to country" (*ATPH* 299). Yet, a shooting version of the script (credited to Ted Tally) attempted to supply the emotion better left imagined under the book's dialogue. Worse, it points toward the title, as if viewers are now incapable of metaphorical reading of any kind. "It all begun with that horse. The good times and the bad ones, too. If I can just find out where he really belongs, then maybe I can start over fresh. Maybe I'll belong somewheres too" (149).[12]

Painful as this is to read, it points to an unavoidable end of the spectrum along which McCarthy is read. But that end of the spectrum remains a powerful area of masculine myth in American culture (indeed, in politics as well). McCarthy's novels express the particularly American mistrust in the social, the urban, in civilization, and an especially American male distrust of the domestic.

Domestic enclosure had been noticed as a salient feature of space in McCarthy even as critics began to devote special attention to his landscapes. In "Reeds and Hides: Cormac McCarthy's Domestic Spaces," Teri Witek saw the normative escape from domesticity in McCarthy's work:

> Nearly all the protagonists in Cormac McCarthy novels flee from or lose their homes. Kenneth Rattner lights out from the cabin he shares with Mildred and his young son (*The Orchard Keeper*), Lester Ballard's family farm is sold out from under him (*Child of God*) as is John Grady's ranch house (*All the Pretty Horses*), Culla and Rinthy Holme strike out from the perverse Eden of their incestuous home (*Outer Dark*), Suttree trades in his family's substantial housing for a houseboat (*Suttree*), and "the kid" leaves his alcoholic father's cabin to wander the practically trackless Southwest (*Blood Meridian*). (136)

Witek's article in *The Southern Review* remains insightful about this common predicament in McCarthy, if less so about its causes. For Witek, McCarthy is "challenging such morally freighted metaphors as the American home" by depicting "dwelling places, and therefore the communities they represent, as impermanent." The implication is that McCarthy intends a form of political attack on cultural assumptions about homes as "emblems of the family" (137).

> I think McCarthy's quarrel is that the metaphors we construct about our existence don't match up with the brutal realities they should rightfully represent and are therefore only a shared delusion. Bent on exposing the chimera by which communities live and lie to themselves, and himself

> a firm proponent of flight, McCarthy is therefore at his most fierce and
> convincing when taking on such conventional images of community
> life as the spaces we choose to call home. (136)

There are perhaps too many objections to raise to this interpretation while
still doing justice to Witek's insights about McCarthian homelessness.
Most may be grouped under the rubric of the intentional fallacy. Whatever
McCarthy may have intended, his works suggest less (or, as it were, more)
than the specific political project of Witek's reading.

For instance, nowhere in McCarthy is there the celebration of freedom that one would expect from a "proponent" of flight. Ironically, Witek's
interpretation reads more like disappointed male idealism than she may
have intended. It may be that Cormac McCarthy is indeed "a firm proponent of flight;" if so, his characters little profit from the fact. They end
up nowhere, or incarcerated; they end up homeless, or dead and improperly buried. This objection could simply mean that while McCarthy is a
"proponent" of flight, he recognizes that civilization forbids or curtails it.
Even so, the resulting interpretation of McCarthy's novels might be complicated further. From a simple reading, in which domesticity is eschewed in
favor of a masculine lack of social and familial connection, we might move
to a deeper reading, which appreciates the recurrent ambivalence toward
both domesticity and flight that suffuses the works. McCarthy's powers as
a descriptive novelist take precedence over his very different (and yet to be
definitely determined) proscriptive and prescriptive powers as a social com-
mentator.

Witek's frustration with the ambiguity of McCarthy's novels is understandable, when it is easy to see how regularly McCarthy portrays characters
in flight from the domestic. Her focus on flight from domesticity (apart
from flight from other spatial constraints), is then easier to pin down with a
theoretical reading of "history:"

> Historically, these images [of domestic places] have been powerfully ide-
> ological. In *The American Family Home: 1800–1960*, Clifford Edward
> Clark argues that by the end of the eighteenth century, for example, the
> rhetoric of family life was that families should work as a balanced com-
> bination of mutually independent parts, as hierarchical and as orderly as
> the Greek Revival architecture so beloved of early colonists, representing
> as it did the imagined reversal of that perceived chaos which greeted the
> first European immigrants. For the Victorians the house was a moral
> edifice, a cornerstone of society which combined the careful display of

> beauty with the sanctuary aspects of church, both presided over by the
> house's guiding angel, Mother. (Witek 137)

The phrases "for example," referring to the end of a particular century, and
"representing as it did," referring to a rather extensive movement in architecture, give away the ideological motive here. Formidable work remains
to be done by cultural historians before we can determine from a complex
past something that can be called "rhetoric of family life." The nature of this
rhetoric here, however, seems informed by assumptions from more recent
culture.

The general anti-Victorian, anti-bourgeois idea here has the horse
stuck behind, pushing a cart filled with ideological assumptions. To be fair,
the prospects of living in a home "presided over by" a "guiding angel," let
alone one that functions in any kind of moral manner, must be repellent to
any free-thinking reader. This is because we now know (as no one, apparently, knew before) that constructions of morality and even ministrations of
angelic guidance ultimately serve to exclude those who do not fit the bourgeois bill, while repressing all those who do. A focus on McCarthy's houses
requires at least some engagement with this widespread intellectual assumption (one that seems sanctioned in academia only in theory)—that houses
are bad things in the world (whatever they are in novels). Nevertheless, when
one looks into McCarthy's novels, with one eye toward that "rhetoric of family life" from which his characters may be escaping, the result is not a very
coherent stereoscopic view of domesticity in America.

If this is because McCarthy intends to present us with a negative view
of what Witek (and Clark) sees as a false bourgeois ideal, then what of the
darkness we see resulting from a character like Ballard's replacement of normative domesticity? Is it nobler to live like an animal than like an imperfect
human being? Here, again, is Witek's guess at McCarthy's "quarrel:" that "the
metaphors we construct about our existence don't match up with the brutal
realities they should rightfully represent and are therefore only a shared delusion" (136). "[B]rutal realities" is a fair assessment not only of Ballard's predicament, but also of any number of stories on the local television news.

Witek adds to this fact two assumptions, however: that the aberrations
that interest McCarthy represent his understanding of the norms of social life
in the twentieth century, and that the "shared delusion" of some better way
of living is addressed by his work in a direct manner. If one must guess at the
author's intentions, it might be easier to infer from his descriptions of flight
from domesticity that the real "shared delusion" he is calling into question
is that flight from social connection automatically grants one an important

existential access to truth. Rather than brave stoics, his characters may as often be described as a series of brave dreamers who insistently attempt to realize dreams that are impossible, or even unhealthy, for them. That would be anything but an advocacy of flight.

The example of Ballard bolsters this argument. But the question of McCarthy's advocacy of flight is equally blunt when put through the example of a character less strange. John Grady Cole, the first fully sympathetic McCarthy hero and notably the first of the characters (from the novels) to make it to the big screen, dies in a "clubhouse made from packingcrates" (*COTP* 256). So much for his brave flight from home.

In *A World Elsewhere: The Place of Style in American Literature*, Richard Poirier describes the struggle of American writers (and architects) to come to terms with both their new landscape and their European heritage.

> From the outset American writers (or architects) who wanted in America to create environments in concert with the formative powers of nature found that they had first to rid themselves and America of styles imposed upon them by history. Even the men who dispossessed the Indian could only possess, could only *see* America through the styles and instrumentalities of the old world. (18)

Poirier then quotes Faulkner's Isaac McCaslin toward a "theme of 'possession' and of 'dispossession,'" which Poirier finds exemplified by

> *The Bear*, where the hero rejects both his historical and his economic inheritance so that he might live in an environment where time (his relation to family and family past) and space (the wilderness, and the plantation life he is to inherit) are redeemed by his sacrifice of profit from either, his relinquishment both of a sexual and of an economic identity. (19)

The distinctive qualities of McCarthy's work apart from the obvious influence of Faulkner are best detailed by Robert Jarrett. But Jarrett sees one difference with which I can only partly agree: that in McCarthy we lose the importance of fathers as we see them in Faulkner. Jarrett argues that, "in McCarthy's early fiction Faulkner's Southern patriarchy has largely disappeared, not only from the sight of McCarthy's protagonists but from the world of the fiction. McCarthy's protagonists may be sons, but they are largely depicted as autonomous—the sons of dead or absent fathers, or in Culla's case, a father who repudiates his own fatherhood" (20–21). This is true in the sense that nothing like the weight of "Southern patriarchy" dominates the sons in McCarthy. Yet, as I will argue further in Chapter Four, a smaller, psychological space of tension between sons and fathers indeed preoccupies McCarthy's characters and has much to do with their reasons for flight.

Few of McCarthy's main characters (save Suttree, perhaps) have any familial identity to sacrifice—except that between the son and the father. Poirier's next statement concerning Isaac McCaslin rings true of Faulkner: "In all respects he gives up the house of his ancestors" (19). McCarthy, however, presents us with a different situation: in most of his novels, the house of the ancestors is unstable, fallen in, or simply empty. This does not, however, prevent a rejecting movement on the part of the protagonists.

The types of spatial constraint in McCarthy's novels vary, and so do the responses of his characters to those constraints. Nonetheless, a cluster of recurring types of constraint and force of flight emerges when one considers the novels in brief. A description of McCarthy characters at the ends of their respective novels suggests they frequently fail to escape at all, or that the only possible escape is to take to an open road, to move:

The Orchard Keeper: Marion Sylder sits in the Knoxville jail (210), while Arthur Ownby is moved from the Knox County jail to an insane asylum (222). Only John Wesley Rattner escapes, leaving Red Branch, Tennessee for "the western road" (246). He leaves through a gap in a cemetery fence.

Outer Dark: Culla Holme reaches the end of the road he is traveling as it terminates in a swamp, wondering, "why a road should come to such a place" (242).

Child of God: The necrophilic murderer Lester Ballard turns himself in to a nurse at the county hospital, having escaped the authorities and hidden himself in a womb-like cave for three days (192). He dies in captivity.

Suttree: Looking "like someone just out of the army or jail" (470), Suttree quits his life of dissolution among the lower denizens of Knoxville and hitchhikes past a highway "ramp curved out into empty air and hung truncate with iron rods bristling among the vectors of nowhere" (471).

Blood Meridian: "The kid" is raped, murdered, and mutilated in an out-house (333) by the leading force of a gang with which he wreaked violence along the borders of the United States and Mexico—until they ran "out of country" (285).

All the Pretty Horses: John Grady Cole is watched riding into the sunset by Indians on the Western plains of Texas—in 1949 (301–2).

The Crossing: After stopping for the night in an abandoned building of "a waystation"(423) in southern New Mexico, Billy Parham is awakened by the light of the first atomic explosion in the distance (425).

Cities of the Plain: Parham rests in the house of a family that has taken him in as he spends his last days wandering the highways of the American Southwest (290–2).

No Country for Old Men: Sheriff Bell, having left the West Texas community he thinks he fails to protect, worries about apocalypse and dreams of his dead father rising into darkness.

In each of these endings, major characters are at that moment taking to the road—or trail—or leaving it (however unwillingly) for some construction of architectural space. Jails, asylums, hospitals, an outhouse, abandoned buildings, the home of charitable strangers, and in the last novel in self-imposed exile, constrain these characters as their attempt to flee some other constraint on their movement gives way to entropy, exhaustion, or the force of a social authority. None of these boys and men simply lives in a house and remains there through the course of a novel. McCarthy's subjects can be restless nomads, antinomians, even murderers, whose regard for civilized society runs from uneasiness to hostility. Even Bell, a lawman, ultimately quits and leaves. His plots are meanwhile the unraveling of such forces as compel these characters to flight, and the constraints on that flight.

One way to read, however tentatively, beyond those plots is to see them in tension between two apparently opposed ideas about America. Particularly in writing on the American West, a notable paradigm shift has taken place in recent historiography. One may read in these novels entwined themes of both a Frontier Myth and its replacements in the New Western History. This is particularly important because critics sometimes dismiss McCarthy's last four novels (while more readers popularly celebrate them) as romantic, even retrogressive narratives of cowboy mythology. Indeed, McCarthy's notable popularity in Europe, particularly in Germany, seems to rest largely on the desire of many readers there to equate the Western novels with a "Marlboro Man Myth." During a panel discussion on McCarthy's reception in Europe at the First European Cormac McCarthy Colloquy, Georg Guillemin introduced American McCarthy scholars to a collection of surprisingly un-ironic German magazine stories that centered as much on the persona of McCarthy himself as on his work.

McCarthy is not, by many accounts, reclusive. He simply does not, as a rule, give interviews or appear in public as an author (Jarrett 6). Readers looking for the persona of the writer as hero, then, must make do with the characters. Although the Western novels are ironic on matters of existential heroism, the loner life of the cowboy, and other romantic notions, McCarthy's Western heroes often seem to buy into a worn mythology. Their dialogue shows them straining at this, however, and sometimes ironically self-conscious about it. In *All the Pretty Horses*, John Grady Cole's patience runs out when Jimmy Blevins overacts his part.

> You never know when you'll be in need of them you've despised, said Blevins.
>   Where the hell'd you hear that at?
>   I dont know. I just decided to say it.
>   John Grady shook his head. [. . .] (*ATPH* 72)

The younger boy is unconvincing. He is saying what he thinks a wise old cowboy should say in his situation. Rawlins, having caught Blevins in a fanciful lie, himself replies in character: "You dont know shit from applebutter" (*ATPH* 58). About to belly up to the bar at the beginning of *Cities of the Plain*, Billy Parham asks of John Grady, "Where's the all-american cowboy at?" (*CTOP* 3). The fact that Billy names him as such belies the title.

The myth of the cowboy is bound to influence even a writer who openly resists it. In 1999, the National Endowment for the Humanities, The Southwestern Writers Collection, and Southwest Texas State University sponsored a "travelling [sic] exhibition" on "Journeys and Transformations in the American Southwest." In a curious combination of old and "New" Western history, the exhibition quoted Wallace Stegner:

> Whatever it might want to be, the West is still primarily a series of brief visitations or a trail to somewhere else; and western literature, from *Roughing It* to *On the Road*, from *The Log of a Cowboy* to *Lonesome Dove*, from *The Big Rock Candy Mountain* to *The Big Sky*, has been

largely a literature not of place but of motion. (qtd. in *No Traveller*, Screen 5)

This is a reliable version of the myth of escape that still dominates popular ideas about the West. Stegner's equation further suggests a relationship of opposition between "place" and "motion." We might even, for a moment, see this opposition in larger terms: "ontology" and "existentialism," or "being" and "becoming."

Western characters—but arguably American characters in general—are characters of action and becoming. When Christopher Newman finds the limits on his actions in *The American*, they are European limits: regardless of how much money he has made, he simply is not the right person—by birth—to be allowed to marry Claire de Bellegarde. He cannot simply expend energy and become otherwise. Neither can John Grady Cole. The attraction of McCarthy's characters, particularly to European readers, may be the insistence of those characters on "motion" rather than "place," on their existential self rather than on their ontological self. They seldom have parents at all. We might even say they do not exist at all, except when they are moving. Stegner's terms suggest an attention to space and motion in McCarthy. The myth of motion, we might call it, is relevant to understanding constraint and flight in the novels.

Using Stegner's terms, we may say that Frederick Jackson Turner's formulation of this myth (in *The Frontier in American History*) imagines the American West as a rather empty "place" awaiting the "motion" of civilizing influences from European settlers. In the last hundred years, the Turner thesis has been disputed back and forth. Yet, even practitioners of so-called New Western History, initially wary of the Turner thesis to the point of dismissing it, have more recently acknowledged the idea's power. Turner's work may be dismissed as mere romantic longing for an Old (open) West, or as the historiographic construction of the putative winners in the (largely) white conquest of the New West. Nevertheless, historians as skeptical as Patricia Nelson Limerick continue to regard Turner's writing as an enduring (if problematic) characterization of America's past.

Limerick's *Something in the Soil: Legacies and Reckonings in the New West* includes a chapter whose very title points to the ineradicable qualities of a theory that sought to account for Westward movement as an integral aspect of American history: "Turnerians All: The Dream of a Helpful History in an Intelligible World" (141). The "Thesis" to historians of an Old West became a "Myth" to New Western Historians, only to be reinstated by Limerick at the last century's end as a "Dream of a Helpful History." In what she calls the "enchanted world" of Turner's writing, abstractions are tangible and virtually animate, right on the verge of speaking for themselves. Conditions, forces, ideals, institutions, traits, types, elements, and processes inhabit the Turnerian world like the weightiest and most settled of citizens. If you bump into a social force or a pioneer ideal, it will be you who gets the bruise. You can, of course, try to refuse the impact. "Neither a 'social force' nor a 'pioneer ideal,'" you can declare, with accuracy on your side, "is the real thing. Both are intellectual constructions. Neither should have the power to bruise."

Yet,

"[a]s they have for nearly a century, Turner's conditions, forces, ideals, institutions, traits, types, elements, and processes remain undissolved by such a challenge. You are free to show [. . .] that these concepts exist without the support of much evidence. You will still have to walk around them" (141).

I would like to point out three things in Limerick's most recent characterization of the Turner myth. First, the obvious personification suggests the idea is alive. That alone, of course, suggests nothing about its veracity as a way of understanding the West. Second, however, Limerick extends this metaphorical device to the point of physical effect—and a violent one, at that. Third, her description of Turner is an unwittingly canny description of much in McCarthy.

That is, McCarthy characters such as John *Wesley* Rattner (with his middle name referring to a cardinal point), and the main characters of *The Border Trilogy*, as well as others, seem driven by an insistent Westward impulse, within their more general impulse away from civilization, away from domesticity. Against this drive, there is much to imagine personified—even as McCarthy avoids that technique—in the settings through which these characters flee. Unfathomable as their interiority can remain, the characters of the *Trilogy*, especially, get the "bruise" when they reach an awakening from their "dream" of a "helpful history" and find themselves confronted with the facts of other cultures, other languages, and other laws in what they took to be a frontier of freedom.

The later John, John *Grady*, finds that beyond the fenced yet still wide-open places of Western Texas lies a set of social customs like Limerick's "weightiest and most settled of citizens." Billy Parham, attempting the romantic restoration of a wolf to its putatively natural home, finds in the Mexican wilderness a medieval society with no regard for his dreams of what is natural and just, and what is not. At the end of *The Crossing*, he witnesses the far-off explosion of the first atomic bomb—a weapon whose operation entails conflating very small space into something whose effect turns places back into spaces.

What bruises these characters, then, is something oddly abstract, precisely the kinds of "[c]onditions, forces, ideals, institutions, traits, types, elements, and processes" that Limerick claims are merely "hardy mental constructions" (141). They are simply more complicated than Turner, fifty years before Parham and a hundred before McCarthy's novels, could have imagined.

In an early work of the New Western History, Limerick draws on her own experience as a resident of Banning, California to join "a grand tradition in western American history [. . .]: taking one's home seriously" (*Trails* 81-82). I can attest that the most indulgent versions of the Turner myth were alive and well able to bruise during the 1960s and 70s in Mesquite, Texas. A glance at contemporary advertising serves as well for evidence: the idea that the American story is one of perseverance in a hostile—if natural—frontier persists even in strategies to sell automobiles that are more likely to carry groceries than cattle.

McCarthy seems to know this, and to have known it even before he moved himself and his fictional settings to the West. The Turner myth is alive and powerful for McCarthy's characters even as the novels underline that myth with irony. Ultimately, McCarthy's works embody both the myth of flight into frontier and its dissolution into the realities of history. This is particularly evident in his figuration of that myth through its essential elements—fences, roads, houses, and cemeteries—in relation to his characters. *Blood Meridian*'s judge Holden suggests the problem of characters pitched against the given world in grand terms:

> The truth about the world [. . .] is that anything is possible. [. . .
>] The universe is no narrow thing and the order within it is not constrained by any latitude in its conception to repeat what exists in one part in any other part. Even in this world more things exist without our knowledge than with it and the order in creation which you see is that which you have put there, like a string in a maze, so that you shall not lose your way. For existence has its own order and that no man's mind can compass, that mind itself being but a fact among others. (*BM* 245)

That McCarthy's characters get bruised as they "lose" their "way" is easy to see. Ultimately, there is no place for home in these novels, not for these young men. How and why they lose their way bears further investigation.

Chapter Two
"Fled, banished in death or exile:" Constraint and Flight in *The Orchard Keeper*

> To leave, to escape, is to trace a line.
>
> (Deleuze and Parnet, *Dialogues* 36)
>
> But it was never his house anyway.
>
> (*OD* 244)

BREAKING GROUND

In Nancy Kreml's "Stylistic Variation and Cognitive Constraint in *All the Pretty Horses*," we see that readers willing to make a binary distinction between different narrative modes can interpret one as an implicit set of directions for interpreting the other (140–143). Kreml argues that an "*opaque*" mode of narration (full of suggestive language) provides a means of interpreting a "*transparent*" mode of narration (bereft of interpretive clues). McCarthy's style is for Kreml the key to reading more depth in his characters than is readily apparent. But Kreml's argument is only necessary because of the primary problem: McCarthy's novels test the ability of readers to venture one interpretation more persuasively than another.

Ascribing any interiority to the characters is difficult. The strongest formulation of this problem is Denis Donoghue's claim[1] that McCarthy characters possess little more than a brain stem, an ability of motor coordination—and violence. Of *The Orchard Keeper*, *Outer Dark*, and *Child of God*, he writes: "The characters in these three novels are like recently arrived primates, each possessing a spinal column but little or no capacity of mind or consciousness" ("Dream Work" 5). Donoghue notes the exception of Suttree, but I find many others within these first three novels. Still, McCarthy's usual refusal of direct psychology highlights his skill at embedding it elsewhere: McCarthy's "high passages" have "much they have to do." "McCarthy's styles have also to speak up for values the characters could not express; for regions, places, landscapes, vistas, movements of the seasons, trees, rain, snow, dawn, sunset, outer and inner weather; and for times not our time" ("Dream Work" 8).

My interest in this chapter is in how attention to the setting, or landscape, of *The Orchard Keeper* provides interpretive clues to the characters in this novel. Why do these characters move so much? From what are they running? And why is it that they fail, with only one important exception, to escape the novel's setting?

Kreml's is one method of reaching into the skulls of the characters, by making "implicatures" out of "codes"—to use the terms from her field of linguistics (Myers-Scotton, Introduction 7–9).[2] We might ask why we need even to *try* to get into the heads of characters who have in common, more than anything else, that they wander an antinomian wilderness, apart from and often in violent contradiction to all laws of civil or moral import. It is interesting to note that Kreml's essay addresses style in the first McCarthy novel to concern a defendable hero, John Grady Cole in *All the Pretty Horses*. Can we extend her methods to understanding *Child of God*'s murderously necrophilic Lester Ballard? What can he have in common with John Grady Cole—higher brain function?

But the process of interpreting one opaque aspect of a text by close attention to something more transparent is neither new nor (outside a particular field) in need of a specialized approach. The very ground, and its demarcation by fences, its "codes" of landscape, provide persuasive clues to the actions of characters in *The Orchard Keeper*. To see this requires close reading. First, a problem of narration makes this difficult.

To use Kreml's term, "the dominant style of the narrative voice [. . .] the transparent style" used to describe simple action in *All the Pretty Horses* is in no way dominant in McCarthy's first novel. *The Orchard Keeper* rather gives us severely elided narration: there is little of the figured bass of an obvious narrator. The nearest exceptions come in lapses of middle-high Faulknerian, and become less frequent in the later novels. The following description of a group of shacks and their inhabitants serves as an example of the darker registers of this tone:

They were rented to families of gaunt hollow-eyed and darkskinned people, not Mellungeons and not exactly anything else, who reproduced with such frightening prolificness that their entire lives appeared devoted to the production of the ragged line of scions which shoeless and tattered sat for hours at a time on the porch edges, themselves not unlike the victims of some terrible disaster, and stared out across the blighted land with expressions of neither hope nor wonder nor despair. (*TOK* 12)

Not exactly anything else, these people, the extras glimpsed this once (but for a few exceptions) are merely a particular level of clay composing the population of Red Branch, Tennessee, the setting of *The Orchard Keeper*. This demographic inhabit buildings that (compared to their occupants and despite their decrepitude) are ironically personified to a slightly higher level of existence:

[. . .] a dozen jerrybuilt shacks strewn about the valley in unlikely places, squatting over their gullied purlieus like great brooding animals rigid with constipation, and yet endowed with an air transient and happenstantial as if set there by the recession of floodwaters. Even the speed with which they were constructed could not outdistance the decay for which they held such affinity. (*TOK* 11)

Though holding an "affinity" for "decay," these shacks have more life in them than those "not Mellungeons and not exactly anything else"—people. What holds more intention, displays more mobility? I have deliberately quoted backwards: in the text the buildings come to us, with their scatological verbal architecture frozen for us, *before* the people stuck with *with* and *nor*: "with expressions of neither hope nor wonder nor despair." This is the first indication we have in McCarthy of the relationship between ground and figure. Here is the foundation on which the style strands both buildings and people: "Gangrenous molds took to the foundations before the roofs were fairly nailed down. Mud crept up their sides and paint fell away in long white slashes. Some terrible plague seemed to overtake them one by one" (*TOK* 11). In *The Orchard Keeper*, buildings as well as people are all *figures* pulled down by a hostile ground.

This is perhaps more Naturalism than Nihilism, contrary to Vereen Bell's study of the first McCarthy novels. Certainly, in *The Orchard Keeper*, the tone shifts slightly and is not always this dark. What is consistent in the portrayal of all *The Orchard Keeper*'s characters, however, is the narrator's preoccupation with relation: in particular, the relation between people and landscape.[3] Four significant characters in *The Orchard Keeper* seem to be in flight from houses, or civilization in general. The gravitational pull of a "blighted land" (*TOK* 12), however, warps the lines of their individual flights into arcs. Kenneth Rattner and Marion Sylder make their living by the road; one kills the other and ends up in prison for a lesser offense. Arthur Ownby and John Wesley Rattner live by the wilderness, Ownby on the mountains and the boy down in mountain streams, trapping. Ownby also resorts to violence and is institutionalized; only Rattner escapes.

THE STONE ARROGATING TO ITSELF [4]

It is an offense to the living to be surrounded by the dead, and an offense to lawful citizenry to be accosted by the criminal. There are two means of dispensing with offenders, both the living and the dead, by enclosing them in (and on) landscape. If dead, they may be buried; if alive, they may be imprisoned or otherwise institutionalized. In *The Scarlet Letter*, Hawthorne recognized the normative function of allotting portions of common land for these purposes: "The founders of a new colony, whatever Utopia of human virtue and happiness they might originally project, have invariably recognized it among their earliest practical necessities to allot a portion of the virgin soil as a cemetery, and another portion as the site of a prison" (49).

   The Orchard Keeper draws our attention to both functions of allotment. Through most of the book, a drifter named Kenneth Rattner lies dead in an insecticide pit, murdered (perhaps) and not properly buried. Marion Sylder, the killer who acted in self-defense against Rattner, ends up in jail for the lesser crime of running moonshine. Rattner's son, John Wesley, never discovers that the man who killed his father was his older friend, Sylder.

   The book begins, however, with a mysterious prologue: three men are cutting a tree and encounter, entangled in the tree, a barbed wire fence. At the end of the book, the workers are gone, but we realize their work has been only recently done, and that it took place in a cemetery. Their work has enabled two things: there is now room for a new grave in the cemetery—not for Rattner but for his wife, John Wesley's mother; and there is a gap in the cemetery's fence. John Wesley steps through that gap to leave forever the novel's setting.[5]

   The novel tells us all this through an ironic chiasmus: an unburied body awaits in a neglected orchard for the enlargement of a cemetery through the cutting down of a tree. The body's location in an insecticide pit extends this irony. What would normally hold poison for insects in a peach orchard holds instead the dead insectile body of a man; what would mark the boundary of the proper cemetery works in a metaphorical sense to contain *The Orchard Keeper*'s living characters as well as the dead. The appearance of the fence to the reader of this novel serves as a structural boundary; it delays and then allows the departure of the young antinomian, John Wesley Rattner. Another listing of the living and dead in the novel will help.

In contrast to the improper interment of the truly criminal Kenneth Rattner in *The Orchard Keeper*'s orchard, his wife Mildred Yearwood Rattner is buried in the Red Branch cemetery once it has been enlarged by the removal of the fence and tree. Arthur (spelled "Ather" by McCarthy, to suggest the local accent) Ownby, a loner who lives among the mountains South of Knoxville by trading roots and herbs at the local country store, also ends up institutionalized (or *interned*). Sylder goes to jail and Ownby eventually to "a place for crazy people" (*TOK* 227). Of the major characters, only John Wesley escapes.

If the central problem of spatial constraint in *The Orchard Keeper* concerns burial, its central element is metal: more particularly, metal involved in a tension of fencing around the novel's landscape. The key appearance of this tension occurs with the novel's opening—in the entanglement of a tree and fence. The release of that tension—John Wesley Rattner stepping through what is now a gap in that fence—occurs when the novel's story catches up to what we realize was a prologue that the reader simply witnesses before she witnesses the story that preceded the workers. The eventual effect is of flashback; the immediate effect is enigmatic. The workers who remove the tree and fence do so, we realize at the end of the novel, just before John Wesley's final appearance to us.

Why does McCarthy show us the beginning of their work before he shows us the first actions of the story that actually preceded it? Because the action of this prologue takes place much later than the bulk of the story that it nonetheless seems to enable, we feel that the prologue is a modernist enigma, an offering of symbolism where symbolism will not be allowed to fully develop.

We see three men cutting a tree at the fence of a cemetery. I write *at* the fence because the fence and tree have, before this scene, become entangled in an interesting way. This entanglement of fence and tree bars the way for the story, even though we will realize much later that McCarthy's workers are doing away with that barrier. I will, as the three men do, save the completion of the work with this strange problem—of fence and tree—for later. For now it is enough to introduce it as McCarthy does: as an interpretive problem that hovers over the main action of the book.

What follows the prologue seems to have nothing to do with that fence and tree, nor with any of those three men. McCarthy's employment of modernist fragmentation in the book's structure heightens this fact.[6] Ironically, the fragmentation is accompanied by markers that suggest architectural plans unspoiled by "[g]angrenous mold:" the novel is divided into four roman numbered books, with several chapters in each, and a significant number of space breaks within those chapters. Transitions between these pieces of the novel are anything but smooth.

In *The Orchard Keeper*, the repeated use of "he" without even an approximate preceding name is employed to an extreme. Beyond a marked disruption in the flow of the story, the technique prevents us from thinking we are keeping up with any one particular character. We might think we are still with Sylder when a few sentences later we realize we are closer to a cat.[7] The technique is ironic, suggesting simultaneously a close and distant stance; we are simultaneously inside a character (sometimes as much as through free indirect discourse) and yet kept outside.

Some of us might have good reason to feel that we are close inside a particular character referred to only as "he:" who thinks of himself by his own name? I am "I" or "me" to myself, and only "Jay Ellis" to others. Names appear in *The Orchard Keeper* (and almost everywhere else in McCarthy's work) only in dialogue, or when a character is in the presence of another character and it is necessary to distinguish one from another character.

That having been said, some of us undoubtedly find it easier than others to imagine ourselves not far from the footsteps of *The Orchard Keeper*'s main characters. Here, as in McCarthy generally, there is a lot of "he" and very little "she." Women, where they appear, are seldom given names at all.[8] This contributes to the sense in which McCarthy's characters are adrift on a landscape outside the bounds of feminine domesticity. Significantly, this late modernist novel has its main characters—all male—alone throughout much of the action. The men and the boy with whom *The Orchard Keeper* is concerned are nearly as often without names as they are without families. Marion Sylder is shown returning home to his wife only briefly, between long scenes of driving, once after a severe wreck that wounds him enough that he needs the care of a woman-as-nurturer. John Wesley hardly sleeps in the house at all with his mother: he moves his bed out onto the porch—that much closer to the wilderness in which he traps fur-bearing animals. Arthur Ownby is home a little more often (in the narration at least), but this "he" is a widower.[9]

Perhaps it is the presence of John Wesley's mother that braces their house. Edwin Arnold, in "'The World of *The Orchard Keeper*," notes the anomalous quality of this house. "Of all the structures" in the book, "the Rattner house seems the most durable" ("World" 4). Arnold quotes McCarthy's description:

> a house of logs, hand-squared and chinked with clay, the heavy rafters in the loft pinned with wooden pegs. [. . .]
>
> The house was tall and severe with few windows. Some supposed it to be the oldest house in the county. It was roofed with shakes and they seemed the only part of it not impervious to weather and time [. . .] for it was sound and the logs were finely checked and seasoned. (*TOK* 62–63)

Arnold's purpose here is to find the house that may correspond to this fictionalized structure. However, a few details unnecessary to that purpose are interesting to recover from the ellipses above. The novel also gives us, after the detail of the "wooden pegs," that there once was a loom upstairs in the loft, but that "it had since been burned piece by piece for kindling." Then we are told of the house, that "[i]t was a huge affair of rough-cut wood that under the dust had retained even then a yellow newness. The rafters still looked that way" (*TOK* 62).

Then the description contains an odd digression—one that in its details of insects invading a domestic space foreshadows a similar problem in *Child of God*:

> In the summer wasps nested over the boards, using the auger-holes where dowels had shrunk in some old dry weather and fallen to the floor to emerge out into the hot loft and drone past [John Wesley's] bed to the window where a corner of glass was gone and so out into the sunlight. There had been mud-dobber nests stacked up the wide planks too but his mother had raked them all down one day and aside from the wasps there were only the borers and woodworms, which he never saw but knew by the soft cones of wood-dust that gathered on the floor, the top log beneath the eaves, or trailed down upon the cobwebs, heavy yellow sheets of them opaque with dust and thick as muslin. (*TOK* 62–63)

Wasps, mud-dobbers, borers, woodworms, and spiders. No wonder the boy takes his bed to the porch when the weather permits. And those "heavy yellow sheets" that are "thick as muslin" might better serve as winding-sheets for the boy's dead father than as sheets for the living son.

This house, sturdy as it is, oppresses ("tall and severe"). And, in the wasp ellipses, it is under attack from nature. Although it seems impervious to mud from below, the mud of the dobbers (a kind of wasp that builds its nest with mud) is brought up to threaten the house with wet rot. Meanwhile, the weather—once dry, and now about to be very wet—has squeezed the dowels out of their fittings. Wasps, taking advantage of this, continue to weaken the wood.

Just before this description, we were told that John Wesley "thought he could remember his father," and then, less certainly, that "[h]e remembered a man, his father or just some other man he was no longer sure" (*TOK* 62). The assaults on this house are too numerous for the mother to thwart; in a country of traditional gender roles, this house needs a man to look after it. Houses rot quickly without maintenance against the climate of such country; that maintenance consists of girding the house as a constraint against the forces of nature: keep out the weather and all non-human creatures that you can. Indeed, even this description of a "sturdy" house (Arnold, "World" 4) includes, within the second set of Arnold's ellipses, admissions of impending doom. It is the roof—close under which John Wesley sleeps, and from which the wasps seem to drive him—that is troubled. This Telemachus, who dimly remembers his father, cannot be held by that roof. It is "the only part" of the house that seems "not impervious to weather and time," because the shakes of its roof were "blackened and split, and now curling in their ruin they seemed victims of a long-ago fire which the house had somehow escaped altogether, for it was sound and the logs were finely checked and seasoned" (*TOK* 63).

Perhaps Mrs. Rattner was not as troubled by the departure of her husband as her son is, as he remembers "his father or just some other man" (*TOK* 62). In any case, the description does show us the most solid house in all of McCarthy's works. Nonetheless, the roof is already troubled and will, by the end of the book, fail.

The outer form of *The Orchard Keeper* seems at odds with its inner stylistic devices. Inside the regularity of the roman numerals that divide the book, inside the chapters, the sentences run on, pronouns without immediate preceding antecedent challenging the reader's ability to keep the story straight. It is, indeed, anything but a straight story. It is as if the characters were entangled with one another, even though most of the book consists of narration following the movements of one character or another at a time—often alone. Something is not right in the novel's structure, and this suits its themes. Just as the workers of the prologue have encountered a fence and tree entangled, the reader is apt to feel that she has encountered several stories entangled.

Marion Sylder's is a story of nearly being killed by and instead killing Kenneth Rattner, dumping the body back in Red Branch in the insecticide pit of the title's orchard, wrecking his car while running moonshine, taking revenge on the constable harassing him, and finally being arrested when the car stalls on the bridge into Knoxville.

John Wesley Rattner's is a story of a boy yearning to leave home and avenge the death of his father—though we get little of this in any reliable action or speech from him. Thus, it is more immediately a story of learning to trap animals for the money brought by their pelts, or turning in a dead hawk for a bounty and then regretting it, of John Wesley's friendship with Sylder, and his eventual departure from Red Branch. He returns at the death of his mother and leaves at the novel's end.

Arthur Ownby's is the story of the orchard's keeper, an old man wandering through the woods, annoyed by a large metal storage tank the government has put up on the mountain where his neglected orchard is located. He is haunted by a strange cat, and by memories of his former life. He is the unwilling caretaker of a body he finds in the insecticide pit of the orchard. Finally, he is shot at, pursued, eventually arrested for shooting the government tank, and sent to a mental hospital.

Of these three main characters, the two grown men are eventually interned, Sylder in prison and Ownby in an asylum. The elder Rattner's bones are discovered, leading presumably to a proper burial (though we do not follow the bones that far). At the novel's conclusion, John Wesley finds that both his mother and her house have been returned to the earth. There seems to be no way out of Red Branch. The people are entangled with their community as is the tree and the fence. Either the ground, or the civic conventions constructed above that ground (against shooting at government property, against running moonshine), would constrain them. This is true also in passages not directly related to the fate of the main characters. The people of Red Branch seem entangled with the very ground beneath them. What more positive spatial constraint could serve them—far better than a prison or a grave—than a simple home?

But homes are unstable here as well. Returning our attention to the buildings that "squat" over *The Orchard Keeper's* landscape, we see that the home is not quite safe from outside trouble, trouble from the dark roads or the dark wilderness. Ownby is haunted out of his fitful sleep with half-dreams of the cat which, if it indeed carries the transmigrated soul of Kenneth Rattner, has put Rattner through a sex change. To Ownby a cat can loom larger than a housecat. The ghostly female panther that troubles his imagination is a "she painter" that "wadn't no common kind of painter." In a scene of outdoor danger, Ownby is nearly killed when lightning knocks a "slab" of tree onto him (*TOK* 172). He is hardly safer indoors, however, where the phantom "wampus cat" tries to come through the window on him (*TOK* 60).

In another scene of indoor vulnerability, Marion Sylder attacks the constable, a man named Lucky Gifford, in the man's own home. Sylder, like Ownby's "wampus cat," uses the window to steal into the home of his nemesis. Sylder first drives past a mausoleum of grand domestic architecture, a mansion for which the surrounding wilderness is protected from unrevenued liquor and unlicensed trapping by the constable Gifford.[10] Sylder drives past,

> the porch posts dead-white as plaster casts of those untrimmed poles, the huge carved lion's head in fierce cameo upon the door, the brass knocker brightly pendant from its nostrils, and the barred panes buckling in the light planeless as falling water, passing out of the glare in willowing sheets to darkness, stark and stable once again. Past his own house, dark but for the light on the porch, and then across the mountain, still slowly, pulling the grades down under the wheels easily. (*TOK* 166)

This depiction of the king of cats in the "huge carved lion's head" is evidence of the taming function of all civilization in McCarthy: civil authority (such as Gifford's) attempts to bring the wilderness into the service of the domestic. The lion's nose is ringed, even, turning him into the servitude of announcing guests. It is an apt example of the efficacy of the constabulary control of both township and its wilderness environs.

Sylder passes these claims to control indifferently, under the cover of darkness and with the power of the road's possibilities beneath him. Reaching Gifford's house, he climbs through the open window, whispering in "mock and inaudible greeting" to the sleeping man in a language Sylder no doubt learned far from Red Branch, and one that Gifford probably does not know: "*Es muy malo que no tengas un perro*" (*TOK* 167). Gifford wakes up just as his nemesis is standing over his bed, "sleep leaving him in slow grudging waves, so that he seemed to be coming up to meet it, the fist rocketing down out of blackness and into his face with a pulpy sound like a thrown melon bursting" (*TOK* 167).

None of the accoutrements of middle class domesticity will protect Gifford if he lacks an animal intermediary for security. *It's very bad not to have a dog*[11]. In other words, there is no security within domestic space unless one has a watchdog—a domesticated animal either allowed to sound alarm from outside the house or allowed inside to protect from intrusion.

Writing on the protection afforded by houses, Gaston Bachelard focuses on two exterior threats to the house's occupant: harsh weather (41–43) and animal aggression (44). Connecting the two threats as one, Bachelard notes,

> that all aggression, whether it come from man or from the world, is of animal origin. However subtle, however indirect, hidden or contrived a human act of aggression may be, it reveals an origin that is unredeemed. In the tiniest of hatreds, there is a little, live, animal filament. [. . .] It is also a terrible trait of men that they should be incapable of understanding the forces of the universe intuitively, otherwise than in terms of a psychology of wrath. (44)

The psychology of wrath in *The Orchard Keeper* is easy enough to infer in the characters by observing exterior effects that border on the pathetic fallacy. Behind the actions of these people, there is both an extended flood (with its dangerous lightning), and a mysterious cat on the prowl. The dying hand of Kenneth Rattner "shrivel[s] into a tight claw, like a killed spider" (*TOK* 40). Gifford lives too far from the magical protection of stone lions, and he does not have a dog. His home is therefore unsafe, as it is unmediated by a domesticated animal.

LINES OF FLIGHT: "WILL YOU GO NOW? WILL YOU GO?" [12]

If we look at any of the central characters in *The Orchard Keeper*, we see them in one way or another in flight from civilization, from other people—and particularly from houses. Sylder spends more time in his car than at home, until his car stalls and he is easily arrested. Interestingly, his car does not simply run out of gas; rather, the gasoline has been watered. The two do not mix, so when the gasoline (which is lighter than water) is depleted, the water kills the engine. If you put water into your gas tank, your car will work just fine—for a while. This means that the fuel taken from the ground and refined for Sylder's car runs out just as it is replaced by the water which elsewhere seems to diffuse the landscape of Red Branch. Fleeing back and forth over Red Branch's surface, Sylder is eventually done in by one of its unrefined elements—water. So, too, as a moonshiner Sylder is hauling clear liquid (that could probably have fueled his car). This strong stuff is, for many of the community's residents, a near replacement for water.

Arthur Ownby's downfall involves a similar confrontation with official authority. Gifford and the local sheriff go to question Ownby about the charred bones in his orchard pit. Ownby runs them off with a shotgun. On a second attempt, Ownby shoots three deputies, and the delegation gives up again (*TOK* 185–6). The third time, Ownby has already fled. "They lobbed teargas bombs through the windows and stormed the ruined house from three sides and the house jerked and quivered visibly under their gunfire" (*TOK* 188). The house, attacked in place of its owner, becomes personified under the assault.

Ownby, like Sylder, is apprehended for a crime other than the one most significant to the novel's plot. Rattner's body has been discovered (again) by children, who this time set fire to it. In the meantime, we have followed Marion Sylder on his moonshine runs through the difficult roads of the countryside around Red Branch. On one such errand Sylder accidentally comes across Ownby:

> When [Sylder] got to the edge of the clearing where the installation stood he could see the man with the muzzle of the gun sticking through the fence-wire. He fired and the barrel came up short, sending waves out along the woven mesh and back. The man jerked under the recoil and the smoke spurted, slowed and billowed in the damp air. There were six neat black holes in the polished skin of the tank, angled up across it in a staggered line. The man broke the gun and picked the shells out. Sylder saw him hold them up for brief inspection before throwing them to the side, and saw them dance in the new light and knew what they were: the brass bases of the shells only, flicking and turning like coins as they fell. (*TOK* 97)

We can only speculate why the man (Arthur Ownby) is shooting at the tower.

This suggests a value exactly opposite the primacy of mentality that we see in Henry James, where a flash of feeling becomes the perturbation in the narrative spider's web. Thought, even feeling, is almost never the primary object of McCarthy's art within a given moment. The only indication of thought in the passage above is the "brief inspection" Ownby makes of the empty shotgun shell casings—and this is at the remove of Sylder's position hiding in the brush. The shells have more evidence of life in them than "the man" Ownby does: they "dance in the [. . .] light." The tank itself has "skin"—even though Ownby is shooting the tank because it is unnatural. That interpretive move I just made, however (that Ownby's motivation issues from the effect of the tank's unnaturalness on him), requires the work of making connections between repeated instances of "metal" and the like in *The Orchard Keeper*; the interpretation cannot be made from inside the single paragraph above. How could we know why the man shoots the tank? We are not in the depths of thought or feeling with this character.

Later, the stance will enter Sylder's consciousness precisely when he is wondering at the reason behind the actions he witnessed. Well after Sylder watches the odd assault on the tank, he wonders, as we must, at the purpose behind the action. Lying in bed, the question comes to Sylder with "a bile-sharp foretaste of disaster. *Why was that old man shooting holes in the government tank on the mountain?*" (*TOK* 168). Reading the novel for the first time, we might know the answer no better than Sylder. This is because the question is insufficiently supported by its context ("on the mountain"). The hint is there—that the novel is deeply concerned with a fundamental conflict between landscape and metal, between natural spaces transformed into unnatural places, and between the natural and unnatural constraint of characters bent on escape—but only the hint.

The decision to allow the reader access to inner questions, but not to inner motivations, is interesting. McCarthy's characters move like arcs in the darkness; we have to see once more the ground against which their actions figure. Because at first we have them simply doing things, we have few clues as to why they do what they do. Character is difficult to see in these novels; setting, however, is not.

This is true even when something other than human beings is what moves across (or in the following case, down) a McCarthy setting. The Green Fly Inn, a roadhouse, is one of the secondary "characters" in *The Orchard Keeper*. It moves, violently. Finally, it dies, burned as much as the skeleton of Kenneth Rattner. In passages dealing particularly with this roadhouse, personification is the natural hint that the Green Fly Inn is more character than setting. But in the larger context of the novel we may also read into the employment of another reference to metal the idea that the Green Fly Inn is a site of contest between the natural land and a construction of culture in a manmade landscape—such culture as a roadhouse offers. Like the human characters in *The Orchard Keeper*, this building is perched precariously above what will later become its grave.

McCarthy's first novel is, like the four that follow it, set within a landscape that is strikingly different from the flat deserts upon which his last five take place. The countryside around (mostly South of) Knoxville, in which the Rattners, Sylder, and Ownby move, is vertiginous. Full of hills and hollows and with few straight lines possible, few places where anything could even move in a straight line, the setting is introduced under a preposition: "Under the west wall of the mountain is a community called Red Branch" (*TOK* 11). The mountain comes first, and then the community built "under" it.

One of the shards of narrative climax toward the end of the novel serves as a good example of the vertiginous quality of Red Branch. Here the character is not human, and the view is therefore closer to the ground and its undulations. This cat, however, is like the human characters of the novel in her compromise with the landscape: her body rolls with the complications of moving over the ground that falls and rises under it; the head moves in contrast, by a different ideal of motion: "Softly and with slow grace her leathered footpads fell, hind tracking fore with a precision profoundly feline, a silken movement where her shoulders rolled, haunches swayed. Belly swaying slightly too, lean but pendulous. Head low and divorced of all but linear motion, as if fixed along an unseen rail" (*TOK* 216). We have one of many identifications of the natural with the artificial, in the head moving "as if along an unseen rail." Is this the same cat that in front of Sylder's speeding car, 185 pages earlier, "stood highlegged and lanterneyed in the road, bunched, floated away over the roadbank on invisible wires" (*TOK* 31)?

That was a bobcat caught in the headlights of Marion Sylder's car as it hurtled down "a narrow strip of asphalt numbered 129 slipping away beneath him like tape from a spool" (*TOK* 31). In any case, Sylder's car is, like the cat, female: it carries the hot liquid of the illegal still. As Sylder and accomplices unload cases of moonshine, we see "the car creaking and rising bit by bit until they had finished and it stood with its rear end high in the air like a cat in heat" (*TOK* 165). Like the cat, the car achieves a dangerous compromise with the road. "In the mountains the road was thin and gravel and he slewed down the curves on drifting wheels" (*TOK* 31). The meaning is that the surface of the road, which would be artificially smooth, is instead loose, more like dirt, its small rocks refusing point-to-point contact with the tires. The result is that the car nearly takes flight, "drifting" through the turns. Later, while Sylder negotiates a "road glazed with ice" we note that he "amused himself by drifting the coupe from curve to curve like a boat tacking" (*TOK* 166).

Elsewhere, Sylder's car is again like the cat in its struggle between undulating earth and the pure space of sky that, with metal, affords straight flight: "The coup dropped, squatted for a moment in the gravel of the lower road, sprang again and slithered away obliquely with the exhaust bellowing from the cutout and gravel popping and rattling in the woods like grapeshot" (*TOK* 19). The personification here is especially interesting, given that the car is at this moment carrying two young "girls" who were identified only as "the taller one" and "the little one" (*TOK* 18–19) when they were picked up by Sylder and June (a man) and taken to an abandoned church (and outhouse) for sex. Here the car, foreshadowing the sex, conducts also an assault on nature, with its "grapeshot" of gravel into the woods.

Sex and flight seem here to be parallel activities. The trick of "anomic" (*TOK* 222) survival in and around Red Bank is to rise up from difficult traction in a jumbled landscape to a line as straight as only metal ("invisible wires") can afford. The bobcat that "floated" away from the threat of Sylder's car will not, however, escape the threat of a purely airborne predator. Returning to the chapter that begins with the description of the bobcat moving with its head "along an unseen rail," we see further evidence of the vertiginous landscape and threat from above. The bobcat is "emerging" "at dusk-dark" "to make her way down the narrow patch as cats go" (*TOK* 216). Note the way the prepositions reinforce, along with the hypotactic syntax, the nouns of a world that is nowhere flat:

> She passed through the honeysuckles by a dark tunnel where the earth still held moisture, down the bank to a culvert by which she crossed beneath the road and came into a field and into a dry gully, the cracked and curling clay like a paving of potsherds, and turning up an artery of the wash, grown here with milkweed and burdock[,[13]] following a faint aura of vole or shrew, until she came to a small burrow in the grasses. (*TOK* 216–17)

Instead of predator, however, the cat becomes prey. She is taken around the same time as Sylder and Ownby are arrested, the same time as the discovery of Kenneth Rattner's body, and just before the first departure of young John Wesley Rattner—all of which is told the reader within twenty pages of the following:

> When she left the rocks, was clear of the overreaching branches of the tree, there grew about her a shadow in the darkness like pooled ink spreading, a soft-hissing feathered sound which ceased even as she half turned, saw unbelieving the immense span of wings cupped

downward, turned again, already squalling when the owl struck her
back like a falling rock. (*TOK* 217)

This animal is more at home in this landscape than humans could ever be.
To her, the landscape provides shelter and food, and predation is something
of the air. Here the personification points to the human problem with death:
we are "unbelieving" when it comes for us. Death, although it suffuses Red
Branch, is preposterous to those for whom it comes. Here the size of the
agent is impressive. Despite the reference by Ownby to a panther (and there
were panthers—also known as cougars or mountain lions—in that part of
Tennessee at that time), the book seems to settle on a bobcat for this animal's
species. A raptor that can carry up a bobcat would be rare, but death does
not bother with proportion.

McCarthy's characters often seem at odds with the facts of nature as
much as culture. As antinomians, they exist in such stark opposition to the
normative constraints of the dominant culture that they seem all the more
dependent on conflict with that culture. They are not, therefore, much more
at home in the wilderness than in civilization. Even Ownby, who knows well
enough how to make his living from nature—well enough to have given up
cultivating it in his orchard for a business of hunting and gathering roots
and herbs—loses sleep over his fear of a mysterious "painter." Moreover, that
he is a "keeper" of the Orchard, albeit without cultivating it, points to the
infrangibility of connection between McCarthy characters and their landscapes. Without recourse to psychology, we can nonetheless determine the
underlying psychological force beneath Ownby: he is ambivalent about his
surroundings. After all, if we must imagine him without connection to the
civilized world, why does he trade his roots and herbs to it? Why, beyond
some sense of moral duty—however different from the sanctioned authority
of the tower against which he rebels—does he keep the unsanctioned grave
of Rattner?

This ambivalence, fixed between the natural land of Red Branch and
its uneasy proximity to the urban civilization of Knoxville, results in repeated
attempts to leave the area: Sylder, near the beginning of the book, had just
given up the idea of leaving Red Branch for good when he picks up Rattner
on the way back. For this reason I see McCarthy's characters as lines across
setting—they are constantly on the move, out for space, because if they stay
in one place they are doomed to alienation and death. How may we interpret
such character lines?

We may first assume that McCarthy, as many have argued,[14] is
significantly a visual writer. John Beck extends this idea, arguing that

McCarthy's Westerns are photographic, devoid of life and line—static. In "'A Certain but Fugitive Testimony:' Witnessing the Light of Time in Cormac McCarthy's Southwestern Fiction," Beck finds in McCarthy's deserts an atemporal fixity: "Analogous to the flattening of space in the desert is the foreshortening of time evident in the practice of storytelling by many incidental characters within the novels, where history does not unfold in temporal succession but is always already here, a surface rather than a line" (126).

Beck means to draw on Barthes in *Camera Lucida*, whom he quotes at the beginning of his article. I would make another connection, to Joseph Frank in his "Spatial Form in Modern Literature:" fiction may achieve a condition one might think possible only in the plastic arts.[15] Our eyes may move along from word to word, but some writers are capable of capturing something outside time on the page: an image, caught almost outside time, an image in a point. Outside of time's line, this image appears to stop time altogether. Those readers who find this to be a valuable effect in reading may remember Flannery O'Connor's advice that writers study "of course and particularly drawing" ("The Nature and Aim of Fiction" 84).

John Beck's understanding of the visual aspects of McCarthy may come more from Barthes than Frank, but whether we consider McCarthy landscapes as something like photos or more like drawings—and paintings—the effect is one of a static image. I prefer painting for my analogy, rather than the photography referred to in Barthes and in many other essays on McCarthy.[16] Regardless of our awareness that photography is not an objective depiction of its subject, we can never quite escape the feeling that photography is less fictive than painting. We think—we understand through a caveat enabled by ratiocination—that photography constructs a world as much or more than it represents one; but we do not yet feel this so much as we now do in painting. Photography is fictive, it is something other than straight representation, because of what it leaves out, and in how it frames what it does decide to show us. In my analogy, I mean to suggest only those aspects of the artist's visual imagination that fit his or her vision—not the reception of sight through the optic nerve, but the visual creation in the mind's eye. In the eye of the mind reading McCarthy (if not in the McCarthy mind's eye) the image of landscape is static. Yet that image is so static, so still, as to resonate with what is missing.

This is part of the tension between McCarthy's landscapes and his characters. Just as we must read the landscapes to infer the psychology of the characters, we must likewise read the flights of the characters to infer the temporality of the landscape. McCarthy's spaces are full of temporal variation and endless possibility. It is in the formation of those spaces into places—sites of architectural constraint—that landscape appears to become static but in actuality gives way to time, to decay. Various characters in the Westerns imagine the land to be free from time, but this is a construction of landscape (of an idea of what constitutes land).[17]

To be sure, the quality of McCarthy's landscapes is difficult to generalize. At key moments, McCarthy's prose is an enactment of visual prosopopoeia:[18] he gives us a canvas of something that is all the more real for its unreality—or its loss. His visual effects are similar to the aural effects in Hemingway: pay close attention to them and they seem odd, awkward, and even false. Yet, they compel as if they were real. Hemingway knew that for dialogue to seem real it could not be truly realistic—if must leave out much of what we real people, less carefully, blurt out. McCarthy's landscapes are similarly false to the effect of presenting themselves powerfully to us. His deserts omit the bumps and declivities that in all real deserts abound. (A desert walked across is entirely different from one seen.) He stretches his settings and they dry into the hard surfaces across which he paints for us the movements of his characters.

It remains to further pursue the function of his characters across that canvas. That movement is not simply a line of time drawn across the static surface of setting, however. Because there are gravities in McCarthy's landscapes, what appears to be flat in his deserts is only flat to the eye. In the Western novels, even the desert landscapes turn out to be warped by gravitational forces that distort the lines of flight of their characters. What would be a straight line of flight becomes curved by the very exigencies that compel and repel the characters in their flights. The courses of their movements across McCarthy's landscapes are therefore arcs: curved lines that begin and end in some form of constraint, and reaching only at their meridians some significant measure of escape from the gravity of setting. Houses, prisons, and graves trap them, and this is little mitigated by the apparent flatness of McCarthy's desert landscapes. McCarthy's characters miniate—in red more often than not. They describe arcs, or die trying to describe, relatively small arcs across the settings of each novel. McCarthy's most compelling landscapes are like narrative particle accelerators: now and then a crack in the tunnel allows a character to fly out into darkness; more often there is no more than temporary flight.

More obviously, though, in the vertiginous landscape of Red Branch, most of the major characters of *The Orchard Keeper* move through lines of flight that become arcs down to prisons or graves. They run trap lines and white lightening in ways that bring them into conflict with the hills surrounding them. The book begins with an aborted escape, which leads to a murder, and when the truth behind that murder is never fully divulged, the narration—more preoccupied with a flood and a curious bobcat—seems to pull the rest of the story into an existential pit.

Alone in escape is John Wesley Rattner, who steps through a fence broken by its having been cut—in the prologue—along with a tree *through* which *the fence* had grown. In anticipation of a growing preoccupation with fences and fencing in *Blood Meridian* and *The Border Trilogy*, the line of fencing on the ground is broken, providing for the exceptional departure of John Wesley at the novel's conclusion. John Wesley Rattner is in flight from the enclosing spaces of his home and even the largest town nearby—the sizable Knoxville, Tennessee. He is also a character in flight from the entrapment of epilogue. Above all, he is in flight from the graves of his ancestors.

DOWN AND CUT TO LENGTHS [19]

Cormac McCarthy's novels are often fenced with prologues and epilogues, often including vivid details of fencing. We might even designate McCarthy's prologues as particularly spatial, in that they introduce not only the setting, the landscape, of the novel to come, but also structural limits of the novel itself. The setting of *The Orchard Keeper*'s prologue is especially liminal: a cemetery. Its limits—a fence—are in question. The prologue is therefore itself a type of fence, if a disturbed one.

Between the two views of graveyard fencing at the beginning and end of *The Orchard Keeper*, there are other, similar markers. Human attempts to partition landscape and cover it with roads become sites of contest between the natural and the manmade.[20] As the passage where Sylder's car throws gravel into the woods suggests, the line between road and ground is uncertain.

The place that Sylder's car is leaving behind in that scene is called a "cutout," a place that is not paved as well as the road and yet pushes back the woods enough that a car can park or turn around in it. One sees this on country roads in the South: rural road building under State budgets cannot afford curbs; rather, the edge of the pavement and the edge of the grass or dirt alongside it are not uniform boundaries. A fence might help to keep the natural world from reclaiming a road, even if its primary purpose is to keep humans and their livestock to one or another side of it. The most that natural land can do to shrug off such human constriction of it is to wait: time and gravity will do their work—as will weather.

What help falls from above falls on the natural and the manmade without distinction, enacting an equal justice: "Still the rain, eating at the roads, cutting gullies on the hills till they ran red and livid as open wounds. The creek came up into the fields, a river of mud questing among the honeysuckles. Fenceposts like the soldiers of Pharaoh marched from sight into the flooded draws" (*TOK* 173). Those fenceposts drown in a red sea across which nothing has escaped. Ironically, our reappearing cat moves through this scene by accepting the high ground already claimed by men, "trod[ing] the high crown of the road, bedraggled and diminutive, a hunted look about her" (*TOK* 174).

We may read this flood as a judgment of fences and their unnatural demarcations, but also of the larger world of Red Branch after the improper interment of Kenneth Rattner's body. This weather impedes the business of running moonshine by Sylder, the man guilty (if understandably so) of killing Rattner. The flood also turns the whole countryside into a version—a Red Branch written larger in the landscape—of the creek where the dead man's son, John Wesley, has laid his traps for mink and other animals.

The flood that begins the fourth major section of the book continues for seven days, after which the main plot points of the novel come to several small climaxes. Arthur Ownby is tracked and arrested after he shoots the deputies who have come to his house to question him about the body in his orchard. Marion Sylder is finally arrested as well, though his part in Kenneth Rattner's death is never disclosed to the other characters. Even the cat, which we have followed from time to time in mysterious passages, is taken into the air in an arc that is opposite that of the humans, whose deaths take them downward. It only remains for John Wesley to trace an arc beyond the environs of Red Branch, to flee, to escape this vertiginous countryside.

The workers of the prologue provide the gap through which John Wesley may flee. They also provide the gap through which the text of *The Orchard Keeper* is possible. In an extra-textual sense, they provide an opening for us into the world of Rattner's story. We might risk inflating their importance even further.

They serve also as guardians of the larger McCarthy oeuvre that follows this first novel. We see these workers standing around the tree "growed through by a fence" (*TOK* 3), and from the distance of the nine novels that follow their first appearance, they assume this larger role: between the moment when their work is stopped by the entanglement of tree and fence, and the gap through which John Wesley walks away from the story's setting, we have *The Orchard Keeper*. Beyond the moment of John Wesley leaving through the gap in that fence, we have the remaining eight novels (as of this printing) of Cormac

McCarthy. There will be little to hold onto, to value without question, within the world of McCarthy's characters. One of the few things of insistent value in that world is work. Manual labor is one of the very few human activities to receive a consistent respect in McCarthy's novels. Much of the manual labor we see in the novels involves the erection and destruction, the keeping and cutting, of fences.

McCarthy accords notable respect to any such work. If all human work with the hands takes place along a spectrum between the natural world and human manipulation of it, then the value of any particular work is unaltered by its position on that spectrum. One traps wild animals, or breaks horses, or mends fences—or burns them. McCarthy presents us with scavengers (the necrophilic Lester Ballard), gatherers (Arthur Ownby), trappers (John Wesley, and later Billy Parham in *The Crossing*), hunters (Billy Parham, John Grady Cole, and Llewelyn Moss), farmers (failing, always, and often the victims of murder, such as the Squire in *Outer Dark*), and ranchers (John Grady and Billy Parham). The respect due all such work is evident throughout in some of the most beautiful language McCarthy has given us.

None of this work, however, is in simple harmony with nature. The cowboy who cuts his way through fencing will later be paid to mend it. Nonetheless, the value of manual labor over less material activity seems reliable. In *The Orchard Keeper*, the social worker who interviews Ownby near the end of the novel is the outsider, a man who clearly does not understand the community he has been sent to study. Marion Sylder is similarly employed in non-manual labor, having been presumably disenchanted by his experience with unskilled manual labor in a factory.[21]

In *All the Pretty Horses,* we know that John Grady Cole has reached his Miltonic Eden (where Adam and Eve had chores to do before the fruit) when we see him ride with Alejandra, at La Purísima. His work and his love are interestingly, even amusingly, entangled in the body of the horse he rides—a stallion whose stall is near the bunk assigned to John Grady in the same barn. Before his value as a "hand" has been noted, however, he is questioned by his Mexican counterparts. The vaqueros of La Purísima are not artificers of words, of how things might be seen or described; they are workers whose respect for empirical reality comes through their hands.[22]

> They listened with great attention as John Grady answered their questions and they nodded solemnly and they were careful of their demeanor that they not be thought to have opinions on what they heard for like most men skilled at their work they were scornful of any least suggestion of knowing anything not learned at first hand. (*ATPH* 95–96)

This description was written by a man who worked at manual labor regularly to support his writing, and for its own sake. According to the first interview that McCarthy gave to *New York Times* writer Richard B. Woodward, McCarthy took on manual labor to support his writing. "I knew I could write. I just had to figure out how to eat while doing this" (30). McCarthy worked in an auto supply warehouse and repaired cars in Chicago. Back in Tennessee, a black family of masons taught him stonemasonry (an experience which led to his first stage play, *The Stonemason*). This apprenticeship taught him the rare skill of how to build using stone that has not been cut to fit—without using any mortar. The barn that he lived in with his first wife, Lee Holleman, was actually a finished-out home worthy of any retiring urbanites looking for a place in the country—all of the renovations done by McCarthy. As a final addition to the building, McCarthy built a study entirely by freestone technique, with no need for weatherproofing beyond the careful fit of the found stones (Luce, "Suttree's Knoxville"). Clearly, McCarthy's education in labor shifted the focus of skilled manual labor from an activity to support his writing, to a value informing his literary work.

In McCarthy's play *The Stonemason*,

> [t]he breakdown of the family in the play mirrors the recent disappearance of stoneworking as a craft. "Stacking up stone is the oldest trade there is," [McCarthy] says. [. . .] "Not even prostitution can come close to its antiquity. It's older than anything, older than fire. And in the last 50 years, with hydraulic cement, it's vanishing. I find that rather interesting." (Woodward 31)

Especially if we consider McCarthy's preference that his works speak for themselves, it is easier to put the importance of work into a larger perspective: McCarthy prefers the hand over the mouth. Apart from the mild comment of "interesting," McCarthy leaves it to simple descriptions of work inside his fiction to argue this value. By contrast, his most talkative character, judge Holden, is a devil not to be trusted.

We may read the choice to open and close many of the novels with manual labor as one of choosing the hand over the mouth. Culture and its artifacts are everywhere in McCarthy viewed with a cold eye. Why write books that seem so regularly to be against books? Or rather, why undertake a narrative that so seriously questions itself in its own endeavor? Perhaps for the sheer craft of moving words, like stones, so that they fit together—with no need of mortar.

It is fitting that the men who make way both for John Wesley's flight and for the story leading up to it are workers. The work they do, despite the tangle of fence and tree, makes possible a rare instance in McCarthy: a character going on to perhaps better things and places than surrounded him in the novel.

> The workers had gone, leaving behind their wood-dust and chips, the white face of the stump pooling the last light out of the gathering dusk. The sun broke through the final shelf of clouds and bathed for a moment the dripping trees with blood, tinted the stones a diaphanous wash of color, as if the very air had gone to wine. (*TOK* 246)

John Wesley looks backward here as we can from a longer view, over the graves of McCarthy characters and over the leavings of those who manage to get farther down the road. The linkage of the sun with blood, of course, will become its own title in the fifth novel and persist beyond it through *The Border Trilogy*. The gathering gloom here, however, foreshadows that light giving way to the "fire in a horn" that is "[a]bout the color of the moon," carried by Bell's father in the concluding dream of *No Country for Old Men* (*NCFOM* 309).

The workers of *The Orchard Keeper* have cleared the way for us as much as for John Wesley Rattner. Two things were in the way: a tree oddly "growed through" a fence (*TOK* 3). The life given to the fence by the writer is interesting, a variation of what used to be done with trees. This tree is not one of Hardy's Wessex varieties, however: there is no President of the Immortals directing it. Unlike Hardy's personification of nature for either a heightened sense of a character's psychology, or an ironic contrast of it, this tree seems less alive than the fence. One might add the use of trees as symbolic of Calvary. The trees over the holly bushes among which Tess seeks refuge from a "well-to-do boor" are a last refuge for wounded pheasants, and therefore suggest themselves as such to Tess (217–218).

McCarthy allows no such symbolic consolation in his woods—Ownby is knocked down by a falling branch, and "[a] clash of shields rings and Valkyrie descend with cat's cries to bear him away" (*TOK* 172). We know better than to trust Hardy's suggestion of salvation. We trust McCarthy's "Valkyrie" even less, despite the modulation to a pagan context. As we find out later, that "cat's cries" might have been literal—and if so, might also have been the calls of a transmigrated thief.

When it is the fence that is personified by the worker, the reader wonders how far to go with that personification. Barbed wire is made by machinery that does seem to give life to woven strands of iron,[23] and the promethean act of carving the landscape with this wire seems here to have turned loose an energy that not only resists the natural encroachment of the tree but actively contests it. The force of the fence prevails even as that of the tree yields: "The tree was down and cut to lengths [. . .]" (*TOK* 3). But the "stump" described on the last page (*TOK* 246) still stands as "the butt of the tree" on the first (*TOK* 3). The change in its description reflects the fact that the workers are forced to give up the proper end of their task.

The tree is tough enough itself: "Damned old elum's bad enough on a saw" (*TOK* 3). The crosscut saw the men are using, however, is a type that could cut the tree down to the very ground around it; this would yield another "section" not only of wood, but, if the stump were removed, would provide that much less impediment to another body's burial—they are working in a cemetery. This cemetery we will not see again until the final chapter of the novel, which resists the formal quality of an epilogue by not being presented in italics (as the first passage with the tree and fence is), and by being entangled with the main character of the book, John Wesley Rattner. This structural complexity affirms my reading of the work these workers do as being both narrative and formal. The last chapter is a "chapter" and not an epilogue also because the workers have invisibly done their work and are gone. What will remain are only "wood-dust and chips," "torn iron palings, and something else:"[24] the workers have created a gap in the fence.

To have given us an epilogue as such (in italics, without the initial capital given the beginning of each major section) would have been an act of closing off the narrative, fencing it in, as it were. Here as throughout McCarthy the implications of action within the narrative are reinforced by the formal aspects of its presentation. The words, in their choice and arrangement and even typographical features, do what they say.

The curious work between the prologue and the book's end is the act of killing a natural thing that has grown up and around a manmade division of the land. The land divided is divided between the living and the dead. Around, or—given the description we reach at the end of the book—along one side of the plots of earth holding individuals "sheathed" within the "crust" (*TOK* 244) of mother earth, we have a fence. We know that it is the tree that has done the growing, at least literally, and that the wire the men find trying to cut the log after they have felled the tree is only incidentally threaded up through the years of growth. Imagine the elm, unnoticed by generations of mourners burying their dead, pulling the barbed wire from the fence up toward the sky as it grew, and then growing over the wound. The men, however, feel otherwise. Speaking of the wire, they see *it* as the agent; one of them says "Yessa [. . .] It most sholy has. Growed all up in that tree" (*TOK* 3).

Carolyn Merchant has written that in the Renaissance,

> all things were permeated by life, there being no adequate method by
> which to designate the inanimate from the animate. It was difficult to
> differentiate between living and nonliving things, because of the resem-
> blance in structures. Like plants and animals, minerals and gems were
> filled with small pores, tablets, cavities, and streaks, through which they
> seemed to nourish themselves. (27–28)

This situation resulted in a generalized paradigm that the earth was alive,
was indeed "mother" earth. Among the circumscriptions on human activity
implicit in such a worldview is that you do not intrusively mine the earth;
you don't rape your mother. One "belief held about mining was the metaphor of the golden tree. The earth deep within its bowels produced and gave
form to the metals, which then rose as mist up through the trunk, branches,
and twigs of a great tree whose roots originated at the earth's center" (29). In
other words, not only was it believed that metal was a living part of the earth,
growing and moving like blood through "veins," metal was in fact understood as something that is not at odds with nature at all—it is nature.

We may now more easily accept that the fence at the edge of the cemetery in *The Orchard Keeper* indeed grew up into tree. McCarthy regularly
uses what would appear to be anachronistic or otherwise uncanny imagery
involving metal with living creatures. It might be possible to take this observation further, to infer that McCarthy's novels are requiems for a lost world.
According to Merchant, that world was "organic." "[O]rganismic theory
emphasized interdependence among the parts of the human body, subor-
dination of individual to communal purposes in family, community, and
state, and vital life permeating the cosmos to the lowliest stone" (1). Perhaps
this could explain the concomitant problems of family, housing, fencing,
and burial: they are often presented in scenes that conflate the natural land
with human constructions of artificial landscape. The lost world was organic,
replaced by a world of binaries, where the constructions of place overwhelm
the voice of space.

If the organic is McCarthy's lost world (and a better one), then behind
the wreckage of humanity across his landscapes, are fences a natural feature?
Perhaps not: the manipulation of the metal by human hands renders the fence
artificial, obviously. It is ironic that, as Frieda Knobloch notes in *The Culture
of Wilderness*, the American Steel and Wire Company of Chicago found a use
for the industrial waste that was a by-product of their primary product: what
was left over from making barbed wire proved to be a deadly herbicide (138).

It is tempting, in McCarthy's novels as much as in our everyday lives, to see an easy dichotomy between the "natural" and the "manmade."

Yet a fence erected to delineate the edge of a graveyard might not be much more artificial than a tree planted there—or even left there—for the same purpose. Both have to go when the ground gets too full in the cemetery. Many aspects of McCarthy's landscape—particularly the skies above it—do not fit a single theoretical interpretation. Ambiguity marks most aspects of the natural world in McCarthy. The planets and stars that wheel around the sometimes personified planet are cold and distant; nature will kill you as soon as suffer you; the fence that frustrates the cowboy in his escape will keep his horses once he's found the new Eden in which to settle.

From the beginning of McCarthy's first novel we would also seem to be returning to something, as a rock thrown into the air reaches the limit of its escape velocity and succumbs to the gravitational pull of the ground below. This returning is suggested as an ironic juxtaposition between John Wesley and Odysseus, returning from the Trojan War. The last two pages of the book, just after John Wesley revisits his mother's fallen house and just before he visits her grave, begin in this manner: "Evening. The dead sheathed in the earth's crust and turning the slow diurnal of the earth's wheel, at peace with eclipse, asteroid, the dusty novae, their bones brindled with mold and the celled marrow going to frail stone, turning, their fingers laced with roots, at one with Tut and Agamemnon, with the seed and the unborn" (*TOK* 244–5). Bones turn back to stone, fingers to roots. Despite the universal, or at least ancient and Classical, claims in this passage, this return to the cemetery is typically American, though American in reality rather than in ideology: it is a return from aborted escape.

The novel begins with a similar return: Kenneth Rattner is thumbing his way to something like home, having mysteriously been on the bum for a year on thirty-one dollars (*TOK* 26). Like a scavenging spider, he had taken the money from the lost pants of men whose drunken perch at the back of the Green Fly Inn would not hold. Thus with the "long creaking sound like a nail being pulled" McCarthy throws down the back porch of a building that cannot altogether defy the pull of gravity in a mountain landscape, and the fall of that porch sets his first full character loose (if we believe Kenneth Rattner) into South Carolina.

THROUGH THE GAP IN THE FENCE [25]

John Wesley is provided with a break in barbed wire. His father was not so lucky. Kenneth Rattner is everywhere in conflict with, and through, metal.

This substance, what Uncle Ather objects to in its presence on the mountain in the government tank, seems to mark the elder Rattner for doom. Of the father, we read, "A low strand of barbed wire had been his undoing" (*TOK* 15). Kenneth Rattner is caught like the owl (*TOK* 143) by metal, and he attempts to kill Sylder with a metal car jack. He supposedly has a metal plate in his head. As we eventually see his bones turned to dust, Rattner returns to the organic. Nevertheless, there is unnaturalness about him. His body in the pesticide pit serves as the constant symbol of the juncture between the natural and the fabricated. Early on, having caught his pants leg in a barbed wire fence, he examines his wound along with the loot from one of his crimes by lighting a "handful of dried weeds," which, after they "had burned to a ball of wispy cinders, still glow[ed] like hot thin wires" (*TOK* 15).

Rattner does not escape mountainous terrain. When we first see him, he is unwittingly headed for a hole in an old man's orchard, an open grave already a wound in the earth, an insecticide pit. If he ever, as he told his wife he would, worked in Greenville, South Carolina, then we are seeing him headed for a time at least *West* in the beginning of this book. In McCarthy, as in American Manifest Destiny, Westward is the general direction of destruction and ruin. It is the direction on this first page of the main narrative, of Kenneth Rattner watched over by a sun that is, "already reddening the western sky," and which has left the road "deserted, white and scorching yet" (*TOK* 8).

Overlapping Rattner's fall home we have another attempt at escape. A lack of sufficient escape force stops Marion Sylder too in his attempt to leave. He gets as far as a roadhouse outside Atlanta and feels "waves of fatigue roll from him." When he picks up Rattner, his car is dangerously coveted, no safer than David Brown's horses (*BM* 287). The ensuing murder, or call it self-defense, propels the action in the rest of the book.

Before Kenneth Rattner meets Marion Sylder in Jim's Hot Spot (*TOK* 15), he finds an earlier victim outside a filling station outside Atlanta. In the filling station Rattner had killed some time pretending to be interested in buying a tire pump. "In a crate at the back end of the counter were jacks, pumps, tire tools, an odd posthole digger" (*TOK* 8). We might follow Rattner's inventory with our own.

All these items except the "odd posthole digger" are present in the murder of Kenneth Rattner by Marion Sylder (*TOK* 37–40). The posthole digger is "odd" because it is not for use in repairing a flat tire but instead for digging holes most often used for fencing. Its presence among the flat tire tools foreshadows Marion Sylder leaving Kenneth Rattner's body in a hole in the ground that is unnatural and intended to contain an unnatural substance—pesticides that in the 1930s would not likely be organic.[26]

Kenneth Rattner's body is interred in a pit that was intended for long-chain molecular compounds—strings of chemical poison that do not break down into their constituent molecular components and thus cannot be safely *put back* in the natural world from which men assembled them. The compounds for which the pit was intended were created by men to kill insects. This is fitting, considering Rattner's insect-like qualities (if we can here consider a spider an insect). When Rattner dies at the end of the fight with Sylder, Rattner "relaxed his hand and the fingers contracted, shriveling into a tight claw, like a killed spider" (*TOK* 40). In this sense Kenneth Rattner is a natural predator who would not necessarily have persisted to the point of killing Sylder as his prey. (Most spiders stun their prey and keep them alive while they extract from them what they want.) When the fight tips away from Rattner's advantage, he pleads for a draw. "For Christ's sake, he gasped. Jesus Christ, just turn me loose" (*TOK* 39). Rattner has become dangerously entangled in his own web and all he wants, if we believe him, is to leave.

If we believe Rattner's plea, then we must agree with Edwin Arnold that Sylder murders Rattner ("World"). More than merely repelling this malicious insect-like predator, Sylder removes it entirely from the natural environment. After murdering the man who might have murdered him but who seemed willing to stop at the point of Sylder's resolve, Sylder does not bury Rattner in the ground.

The corpse of John Wesley's father is thus left to rot in the open pit. Accidentally cremated, Rattner is further reduced to a bag of bones given to "him who placed them in a clean bag of white canvas" (*TOK* 234). The "him" they are given to is a pronoun impossible to connect to a character. In McCarthy's sometimes frustratingly modernist suspension of clear relation of pronouns to names (or in any other way to identifiable characters), this example of kenning—no pun intended—removes the few remaining bones of Kenneth Rattner even farther from a natural grave. Like the dissected remains of Lester Ballard, Rattner's body has been processed by institutional authority. Both Rattner and Ballard were criminals who crossed the lines from behavior acceptable to society. Fittingly both criminals, the first through grotesque accident, the second through the cool administration of formalin and the work of autopsy tools for the instruction of "state medical" students, are rendered to bags.

This brings us back to the open gap that ends *The Orchard Keeper*. Once the work is done of removing the entangled fence and tree, there is room enough in the cemetery for the headstone that drew John Wesley to a last look before leaving. It is John Wesley's mother, not his father, whose body has been interred in the cemetery. Her interment, however, seems to justify the alteration of the fence. The fence is unlikely to be pulled down but rather repaired or moved to make more room for the dead, those who "are gone now. Fled, banished in death or exile, lost, undone" (*TOK* 246). John Wesley is simply the first for exile rather than death (or prison). The entire book therefore turns on the motifs of housing, fencing, and burial.

To return briefly, as does John Wesley, to the seemingly solid house of his mother, we see that the work of "weather and time" (*TOK* 63) has been too much for its roof. The book's last chapter begins with this description:

> The few small windows were glassless but for a jagged side or corner still wedged in the handmade sashes. The roofshakes lay in windrows on the broad loft floors and this house housed only the winds.
>
> Dervishes of leaves rattled across the yard and in the wind the oaks dipped and creaked, and in the wind even the spavined house hung between the stone chimneys seemed to give a little. The doors stood open and wind scurried in the parlor, riffled the drift leaves on the kitchen floor and stirred the cobwebbed window corners. He did not go to the loft. The lower rooms were dusty and barren and but for some half-familiar rags of clothes altogether strange. (*TOK* 243)

The *Oxford English Dictionary* tells us that "spavined" comes from the Middle English "spaveyne," "Either of two diseases afflicting the hock joints of horses: A. Bog spavin, an infusion of lymph that enlarges the joint. B. Bone spavin, a bony deposit that stiffens the joint." These suggest a house alive, but old, diseased, even if stubborn in strength. Yet, the word can also refer to "a row, as of leaves or snow, heaped up by the wind." The many references to the wind in this last description of the Rattner house suggest a slight teleology: the wind has effected this change. Meanwhile, the first definitions recall the house's interior situation I observed earlier in this chapter: the house of Mrs. Rattner was strong, yet severe, while the roof over her son was too troubled—and neglected—not to suffer.

The image of this roof, "hung" between the two chimneys, suggests the diseased and sunken back of a horse. It is little wonder now that the boy who once slept on its porch when he could (avoiding that loft) has now been gone from the house for seven years. We must wonder, however, how much the house has deteriorated before the death of the mother brings him back for this last visit before his final escape.

We might at this point read the title of this novel as both the literal description of Arthur Ownby, who "keeps" the orchard by tending the insecticide pit-grave of Kenneth Rattner, and as a description of the novel's meta-narrator himself: the title of "Orchard Keeper" goes to him who minds and mends the rifts between broken houses and graves. These two worlds include animals and men,[27] trees and fences, so-called "natural" and "unnatural" limitations on space.

Just before we see John Wesley return briefly to see his mother's grave, the novel treats us to the comic distraction of a simple-minded deputy named Legwater digging out the insecticide pit in search of the valuable metal plate that was never really in Kenneth Rattner's head. The arcs of *The Orchard Keeper* are of metal touching life and if not killing it, growing through it. As unrefined metallic meteors naturally "cannonade" the top of the mountain in an astronomical arc from the heavens to the land that reaches toward them, an old man assaults a government tank with smaller, unnatural metallic missiles from loads of buckshot. Between these assaults, from heaven and man, fly the arcs of mortality, the lives of the characters arcing down to death. McCarthy's development of this last arc is close to Sophocles and Shakespeare, with proper burials forestalled and a fool in the grave looking for loot.

Chapter Three
Unhousing a *Child of God*

> What's your plans now? said the sheriff.
> Go home, said Ballard.
>
> (*COG* 55–56)

DERANGEMENT FROM LAND AND SENSES

McCarthy's third novel opens with the procession of an auction to the dwelling of a man who will resist that auction, unsuccessfully. At first, there is no mention of the protagonist. This is not unusual, but it is notable that the book's first paragraph opens against him: the reader follows the movement of folk from a community on its way to the dispossession and sale of the main character's family home. From the beginning, we are implicated in his unhousing, before we even meet him.

When we do meet him, he is described like an animal on display. "He is small, unclean, unshaven. He moves in the dry chaff among the dust and slats of sunlight with a constrained truculence. Saxon and Celtic bloods" (*COG* 4). We might next expect to see the added information, "Homo Sapiens," if not indeed quite "Homo Sapiens Sapiens." The words "constrained truculence" point to the fundamental oxymoronic character of Ballard: his propensity to fight is inappropriately housed; he is too small for it, and he is (at least for the moment) quartered in housing intended for domesticated animals—nothing sturdy enough for the wild beast suggested by "truculence." Standing in a barn, he is watching the approach of those who will take his home from him. Already "constrained" in the domicile of animals, he is already outside his suicide father's house, and we may imagine him having retreated from house to barn as he watches the approaching parties of the auction. It must then be pointed out to us by the narrator that he is, none-theless, "[a] child of God much like yourself perhaps" (*COG* 4).

My argument on *Child of God* is that whatever the mental insufficien-cies and psychological deformities of Lester Ballard, the plot is launched by this action of unhousing; every subsequent action of Lester Ballard—includ-ing necrophilia—follows from that initial scene. Ballard is a child of god without a home because it has been auctioned away from him.

This reading is similar to an earlier argument by John Lang, although I would not go as far as Lang in psychologizing Ballard. For Lang:

> *Child of God* testifies not to the anomalous outrages committed by Lester Ballard but to the potential for violence inherent in all human beings. Lester's actions are often shocking, but they are not, unfortu-nately, unique. By endowing Lester with a psychological and emotional history, McCarthy reminds us of his protagonist's underlying humanity. (94)

Lang also draws attention to the loss of the house, and the father's suicide, as episodes of "trauma" that must be considered in Ballard's case (89), and he also suggests that the book's structure has something to do with Lester's humanity (88). What I would like to add in this chapter is a lengthier consid-eration of the details of Lester's unhousing, but also attention to the domestic and natural spaces through which Ballard falls. As I will argue, underground spaces add much to Ballard's problems.

Vereen Bell focuses somewhat on Ballard's housing problem, but does so in mostly psychological terms apart from details in the text. Bell does note the indirect narrative approach of the book:

> The strangeness of the story [. . .] begins [. . .] with the way the story is told. Even by McCarthy's ordinary standards, an unusual degree of unassimilated raw material impedes—or seems to impede—the cen-tral narrative flow. We are nearly halfway through the novel before the shocking main theme of the story—Lester's necrophilia—is securely under way; and even from that point forward [. . .] the material of the story itself is not much more than would flesh out a long short story. Before that point the narrative is so aimless and fragmented that an innocent reader might wonder if there is even to be a plot. (53)

Bell takes the material that is "outside" the main story of Lester Ballard's necrophilia to be somehow unrelated to that story. Although his reading provides several insights into Ballard's unhousing, Bell's early assessment focuses first on this problem as a point of narrative structure suggesting a metanarrative value, and second on a generalized psychological ambiguity in the novel. "Lester makes his life with a story in a novel that is partly *about* stories and storytelling and thus passes over the edge from fact into fiction, where behavior is no longer required to be restrained—any more than stories are—by taboo" (55, his emphasis).

My reading is simpler. First, the quality of any novel's indulgence in stories—that it is "*about* stories and storytelling"—seems to me overdetermined. Much ink has dried in arguments that so-called metafiction works, despite an apparent lack of plot, because it is somehow about itself as fiction. The only such fictions still read, however, retain something of a plot. In other words, if a novel contains an interesting story, that makes it compelling. If it contains interesting stories that seem to be about storytelling, that fact alone does little for their interest. Bell's appraisal also misses the point of the novel's division into three sections (each with a roman numeral). The first section contains most of the "stories" that do not directly relate to the plot; the second section in comparison presents a relatively ordered series of scenes, most of which are directly related to Ballard's descent into full violence; the third section begins just after we learn that Ballard's violence has reached serial habits, and it follows his capture, escape, and surrender.

Second, McCarthy's structure seems clear to me, and to lead to a less complicated psychological reading than the book has so far received. It is true that jumps in narrative stance mark the first section, and that the second and third have none of these. It is also true, however, that a sure-footed progression of action constitutes the plot of the entire book.

The first section sees Ballard moved from his father's house to take up residence in an abandoned house; the second section sees this second home catch fire and Ballard go literally underground; the third section sees him arrested out of his cave, escaped back to it, and finally housed in an institution—until his death. Ballard's identity slips down, from the status of an evicted homeowner, to a homesteading squatter, to a cave dweller. These changes in identity match his eviction from society in Part I, his uneasy existence at the margins of society in Part II, and his total depravity and criminality in Part III. Yet another way to see the sections is that in Part I he is legally evicted; in Part II he is unlawfully arrested for something he did not do, picked up again but let go and told he must "find some other way to live or some other place in the world to do it" (*COG* 123); and in Part III he follows that advice—until his behavior is so egregious from societal allowance that he is finally legally interned, and interred.

The three sections also parallel his mental states in three phases: he cannot "hold his head right" (*COG* 9) and is himself not "right" (*COG* 21) in Part I. Part II goes from this occultatio to a medial condition: he is said by the narrator to appear "half crazy" (*COG* 15). By the ending in Part III, his sanity is completely gone. I argue that Lester's story is one of an unhousing that parallels blows to his head and that these actions remove his senses from him. I will make that argument mostly on particulars, but it is also supported by the larger structure of the book.

That structure is not incidental, and it is more valuable as an internal indicator than as a mark of metafiction. Bell's attention to the unnamed narrators among the community (apart from the omniscient narrator) is warranted. Yet there is nothing charming enough about the stories in Part I (and very little detail given concerning who is telling them or to whom) to make them worth anything *as* mere storytelling. I will read their details rather for something else: they are the voices of a community that has rejected Ballard well before his descent into the darker and deeper moral (if we should use the term for a man reduced to an animal state) and geographic locations he will inhabit in Parts II and III.

Third, although Ballard's psychology is certainly something to worry over, the severity of his problems is exacerbated by two events presented in the novel's opening: he is driven from his home, and he is (if not for the first time, not for the last) hit in the head. He is thus doubly unhoused, or deranged,[1] by the auction; everything that follows is connected to that first scene in the novel.[2]

Bell reads the novel as one part loosely narrating various scenes that are only somewhat illustrative of Ballard's character, and second and third parts committed to the story of his crimes. Instead, I suggest that the many details concerning domestic constraints on space in all three parts point to Ballard's need for a home. As the novel progresses, the natural order of a home within a house is so lost to him that he takes up home underground, in a cave. Ultimately, Ballard's attempt to recreate a domestic home in the unhomelike conflates graves with houses, and living family with dead strangers.

This is hinted at in another detail in the novel's introduction of Lester in the barn. Although only the most careful reader would notice it in its initial description, we later learn that the "rope hanging from the loft" (*COG* 4) in the barn was used by his father to hang himself. We learn this from voices that seem to belong to otherwise invisible characters. As Bell reads it, these are "unidentified narrators speaking at times to unidentified friends" (53). Or, perhaps the interlocutor is the main narrator (and perhaps originally McCarthy, as he took oral histories for his research).[3] According to one such source, for instance, Ballard's "mother had run off" and Lester "was never right after his daddy killed hisself" (*COG* 21).

This points directly to the same conditions behind all of McCarthy's main characters: none of them has a happy family life behind them, and most have a remarkably incomplete, or quite perverted, family if any family at all. Perhaps neuroscience may one day explain the type of behavior at issue in Lester's killing and raping of his victims, and I will suggest that damage to Lester's brain does lie at the root of his actions. Here, McCarthy's slips into suggestions of determinism are more sociological than psychological. (Both *The Gardener's Son* and *The Stonemason*, obvious as they are in the transparency of their ideological treatment of labor issues, offer strong evidence of this outside the novels.) The notable sociological force behind *Child of God* is a negative one, a social vacuum: it is the absence of a home—a different thing than a mere house—from which Lester could be evicted.

Given the nature of Lester's later crimes, it is not too far a stretch to imagine that something untoward befell his mother. Our source tells us that she left "I don't know where to nor who with" (*COG* 21). Perhaps Lester's crimes begin before the opening of the novel, or perhaps they follow a crime of his father's. While I find no textual evidence for either, it is notable that Lester's mother is gone from his life. By the time we meet the *child*, the father has killed himself. The social structure of the home was broken so well that we never even see its physical house until the man who buys it is living in it and Lester is spying on him (*COG* 109). Even Lester's father— supposedly deserted by his wife—seems unfit for domestic constraints, as he goes out into the barn to hang himself in that quarter for animals. It is a more practical space to throw a rope, but McCarthy also chooses to introduce us to Lester in that space. It is therefore difficult even to imagine Lester the man in the family house, let alone as a boy. Indeed, the few stories of his boyhood related by other "unidentified narrators" always place him out of doors (Bell 53).

As we meet Lester standing in the barn, he is therefore (already) marginally housed. He is about to become fully unhoused in two ways: by the auction, but also a literal blow. In the single paragraph of the book's second chapter, we are told after the fact that Lester's armed challenge of the auctioneer ends in Lester being laid out by a blow to the head with an axe by a man named "Buster" (*COG* 8–9). It is obvious that Buster hits Lester with the dull end of the axe, but the heaviness and hardness of the weapon amounts to more than a minor detail. Given the subsequent events of the novel, this blow deserves investigation.

It would be nearly impossible, and it is certainly improbable, to hit a man over the head with an axe *handle* while holding the business end of the instrument. Anyone who has put an axe to work knows that it is the weight of the thing, as much as the sharpness of the blade, which does the work. Focus on strength while chopping wood and you are certain to run out of energy. Instead, one uses gravity and momentum; in a single-bit axe the tool's potential resides in the heaviness of the hammer-end of the iron. Hit a man with the blade and you are almost certain to kill him. Hit him with the dull end of the bit—in an emotionally charged moment where the man you hit seems about to kill someone—and it will be remarkable if he survives. Remarkable, yet possible.

The word used is "axe," and whenever an iron bit (single or double-bit) is missing from the end, one refers to an axe *handle*. Clearly, Lester is hit with the blunt end of an axe *bit*. Lester's challenge to the auctioneer, after all, is serious: he threatens to shoot "C B," the auctioneer (*COG* 8), if C B refuses to step down from his perch on a wagon. Buster's blow would also have to be fast, if he intends to disarm Lester before Lester can fire. This means that Lester Ballard, our child of god, begins his descent into psychopathic violence with a quick blow to the top of his head with the blunt-end of a full-sized single-bit axe: "Lester Ballard never could hold his head right after that. It must of thowed his neck out someway or another. [. . .] He was layin flat on the ground looking up at everbody with his eyes crossed and this awful pumpknot on his head [. . .] and he was bleedin at the ears" (*COG* 9).

Three details here suggest the seriousness of the injury: his spine at the neck is permanently injured, his eyes are affected, and the blow is severe enough to cause bleeding inside his ears, and therefore most likely inside his brain. The physical aspect of his derangement is partially accomplished by this blow. The reader's patience need not be tested by forensic medical evidence linking serial murderers to head injuries to accept the likelihood that half of Lester Ballard's derangement is internal but *cerebral*.

The importance of the axe is reinforced in an ironic chiasmus toward the end of Part I. McCarthy, who regularly bestows reverence on human activity only when it entails skilled work with the hands, devotes a full chapter (of substantial length, relative to the many shorter chapters in the novel) to a description of a blacksmith sharpening an axe for Ballard. Significantly, Ballard, who was on the receiving end of the axe in the first chapter, has found only "a rusty axehead" (*COG* 70). The smith, instead of trying to sharpen the damaged iron, talks Ballard into a transaction that allows McCarthy to describe, beautifully, one of the skills lost to the modern age that so troubles his characters. Instead of dumbly having the smith sharpen the bit, or spending slightly more for a new axe, the smith suggests that Ballard have it forged anew. He promises that a reworking of the old axe, fitted with a new handle to suit this skilled labor, will be worth more. "I'd better to have thisn and it right than two new ones" (*COG* 71). What follows is sad, as it hints at the possible redemption of Ballard himself. The man, however, is inadequate to the opportunity.

Speaking of the axe, the smith (who would show Ballard the skill to do the work himself one day) says, "Some people will poke around at somethin else and leave the tool they're heatin to perdition but the proper thing is to fetch her out the minute she shows the color of grace" (*COG* 72). The axe is, of course, personified further as "she," creating further irony in the handling of the axe "head," as Ballard's own problems will be taken out mostly on women.

Ballard, hammered repeatedly throughout his life, has himself been overlooked; the community around him leaves him to perdition after casting him into the fire of homelessness. Only the smith suggests the possibility of "grace" for Ballard, in the only description the novel gives us of the man standing in a position to learn something. The smith, a typical teacher, overestimates his powers and the ability—or desire—of his student. After heating and tempering the bit, the smith tells Ballard:

> Now. We polish it and draw the temper.
>
> He brightened the bit with a stick wrapped in emery cloth. Holding the head in the tongs he began to move it slowly back and forth over the fire. Keep her out of the fire and keep her movin. That way she'll draw down even. Now she's getting yeller. That's fine for some tools but we going to take a blue temper on her. Now she gets brown. Watch it now. See it there?
>
> He took the axehead from the fire and laid it on the anvil. You got to watch her close and not let the temper run out on the corners first. Shape ye fire for the job always.
>
> Is that it? said Ballard.
>
> That's it. We'll just fit ye a handle now and sharpen her and you'll be on your way.
>
> Ballard nodded.
>
> It's like a lot of things, said the smith. Do the least part of it wrong and ye'd just as well do it all wrong. He was sorting through handles standing in a barrel. Reckon you could do it now from watchin? he said.
>
> Do what, said Ballard. (*COG* 74)

In *Cormac McCarthy and the Geology of Being*, Thomas Young calls this reply the revelation of "the full extent of [Ballard's] cultural dispossession" (117). Young focuses on Ballard's dispossession of the farm, and on his nature as pre-destined by his family history; he is a "congenital misfit" (118). This scene, however, also echoes the literal blow. It is too late for Ballard, as the "least part" of his childhood and early adulthood has gone so tragically "wrong"— but also particularly too late when it comes to axes. So, too, the novel's Part I (the least part of all three) has gone wrong for Ballard, and he is mentally ruined for anything but what follows.

As the axe blow removes what senses Lester had from their cranial home, an invisible civic blow, through the function of the auction, removes Lester's body from its architectural home. A detail concerning the new owner of the property adds to the linkage of social identity with topological location. Lester, having not paid taxes on the land, his family gone, has no rightful ownership of the property—at least in the eyes of the community. A spokes-man for that same community, in the form of the second chapter's narrator, tells us that John Greer (the man who buys the house) is himself from out-side the local area: "from up in Grainger County. Not sayin nothin against him but he was" (*COG* 9). This is occultatio, saying something against the man by claiming not to say "nothin against him;" Greer is an interloper. The implication here is that local identity requires precedence. Ownership of the property accomplishes both psychological self-possession and social accep-tance, and this narrator betrays hints of guilt at Lester's treatment: the knot on Lester's head is "awful" (*COG* 9) and the detail about Greer hints that he may, after all, have less natural right to the land than Lester.

The speaker who conveys this suspicion about Greer aligns himself with authority even as he distances himself from the violent action of that authority. This suggests an ambivalent attitude toward the events. "I didn't see Buster hit him but I seen him layin on the ground. I was with the sheriff" (*COG* 9). Lester, who is "less" than "Bus*ter*," goes unnamed here[4]. Presum-ably, the sheriff was not the one who dealt the blow, yet it comes from a legal direction. This violence is legal because Lester is attempting to stop a legal auction, and he is threatening to kill the man acting out that officially sanctioned proceeding (Lester has apparently failed to pay taxes on the prop-erty).[5] While Lester is still watching from the barn, the auctioneer extols the abstract value of the ownership of property in hyperbolic terms: "There is no sounder investment than property. Land. You all know that a dollar won't buy what it used to buy. [. . .] But real estate is goin up, up, up" (*COG* 6).

The auction's emphasis on property ownership adds to our understand-ing of Ballard's actions. Already in the introduction of this character, *Child of*

God has refused to judge Ballard on moral terms. His inadequacies before the axe blow lie elsewhere, in his relation to his surroundings. Between the carnivalesque description of the arriving auction, and the first scene of violence, we see Ballard in relation to his immediate spatial constraints, looking out at those who will displace him:

> To watch these things issuing from the otherwise mute pastoral morning is a man at the barn door. [. . .] A child of God much like yourself perhaps. Wasps pass through the laddered light from the barnslats in a succession of strobic moments, gold and trembling between black and black, like fireflies in the serried upper gloom. [. . .] [Ballard] moves along the barn wall, himself fiddlebacked with light, a petty annoyance flickering across the wallward eye. (*COG* 4)

What is wrong here is not yet primarily internal to Ballard (though the auction will fix that). Rather, he is described in details that make it clear that he is out of place. What agent of perception in the barn, for instance, is "annoy[ed]" by his presence? Is it the narrator, the reader, or the light itself? This is an unusual passage for McCarthy in the suggestion of there being someone external to the narrative to look at Ballard.[6] That "wallward eye" is almost subjunctive. It assumes an onlooker who is him-or herself outside the narrative. Yet the wasps belong. They are even beautiful, if vulnerable, in their "strobic moments, bold and trembling." Are they trembling at the presence of this man who does not belong in this space?

A SECOND HOME

After his eviction, Ballard takes possession (by trespass) of an abandoned house. He accomplishes this first on an animal level, by defecating behind its barn. This fourth chapter (of Part I) begins with a description of "[a]ll that remained of the outhouse"—"a few soft shards of planking grown with a virid moss and lying collapsed in a shallow hole where weeds sprouted in outsized mutations" (*COG* 13). The combination of decay and fecundity foreshadow the intensification of Ballard's ambivalence, which will later be played out in necrophilia inside this house. The house, and therefore presumably the area of the outhouse as well, is invisible to the road, hidden by weeds. Yet, Ballard hides himself from the house itself by going behind the barn to do his business; with the outhouse collapsed, he would be exposed to view from the house—as if it possessed some scopophilic power of its own. He is taking possession of a dwelling for humans, and acts accordingly to keep his bathroom not only well away from it, but also out of sight from it.

After relieving himself well away from where he will sleep, Ballard next claims the house from the wasps that seemed more fit than he for his father's barn: "A hornetnest hung from the corner of the porch and he knocked it down. The hornets came out one by one and flew away." He cleans the "dried dung of foxes and possums" from inside the house and then, finding another living creature already a tenant, burns a spider out of the chimney (*COG* 14). These are landlord actions of eviction, chasing the wilder creatures out to make room for a man still clinging to domesticity. It creates a sad chiasmus with his own dislocation by the auction: Ballard evicted, evicts a spider. Of course, the spider is itself an opportunistic predator, much as Ballard will be.

Ballard finds a mattress but seems unequal to it, as the narrator tells us the mattress itself "forded the brake toward the cabin. It was hinged over the head and shoulders of Lester Ballard" (*COG* 14). "By dark he had all he owned about him in the barren room [. . .]." He blackens potato slices over an oil lamp but manages to burn his mouth without cooking the insides of the potato slices. After this dinner, he smokes and reads—or at least, he looks at old newspapers and "mutter[s] over them, his lips forming the words" (*COG* 15).

Everything Ballard does in this passage is directed toward the replacement of a lost home, what Thomas Young calls a "parodic diminishment of domesticity" (118). Yet, the narrator also tells us straight out that Ballard here "looked half crazy" (*COG* 15). Ballard has descended to half, but is on the way to full, insanity—full derangement in both the topological and mental senses of that word.

In mockery of his attempts to homestead, hunting dogs run through this house. The fox they are chasing (another predator) has already escaped through the glass-less window, yet once inside the doorless door, the dogs seem confused: they "circled once with rising volume dog on dog and then swept out the window howl on howl carrying first the muntins, then the sash, leaving a square and naked hole in the wall and a ringing in his ear" (*COG* 24).

This attack on both the window and the ear throws Ballard back from the domestic, closer to a dog's identity. He catches one of the slower dogs and beats it savagely, and the sound of this fuses Ballard's exasperation with the dog's pain: "It set up a piteous howling. Ballard flailed blindly at it with his fist, great drumlike thumps that echoed in the near empty room among the desperate oaths and wailings" (*COG* 24). The dogs have removed even the suggestion that this is a home: they leave "a square and naked hole" where the window was, and the verb "leaving" works a zeugma on Ballard's brain, "leaving" also the "ringing in his ear." The man is already down at the beginning of this chapter: "Were there darker provinces of night he would have found them" (*COG* 23). Invasion by hunting dogs drives him only farther to derangement.

Mental derangement is brought up by association with Ballard in a later chapter. To establish Ballard's insanity, one of the unnamed local narrators tells the story of a man named Gresham who, after his wife dies, stands up at the funeral and sings "the chickenshit blues" (*COG* 22). Gresham, who is not "a patch on Lester Ballard for crazy" thus mars one of the few otherwise standard burial services in a McCarthy novel. The man's wife is physically interred (more successfully than many a McCarthy character), but Gresham perverts the speech act that would properly accomplish her burial as a placement of her social identity along with her bodily interment. Gresham's singing of "the *chickenshit* blues" (my emphasis) is also not the blues one might expect. The lyrics to this blues lament the "trouble" of trying to control several women.

What Ballard wants at this point in the novel is a living woman, but he is already outside the boundaries of normative society. We have witnessed the dual blows at the auction that ostracize Ballard as a non-taxpayer; two other chapters ostracize him for other actions unacceptable to society. One brief chapter describes a story of brutality committed by Lester as a boy, and another describes how calmly Lester relates the news of his father's suicide; both of these come from unnamed narrators, still in Part I.

We gather that Lester stood outside society from the time of that suicide, "about nine or ten year old at the time" (*COG* 21). It is remarkable how well McCarthy occludes what should be a central question in Lester's case: who watches over him for the next ten years or more? A social worker comes to check on the antinomian Uncle Ather at the end of *The Orchard Keeper*, though the old man wants nothing from the government and is in fact in jail for assailing one of its structures.

Yet the "nine or ten year old" Lester seems to have been on his own, living alone in the house that his mother had already abandoned, well after his father hangs himself in the barn. That no one seems to have raised him is alarming. Even the kid in *Blood Meridian* has a father five years longer than Ballard. Lester, the least sane of McCarthy protagonists, has the least family background. Rather than someone coming to care for the child, the people of the community appear to show up only to run Lester the adult off the property when he fails to pay its taxes. Had he paid them before? That is unlikely. Had anyone thrown him off the place before he reached adulthood, however, he or she would have had to do *something* with him; they would have had to provide him with a home. Instead, he seems to have been left there until he is deemed old enough to be kicked off without any bother to the community.

We are told, then, that Lester "never was right after his daddy killed hisself" (*COG* 21), but the first local narrator has already told us that "Lester Ballard never could hold his head right" after the blow at the auction. This betrays the liberal politics that are relatively much more obvious in McCarthy's plays: the implicit argument of *Child of God* is that Lester Ballard is *made* a necrophilic murderer by the circumstances and forces of the society that refuses, repeatedly, to claim him in the absence of his family. Abandonment by the mother, witness of the father's suicide, forced homelessness, and several blows to the head are the recipe for the Ballard we see by the end of the book. His craziness is then not something outside us, but implicitly the symptom of more subtle societal sicknesses. The McCarthy of this book seems not quite as tough as the man who wrote *Blood Meridian*.

The impossibility of Ballard finding a living woman (with whom he might make the family he needs to replace the one that we all lose) leads this outcast to an interesting position. Outside society, he dumbly begins to witness life as a voyeur, and eventually he attempts to replicate first a romantic and sexual relationship, and then family life, with the dead—those ex-members of the very ranks of society that failed in life to accept him.

The voyeurism is the first step, while he is still only "half" crazy. In search of satisfaction, he literally stands outside a car, peeping at a couple in the back seat. Ballard sees that the woman is white but mistakes the man for an African-American. Thus, this couple would themselves be permitted intimacy only when parked on the side of the road, well outside the town. The man who leaps from the car and chases Ballard, however, is white. He does so, of course, because he realizes that he has been watched; but he has found this out because it is Ballard's surprise that gives away the peep. This is a mistake of double ignorance: Ballard is first factually ignorant of the other man's "whiteness," and second culturally ignorant in his racist surprise after the first mistake. Though Ballard is himself outcast from the dominant culture, he keeps the racial tenets of that culture, and in his surprise when he thinks he is a witness to miscegenation, he cannot keep himself quiet. "It's a nigger," he whispers (*COG* 20).[7]

These first victims of Ballard (if only of his eyes) come to him: for whatever reason, they are having sex on the side of the road, outside Knoxville and the small towns around it. They have left the town that has rejected him and are closer to his makeshift home than to their proper beds. Ballard only enters another's home to take a victim when he first resorts to murder, later in Part II. In the meantime, he escapes when his peeping goes wrong for him.

Ballard's next scopophilic target is a woman yet farther outside putative societal norms: he finds her alone, passed out drunk, and well outside the town. Ballard defends himself from her outrage at his curiosity, but she maintains the pretense. Indeed, the police later pick him up for raping her. Clearly, the woman has two other men in mind as guilty parties in that crime, yet she takes everything out on Ballard. The word "scapegoat" is perfect for him (as I will explain more fully later): Ballard is cast out of society and blamed for things he did not do—before he then does them. Even in church, he is hardly tolerated (*COG* 31–32).

Thomas Young recognizes the scene of Ballard's discovery of the drunken woman as one of several that points to Ballard's "problematical heroism." For Young, Ballard lacks much yet still bears comparison with the "criminal heroes of Hugo or Dostoevsky." This heroism, however, is earned only by Lester's libido. He is heroic in the Freudian sense that he "reconstitut[es] [. . .] one man's instinctual life" (113). Young's Ballard is heroic simply because his libido persists outside the boundaries of civilized life—to the point that Ballard's satisfaction of that libido necessarily compels him to carry members of civilized life outside their accustomed boundaries, away from their accustomed enclosures of automobiles and houses, into the underground, unsanctioned, alternative spaces to which he runs at the end of Part II.[8] Young is partly right about Ballard's drives. His libido (not his hunger) runs him to ground; but there are too many other references to his homelessness for us to understand his actions as only motivated by the sex instinct. Surely, Freud went too far with a good idea: the sex instinct may be quite powerful, but there are other, perhaps more fundamental, drives. Staying out of the rain is one of them.

In any case, while I agree that Ballard is a sympathetic character in scenes where he is disenfranchised, shunned, and unfairly abused by the community that refuses him a place within it; the fact that he displays animal instincts to procreate—no matter how far he falls—hardly qualifies him for "heroism." Young's argument is largely sound in the particulars, as far as it goes. To his argument that this novel is the first (and I would add only) novel from McCarthy whose primary "focus [. . .] becomes human sexuality itself" (113), however, I would object that it is precisely because of his dual derangement that Ballard is unacceptable to women. With no house (or car), and with fewer senses every time he gets knocked in the head, he stands no chance with the opposite sex.

Young's close reading of Ballard's first encounter with a woman leads up to Ballard's arrest for rape, and includes most of the subsequent fight in the sheriff's office. Ballard attacks the woman, she begins to best him, and a deputy tackles our problematical hero with an arm hold and "one knee in the small of Ballard's back." What happens next, as with the auction, needs looking over in slightly more detail: "The woman had risen. She cocked her elbows and drew back her foot and kicked Ballard in the side of the head." The deputy objects, "Here now," but continues to hold Ballard. "She kicked again" (*COG* 52), we are told. Clearly, the deputy's anxiety derives from the fact that the Sheriff does not step in to control the woman. Add two blows to that of the axe.

Ballard is then housed in jail for "[n]ine days and nights" (*COG* 52). The food is better than what he managed on his own. In a second occasion of whiteness offset by the supposed identity of a black man, Ballard meets an African-American fellow inmate.[9] "John" parallels Ballard and contrasts him at once: "I'm from Pine Bluff Arkansas and I'm a fugitive from the ways of this world. I'd be a fugitive from my mind if I had me some snow" (*COG* 53).

Although Ballard is from Sevier County (and thus not the outsider that Greer—the man who buys his house—or John is), we will be told by a community narrator at the end of Part I that the Ballard family's past is a fugitive one, characterized by a liminal relationship with society. Ballard's grandfather Leland dodged the unofficial draft for the civil war, yet "was a by god White Cap"—a member of a Tennessee equivalent of the Ku Klux Klan. This grandfather Leland also died by a rope, but not by his choice; "he was hanged in Hattiesburg Mississippi. Goes to show it ain't just the place. He'd of been hanged no matter where he lived" (*COG* 81).

Like John, then, Ballard is ultimately out of place in origin, and behavior, "a fugitive from the ways of this world" (*COG* 53). Unlike John, however, Ballard is already "a fugitive from [his] mind," though not through drug use. Whatever blows to the head John has received, they have not separated him from his senses as much as he would like to achieve with cocaine.

Ballard confesses to something more than the crime for which he is jailed: "I was supposed to of raped this old girl. She wasn't nothin but a whore to start with" (*COG* 53). Ballard is jailed for what he was "supposed to" have done, and will be released when the woman accusing him disappears. The sheriff asks Ballard where she was from, and Ballard does not know; she, too, is apparently homeless.

John, on the other hand, is jailed for something much more serious: he has decapitated a man "with a pocketknife." The extremity of this crime along with the singing John is about to do suggest insanity. John also suggests he is guilty of a crime that, in Sevier County, Tennessee, within the living memory of characters who regularly mention White Caps, would likely be considered as serious by the authorities: miscegenation. After Ballard tells him what he was "supposed to of" done, John comments that "White pussy is nothin but trouble" (*COG* 53). In that town and time, a black man having had sex with a white woman—let alone actually raping her—would likely put that man in a noose. When the sheriff takes John away, he suggests as much: "You'll be flyin all right [. . .] Home to your maker" (*COG* 54).

This comment extends the metaphor John has already been using, in song, for the week that he shares confinement with Ballard. John sings,

Flyin home
Flyin like a motherfucker
Flyin home (*COG* 53)

The obscenities from John serve the ironies here. The home he sings of, the one the sheriff agrees he is headed for, is the only one in which Ballard will finally find rest. And the obscenity in the song points to a taboo as serious as Ballard's, as well as back to his crime, that he "cut a motherfucker's head off [. . .]" (*COG* 53). This separation of the body from the mind is the opposite of Ballard's future crime, because Ballard's necrophilia occurs in an attempt to put back together the bodies of the dead with their living social arrangements, through pretending they are not dead. The word necrophilia is in one sense inaccurate for this; Ballard loves the dead by pretending they are alive, and that they have not rejected him. John seems not to have had this problem at all, including in relations with white women. Ironically, the white Ballard will not experience sex with a living woman and will not be caught so soon as John; even then, unlike John, he will not be killed for his actions.

After Ballard's release, the sheriff stops him on the street to ask his plans. "Go home," he replies. The sheriff guesses according to a moral suspicion of Ballard, rather than an animal understanding of what will most likely follow first: "I guess murder is next on the list ain't it" (*COG* 56). Ballard's first murder, however, is preceded by his first necrophilia. That it involves no murder bears witness to Ballard's actions as conditioned by his station: he has no urges (yet) to kill and operates at first by opportunity. This fits his station in the abandoned house; however sorry its condition, it is still a medial state between a true home and the caves he will run to when he becomes a full predator. Meanwhile, he is something closer to a scavenger.

When the hunting dogs (true predators trained to their work) invaded his house, the dog he bests is presumably the weakest of the pack—slowest to arrive and easily turned from predator into prey. Ballard was therefore farthest behind the primary prey, a fox, itself a predator. Even among a dog pack, Ballard can only best the runt.

In his first sexual encounter, he is similarly far down the chain of predation. He is unable to woo even the outrageously promiscuous daughters of the "dumpkeeper," (who, in nonsensical synecdoche chosen from a discarded dictionary of medical terms, has named them "Urethra, Cerebella, [and] Hernia Sue"). One of "[t]hese gangling progeny," who move "like cats and like cats in heat" (*COG* 26), teases Ballard. He stands no chance, however, even with her. His visit to the church follows this failure at the dump, suggesting, however slightly, that Ballard may yet feel some shame for even his natural urges.

Part II begins with his discovery of a couple, dead in a car whose engine is still running in the morning, presumably, after parking for a date the night before. Like the first couple spied on by Ballard in the act of sex, this couple has come to the turnaround by the road for this purpose alone. The man of the first couple chases Ballard away; this man cannot. A leak in the car's exhaust system has poisoned them with carbon monoxide during their copulation. Their location suggests a furtive assignation; their condition furthers their estrangement from society. Beginning as biologically natural yet socially illicit lovers, their copulation has presumably slowed in progress until they passed out and crossed over fully from the realm of natural, and socially sanctioned, sex—into the realm of the fully taboo: sexuality in death. The radio of the car, now playing a Sunday morning show, eulogizes them: "Gathering flowers for the master's bouquet. / Beautiful flowers that will never decay" (*COG* 86). Because they are dead, these victims are frozen in time for Ballard.

If in desire there is something that wants time to stop, Ballard has up until now been completely frustrated. He never even begins a normal relation with a living human being. Even his attempt at scopophilic satisfaction has failed, as he was interrupted when the tableau before him broke, the man getting out of the first car to chase him. By finding a dead couple, Ballard's scopophilia is perfectly satisfied because the moment "will never decay." His slow awareness of this leads him to step back from scopophilic remove to active engagement; as time for the couple has stopped, for him it is just beginning.

Coldness and stasis go together. We describe the appearance or feeling that time has stopped as a moment "frozen in time." McCarthy's description of this scene includes the word "cold" seven times (referring directly to the weather), as Ballard goes from voyeur, to robber, and finally to sex with the girl's corpse. From here on, no more community narrators intrude; the narrative for the rest of the novel comes from this one omniscient voice. It is as if the voices of others in the community are too far away, but it is also the case that such intrusions would suggest a normal flow of time. Even the birds are quiet as Ballard takes the body of the girl home.

A SECOND EVICTION

Ballard is discovered in his second home not as a necrophiliac, but as a squatter, by two boys with permission to hunt around the house. This makes it clear that his home belongs to someone else and that the legal owner is alive and able to grant permission to the boys (and that he has not granted permission to Ballard). It also means that Ballard cannot keep his first prey in the house with him, even in the cold of the room adjacent to his living quarters. Instead, he stores her in the attic. Later, he will drag his victims into the secret places of the earth.

This first, found, victim, however, represents an ideal that cannot be equaled once he descends into spelunking and murder. It is appropriate that he places her in the attic, above the rest of the house. To Ballard, she is a gift; like the house, he has found her by chance and will take possession of her through ritual, as he has taken possession of this abandoned house. Indeed, I read the careful attention to detail in the description of Ballard's possession of both the house and this unlucky woman as indicative of his feeling that for once, the universe has smiled on him. Together, the found house and the found woman—both dead to the rest of society—offer him a chance at the courtship rituals, the spatial constraints, and the spatial distinctions between inside and outside, that contribute to domesticity.

Accordingly, Ballard does not rush in. Although he has already indulged his sexual desire in the found car, he realizes, eventually, the long-term possibilities. He buys clothes for her, and then buys food almost as if she could eat with him: "two loaves of bread [. . .] and a box of cakes" (*COG* 99). The grocer's name is Mr. Fox, a curious reminder of what the hunting dogs were chasing, and that their prey was as alive as the grocer—unlike the girl.

The clothes Ballard buys, and his other preparations, suggest an act of prosopopoeia. Ballard wants to bring this young woman back to life in a new role. He is imagining a larger life around the moment for which he is preparing, and that moment must be led up to as if it existed in normal time, even as the decay brought on by normal time would spoil the girl's body. Ballard therefore attempts to manipulate, carefully, the weather; by controlling the temperature inside his second home, he can stop and start time for the girl.

Outside, it is exceedingly cold. Inside, Ballard divides the house into two parts: he furiously heats the half in which he must dwell to stay alive, and into which, at the right time, he brings the girl. The other half of the house is left cold, static, a storage space for time, and his hedge against the fact that the girl is dead. In an attempt to prevent the discovery of the girl's body by an intruder (such as the hunting boys who have already almost seen her), Ballard has put the body into the attic. She is therefore in the house, but not within its living space. Ballard will have to move her at just the right time for his tableau.

When he builds a fire for his macabre date, he burns "whole lengths of fencepost with sections of rotted wire hanging from their staples" (*COG* 102). This sacrifice of the outside enclosure of the grounds around his found house foreshadows its inevitable loss: the natural order is inverted here, with fencing brought outside to fuel the heating of the inside. Ballard will heat his passions with a fuel derived from the remainders of natural life, sacrificing them in the long run for a scene meant to stop time—for what the French call a "little death."

The narration mocks the domestic scene Ballard is trying to recreate, by describing his movements of her body without mentioning him: "She came down the ladder [from the attic] until she touched the floor with her feet and there she stopped." Then we read, "He paid out more rope but she was standing there in the floor leaning against the ladder. She was standing on tiptoe, nor would she fold." Even now, the scene seems to be one in which it is the corpse that insists on a life-like will. Only the word "fold" is out of place, and only slightly so, following "would." "Then he dragged her into the other room and laid her on the hearth" (*COG* 102). It requires the brute force that spoils his fantasy to move her from the frozen attic (the only way to keep her) into a temporary encounter in the room that he (in order to keep himself alive) must heat. He curses her for this, much as if he were failing at bending even a dead woman to his romantic will.

In the rest of this scene, Ballard continues to behave like the natural suitor that he is not, given the situation. He exhibits what is for him an unusual patience, both willingly and unwillingly. (This man does not wait for his food to cook through, yet he waits for her.) He has to wait on her to thaw, "past midnight" (*COG* 102). Instead of taking a while to loosen her resolve, it takes a while to loosen her limbs. "He would arrange her in different positions and go out and peer in the window at her" (*COG* 103). The tense, "[h]e would," suggests that he does this more than once. This practice does more than connect his existing voyeurism with this new pathology; it also reconstitutes the domestic scene that is missing from his life: the window in this small house is likely the same one ignored as such by the hunting dogs. By going outside and looking at the girl, he first establishes—for himself, if not the reader—the believability that this is *not* an aberrant situation: leaving the scene where he dresses and prepares her allows him to then enter the house as if she had come to be there without his will behind her movement.

When he stays inside the house, he still takes his time. "After a while he just sat holding her, his hands feeling her body under the new clothes. He undressed her very slowly, talking to her" (*COG* 103). He has already, in the car when he found her, "poured into [her] ear everything he'd ever thought of saying to a woman" (*COG* 88). The words here make it clear that he has never been with a living woman, and that he is *full* of what he wants to say; of course, this is a pathological romance, as much as pathological sex. The scene is easy to maintain a comfortable distance from if the reader dismisses all of Ballard's behavior as equally aberrant; but McCarthy challenges us to recognize that the natural longings of any lonely person are present here: the desire for home, companionship, romance—and only then, sex. The moment is obscene, yet the words he finds for it are merely desperate, indicating not insanity so much as a desperate loneliness. They suggest a narrative that Ballard has been lacking that precedes sex (and therefore a drive that is not primarily sexual, but social in its own right). He must even imagine a past to bolster this fantastic moment: "You been wantin it," he says to her (*COG* 103). The tense is telling. In the act of psychological projection that is common to all lovers, he imagines that the past of his longing is the past of hers.

No house can hold such a macabre scene of courtship ritual. In a metonymy of house and attic against Ballard and his dead beloved, the transfer of heat is too much. The weather seems almost personified to protect this dead girl, insisting that she is dead by falling "to six below zero" (*COG* 103). The fire and Ballard's purpose for it (that it is hotter than he needs merely to survive) only enrages the house: "The flue howled with the enormity of the draw and red flames danced at the chimney top." Ballard treats it like a body, ramming more fuel "up the chimney throat." Then he personifies the night and dares it to "freeze, you son of a bitch" while fighting the cold and the night unnaturally, until it is "bright as day in the cabin" (*COG* 103). When a brick falls into the flames, we know the division between that part of the house for him, warmed by the fire, and the cold attic for her, has been breached. The house burns, with her inside. It is no burial, but a proper cremation, and the house has to go to the flames to accomplish it.

After warming himself on the hearth of the incinerated house—much as he warmed the body of the girl—Ballard is reduced to sitting on "a nest of weeds he'd made on the hearth." He finds nothing of the girl's body, "as if she'd never been" (*COG* 107).

THIS SEEMS A HOME—
AND HOME IS NOT—[10]

Homeless again, Ballard moves to a cave. But before we examine that spatial constraint, we should consider the connection between his last house and his first murder, and at the depiction of the ultimate product of domesticity in a wholly negative light. The domesticity he conjures with his first, found, victim requires the spatial constraint of a house. It is not so surprising, then, that Ballard's transformation to predatory (rather than scavenging) necrophilia occurs in another peculiar relationship to a house, or that it so obviously includes the woman he wants and excludes the child he does not.

Ballard first enters this house in the novel's first section, in one of many significant precursors to his finding the dead girl in the car. He is welcomed into this house first by the mother, though "his eye was on the daughter" (*COG* 76), so that he can wait for the patriarch, a man named Ralph. (Ralph never shows up.) Ballard has caught a robin in the snow as it feigns injury (as many mother birds do to lead a threat away from a nest of fledglings). The weather, "very cold" (*COG* 75) with deep snow, puts this particular bird already out of place; it is too early for signs of spring, such as this robin on the ground. Ballard's pursuit of the bird is childlike, as he falls and runs "laughing" (*COG* 76). He goes to Ralph's house to present the bird as a gift for the daughter's bastard child.

As has become obvious in *Outer Dark*, the novel preceding this one, McCarthy's depiction of problematic domesticity includes a severe disdain for children.[11] As Rick Wallach puts it, "a Cormac McCarthy novel is the last place you would want to turn up if you were a child" ("Prefiguring Cormac McCarthy" 19). Lester Ballard may be a child of god, but through the narrator's eyes, the child to whom Lester gives the bird is "the thing in the floor" (*COG* 77). This may be free indirect discourse or at least a stance of narration closer to Ballard's point of view than the more gracious narrator, who claims a murderer for a child of god. In any case, descriptions of the child suggest that it is developmentally impaired. McCarthy's narrator then employs eloquence far beyond Ballard to describe the child in an unpleasant light:

It didn't look. A hugeheaded bald and slobbering primate that inhabited the lower reaches of the house, familiar of the warped floorboards and the holes tacked up with foodtins hammered flat, a consort of roaches and great hairy spiders in their season, perennially benastied and afflicted with a nameless crud. (*COG* 77)

Interestingly, this child's obvious mental deficiencies do not afford it the same sympathy that Ballard gets for his. Perhaps this is because its insufficiencies are congenital, and not directly due to the kind of social injustice so regularly handed to Ballard in the course of the narrative. We might also infer that the child is the product of incest, as its mother is only referred to as "the daughter" (*COG* 76), and she is remarkably vehement (unnecessarily so, for that socio-economic quarter) that the child is not a bastard (*COG* 116). She may therefore be keeping a darker secret.

It is not merely the narrator looking through Ballard's eyes who sees such a "benastied" creature. Even the robin's point of view frames a monstrosity: "The robin started across the floor, its wings awobble like lateen sails. It spied the . . . what? child? child, and veered off toward a corner" (*COG* 77). The ellipses are McCarthy's, and they (along with the awkward interpolations of question marks) are uncharacteristically sloppy of McCarthy, indicating too obviously the bird's (or the narrator's) difficulty in identifying the child as an immature human. This stylistically uncharacteristic dip into consciousness—that of the bird—is all the more notable for its sympathy toward the non-human animal (anything but a baby for sympathy here). Yet no character in that house, least of all the bird, knows what a "lateen sail" is. The view of the baby, then, veers on that of authorial comment.

Ballard catches the bird again and hands it to this child, who simply bites off its legs. As Ballard explains, "He wanted it to where it couldn't run off" (*COG* 79). So much for constraining one character trying to escape the jaws of domesticity.

Ballard clearly thinks of the gift to the child as part of a courtship ritual. To the household, it would be acceptable for him to bring a gift to the child before giving one to the "daughter." The dialogue foreshadows more than Ballard yet intends, however. Before the child attacks the bird, the "daughter" warns him that this intrusion of something naturally free, and wild, into the domestic space will result in violence. Ironically, in the case of the child, the violence is inherent toward that which it cannot easily possess.

He'll kill it, the girl said.
Ballard grinned at her. It's hisn to kill if he wants to, he said.

> The girl pouted her mouth at him. Shoot, she said.
> I got somethin I'm goin to bring you, Ballard told her.
> You ain't got nothin I want, she tells him. (*COG* 77)

The next time Ballard visits this house, he will indeed "shoot." The girl pouts her mouth *at* him; he will point a gun at her (though not when she can see it). On his next visit, Ballard has premeditated murder on his mind, but it is not at all clear that he sees this murder coming at the earlier event of this ironic dialogue. These words suggest a narrative predestination at obvious work, limiting the options of this outcast trying to flirt with someone; Ballard's actions are constrained by the ironic weight of the dialogue in which he is already caught. They are both, in different ways, doomed.

This scene also creates a chiasmus between Ballard, the child of god, and the idiot child of the floorboards. Ballard has grown up enough to want his possession sexually; the child is too unpleasant to retain any of the innocence we associate with even unfortunate children, but it still wants its possession orally. By eating the legs of the bird, the child constrains the bird so "it couldn't run off," Ballard will kill the child's mother so he can keep her. The bird is a gift from him to the child; the child's mother is stolen from it by Ballard. Meanwhile, McCarthy's dialogue has cut the legs off our main character, as that dialogue hits us with an ironic foreshadowing of the man's future actions.

By his second visit to this house, Ballard has found and lost his first corpse, and it is not too surprising that he is ready to take the next one by force. What is interesting, however, is that Ballard adopts—like a rogue animal—hunting habits learned by accident. These new habits lead him not only to murder, but also to arson. He can only appropriate the young woman by killing her, but he must also cover his tracks. To do this, he burns the house—and the "idiot child" who is alive and "watching him" (*COG* 120). It is as if Ballard, constrained to the action of murder foretold by narrative foreshadowing, does what he can to learn from another, interpolated, event—the fire in the chimney of his squatter's house—at least to hide the evidence.

An odd detail in the description of Ralph's house, before and during Lester's assault on it, suggests something is already not right with it. By synecdoche, McCarthy suggests that the domestic order of the household is uneven (with the daughter having an idiot bastard child, perhaps by her father Ralph), but he does this mostly through description of the house's appointments. The detail is odd in that it may not be easy to imagine if one has not seen it before: the floor of the front room in Ralph's house is wooden, and is partially covered with what the novel calls a "yellow linoleum rug" (*COG* 119). Linoleum is a stiff material, of course, used in cheap coverings ordinarily glued down to cover the less dazzling surfaces beneath them. It is sold in sheets, and if a sheet of it is too small to cover the entire area of a floor or counter, it is likely to curl up at the edges; it is unintended as and unsuitable for a "rug" and is intended instead to have its edges covered by floorboards, counter trim, or some other device working as a border. This mismatch of material to purpose suggests not just the relative poverty of Ralph's household, but another ironic distinction from Ballard, who upon his second visit to this house has no house of his own. Ballard's homes are increasingly wild spaces decorated with the smatterings of domesticity and civilization; Ralph's house has been decorated beyond practical necessity with a flooring that is synthetic, but of inadequate size to completely cover the natural materials (the wooden floor made from the woods outside) that lie beneath it.

The third sentence of the chapter for this second visit tells us "[a] pale yellow trapezoid of light lay in the mud beneath the window. Within, the idiot child crawled in the floor [. . .]" (*COG* 115). The preposition "in" is odd, as one could more easily crawl *in* yellow mud than a yellow linoleum floor. Here, the "idiot child" is warm inside a domestic space, and the child of god is outside, wanting in.

McCarthy then heightens the sense in which Ballard's murder of the girl is an invasion of wilderness desire into the domestic by giving us this odd floor, whose boundaries are made of wood, in an odd house that may have failed already in keeping its inhabitants constrained by the usual civilized taboos. Ballard eventually shoots the girl, and we see that "[a] thin stream of blood ran across the yellow linoleum rug and seeped away darkly in the wood of the floor" (*COG* 119). This wood is untreated, and at its outer edges, closest to the walls of the domestic space, it soaks up what would remain pooled, and more garish, on the linoleum. The floor already suggests an insecure boundary between cultivated materials and the plain, untreated, wood of the wilderness.

The fire to warm this house is hardly contained within the constraints of the house's outer walls. Because the child cannot be trusted not to turn over the wood stove and burn the place down, the occupants have installed a fence around it—an indoor fence of "chickenwire" (*COG* 116). Chickenwire is a material for penning *in* domesticated animals, but not usually within the same house inhabited by humans. Here it serves to protect the domesticated fire and its wood stove container from the inevitable product of domesticity: a child. In this case, the child is unsuitable for domesticity, in as much as it (like Ballard) is not intelligent enough.

"The posts [of the fence] were toenailed to the floor and the fencing was nailed down as well." This suggests desperate measures to keep the child out of the fire, yet such a fence can hardly keep out such a child. Ballard comments,

"I bet he could push this over if he wanted to" (*COG* 116), and again we have foreshadowing with an ironic connection between the idiot child and our child of god. After he shoots the girl, Ballard indeed pushes the stove over to burn down the house. By burning the house, Ballard erases the domestic space he has been denied, immolates the offspring product that he is also denied (sex with cadavers provides him the illusion of intimacy without the danger—as I will later argue it seems to McCarthy men—of having a baby), and obliterates the evidence civilization might use against him. That evidence has "seeped" into the wooden floor (*COG* 119), and thus evaporates in the floor's fire. House, baby, and the blood of Ballard's new beloved all go up in smoke and down in ashes.

The girl has already referred to both the child of god and the idiot child as insane. When Ballard asks about the idiot child, she replies, "He's crazy as ever" (*COG* 116). Shortly after, Ballard pushes his flirtation too far and she warns him that she will tell her father. "Shoot, I was just teasin ye." This time, it is Ballard who says, "shoot." "Why don't you go on," she tries. "I guess you too young to know when a man's teasin ye," says Ballard. Her reply places him again in connection with the idiot, refusing him male adulthood and sanity: "You ain't even a man. You're just a crazy thing" (*COG* 117). In this exchange, Ballard is now like the idiot child, both "crazy" and an inhuman "thing." When she insists that Ballard leave the house, she stamps her foot, the way one runs off an animal (*COG* 118).

As for the girl, she appears to us in the second visit momentarily like the bird that, its legs chewed off, could not escape the hunger of the idiot child. "She was wearing pink slacks of cheap cotton and she sat in the sofa with her legs crossed under her and a pillow in her lap" (*COG* 116). For Ballard, she will need no legs. When her son bites off the legs of the robin, Ballard sees "[s]mall red numbs work[ing] in the soft down" (*COG* 79). Now, the girl on the sofa appears equally unable to run away. She is also oddly "in" the sofa (as her son was described as "in" the floor), and where what was left of the robin's legs disappeared in its own "soft down," the girl has a pillow (presumably full of feathers) covering her lap. The domestic space of this paltry house contains and constrains its inhabitants, such that the preposition "in" predominates spatial arrangements. Ballard simply wants in.

When the girl stands up, eventually stamping her foot to get Ballard out of this place, she exercises her legs for the second to last time. The last time comes when Ballard has gone outside. Again, his prey is back in the sofa, which from the rear covers all but "the back of her head." Ballard "raised the rifle and cocked it and laid the sights on her head. He had just done this when suddenly she rose from the sofa and turned facing the window. Ballard fired" (*COG* 118). Her standing and turning is the action Ballard's first victim might have taken when he looked at her from outside his second, lost, house—had she been alive. It is this young woman's last action of resistance: looking out of the window at the wildness, she senses that it is about to attack the house.

Because she stands, Ballard's shot hits her in the body rather than the head. The glass is "spidered" (*COG* 119) where the bullet goes through, referring back to the predatory squatter that Ballard ejected—with a burning newspaper—from the chimney of his second, lost, home. Before Ballard leaves with his prey, he finds "newspapers and magazines" to spread around the wood stove before kicking it over. The fire catches the wood first, "at the edge of the linoleum" (*COG* 120). As he leaves, the dead girl over his shoulder and his rifle in hand, the house raises a last domestic resistance, in an image of the loosed fire as "painted." "As he whirled about there in the kitchen door the last thing he saw through the smoke was the idiot child. It sat watching him, berryeyed filthy and frightless among the painted flames" (*COG* 120).

Like the problem with children, the problem with living women in *Child of God* has its history in *Outer Dark*. Nell Sullivan traces it even earlier, to McCarthy's first short story publication, "Wake for Susan," in a 1959 student literary journal at the University of Tennessee. McCarthy's rejection of this early work reportedly employed a trope with intriguing irony: when the *Virginia Quarterly* offered to republish "Wake for Susan" and "A Drowning Incident" (which involves the killing of puppies), McCarthy told them he "hoped to be long buried and mouldering before they were published again" (Wallach, "Prefiguring Cormac McCarthy" 15). Rather than allow a new home for his first literary progeny (now disowned), McCarthy prefers the grave.

In "The evolution of the dead girlfriend motif in *Outer Dark* and *Child of God*," Sullivan notes that McCarthy began "Wake for Susan," and thus his publishing career, with an epigraph from Sir Walter Scott:

> "Who makes the bridal bed,
> Birdie, say truly?"
> "The grey headed sexton
> That delves the grave duly."
> (Sullivan 68)

In the story, the title character is a "long-dead woman onto whom a young man at her graveside projects his fantasies." Sullivan's reading of this—and much theory besides—leads her to some monosemantic interpretations of McCarthy's depictions of women. Her point is more accurate as it identifies a general theme (or problem) in McCarthy than in her particular reading, especially of *Outer Dark*. The general idea, however, remains persuasive:

> With their conflation of the bridal bed and the grave, the lines from Scott's
> "Proud Maisie" introduce a theme echoing throughout most of McCar-
> thy's fiction: the theme of female sexuality inextricably bound up with
> death and, therefore, posed as a source of masculine dread. This insidious
> association leads inexorably to the narrative death sentence for most young
> women in the McCarthy canon. Moving from its gentler to most egre-
> gious articulation, the transition from *Outer Dark* (1968) to *Child of God*
> (1973) marks the crystallization of the "dead girlfriend" motif in McCar-
> thy's mature fiction. (68)

For Sullivan, this motif originates early, in a pre-existing pathology not only
evidenced in McCarthy's work, but also in a larger tradition. She quotes Gail
Kern Paster, on a "female body [. . .] perceived in the Western canon as
'naturally grotesque—which is to say, open, permeable, effluent, leaky' [.
. .]. That [Rinthy, in *Outer Dark*] is 'open' and 'permeable' —that is, preg-
nable—has rendered her an outcast in Johnson County and determined for
her the life of misery that the novel details" (69).

This is about half right. Rinthy's body does indeed leak throughout the
book, but this can be read as a pathological condition connected to the incest
between her and her brother, rather than a normative but repellent condition
of all females. The fact that her breast milk comes in and continues becomes a
problem only inasmuch as her baby has been taken from her; indeed, her pain
in this condition serves as a reminder of the pain suffered by women abused by
men: their bodies bear visual witness to the abuse. (To this reader, her condition
is sad, arousing sympathy, rather than revulsion.) Rinthy first appears outcast
while still in the cabin, where she is hidden because her obvious pregnancy bears
visual witness to incest that was possibly forced. On the road, she is outcast in
her inability to stop her breast milk: a mother obviously missing her child must,
presumably, keep moving to find it.

She only owes this sad condition, of course, to her brother Culla for
having taken the baby and left it in the woods. Outcast by the narrative,
she is nonetheless sympathetically received by some of the people she
encounters. In searching for the child, she actually moves through towns,
and is occasionally helped by people there. Sullivan, who sometimes fails
to distinguish between McCarthy, his putative intent, and the reasonable
inferences one may make from his novels, sees an unredeemed male author
in the monologic act of casting women out from his books—particularly
living women.

It is at least equally plausible (and as I have argued, more likely) that
McCarthy's work does contain no small measure of social criticism, despite

the fact that such criticism is, in the novels, limited to implication. His men live generally unpleasant lives frustrated for comfort and harried by violence, particularly in the degree to which they reject the values of domesticity—values that, historically, have been constructed as the gender-specific domain of women. The "'dead girlfriend' motif" that Sullivan sees crystallized before McCarthy's third novel (*Child of God*) may be more complex after all.

Sullivan uses the word "romantic" quite naturally to characterize the female lead in a short story where "a young man" "projects his fantasies" by her grave. Even if one needed to deny McCarthy his wish that we would leave these short stories in the grave before he arrives there, one can see a gulf of artistic development between this scene from "Wake for Susan" and those scenes of dead "girlfriends" in *Child of God*. As I have argued, Lester Ballard conjures a romantic anticipation of domesticity, as much as sex, outside the window of an abandoned house that contains the dead woman he means to possess. If one must, it is not difficult to see an equal movement between the social criticisms implicit in these very different scenes. The first scene (written by a young McCarthy) imagines the romantic attachments of the heart to an uncomplicated love of a dead woman long gone. The later scene captures, with an older, colder eye, an entire world attached to the narrative of possession that Ballard conjures for himself. Ballard wants much more—an entire world of not only sexual possession but also feminine companionship and the comforts of domesticity (all of which his actions seek to replicate even if apart from the society that has rejected him). It is this world that Ballard sees through the window that, for the reader, frames only another "dead girlfriend." Finally, however unpleasantly women may be depicted by McCarthy, Ballard is certainly nothing appealing. If his narratives regularly hew close to the situations of male main characters, it does not follow, however, that we are not to empathize with any other of the characters.[12]

A THIRD HOME

Through half of Part II, Lester Ballard lives in a cave. The narrative through that section of the book, however, hardly mentions this cave. As if the narration shuddered to follow him to his farthest reaches away from society, we see his coming and going without reference to his new home, with only a few dramatic hints as to what he does there. With his first murder, and the loss of the home he inadvertently burns, we know him to be moving farther from the norms of society. Outside the cave, however, there are curious details of his interactions with living people. He lacks any intimate relations with the living whatsoever. He nonetheless attempts to carry on more business-like connections with them.

His credit at the country store is in arrears. At first, his debt seems far beyond his ability to pay, until we realize he is unwilling to pay what he eventually slaps on the counter (*COG* 125–126). We might imagine that he is reluctant to show the money he must be taking from his victims, yet he dares to wear "black lowcut shoes that were longer than he needed" (*COG* 129). Daring to wear the shoes of your victim might be worth daring, with the weather as cold as McCarthy describes it. Then, in the same store that he is reluctant to pay for his groceries, he sells three men's watches, certainly taken from victims (*COG* 129–132). Ballard's position in the transaction is weak: one of the men offers him a low bid for one watch and adds that he "won't ast [him] where [he] got it" (*COG* 131). Ballard bargains poorly, getting eight dollars from a man who immediately, as if to shame the seller, sells two of the watches to his friends at a small profit (*COG* 132).

Ballard's bad luck with money here reminds us of his dispossession of the family home: he feels he has been dealt an unfair hand, not just a bad one, and thus he makes no distinction between fair play and cheating. Rather, he is out to get what he feels he deserves, and to pay as little as possible for it. Unlike many scenes of social interaction in country stores in McCarthy's Southern novels, Ballard is never included in the arrangement of bodies around a fire, and no one ever offers him a drink. Drink, a seat, and conversation are offered even the outcast Gene Harrogate in *Suttree*.

Ballard, unwelcome at any social activity, is unwelcome even to the temporality of the community from which he is exiled. By temporality, I mean the passing of time in all activities of a social nature that therefore require timekeeping. The men in the store know this on some level, and they tease Ballard by including in their comments unconscious references to the fact that Ballard's life is not marked by a career—a course, or movement, that might be directed through time with intentional goals. They do this simply by including references to selling watches at this particular point in time: "Ain't you goin to get in the watch business today, Orvis?" one man teases another, who answers "I cain't get my jobber to come down" (*COG* 131). They all think that Ballard is a "jobber"—a middleman—of nothing; or at least they prefer to think that rather than to confront the alternative that he is a "jobber" of dead men's watches.

Ballard needs not even one, let alone three, of the watches owned by his victims; he has the sun, and for a man outside society, the sun and weather are all the timekeeping needed. The lives of his victims, now stopped, afford him some relationship to the social time in which they took part. Their timepieces, in contrast to their hearts, go on ticking. The watches belong therefore among the community of the living, rather than to Ballard. Sold by a man living among the dead, the watches naturally go for a low price; in the land of the living, the watches of the dead find a buyer's market.

By including these details of awkward social interaction, McCarthy accomplishes two things. First, he builds dramatic tension by not telling us exactly what new crimes Ballard is up to, preferring instead to give us physical evidence and clues in dialogue. None of the physical evidence would be conclusive, and the clues in dialogue are somewhat opaque. We want to know more, and this propels the novel's economical plot.

Second, however, he implicates us in something more complicated by now refusing us the direct access we had to Ballard's home life, such as it was, up until his first murder. This secrecy places Ballard at a further remove from the reader. We may reassure ourselves that he is Ballard, the murderer who is not we, even if we remember him as "a child of god much like [ourselves] perhaps" (*COG* 4). Our certainty of Ballard's deeper guilt nonetheless pricks our awareness—dim, as we have yet to go inside—of his residence in a deeper, third home. We go there with him, finally, toward the end of Part II.

On a tour of underground space, we arrive at the vision of his life as he will find and order it in Part III. Gone are the squalid details of Part II, the particulars of real houses, the quotidian and comical details of domesticity even as ragged and amoral as we found the domesticity at the dumpkeeper's place. What we find instead is a deeply symbolic space, carved by nature in chance and chosen by Ballard in desperation, but also appointed by him—decorated even, in the slight free indirect discourse of McCarthy's descriptions of it—in the compromised life of Ballard's third, penultimate, home.

Ballard's deepest urges are those of many humans: to subdue nature, the better to participate in culture. Not only do we need shelter, we need paths, places in which to meet. Ballard's third home exhibits some of these distinctions, and addresses his inability—our inability—to live in an unmodified natural world.

> Coming up the mountain through the blue winter twilight among great
> boulders and the ruins of giant trees prone in the forest he wondered at
> such upheaval. Disorder in the woods, trees down, new paths needed.
> Given charge Ballard would have made things more orderly in the woods
> and in men's souls. (*COG* 136)

When we follow Ballard into his third home, we see how much he has done to make "things more orderly," to turn underground space into domestic places. Regressing to a more primitive state of existence, however, losing distinctions between himself and his victims, Ballard's relationship with his third home conflates the agency between himself and nature. Much as he "would have [. . .] things more orderly" in his own life, his is still a negotiation with the chance arrangements of things. He has therefore arranged a home within a cave. But it is the cave's own slower processes that have predetermined the features to which he must accommodate himself—and his victims. These arrangements are notable.

As we follow Ballard into his cave for the first time, we enter a living organism that is also a house, described in terms of a house and its appointments, albeit alive. "The nearer walls of the cavern composed themselves out of the constant night with their pale stone drapery folds and a faultline in the vault's ceiling appeared with a row of dripping limestone teeth" (*COG* 133). In just two pages, the words "walls" (twice), "drapery folds," "ceiling," "room" (twice), "urns," and "floor" (twice), all suggest a built environment (*COG* 133–134). It might be objected that caves are regularly referred to in terms of walls, ceilings, and floors, but then we may suppose that our words for these aspects of built environments are actually connected to our first, found, shelters in caves.

The tour we take of Ballard's third home leads through these domestic terms of description—and then away from them, as he passes from his dwelling to another place: the new home for his victims. We read that he travels "perhaps a mile," and then farther, all underground, until he reaches the holy spot in which he has arranged (by my count) at least half a dozen bodies. With some amazement we realize that he must have carried them throughout the long trip, even somehow thrusting them through the narrower passages that he negotiates "sideways like a fencer and through a tunnel that brought him to his belly" (*COG* 134–135). More amazing, just before he arrives at his sanctuary he must climb "up a chimney to a corridor above the stream" that he has been following (*COG* 135). There is no suggestion (including when these bodies are accidentally found at the novel's end) that there is an alternative entrance to this sanctuary.

Two words here help create the distinctions between Ballard's new home, the long passageway, and the sanctuary: when we are nearest the home or the sanctuary, we pass through "corridor[s]" (*COG* 134 and 135). By contrast, when we are following him through the long passage between his home and his replicated society of saints, we endure a "tunnel" (*COG* 134). If this seems a minor distinction between the passageway of a house and one that is never in a house, we may also note that just before Ballard climbs the "chimney" he is on his "belly, the smell of the water beside him in the trough rich with minerals and past the chalken dung of he knew not what animals" (*COG* 135). To move from home to social space,

Ballard passes through a bestial space, much as he would travel through the woods from home to the store in his former life above ground.

This is the world underground, though. Indeed, Ballard's trip up the chimney recalls the spider that he had, in a more civilized domestic space, evicted with a burning bit of newspaper. Ironies abound here. This time, Ballard is now the predatory arachnid. Here, the social life of various people who are not Ballard yet who are gathered in a social space awaiting his coming and going is really a still portrait of society, a dead depiction of something that can only really occur in life. Perhaps this is why the word "saints" is used to refer to them: we find them lying "on ledges or pallets of stone" (*COG* 135) where they might be "entitled to public veneration and capable of interceding for people on earth" (*American Heritage*).[13]

Ballard's third home, therefore, replicates more than his lost home (which he begins to spy on increasingly). His homesteading in the cave also replicates the social world that long ago cast him outside its approved boundaries. McCarthy further emphasizes the difference between Ballard's home cave and the sanctuary cave with prepositional anaphora:

> Here the walls with their softlooking convolutions, slavered over as they were with wet and bloodred mud, had an organic look to them, like the innards of some great beast. Here in the bowels of the mountain Ballard turned his light on ledges or pallets of stone where dead people lay like saints. (*COG* 135)

This anaphora ("Here [. . .]") also announces the magical aspect of the space and its inhabitants, through an incantatory rhythm, a real estate liturgy for a house of the dead. In *The Practice of Everyday Life*, Michel de Certeau notes the work of C. Linde and W. Labov on the way New York City residents describe their apartments. Linde and Labov discover two types of descriptions: tours and maps. Tours are stories, and they tell someone what it would be like to be in a place. Maps, on the other hand, are more abstract: rather than tell of "operations," maps distill a "path" into "a series of units that have the form of vectors that are [. . .] static." The map "*tableau*," it turned out, was much less common than the tour's organizing "*movements*" (119, their emphasis).

The anaphora "Here" at first indicates a map description. In its unusual location, however, the static place described to us as "here" seems to be alive. Both dead and alive, the space created by the static place of a living cave through which moves a necrophiliac carrying dead people to a sacred place collapses into both tour and map, both generative personified space and dead static place. Indeed, the cave is more alive than are the people in it, and the narration's description further suggests a womb-like space that has been perverted to the intestinal, fecal place; it is wet and bloodred like a menstruating uterus (or a womb in miscarriage), yet these are the "bowels of the mountain." This fits Ballard's inverted, perverted, and generally pathological construction of space.

Nell Sullivan notes, "the caves resemble the generative female body" (76). We can also see by now how the narration conflates that generative space with the end of the alimentary canal. Rather than suggesting a misogynistic attitude toward women, however, this conflation—embedded as it is in descriptions of setting that imply Ballard's psychology—suggests the horrifying depths of his impacted psyche. Ballard stands as the ultimate example in McCarthy of a man afflicted with unachieved ambivalence toward the mother. Dianne Luce further makes the connection between Ballard losing his parents at an early age, and the background in clinical cases of necrophilia, "many of whom had lost parents to death when they were young, and for whom the corpse represented the lost mother" ("Cave" 173).

To bolster this portrait of mental illness, the narrative projects the maladies of the child onto its adopted mother. Ballard therefore falls from the condition of literal orphan to a deeper orphaning, a spiritual rejection by the earth itself, forever the child of an ambivalent earth that keeps him in a kind of excretory womb, a conflated replica of both the domestic situation that might produce children and the domestic excretion of waste from them and their mother.

In case the reader misses this, descriptions of the bodies eventually retrieved from the cave extend the conflation of birth and excretion by adding the imagery of a hellish kitchen to those of a womb and bowel: eventually, as it were, mother earth will not even digest, let alone hold in its alimentary canal, the taboo children of Ballard's ambivalence.[14] No real child can be born from the caves Sullivan identifies with the female body. Instead, the bodies discovered and removed by the sheriff's department later in the book are described in terms of food gone bad, "covered with adipocere, a pale gray cheesy mold" with "scallops of light fungus" grown on them (*COG* 196). After they have been wrapped in muslin, they are described as "enormous hams" (*COG* 197).

Unpleasant as these descriptions are, they bring closure to the three elemental needs that drive Ballard before the discovery of his sanctuary: food, shelter, and companionship (including sex). In life, Ballard's loss of shelter parallels his loss of any hope for relations with a woman. He is deft, however, with a rifle. Procuring food (if not sex) is easy for him. Although his predation on women (and men) is ultimately sexual, it is more immediately akin to acquiring food in the manner that early humans must first have acquired it. First, he gathers what he finds, then he kills for what he needs, and finally he arranges a living space around a steady life. That found space is turned into a domestic place from which he can hunt, and within which he can hide his prey, conjure social relations, and even perform magical services. His final outrage among the living above ground, therefore, requires him to perform several acts that gather the threads of these three drives—food, shelter, and sex—even as they complete the chiasmus of his trajectory against that of normal society.

John Greer, in some measure, has been the cause of Ballard's first literal homelessness. Before that auction, of course, Ballard's mother had deserted the family (again, assuming nothing worse came to her), and his father had committed suicide. His home was already empty of family; the auction was only required to take away the space of a house that the family had once made the place of home—however meager. Deprived of mother, then father, and finally his home, Ballard's journey leads inexorably to the underground duplication of these needs in an ordering of things comestible, sexual, and domestic, providing for all his needs. In the end, however, even Ballard is not so strange as to find contentment in this reversal of fortunes. Even as he perfects his underground life, he imagines that he hears "his father on the road coming home whistling" (*COG* 170), a memory from before the auction.

His dreams further conflate the natural world with the world of people, in a rebuke of the living against the dead. In one dream, he rides a mule through a wood:

> Each leaf that brushed his face deepened his sadness and dread. Each leaf he passed he'd never pass again. They rode over his face like veils, already some yellow, their veins like slender bones where the sun shone through them. He had resolved himself to ride on for he could not turn back and the world that day was as lovely as any day that ever was and he was riding to his death. (*COG* 170)

There are many reproaches here. Not only is he failing in his attempt to escape time, despite having stolen his corpses from time by removing them to an underground stasis. He is also ridden over by leaves, even though he is the one on the mule that would ride over the leaves after they fall. Their "veins" and "slender bones" not only enact a symbolic revenge of power by the dead over their living tormentor; they also punish him with a realization: only that which is passing can be truly beautiful, and he is living a lie.

He has therefore failed to replace his home, and he remains bent on recovery of that home and revenge against the man he blames for its loss. At the end of the novel's second section, the end of winter sees him spying on the house "every day. [. . .] He laid queer plans. His shuffling boot tracks trampling out the prints of lesser life. Where mice had gone, or foxes hunting in the night. The dovelike imprimatur of a stooping owl" (*COG* 140). In his coveting, he rises above "lesser" animals.

Indeed, his sexual and social needs have blurred his identity into that of the living women missing from his deathly life: "He'd long been wearing the underclothes of his female victims but now he took to appearing in their outerwear as well. A gothic doll in illfit clothes, its carmine mouth floating detached and bright in the white landscape" (*COG* 140). This cross-dressing emphasizes the blurring of Ballard's sexual identity, through the projection of himself onto his victims, and vice versa. The landscape that he also desires—the valley and hills of his lost homestead—further mirrors this "gothic" mask. Immediately following the description of Ballard in drag, we see: "Down there the valley with the few ruststained roofs and faintest wisps of smoke. The ribboned slash of mud that the road made up the white valley and beyond it the fold on fold of mountains with their black weirs of winter treelimbs and dull green cedars" (*COG* 140–141). The "slash of mud" suggests red fecundity against the white skin of the ample "fold on fold" of the mountains, below their limbs of trees and hair of cedar.

Ballard's nurse in the hospital, where he convalesces under guard after John Greer shoots off his arm, mistakes him for a man completely unhinged. About Greer's fate, she tells Ballard, "You really don't care one way or the other do you?" Ballard corrects her: "Yes I do [. . .]. I wish the son of a bitch was dead" (*COG* 176). To Ballard, that is less a wish that Greer leave the living than that Greer join the dead. In this way, Ballard might not only exercise the complete control over Greer that he has accomplished with his other dead; he may more thoroughly conflate his own identity with that of Greer, just as the "frightwig and skirts" (*COG* 172) Ballard wears in his attack on Greer conflate Ballard's identity with that of the female necessary to domesticity.

The stance of the writing in the attack on Greer is close to him, not Ballard. Now the narrator renders Ballard down to an "it" in Greer's eyes, with Greer "looking at whatever it was standing there cursing to itself while it worked the lever of the rifle" (*COG* 172–173). Ballard shoots Greer twice as he chases the man into the house. Ballard gets only as far as the door, however, where the house seems to spit him out of its mouth, Ballard "swallowed up in the door and discharged from it again almost simultaneously, ejected in an immense concussion backwards" (*COG* 173). He has come home, only to be put out again, this time with a shotgun blast that claims his right arm.

A DECENT BURIAL

A mob takes Ballard from the hospital to frighten him into leading them to the bodies. "You show us where you put them people so they can be give a decent burial [. . .]," they tell him (*COG* 182). These men are following the custom that cannot imagine a body uninterred to be "decent." Decency for the dead requires a bodily fit within an approved space away from the living. Ballard's violation of these bodies is a violation not only of the sanctity of each individual, but a breach of the proper requirements for spatial constraints around the bodies of the dead, constraints that are particular to the dead and circumscribed from the living.

To obtain the whereabouts of the dead from Ballard, they threaten to lynch him with an oiled cable. They are on the verge of doing just this when he relents, only to slip away from them in a cave. In refusing to enable the burial of his victims, Ballard nonetheless escapes a noose so firm as to be made of woven metal; in doing so he of course escapes his own grave. This scene begins Ballard's last habitation of a home outside society, but the ambiguous nature of this last cave space will terrify him.

Gaston Bachelard, in a close reading of a prose poem by Henri Michaux, concludes that life (or as he names it, "being") without some certainty of space is terrifying, a hell where being has been "overthrown" (217). "Being is alternately condensation that disperses with a burst, and dispersion that flows back to a center. Outside and inside are both intimate—they are always ready to be reversed, to exchange their hostility" (217–218). Lester Ballard's condition is fraught with an exchange of inside for outside in three notable ways: bodily and kinesthetic, psychologically, and socially. Ballard sought a balance the only way he knows how: a perverse balance in exile. His desperate strategies of the resistant scapegoat, and his arrangements of compromised domesticity above ground, crumble beneath him with every step he takes toward the cave. That cave is sought for a home, but it expels him from its bowels as surely as the family house spits him out of its front door mouth. When Ballard returns to the cave, it becomes both a womb and grave. Because of this conflation of generative with degenerative spatial properties in descriptions concerning the womb-cave, I will refer to this space as the *womb-grave*.

Ballard's body, already garbed in the clothing of identities that are not his own, has been dismembered. Bodily and kinesthetically, he has not adjusted to this new reality. Although Greer's shotgun blast has severed Ballard's arm, Ballard cannot imagine an empty space in place of the pain he feels in an arm no longer there. He even asks the nurse about the arm's location:

"You got it shot off," she tells him. "I know that," he replies, "I just wanted to know what all they done with it" (*COG* 175). The narration's stance here is sympathetic. It captures the cognitive dissonance between Ballard's mental will and his proprioceptive experience. A proprioceptor is "[a] sensory receptor, found chiefly in muscles, tendons, joints, and the inner ear, that detects the motion or position of the body or a limb by responding to stimuli arising within the organism" (*American Heritage*). A loss of proprioception is thus an inability to accurately accord for the spatial relationship between a part of one's body and the world around it.

"He [. . .] raised his hand. No hand came up" (*COG* 174). As he sits in the truck with the lynching mob, "[h]is arm hurt" (*COG* 180). Instead of the place his arm created in the world, he is left with nothing but an empty space. Yet Ballard does not feel this; his arm, he thinks, must still exist somewhere—it must be turning some space into a place— and he cannot give up the absurd desire for an intelligence of its location. Deprived of accurate proprioception, he insists on a less connected knowledge.

Psychologically, repeated descriptions of Ballard's body (deprived as it is of the women's clothing he had worn in the attack on Greer) emphasize the diminution of both that body and whatever biological space it might house. In the truck, one of the vigilantes shows some compassion for Ballard's well being, as his charge sits through a cold night in nothing but a hospital shift. He gives Ballard clothes, very likely the same type of clothing that they wear: overalls and a work shirt. Previously, Ballard has struggled with the buttons on a dress he put on one of his dead victims. Now he struggles, one-handed, with the buttons of the costume he is forced to put on. "He'd never tried to button a shirt with one hand and he was not good at it. He got the overalls up and the straps fastened. [. . .] [T]here was room inside for a whole Ballard more" (*COG* 180–181). His appearance, as well as the paucity of his entreaties and denials in bits of conversation, reveals him as a pitiful object, fallen into the hell of a hostility between inside and outside identity. Indeed, at this point he is so fallen from any accepted place within society that the very clothes he has been handed are seemingly empty—with room for "a whole Ballard more" in their space.

Socially, Ballard is in one ironic detail better off than he would be on his own. Rather than turning a burnt potato on a coat hanger over an open fire, he sits in his hospital room "unrolling *his* silver from [a] linen napkin" (*COG* 176, my emphasis). In captivity, he is shown both contempt and compassion; in any event, they certainly have a space in which to put him, even if he seems unlikely to fill it. Ironically, the accoutrements of domesticity are freely given to this man to whom they were previously denied.

In *Space and Place: The Perspective of Experience*, Yi Fu Tuan describes a movement through human cultural development from the most intimate to the most public spaces, by tracing the development from living in primitive earthen shelters to the construction of elaborate architecture that requires planning, imagination, and—most of all—language.

> Consider the sense of an "inside" and an "outside," of intimacy and exposure, of private life and public space. People everywhere recognize these distinctions, but the awareness may be quite vague. Constructed form has the power to heighten the awareness and accentuate, as it were, the difference in emotional temperature between "inside" and "outside." In Neolithic times the basic shelter was a round semi-subterranean hut, a *womblike* enclosure that contrasted vividly with the space beyond. Later the hut emerged above ground, moving away from the earth matrix but retaining and even accentuating the contrast between interior and outside by the aggressive rectilinearity of its walls. At a still later stage, corresponding to the beginning of urban life, the rectangular courtyard domicile appeared. (107, my emphasis)

When juxtaposed with the story of Ballard's housing, several aspects of Tuan's three-part account of normal human social development stand out.

First, the story of Ballard's housing is initially regressive but eventually circular. Beginning on a family farm, and thus at a remove from the urban, the story moves away from urban development. The family farm has presumably held the urban at a distance, as Ballard has either refused to pay, or been unable to pay, taxes required by the larger community. In retribution, that unpaid community invades and takes over this rural home, with its division between house and barn. Ballard's second home is akin to the hut; animals enter this house as readily (or more readily, as far as we are told) as they enter its barn. His last home is further regressive: more "womblike" than he intends, it constitutes a dead end beyond which he must either succumb to death and burial among ancient animals or against which he must struggle to be born back into the light of civilization. That light will judge him harshly, and yet he chooses it, struggling his way out of the womb-grave. This space finally births him back into the extreme constraints of a public housing that is as much penitential and judicial as medical. Having reached the nadir of regression away from civil society, Ballard's return to civil authority means that his housing journey is finally recursive: the civil requirement that he had evaded (paying taxes) is then replaced by a more strict confinement for more serious crimes.

Second, Tuan's further analysis of architecture's distinctions between inside and outside, between private and public places, emphasizes two abilities of complex architecture. Architecture of sufficient complexity reinforces distinctions between inside and outside even as it enables greater freedom of movement between the "emotional temperature[s]" of outside and inside. In Ballard's womb-grave, inside and outside are conflated through the impossibility of his remaining in that space and place. Because the womb-grave is both generative and degenerative, he must either be born from its space, or die within its place. Its spatial possibilities are about to collapse, unless Ballard escapes them.

As if mirroring these aspects of Tuan's reading of spatial constraints, Ballard's escape into the last cave leads him to contact with Paleolithic hunting. He finds "a long room filled with bones. Ballard circled this ancient ossuary kicking at the ruins. The brown and pitted armatures of bison, elk. A jaguar's skull whose one remaining eyetooth he pried out and secured in the bib pocket of his overalls" (*COG* 188). These three animals have been extinct from Tennessee for nearly a century when Ballard finds this evidence of their earlier hunters.

Then he finds a hole, "a sheer drop" whose incredible depth suggests that by falling into it he might have fallen back to the beginning of time itself. When Ballard finally finds some means of exit from the cave, he has to claw his way out, first barehanded, then with the first tools humans ever used: rocks dug up with the hand that become more suitable than the hand for digging out more rocks. Using "the larger chunks to pry and dig with," he finally escapes the dangerous ambivalence of the womb-grave. But first, we see him pitifully caught in that ambivalence.

McCarthy's sympathetic phrase for Ballard—"A child of God much like yourself perhaps"—echoes cruelly in this cave. The narrator steps in to find Ballard asleep, a "drowsing captive [who] looked so inculpate in the fastness of his hollow stone you might have said he was half right who thought himself so grievous a case against the gods" (*COG* 189). In this second sympathetic view of Ballard, he is no longer the child of a singular god, but rather someone with a case against numerous "gods." With the word "inculpate"—which means, "[t]o incriminate" (*American Heritage*)—McCarthy takes the freedom to render a transitive verb into an adjective. It is like saying *he looks accuse* or *he looked so incriminate*, an

odd way to suggest the ambiguous colors with which the narrator is painting this scene. It is Ballard, of course, who has been accused of horrible
crimes; yet we are to remember that he is "half right" in his own thinking,
which accuses "the gods" of a "grievous" injustice: his unhousing has led
to this underground housing in a womb of bones in death.

The imagery used in this passage is worth another look.

> In the night he heard hounds and called to them but the enormous
> echo of his voice in the cavern filled him with fear and he would not
> call again. He heard the mice scurry in the dark. Perhaps they'd nest
> in his skull, spawn their tiny bald and mewling whelps in the lobed
> caverns where his brain had been. His bones polished clean as egg-
> shells, centipedes sleeping in their marrowed flutes, his ribs curling
> slender and whitely like a bone flower in the dark stone bowl. (*COG*
> 189)

Here, it is Ballard's bones that will be part of the "ossuary" of the underground world (*COG* 188), a world once belonging to Paleolithic humans
but since left to animals alone. Mice, and their offspring, will sleep in
his empty head. If he dies here, his rib bones will remain a darkly ironic
memorial to his problem. Home to insects, Ballard's bones will nonetheless resemble a sad remnant of human domesticity: a cut flower placed
in a "dark stone bowl" serving as a vase—engendering nothing itself, yet
home to the domesticity of rodents.

Against this eventuality, Ballard escapes the dead end of the underground world to which he had run. Indeed, after he claws his way out into
a foreign landscape, he is immediately confronted with the aboveground
ordering of spaces that include an opposite relationship between humans
and animals than what he imagined in the womb-grave. "The first thing
he saw was a cow. [. . .] and beyond the cow was a barn and beyond
that a house. He watched the house for signs of life but saw none. He low-
ered himself back into his hole and rested" (*COG* 190). It is too light for
this macabre figure to present itself to even a farmyard.

After dark, he notes lights at the farmhouse. He chooses the down-
hill course of the road he finds, using it to return to the town. On the way,
he sees his doppelgänger staring through the back window of a church
bus,

> a small boy [. . .], his nose puttied against the glass. There was noth-
> ing out there to see but he was looking anyway. As he went by he looked

at Ballard and Ballard looked back [. . .] Ballard climbed into the
road and went on. He was trying to fix in his mind where he'd seen the
boy when it came to him that the boy looked like himself. This gave
him the fidgets and though he tried to shake the image of the face in the
glass it would not go. (*COG* 191)

The child of god has come full circle. As the "nothing" adult Ballard that
his "small boy" doppelgänger has looked at walks on, roosters outside the
town reinforce this sense of conflation and recursion by calling out in the
darkness far too early for the coming dawn. Ballard "kept watch eastward.
Perhaps some freshness in the air. Everywhere across the sleeping land they
called and answered each to each. As in olden times so now. As in other
countries here" (*COG* 191). This rooster passage resembles the ending of *The
Orchard Keeper*, with its turning earth full of the bones of the long dead, and
its broken fence giving way to a Western road. It is McCarthy in his mode of
archaic incantation, verging on the tendentious. Yet it sets up a fitting ending, with rhetorical flourishes that give a sense of eternal return, the inevita-
bility of death, and peace in a country where what is dead is buried and what
has been robbing the dead is headed to turn itself in to the authorities, who
will keep him far from fresh air.

BALLARD INSIDE OUT

Returning to the place of his confinement (and convalescence), Ballard
appears before the night nurse at the county hospital. "A weedshaped one-
armed human swaddled up in outsized overalls and covered all over with red
mud. His eyes were caved and smoking. I'm supposed to be here, he said"
(*COG* 192). To the nurse, Ballard is a newborn, however deformed. Covered
with the blood of the womb-grave, he has been reborn to captivity. The spatial constraint he has failed to flee is now internalized in his own skull, his
eyes "caved."

Nell Sullivan notes that Ballard's appearance resembles that of "a
newborn suffering birth trauma," and her reading includes the dual nature
of the cave from which Ballard has birthed himself: it is "at once mother
and mausoleum." Sullivan, however, negates the ambivalence in the novel
by arguing that Ballard is in full flight from "the figurative generative female
body" (76). As her reading elsewhere suggests, the images of females in
McCarthy are not simply "generative" but include the implicit threat to
males of smothering enclosure, or constant leakage—women are at once
improperly contained even as they threaten the young males of McCarthy

novels (and short stories) with eternal containment (68–72). It's too bad that good reading of the particular imagery of feminine spaces and—as Sullivan focuses on them—"dead girlfriends" (68), is forced to fit under a simple condemnation of the novels as the work of a misogynist; Sullivan otherwise has made invaluable contributions to feminist work on McCarthy.

As she also notes, there are frequent images of both "young women arrayed for death" and "threatening landscapes personified as female" in McCarthy's work (76). There is, however, another way to understand these images. As I have argued, Ballard's desire for dead women is a pathetic transference—even sublimation—of his desire for a live woman. His need for a home leads to his enclosure in a womb-grave that would be a threatening enclosure for anyone. Ballard's retreat to a hiding place in a primeval shelter runs him back toward death, in a regressive move that reverses the natural evolution of human culture as it adopts increasingly complex and sophisticated spatial distinctions between inside and outside.

We might theorize with Sullivan an idealization of natural spaces identified with female bodies. Then we might speculate on the misogyny in telling stories of males avoiding those spaces. Ballard seems to me, however, to have sought out domestic enclosure, and to have sought out some frightening replacements for real female companionship only when he fails, pitifully, at a normal way of finding companionship with a living woman. Ultimately, Ballard seems to me to have tried to replace his departed mother with the earth, only to be ambivalently born from her into the constraints of a civilized society that has no place for him that is not narrowly circumscribed for the criminal and the insane. He moves from the impossible constraints of the womb-grave to the impossible constraints provided by institutions for the deranged.

Ballard's attitudes toward women, and caves, are more ambivalent than we might suppose. Ballard "belongs," as he puts it, in the institutional enclosure of the hospital because he has been run to ground, and if he continues to live in the ground, he will die. Further generalizations about the attitudes of McCarthy's males toward women, and "threatening landscapes personified as female" (Sullivan 76) further miss the mark in other McCarthy novels. What, for instance, is the relationship between John Grady Cole and Alejandra, with her landscape of the Bolsón de Cuatro Ciénegas, generative in water and Edenic promise? In considering *The Border Trilogy*, I will argue that when John Grady Cole attempts to take these prizes in a social situation that refuses to recognize his right to them, he too finds only rejection.

We may see Ballard as a simpler reject of civilization: a man deprived of house, and thus home and family. That he is no noble character easy to identify with may make him even more appropriate a figure for McCarthy's implicit claim that he is *nonetheless* a child of god. There is a Christian gesture here: Ballard is certainly the least of creatures to endure deprivation of suitable domestic constraint. As he flees the constraints of prison and hospital in search of domesticity on his own terms, ironically the earth itself forces him to yield, finally, to return to the meager constraints allowed him by society. Before we proceed to more heroic figures who suffer these problems, a return to the novel's claim that Ballard is a child of god reminds us to think of this least sympathetic of all McCarthy's characters as the least of a group. They are all young men suffering something that McCarthy's books suggest is a common problem in the modern world.[15]

Thus there is much irony in Ballard's statement to the nurse that he is "supposed to be" in the hospital. He may look like a newborn, but he is headed for death as surely as he would have been had he not escaped the cave. The only difference is that his death—and burial—will now occur within the constraints society provides for its outcasts. In modernity, outcasts are no longer "cast out." Perhaps because we have so thoroughly filled even the most distant spaces, we instead constrain our outcasts. We put them into places that keep them from wandering in the open.

Indeed, Ballard is shuttled from the county hospital to another, state hospital. Too much a problem for the local community, he is constrained by the next largest government authority, and is "there placed in a cage next door but one to a demented gentleman who used to open folks' skulls and eat the brains inside with a spoon" (*COG* 193). Note the recurrence of the skull as the bodily home, that this cannibal is an invader of the skeletal house for the mind, and the reference to silverware that recalls Ballard's possession of the same accoutrement of domesticity. Finally, there is the irony that Ballard is treated at once like an animal and a human. He is caged like an animal and yet housed like a human "next door" to this maniac of possession.

Even as the narrative indulged in the playful antinomy of "gentleman" for a cannibal, it turns away from such ironic high-low diction to side with Ballard, regarding this neighbor as "a crazy man" (as if Ballard is not), to whom Ballard "had nothing to say"—and with whom he presumably has nothing in common. This is the last moment of connection between the narrative stance and the cognitive point of view, not to mention the feelings, of Ballard.

Ballard soon falls ill, and from then on, the narrative abandons such sympathy in favor of both meiosis and an entropic deceleration to ontology (and nowhere in McCarthy is ontology preferable to the uneasy movement of existentialism). Worse, the "to be" verbs in this passage act upon Ballard, thus rendered into an object before he can be at all accepted—even as outcast—by society. The narrative stance itself follows the dictates of the state, relegating the child of god to the objectivity of a thing moved around by the helping verb "was:"

> He contracted pneumonia in April of 1965 and was transferred to the University Hospital where he was treated and apparently recovered. He was returned to the state hospital at Lyons View and two mornings later was found dead in the floor of *his cage.*
>
> *His body* was shipped to the state medical school at Memphis. There in a basement room he was preserved with formalin and wheeled forth to take *his place* with other deceased persons newly arrived. He was laid out on a slab and flayed, eviscerated, dissected. His head was sawed open and his brains removed. His muscles were stripped from his bones. His heart was taken out. His entrails were hauled forth and delineated [. . .] At the end of three months when the class was closed Ballard was scraped from the table into a plastic bag and taken *with others of his kind* to a cemetery *outside the city* and there interred. (*COG* 194, my emphasis)

This is almost technical writing, treating the body of the condemned to worse than he would have found underground: dying to provide a home for mice in your bones is better than being so treated and so studied. Worse, he is allowed no single residence, as these movements from hospital to hospital make for more moves than he endured in his homeless life as a criminal stray. Worst of all, his body is dissected into pieces that belong to him so tenuously that they require the possessive pronoun. Linked to "Ballard" by "his," head, brains, muscles, bones, heart, and finally entrails are all removed from the natural relationship that creates something the narrator returns to calling "Ballard" only as a mysterious collective.

The "Ballard" that is "scraped from the table" depends on its synergy in life. In death, he needs a new container. The place of his body had lost its possibility to tour, and he has been cut into the pieces of a map. First outcast into homelessness, he is now bodily unhoused. Because he is an outcast, he is so disassembled that before he can even be placed in the constraint of a grave, he needs "a plastic bag." (The placement of his body in a bag further recalls the treatment of Kenneth Rattner.[16])

Instead of a return to the earth, where they might house mice, Ballard's bones are also bagged uselessly, in the smallest constraint to which a human being can be relegated. That he is not permitted burial within the town is fitting. Even his bones, once scraped and studied, must be rejected and removed from the civilized space of the living and the dead; doing so restores order and distinction between the living and the dead. Burying a murdering necrophiliac in a cemetery within the city limits might stir a plague upon the people.

The word "scapegoat" is perfect for Ballard, as in one sense of the original Greek *pharmakos*. Jonathan Culler describes the problem of the scapegoat as one of social reinforcement against aberration. To maintain necessary civic distinctions,

> [t]he *pharmakos* is cast out as the representative of the evil that afflicts the city: cast out so as to make evil return to the outside from which it comes and to assert the importance of the distinction between inside and outside. But to play his role as a representative of the evil to be cast out, the *pharmakos* must be chosen from *within* the city. The possibility of using the *pharmakos* to establish the distinction between a pure inside and a corrupt outside depends on its already being inside [. . .]. (143)

No wonder, then, that Ballard, rejected in life, is penultimately fully integrated into the complex of hospitals in sickness and death. Before he can be cast out, he must be made a part of the city that had rejected him, even if that means keeping him in a place circumscribed from normalcy. His body, if not his mind, becomes a willful participant in the system that helps maintain distinctions between inside and outside, living and dead, and proper and improper. As Michel Foucault noticed, "the modern instrument of penalty" is hardly distinguishable in its particular forms. "Is it surprising that prisons resemble factories, schools, barracks, hospitals, which all resemble prisons" (228)? It is, after all, in the state hospital that Ballard is put in a cage. In death, he is moved from a hospital intended to confine him (presumably with little treatment), to a teaching hospital, where he becomes a simple study in the anatomy of a scapegoat.

No better than the spider he once killed, his entrails are inspected by "four young students who bent over him like those haruspices of old [. . .]." The dictionary tells us "haruspices" were priests "in ancient Rome who practiced divination by the inspection of the entrails of animals." Undeterred by the fact that anthropometry should be a discredited science for them, these students "perhaps saw monsters worse to come in their configurations" (*COG* 194). A child of god indeed, better constrained than not.

Chapter Four

Sins of the Father, Sins of the Son in
Outer Dark, Suttree, and *Blood Meridian*

> I believe in takin care of my own [. . .]
> (The bearded one, *OD* 181)

> You think my father and his kind are a race apart.
> You can laugh at their pretensions, but you never question
> their right to the way of life they maintain.
> (Suttree, *S* 19)

> Dont you know that I'd have loved you like a son?
> (Holden, *BM* 306)

PARENTAL ANXIETY IN *OUTER DARK*

Beneath the actions of McCarthy's main characters, we find that their primary drive stems from a general spatial ambivalence. Wanting freedom of movement, they roam. Ballard may want a home, but both the Rattner males, as well as Marion Sylder and Arthur Ownby, require a larger range. For Ballard, the degree to which he is at ease in the woods serves only as some compensation for the cycle of forfeiture that deprives him of his senses and his literal home. His ability to create a simulacrum of that lost home inside the caverns of the natural world becomes dangerous even to him. For John Wesley and Ownby, this movement in its ideal form occurs through a natural world unmitigated by anthropocentrism. Kenneth Rattner and Marion Sylder display the modern variation of that escape into wilderness that powers so much of masculine American fiction, as they take to roads; they even fight to the death over Sylder's car, the tool for those modern roads.

In *Outer Dark*, we have at once the strongest expression of a road narrative within the Southern novels, and the strongest indication of the more particular psychological force behind the movements of these male characters: anxiety over relations between a son and father. As the domestic space of the Holme cabin collapses through endogamy into taboo, it comes into conflict with the larger social space that cannot tolerate incest, setting both Rinthy and Culla Holme onto the road. This flight therefore originates as a break from the psychological constraints of Culla's conscience. Social conflict, however, arcs over the collapsing psychological space of Culla Holme's guilt over the incest, and his fear of his own child. Rinthy and the child seem to be the victims of that conflict. It only remains for the triune, a magical force deeply connected to Culla's guilt, to enact the terrible justice on a child for the sins of its father.

The roads here, unlike a few in *The Crossing*, have yet to be paved. Although *Outer Dark* includes a few notable references to the history of its setting,[1] that setting remains more mythic and archetypal than in most McCarthy novels. Certainly, its road narrative lacks the historical reference that informs *The Border Trilogy* (however ignorant of that history are its main characters). Georg Guillemin makes a persuasive case for reading *Outer Dark* as a gothic, rather than a pastoral, novel. The book's "characters are grotesque in the manner of solitary gargoyles, woven into the text not so much as individuals in their own right but rather as typological variations on gothic archetypes" (55). Guillemin also notes the surpassing of pastoralism in the setting: "Images of ruins and decay commonly reflect pastoral nostalgia in Southern literature, yet in *Outer Dark* pastoral decay escalates into universal desolation" (57–58).

True, and I would add that the story itself reaches back to myth. But here is where myth arcs over what may be the most personal and confessional moment in McCarthy: the confluence of the myth of Oedipus and McCarthy's own anxiety over fathering a son. By this last phrase, I do not mean that I intend to go very far into biography. But just as the setting for this book—for all its archetypal qualities and resistance to simple realism—nonetheless has its geographical and historical reference, so too Culla Holme's name betrays echoes of McCarthy's first marriage and first son.

The correlation of *Outer Dark*'s plot with the Oedipus myth is the first things we notice: Culla Holme leaves his own son in the woods to die. Instead of a shepherd, a tinker (the post-industrial version of the classical or pastoral nomad) rescues it. At this point, the plot departs from the myth, although it returns to it later, with Culla's eventual punishment.

In the meantime, instead of the child living and returning to kill his father and marry his mother, the child is intercepted, as it were, by a violent force that is safely removed from the direct agency of the father.[2] The father is guilty of rejecting his own son, a rejection leading to his son's murder, albeit at someone else's hands. The threat seems less that the son will grow up to kill the father than that the son's mere existence bears witness to an initial union that already broke the taboo of incest. Because the son is the actual product of incest, rather than its future perpetrator, his presence in the cabin, let alone that knowledge of his existence might reach a larger social space, creates more of a direct threat to Culla than does the birth of Oedipus to King Laius. Culla cannot allow this child's existence to reach beyond the cabin and immediately surrounding woods in which he has committed this crime with (or upon—the book is unclear on this) his sister Corrinth. No soothsayer warns him of some future crime; the crime already belongs to the father in his own sin.

Indeed, Culla and Rinthy live so alone in the woods that they seem to inhabit their own fallen Eden.[3] Guillemin thinks, "the evil irrupting from within the pastoral world of *Outer Dark* mocks the very distinction between good and evil, between outside intrusion and civic strife. The sense of evil remains vague and endemic" (55). But I have to disagree on this. As the setting of a fallen Eden in *The Orchard Keeper* suggests a magical ruination of the land through the accomplished death of the main character's father, *Outer Dark*'s gothic darkness and desolation point directly to Culla Holme's breaking of an ancient taboo. This is why his dream evokes not only an early human fear—that the sun might fail to reappear after winter, or even more so after an eclipse—but also the first fear this father has of his own son: that the son's existence will eclipse his own.

Instead of giving us a soothsayer looking into the future, the nightmare that begins the main text of this novel passes judgment on Culla's past misdeeds. As Edwin Arnold notes, "Culla's opening nightmare tells us all we need to know of his suppressed guilt—he is McCarthy's version of Hawthorne's Reverend Dimmesdale, with the leader of the dark triune filling in for Chillingworth" ("'Go to sleep'" 42). We do not yet know what Culla has done; he does, and yet his suppression runs so deep that instead of dreaming of his guilt, he dreams that he is the passive recipient of some "affliction."

The dream feels like Hawthorne with only a slightly surreal tint. A "prophet" stands before a "beggared multitude gathered" in hopes that an impending eclipse will cure them. Culla, himself was caught up among the supplicants and when they had been blessed and the sun begun to blacken he did push forward and hold up his hand and call out. Me, he cried. Can I be cured? The prophet looked down as if surprised to see him there amidst such pariahs. The sun paused. He said: Yes, I think perhaps you will be cured. Then the sun buckled and dark fell like a shout. The last wirethin rim was crept away. They waited. Nothing moved. [. . .] The sun did not return. It grew cold and more black and silent and some began to cry out and some despaired but the sun did not return. (*OD* 5–6)

Whether the prophet sees this shift in the arrangement or not, the sun must fail for the others in order for Culla to go on in endless wandering through a perpetual darkness. The eclipse is understood by the "delegation of human ruin who attended" the prophet in a square (a civic space) as a period of magical erasure and rebirth: "This hour the sun would darken and all these souls would be cured of their afflictions before it appeared again" (*OD* 5). Not only the tense here, but also the prophet's surprise at the appearance of Culla "amidst such pariahs" suggests that this magical healing of blindness and leprosy would have taken place. The sun's reappearance would, as in the natural world, renew health and life.

But Culla's sin, which has blackened not his eyes and not literally crippled him, but rather blackened his heart and crippled his conscience, proves too great for this magic. The prophet tells Culla that, "Yes, I think *perhaps* you will be cured" (my emphasis), but we have already seen that, "[t]he sun paused" at Culla's appearance for this miracle. As soon as the prophet says that Culla, too, may be cured, "the sun buckled and dark fell like a shout" (*OD* 5). We twice read that, "[t]he sun did not return," meaning that not only was its disappearance brought on by Culla's guilt, but that his crime is so serious that it circumvents the pleading of the other supplicants. "Voices were being raised against him. He was caught up in the crowd and the stink of their rags filled his nostrils. They grew seething and more mutinous and he tried to hide among them but they knew him even in that pit of hopeless dark and fell upon him with howls of outrage" (*OD* 6). The terror at this judgment is what brings Culla's "hollerin" to the point where it wakes up the sister he has impregnated.

Remembering the innocence of the father's loss in young John Wesley's case, we can now see that the first two adult main characters to follow John Wesley and *The Orchard Keeper*—Culla Holme and Lester Ballard—both commit egregious crimes of sexual taboo. Lester's has been occasioned by a second death of a main character's father, when Ballard Senior hangs himself

in the barn. That suicide may hint at no more guilt on the part of the son
than did the murder of Kenneth Rattner by Marion Sylder, but it occurs
uncomfortably close to home, and in any case, suicide always occasions guilt
on the part of any surviving family member or close friend. The nature of
the sexual taboo reverses itself, although not fully, in Culla's crime. Whereas
Ballard innocently loses the domestic space that eventually leaves him reas-
sembling a negative domesticity founded on murder and necrophilia, Culla's sex with his sister Rinthy violates the supreme taboo within a domestic
space—incest.

For children within a domestic space well away from a community, the
quickest path to sex still can only be realized in a domestic space that is somehow incomplete. It occurs only where there is no controlling authority—
no mother, and no father—to prevent it. The parents of Culla and Rinthy
Holme are indeed so completely absent (we have no mention of their deaths,
their graves, or their leavetaking) that their very existence seems called into
question. In this way, Culla's fears that his son's existence might eclipse his
own seem confirmed: we see Culla, but never his father. The remoteness of
the cabin suggests either a space of retreat for these siblings—that they have
been cast out by their parents—or that the parents and their children already
lived outside the bounds of society.[4] If indeed these siblings arrived at this
cabin as scapegoats, then presumably Culla's own father has rejected him. If,
instead, the parents are dead, then Culla has indeed eclipsed his own father;
that precedent would add to his anxiety over a son.

Either way, no wonder Culla's terrible punishment is condemnation
by a community of which he was not already a part, that is itself already
fallen, and yet that he joins in an attempt to evade responsibility, to treat his
sin as an "affliction" ("the dreamer himself was caught up among the supplicants" *OD* 5). This dream punishment for violating a social taboo, however, is that he is also inextricably surrounded by that society he had hardly
joined. "They grew seething and more mutinous and he tried to hide among
them but *they knew him even in that pit of hopeless dark* and fell upon him
with howls of outrage" (*OD* 6, my emphasis). His condition at the end of
this nightmare directly contradicts the situation in which he awakes: alone
with his sister rather than "among" (*OD* 5, 6) a community, secretly feeling
victimized rather than publicly known as guilty, and sentenced to an endless
outer darkness rather than the inner darkness of his dreams and the "quiet
darkness" of this incestuous domesticity.

For tribes, let alone clans, let alone single families, exogamy is only
possible where there exists outside the immediate domestic space some larger
social sphere in which one can accomplish endogamy. Although the end of

Culla's dream has just indicated his guilt, Culla persists in seeing evil outside, rather than inside: "he heard the tinker's shoddy carillon long through the woods and he rose and stumbled to the door to see what new evil this might be" (*OD* 6). The cabin's isolation, existing in its own space so far from any social space that when the tinker arrives, "[t]here had been no one to [it] for some three months" and "so remote a place" that he has to take a four mile trip to the nearest store, enables but also adds to the sexual pressure toward incest.

This isolation also returns us to the mythic quality of the story, as Culla and Rinthy seem to exist in their cabin like a post-lapsarian Adam and Eve—except that they seem at the same time to be the offspring of Adam and Eve. This, after all, is the implicit problem in the Judeo-Christian origin myth as it first confronts sex: with whom can the son and daughter of Adam and Eve reproduce without committing incest? These siblings seem to be the only people in an inner world surrounded by the outer world of *Outer Dark*, even after the visit of the tinker, who is repelled by Culla in two ways. First, Culla literally lies, but figuratively tells the truth, in telling the tinker that they "[g]ot sickness" there (*OD* 6). Second, he refuses even the commercial transaction that at least connects remote settlements to a larger society, telling the tinker that he needs nothing, but also that even his supposedly "mendin" sister needs none of the tinker's medicines (*OD* 7).

After Culla abandons the child in the woods, rather than the son returning to kill the father, the son is taken away forever. Rinthy of course follows to rescue him. Culla, however, journeys perhaps to recover his sister, but more likely in simple wandering. Sickness has no one left to claim in the Thebes of their abandoned cabin, and instead, the outer world of the novel proves already to have been infected by the same concerns. The world outside what the tinker sees as a "ruined shack" (*OD* 8) proves to be both temporally and spatially indeterminate. As Vereen Bell sees it, *Outer Dark's*

> topography is vague, dreamlike, and surreal in a way that imposes an unwholesome, deranged aspect upon the entire scene. The distances are all walking distances, and the time span covered cannot be more than a few months; but within those limits the characters encounter bafflingly incongruous aspects of landscape—sluggish rivers, mountains, moss-laden trees, swamps, precipitous gorges. This, of course, reinforces our sense of the characters as utterly dislocated and homeless not only in their negotiated space but in the world as well. (33)

The triune's further disruption of proper spatial relationships arguably only highlights the spatial concerns that already exist in this "negotiated space." When they invade old man Salter's home and murder him, he has opened the door somehow expecting a minister in the middle of the night (129). When they rob the dead of their clothes, they go further than a mere disruption of civilized society's separation of the living and the dead; they arrange two of their victims in a pose that calls into question every social distinction on which the town presumably relied.

> Someone should have cared more than to leave an old man halfnaked in his burial box beneath these eyes and such a sun. But that was not all. Across the dessicated chest lay a black arm, and when Holme stood on his toes he could see that the old man shared his resting place with a negro sexton whose head had been cut half off and who clasped him in an embrace of lazarous depravity. (*OD* 88)

The first sentence here might be dialogue, but might also be the narrator's judgment slipped into the description. It could be free indirect discourse for Holme, and yet that feels wrong: he regularly remains too preoccupied to notice much that does not directly relate to him (although this crime will soon be charged at him). The "old man" here is the second of several bodies described in this line-up of victims after the triune's grave robbery. The way this man's legs are described as having "gone a dusty brown" not only implies a white narrator but also assumes a white reader. The "black arm" hints at low-level racism underlying the reader's supposed reaction (indeed its owner is described specifically as a "negro" before we are given his job title). As the coat and tie taken from the "old man" seem to be the clothing that, worn by the bearded man, lead people to take him for a minister, his embrace by the "negro sexton whose head had been cut half off" not only suggests a deviant sexual relationship between a former employer and his employee, but also reminds the "eyes" of whoever is looking at this scene that the black man would have paid the price for crossing such boundaries with a white person of either sex. The tableau presented to "these eyes" doubly violates the boundaries that would have existed between these two men in life, suggesting nothing less than homosexual miscegenation.

The phrase "lazarous depravity" recalls the taboo broken by Ballard, but it also makes clear that what the triune are about does connect deeply, if magically, with Culla's crime: not only the eclipse of other human beings (through murder) and the transgression of spatial boundaries (through home invasions and grave robbing), but also the violation of sexual taboo is at loose in this country. The two figures in the box, we are to assume, would not have made sexual partners in life for several reasons. So, too, Culla and Rinthy were not to have made sexual partners for one significant one. This only adds to the irony when Culla is assumed guilty of robbing the graves: he has transgressed the social boundaries with his sister and then left his son to die, and be left unburied, in the dark woods.

The phrase "these eyes," referring to the scene of the unearthed coffins and their dead, remains mysterious, but certainly the eyes and "such a sun" both recall, and contrast with, the blindness of the supplicants in Culla's dream, and the absence of the sun in that dream. Although the words "sun" and "son" share nothing but accidental etymological heritage, their homophony has led to innumerable serious puns, often reinforcing a fundamental trope of Christianity, where the sun is regularly represented as the son of god.[5] Like the best of McCarthy's titles, then, *Outer Dark* refers to several arcs of space in this novel: to the darkness outside Culla within the dream, but also to the darkness outside the dream, extending well outside the incestuous cabin and into the gloom in which the book comes to a dead end; yet always this darkness—this absence of the sun, after it "buckled and dark fell like a shout" within Culla's dream—corresponds to the rejection of Culla's son.

When killed by the bearded man, this child is "watching the fire." The cutting of the child's throat is described with several metaphors of sight and facial features all collapsing into a simultaneous description of the animated knife, the child's face, and his eyes: "Holme saw the blade wink in the light like a long cat's eye slant and malevolent and a dark smile erupted on the child's throat and went all broken down the front of it. The child made no sound. It hung there with its one eye glazing over like a wet stone [. . .]" (*OD* 236). The description murders the child even before the knife moves, as "the blade" is already more alive than the child, alternately referred to as "the child" and "it." That "its" "one eye" (that is visible to Culla, and therefore to us) is first merely "watching" and then is "glazing over," is contrasted by the animated "wink" of the blade even as it echoes the sensorial and expressive limits of "the mute one" in this scene. Of the three men, "the mute one" most of all stands as the bearded man's grotesque ethical reproach to Culla.

The scene is arguably more repulsive than anything in McCarthy's novels, including Lester Ballard's necrophilia, or any of the many murders in *Blood Meridian*. This is because the victim is a child; it (or he) cannot help itself and, outside of the illogical equation of typological father and son guilt, is guilty of nothing. Here, the son has been forsaken by the father, while another, outwardly darker father enacts the sacrifice of that son when "its" father will not name him. This slaughter takes place only well after the bearded man has, in his own rough terms, defined to Culla through the transaction of the boots a primordial foundation for fatherhood: "I believe in takin care of my own," he tells him (*OD* 181). I have already examined some mythogical and social interpretations of Culla's response to the incest. But the horror of this scene remains unaccountable without reading for additional forces at work here. Given the consequences of inaction when confronted by the bearded man holding his own son, what are we to make of Culla Holme's refusal to name him?

WHAT'S IN A NAME?

The names "Culla" and "Holme" echo the names of McCarthy's immediate family during the likely composition of *Outer Dark*—too closely not to invite some speculation on how this author's remarkable imagination might have transmogrified into extreme fiction the mild—but exhausting—problems of responsibility for a small child. We know that as of this writing McCarthy is married a third time, with a young son. A first son, however, named Cullen, was born in the early sixties to McCarthy and his first wife, Lee Holleman. *Outer Dark* was published in 1968, four years after McCarthy's marriage to Holleman.

The family name in *Outer Dark* of "Holme" includes several resonances. The first leads us into biographical literary onomastics. "Holme" suggests a reduction and slight transliteration of "Holleman," the family name of McCarthy's first wife. It is her family name with the "man" cut off (or with the "m" that makes the article "an" the masculine personal pronoun). In English and Irish names, the suffix "man" of course connects a person to the place or trade referred to in the first part of the name: in this case, the original name could have simply indicated a "man" from "Holle." Where or what is "Holle?" In pronunciation, it can run close to "holler."

> One feature of Upper Southern English and specifically of Appalachian English is its pronunciation of the final unstressed syllable in words such as *hollow*, *window*, and *potato* as (-er). *Holler, winder*, and *tater* [. . .] are merely variant pronunciations reflected in spelling. A noun *holler* has the specific meaning in the Appalachians of 'a small valley between mountains [. . .]' (*American Heritage Dictionary*)

This trail leads back to "hollow" and eventually to "Middle English *holwe, holowe*, from *holgh*, hole, burrow (influenced by *hole*, hollow) from Old

English *holh*" (*American Heritage*). If we read (or hear) "Holleman" as a name for a man (or woman) who lives in a holler, it seems all the more natural a family name for a young woman McCarthy would meet in Tennessee.

As a play on the word "home" conflated with an exterior place ("holler"), the name "Holme" resonates with inferences about the untold story that leads up to the opening of *Outer Dark*. We might imagine that Culla and Rinthy did indeed once live in a holler, and that in the opening of the novel we are now finding them in exile, in "the glade" that now surrounds their home: "Holme" in this reading retains a letter from its earlier permutations from the Indo-European "kel" so that we are reminded that their original home remains elsewhere.

But that Indo-European "kel" also led to the Old English "Hell." If we add an umlaut, we get German for "hell:" "hölle." Also in German, "man" indicates not a male person specifically, but is rather an indefinite pronoun indicating "one, you, we" or "they, people." This means that "Holleman" as much as "Holme" can suggest "people from hell." Indeed, as the archetypal fallen children of Adam and Eve, Culla and Rinthy are "people from hell." Culla's extra share of the guilt for incest is suggested by his first name's echoes of "kel."

Another place name resonance in "Holme" leads away from any biographical interpretation and back to the plot of *Outer Dark*. "Holme" can be seen as merely the word "home" with an extra letter. The name is a perversion, as it were, of the word "home," just as the inbreeding between Culla and his sister Rinthy is a perversion of the home they inhabit. In a cabin inhabited only by siblings, that vertical stem of consonance—"l"—is orthographically out of place; it even perverts the tongue's rest at the bottom of the mouth in pronouncing "home," lifting it to the roof and toward the opening of the mouth. As a character's name—something that needs to sound in the heads of readers—it is an awkward choice, more visual than aural. Yet, that awkwardness keeps us from forgetting the perversion of the simple word "home" in their name.

The loss of heterozygosity in the offspring of Culla and Rinthy's relations even seems to require the interpolated orthographic aberration from "home" to "Holme." Inbreeding does not in itself create birth defects. Rather, in reducing heterozygosity, or the variety of genetic variation in an offspring, it increases the chances that recessive genes will be duplicated and thus become pronounced. The "l" hidden within the word "home," then, is apparent in the author's name for characters that are both siblings and parents. In this sense, their transgression of the taboo against inbreeding seems prefigured in their family name, "Holme."

Finally, Culla and Rinthy's family name shares some affinity with another proper name, this one centering on Rinthy (and therefore only recalling McCarthy's first wife's family name as it calls our attention back from Culla to his partner, Rinthy). In Northern European mythology, Holle "is also known as Holda or Hulda. A triple goddess, Holle is the Maiden, the Mother and the Crone—the embodiment of the three stages of womanhood. [. . .] Holle's name is linguistically related to the word Halja, which means 'covering,' and is the ancient Teutonic name for Hel, the Norse land of the dead" (Kleinschmitt). Thus, we come back around to the place name connection for main characters in a novel of nether regions, but with the name now carrying deeper resonances for both Rinthy and Culla.

Where "Holme" recalls "Holleman" most is in the first name "Culla," which is quite close to "Cullen," the name of McCarthy's first son. Here, it seems impossible to go further without some tentative speculations back in the direction of biography. Confronted with a main character whose name suggests a man from a hellish region, coupled to his own sister in a mythical story (her own name recalling better places and higher resonances), and unavoidably recalling the names of McCarthy's first wife and son, we might then imagine anxieties occasioned by the birth of that son to the author and Lee Holleman. McCarthy's second wife, Annie DeLisle, has told an interviewer that Cormac "couldn't have had children, it would have driven him crazy" (in Jarrett 3). Nevertheless, when McCarthy married the woman who said this, he had already had one. The tense is thus ironic: he *could not have had*, yet *he had had*.

The first interview McCarthy gave (and notably regrets) includes this exchange: "Asked if he had ever paid alimony, McCarthy snorts. 'With what?' He recalls his expulsion from a $40-a-month room in the French Quarter for nonpayment of rent" (Woodward, "Cormac McCarthy's Venemous Fiction" 30). Alimony is not child-support, and yet the conflict is already clear in this first interview: maintaining the freedom to write without the constraints of a job that would both pay the rent and the alimony is the chief value. To be fair, this necessity of putting writing above every other consideration seems to have been the case for a long time, with many writers. In a second, more recent interview again conducted by Richard Woodward, McCarthy apparently spoke more directly about his first family. But Woodward seldom quotes him directly on this topic, instead offering observations highlighting relatively few quotes from the interview. Describing McCarthy's latest home in Santa Fe with his third wife, Jennifer Winkley, and their six-year-old son, John, Woodward writes that McCarthy, "seems settled here and yet not. He dotes on his son, whose bedroom is stuffed with books, maps, and models.

One has the sense that he wants to atone for his shortcomings as a parent earlier in life. He seldom saw his first son, Cullen, after his first marriage dissolved" (104).[6]

I hasten to recognize, of course, that all parents feel they could do better with a second chance. And no one knows what happens in a marriage except those inside it. *Outer Dark* at least expresses archetypal anxieties, if not any serious ones from the author's life, over the inevitable conflict between a father's independence and a son's existence. It seems silly, however, not to explore the possibility that McCarthy, as any creative artist usually does, may have drawn on his own domestic life in this, and other novels. If any of Culla's inability to care for his son, to name him, to in any way recognize him before his murder, originates in any anxiety that a serious young writer hardly thirty years old may have felt at the birth of his first child, that seems an honest and brave admission. And of course, it is equally possible that, as creative artists also regularly do, McCarthy simply took the clay of life—including the accidents and intentions behind names—and molded it to a dramatically extreme variation of that life.

Ironically, it is the name of the father in *Outer Dark*, Culla, that echoes the name of the author's son, Cullen, in life. This connection, rather than surprising, only fits the uncanny equation involving father and son identity that recurs in these novels. And it again strengthens the sense in which McCarthy's exploration of father and son trouble reaches back much farther than mere family histories. Indeed, the conflation of son and father in an equation of guilt is typological. The Old Testament's book of Isaiah demands such a connection: "Prepare slaughter for his children for the iniquity of their fathers" (14:21). The connection, therefore, between the guilt of a father who first actively rejects his child and then, refusing to acknowledge him, passively witnesses the son's murder; and the rebellion of a son against a father whose ethical, moral, and philosophical positions he abhors; only reinforces the continuing arc of this psychological force behind character flight—particularly as I will trace these next in *Suttree* and *Blood Meridian*.

Meanwhile, we must note that *Outer Dark* continues a less ambiguous general characterization of babies throughout the novels in negative terms. The child in *Outer Dark* is unnamed not only by Culla, but also by the narrator. That child is regularly an "it," or worse: "the nameless weight in [Rinthy's] belly" (*OD* 5). Still, *Outer Dark* intensifies this negative characterization to a pitch beyond that in the other books. *Blood Meridian* gives us babies impaled on a tree, but their number spells out a larger social atrocity even as it is impossible to see any one particular child. The baby in *Outer Dark* is, by contrast, particular. We are challenged to imagine him so (and

McCarthy's use of "it" for the child makes it easy to forget its sex), because McCarthy takes his avoidance of direct psychology to an extreme. We are told nothing of what the father is thinking or feeling in the scene of the child's murder—its effect would be impossible to film (which might be argued for all McCarthy's novels). Yet the violence is *hypo*-bolic, under thrown.

This is a difficult passage to quote again, but necessary to look at once more so as not to go too far astray in the already suspicious business of imagining the author's intent:

> Holme saw the blade wink in the light like a long cat's eye slant and malevolent and a dark smile erupted on the child's throat and went all broken down the front of it. The child made no sound. It hung there with its one eye glazing over like a wet stone and the black blood pumping down its naked belly. The mute one knelt forward. He was drooling and making little whimpering noises in his throat. He knelt with his hands outstretched and his nostrils rimpled delicately. The man handed him the child and he seized it up, looked once at Holme with witless eyes, and buried his moaning face in its throat. (*OD* 236)

If one could manage a full analysis of such a scene, one might begin with the author's use of meiosis.

But what immediately follows this infanticide is as complex as it is shocking. At first, the queasy reader is given reason to hope that the "mute one" is upset by the act of the triune's leader. Again, the murdered child's "one eye glazing over like a wet stone" is reflected in the "witless eyes" of "the mute one." The baby makes "no sound" and the mute one can only make "little whimpering noises in his throat"—which synesthetically echoes the visual description of the knife cut at the *baby's* throat. The reader's first desire, after such horror, is to see someone in the scene act out our shock and grief. There is cause for more unease as the mute one's "nostrils rimpled delicately." Then the mute "burie[s] his moaning face"—which could still be an act of grieving—"in its throat." Exactly where the mute buries his face, however, clarifies a more elemental intent than an expression of grief; it is animal hunger. Rather than grief, we witness vampirism.

As Rick Wallach observes, "a Cormac McCarthy novel is the last place you would want to turn up if you were a child" ("Prefiguring Cormac McCarthy" 19).[7] Baby trouble occurs throughout the novels. Only *Outer Dark*, however, expresses a direct anxiety on the part of a father over his son's existence. (Usually, as we have seen and will see in every other McCarthy novel, the anxiety resides in a main character that is only a son, or more son than father.) This anxiety rests in Culla alone, though, as even the parodic fatherhood of the bearded man throws into yet darker relief Culla's inability to own his son. In other characters, too, there is nothing of the grotesque in their views of the child. And McCarthy's avoidance of sentiment in descriptions of the child serves, in scenes without Culla, as meiosis that beckons the reader's feelings forward.

Indeed, *Outer Dark's* descriptions of Rinthy, her suffering, and even of the child as it passes from the tinker's cart to the arms of its first foster mother, are sometimes emotionally moving. When the child's first foster parents—the tinker and his woman friend—set forth to pass the child on to the new mother, Mrs. Laird, the narration risks an astonishing degree of sibilance to ease their way:

> Setting forth in the faint moonlight, the tinker now at her elbow and her carrying the child wrapped completely from sight, they appeared furtive, clandestine, stepping softly and soft their voices over the sandy road in shadows so foreshortened they seemed sprung and frenzied with a violence in which their creators moved with dreamy disconcern. (*OD* 23)

The stance here manages at once to convey the unsentimental truth that "their creators" remain "disconcern[ed]" with the problem of theodicy afoot in this, and indeed all, of McCarthy's novels. The form "disconcern" does not appear in my dictionaries, but it seems to follow "disinterest" in its equanimity and remove from passion; these "creators" may have "sprung" the shadows of these odd foster parents, and may even move "in" a "violence" that "frenzie" those shadows, but they do so "with dreamy disconcern"—with no feeling one way or another for their safety. These are simply the creators of all: these protectors of the orphan child and the mother in search of him, but also the unwilling father who has abandoned him, and the triune. Evil threatens this scene of a provisional family, but the language seems sympathetic to their situation, even as it indicates that "their creators" are not.

This departure ends a scene that clearly indicates the basic decency toward a child in need, a decency never felt by Culla. When the tinker appears at the door of this woman friend, she answers the question as to whether the new mother, Mrs. Laird, will agree to nurse this orphan. "She aint got nary choice," she says. Indeed, McCarthy makes it clear that this is the normal reaction for anyone toward a child in need. So, too, the tinker's trouble in finding the child is clearly altruistic: he gains nothing by this discovery of the secret he suspects of Culla. In fact, this act of kindness will eventually cost him his life. You do not do the right thing, therefore, because it will do you any good, or even in hopes that it will make a difference. You do it because you "aint got nary choice" (*OD*

22). These stoic country ethics foreshadow a cowboy version in *The Border Trilogy*.

When Culla leaves his son in the woods, his fear of Oedipal retribution is, as I noted earlier, temporarily obviated. Indeed, in the scene of the child's murder, Culla essentially trades the life of his son for his own life. Yet, precisely here is where the book returns to the myth of Oedipus. First, the father is punished by having to witness the killing. Then the father receives the same mythic sentence as the official punishment given to Oedipus. Like Oedipus, he must wander forever; unlike him, however, he never blinds himself. In a reverberation of Culla's nightmare, he remains sighted even as those around him seem to have been blinded long ago and are only denied relief by the contagion of his transgression of the incest taboo.

Holme is not literally blind, and yet he seems to see less than a man whose blindness is literal. McCarthy finishes the book by returning to overt variations on the tropes of blindness and prophecy—tropes rivaled only by those of darkness and light for the central pressure in this book. "In later years [Culla] used to meet a blind man, ragged and serene, who spoke him a good day out of his constant dark" (*OD* 239). Holme tries to avoid speaking with this Tiresias figure, and denies having spoken with him before. The blind seer claims to remember him—or in some other way to have known him or known about him: "They's lots of people on the roads these days, Holme said. Yes, the blind man said. I pass em every day. People goin up and down in the world like dogs. As if they wasn't a home nowheres. But I knowed I'd seen ye afore" (*OD* 240).

The man goes on to ask if Culla needs anything, and tells him "I'm at the Lord's work" (*OD* 240). Culla claims to need nothing, and goes on, but can't get far before he's told a parable about a preacher.

> A healin preacher wanted to cure everybody and they took me up there.
> [. . .] and they told it he could make the blind see. And they was a
> feller leapt up and hollered out that nobody knowed what was wrong with.
> And they said it caused that preacher to go away. But they's darksome ways
> afoot in this world and it may be he weren't no true preacher. (*OD* 241)

The blind man suggests that the preacher may be false, but the putative reason for the man's departure is in whatever the "feller" "hollered out."[8] Presumably, if the preacher is false, he leaves because he is in some way denounced. But in addition to the dream that opens this novel, there is a similar scene to test against this one, in McCarthy's fifth novel, published years later.

When we first meet the judge in *Blood Meridian*, it is in the tent of the Reverend Green. We hear the judge's actual words, humorous in their particular charges of "congress with a goat," but in that particular charge there is evidence (especially given the regularity with which McCarthy suggests a devil's presence through the description of hoofprints, cloven hooves, etc.) that Green is indeed, as the judge names him "[t]he devil. Here he stands" (*BM* 7). We soon find out, however, that the judge claims never to have seen the Reverend. "I never laid eyes on the man before today. Never even heard of him" (*BM* 8).

This is a devil's trick, and something of a devil's calling card: he is a false prophet who purports to unmask the real prophet as an imposter. The blind man at the end of *Outer Dark* seems to be another such devil trickster. It may be uncertain as to whether the blind man is, in his own terms, a prophet or false prophet, but Culla's own ungulate nature—and a reminder that perhaps, as one reading of the name "Holme" suggested to us, Culla may be "from hell," is evidenced by his "toed tracks soft in the dust among the cratered shapes of horses and mules hoofs" (*OD* 241–242).

Is Rinthy also from hell? No. In its remarkable passages following Culla's sister, *Outer Dark* gives us a refreshing break—early on—from the otherwise unbroken preoccupation with men and their problems in McCarthy. Yet, as Nell Sullivan has pointed out, Rinthy Holme is described in terms that keep her at a greater distance than that reserved for Culla. Quoting Gail Kern Paster, Sullivan notes the typical Western canonical depiction of women as "naturally grotesque [. . .] open, permeable, effluent, leaky" (Sullivan 69), and goes on to note that Rinthy "leaks constantly [. . .] tears, blood, and milk, the three often combined and conflated" (69).

I can only add to this that the book ends in a swamp. As much as I might like to have found Rinthy closer to the center of this novel, that would not fit, and extend, McCarthy's explorations of son and father anxiety throughout his work, nor would it give him the artist's due: to explore and focus on what he or she will. Ultimately, *Outer Dark* is of course another novel about the problems of men and space: Rinthy serves as much as an indication of the threats of parenting felt by Culla, as she does anything else—with the strong exception that in her suffering, we do see that another victim of an unwilling father is the mother equally abandoned.

What are we to make of Culla's dead end in such wet territory, after he is passed by a blind devilish trickster out of both Hawthorne and Sophocles? The novel begins and ends with Culla, the failure of a father, even if McCarthy achieves a wonderful sympathy with the wandering mother in the interim. In McCarthy's last reference to Rinthy, she is called "little sister" (*OD* 238). Whether you find that condescending or tender, the narrator is taking away her motherhood with the slip into free indirect discourse for Culla; the narrator has no such term of endearment for Culla.

Edwin Arnold's reading of "McCarthy's Moral Parables," and Robert Jarrett's study of "parodic families" in McCarthy, both find the leader of the triune a judge of Culla, and an ironic father-figure who believes in "takin care of [his] own" (*OD* 181, Jarrett 17). For Jarrett—who also identifies Ballard, Harrogate, and Suttree as criminal orphans (39)—Culla runs from the child because it is proof of his incest; for Arnold, Culla's inability, or refusal, to recognize his own son puts Culla into the "cast of sinners" Dante finds as "neutrals" who are left "'nowhere,' in a state of nothingness" (51–52).

But because we last see Culla in a wet end of the road, I wonder if he isn't consigned to something more befitting a man who gets his own sister pregnant, only to take her baby from her, abandon it, deny it, and watch it die: as he has repudiated his fatherhood, he is placed in his own personal hell: a feminine wetness of that "mire before him" that "rose in a vulvate welt claggy and sucking." As Nell Sullivan has made clear, this is a territory more appropriate to Rinthy, as the narrator has described her. Is there irony, then, in this failed father coming to the end of his road in a miasma of femininity? What's more, the place is a "faintly smoking garden of the dead" (*OD* 242). I take that to mean that it is both fecund and morbid at once. This scene recalls the cemetery at the end of *The Orchard Keeper*, then, from which the son is freed, as well as the womb-grave cave of *Child of God*. Culla Holme may have managed to outlive his own son, but as a portrait of a guilty father, he demands less sympathy than the relatively innocent, though crazed, Lester Ballard. In this early and, so far, only full portrait of the father's end of the anxiety over domesticity, the father comes out worse than even the murdered son.

Outer Dark's revelation of son and father trouble points to the father's ambivalence, more than any other McCarthy novel. "Going back the way by which he came," however, "the blind man tapping through the dusk" met by Culla Holme is also himself, his blind doppelgänger with the cane of Oedipus (*OD* 242).[9] So too, the equation of guilt collapses the identity of the father into that of the son—a typological echo of that verse from Isaiah, which goes on to provide the reason for the punishment of a child for its father's sins. The reason for such punishment is ultimately social, born from the assumption that there can be no children fully innocent of their father's sins. The aim, therefore, is to stop the line of begetting, even to the point of erasing all possibility that the contagion might spread: "Prepare slaughter for his children for the iniquity of their fathers; that they do not rise, nor possess the land, nor fill the face of the world with cities" (14:21).

SINS OF THE FATHER AND SON IN *SUTTREE*

The imaginative varieties through which McCarthy grapples with anxiety over his father's profession, and its lasting effect on the natural environment, the landscape, and the people in the countryside around Knoxville, Tennessee, remain a testament to this artist's abilities to send something from life through a prism. Whatever comes into that prism from life grows stronger through the progression of the Southern novels, culminating in the fourth book, *Suttree*.

Before *Suttree*, McCarthy refracts son and father anxiety through a prism that is mythological and archetypal. What connects the sins of the father and the sins of the son also remains relatively remote—biblical, especially in *Outer Dark*, but nowhere yet causative, or reflected in some specific activity of the son. As we proceed through the Southern novels, the space of son and father anxiety enlarges, while the seriousness of their sins (or crimes) deepens. We move from familial tensions, through social problems, up to philosophical problems; from relatively petty crime, through taboo, into serious social impact directly affecting thousands, upward and onward out of the Southern novels altogether, to historical and philosophical justifications for killing millions—all the way to *Blood Meridian*. By the time we have reached *Suttree*, the son's behavior seems related directly to the sins of the father.

The Orchard Keeper's father, Kenneth Rattner, is guilty of relatively small-scale crimes. For John Wesley, this simply means that his father is murdered in a fight over a car. He never knows the truth of this (certainly his behavior does not deeply reflect that of his father), and he is not punished for those crimes. In the suicide of Lester Ballard's father, however, an existing problem in the domestic space speeds and widens the process of Lester's derangement in *Child of God*. And, of course, Lester's crimes are outrageous. In both of these first two novels, transgressions are social offenses—crimes. But they are small in scope and effect. In Rattner's case, for instance, nothing he does compares with the acts, and philosophies, of an Anton Chigurh, let alone judge Holden. In Ballard's case, the psychological, social, and even medical reasons I detailed for his insanity would seem silly explanations, compared with the philosophical justifications of Chigurh and Holden. But such is the difference between criminal insanity and a fully lucid, but amoral and antinomian, commitment.

As I have argued, the breaking of the incest taboo in *Outer Dark* accomplishes a more serious departure from social norms—and, hard as this is to argue, I have—Culla Holme's transgressions warrant less sympathy than does at least the underlying needs behind those more horrible crimes committed by Lester Ballard.[10] Indeed, Culla's behavior rightfully calls up the term "sin," and socially his transgressions (because they constitute a rejection of civilized connection with a world outside the family, rather than merely trying to recreate a family of which he has been deprived) run the deepest so far, so much so that his entirely innocent son pays the biblical price for them.

Consequently, Culla's sentence compares interestingly with those of both Rattners and Ballard. The younger Rattner may seem as much freed from Red Branch as ejected from it, while his father's bones end up in a bag only after they rest during much of the narrative within the larger community. Ballard, by contrast, is imprisoned (like both Sylder and Ownby), then mutilated in death with the remains bagged (like Rattner), and finally also ejected from the community when he is buried outside the city limits (*COG* 194). By comparison, Culla Holme is doomed to a life of wandering (perhaps even in a circle) well outside any community that would recognize him. Like Oedipus, he must leave the space of civilized community even before his death. And his son pays the ultimate price for his father's sins, while ironically rejected by him, profiting from them not at all.

Whether or not any real father's guilt informed *Outer Dark*, however, a strong sense of the guilt of Cormac McCarthy's father seems to have informed *Suttree*'s vision of a young man attempting to break free from the entailment of his father's sins. We can only guess at the reality of both fathers, of course, through the feelings of their sons. It goes without saying that the elder McCarthy, especially (because he lived outside the pages of a book and is also no longer alive to offer a counterargument to what I infer from *Suttree*), remains a mystery to us. McCarthy Sr. may have been a loving father at home and, in his professional life, a wholly altruistic and philanthropic man. All I claim to argue here is that the author of *Suttree* may have felt no better about his father than did the main character of that novel about his. As I infer anything about the man who was Cormac McCarthy's father, then, I mean to do so only as if *he* were a character in a novel, as much as Suttree's father. The reason for going even so far as to make any biographical inference at all should become clear when we look into the novel. Still, I only intend such inferences to work as indications of possible feelings on the part of the author of *Suttree*.

The sins of the father of Cornelius Suttree, and strong hints of the sins of McCarthy's father (as we infer them in *Suttree*), are socially wide in scope. The sins of both might also, presumably, have profited both sons substantially. Indeed, they seem to have done so, at least at the level of their education and freedom from material want. Although legal (as far as my research on McCarthy's profession suggests), neither the sins of the fictional, nor the real, father are social except at the highest level of society's requirement of ethical behavior. Without outraging the upper or lower classes through violating taboo, or by thieving their wallets, both Suttree Sr. and McCarthy Sr.—in fact through fortifying their positions at the top of society—seem through *Suttree* only to have been guilty of snobbery and indifference to the suffering of those less fortunate than them. By judging their inferiors as less deserving, however, they give them less. And that includes family members, as well as the poor.

What do we call these transgressions, particularly as they seem strongly felt by the son, but are, at least superficially, respectable to higher society (especially when convenient to that society)? Mere ethical lapses? "Ethics" seems an odd word for any McCarthy novel, and yet it fits better than "sin" (or "morality"). Sin, after all, suggests the religious tenets from which Cornelius Suttree (and McCarthy, in this most easily autobiographical book) is trying to break free. Quite apart from the value of Christian charity, Catholicism, as a repressive system of behavioral regulation, is one of the hard targets here. It does not follow that religion per se is under attack in *Suttree*. "Sin" certainly won't go away as a useful term here, then: indifference to the poor is more important than sexual purity, for instance, to the Jesus of the Gospel of Mark. Nonetheless, whatever values one might find within both this book and Christianity in general might as well be characterized in the terms of another religion altogether, or in the wholly secular terms of civic life: ethics.

William Spencer has argued for both these idioms in understanding the best behavior of the notorious son, Cornelius Suttree. In "Suttree as Social Nexus," Spencer reads the regular visits that Suttree makes to Ab Jones, Gene Harrogate, and many of the other down-and-out denizens of McAnally Flats as akin to the rounds of a social worker. Alternatively, Suttree's name suggests for Spencer nothing less than a perfect Buddhist. Suttree, who has rejected his legacy in order to live among the poor, reminds us of an enlightened being who forgoes nirvana in order to help those less fortunate than himself. Spencer's "Suttree's Unknowable Self" links the nickname and last name "Buddy Suttree" to "Buddha sutrah," and then on to "bodhisattva." Indeed, in the major events of Cornelius Suttree's life Spencer finds remarkable parallels to the story of Siddhartha Gautama. Suttree's origins as the protected son of a powerful father whose protection he rejects, his sojourn through both deprivation from and indulgence in physical pleasure, his relationship with a prostitute (and birth of a son), and of course his relationship to the river all echo key elements of the life of the Buddha.

Both ways of seeing Suttree—as social worker and as a bodhisattva—focus on Suttree stepping down from a relatively superior position in order to minister to the needier people around him. In *Suttree*, this means a serious break with the father. As Robert Jarrett notes, "Suttree has repudiated his wealthy and socially respectable father, partly in response to his father's contempt for his lower-class wife and her family" (39). This repudiation comes in a reference that feels strongly autobiographical in the specificity of three professional realms:

> In my father's last letter he said that the world is run by those willing to take the responsibility for the running of it. If it is life that you feel you are missing I can tell you where to find it. In the law courts, in business, in government. There is nothing occurring in the streets. Nothing but a dumbshow composed of the helpless and the impotent. (*S* 13–14)

This passage of interior monologue fully breaks the usual practice of avoiding the interiority of characters, and serves as a model for the regularity with which *Suttree* enters the thoughts of McCarthy's most autobiographical character. On this and other accounts, the book demands innumerable critical comparisons to Joyce. Like *Ulysses*, this peripatetic novel follows a troubled son and a troubled father. The son (Stephen Daedalus) and the helpful father (Leopold Bloom) of *Ulysses*, however, are here conjoined in the same person of Cornelius Suttree. Suttree rejects the church and its authority as much as does Stephen Daedalus, but he also ministers to a younger man's need for a father figure (as does Bloom), in the form of Gene Harrogate. Furthermore, as Bloom has already lost a child before the action of *Ulysses*, Suttree will lose his son during the novel. Only in the sense that Stephen, the poet, is echoed by Suttree's rejection of the world of business, and Bloom's advertising job at least approaches the obvious "running" of the world in law and government, do Cornelius and his father echo Stephen and Bloom separately.[11]

In the letter's disparagement of "the helpless and the impotent" (*S* 14), Suttree's father certainly suggests the high-handedness he seems to have shown toward Suttree's mother. This social tension quickly returns when her brother, the uncle John to Cornelius, visits Suttree on the houseboat—either nearly drunk or confident that he will soon get that way. The scene recreates a more finely honed family dialogue, if scalpel-sharp but small, than anything else in McCarthy. Suttree's ambivalence toward his family, himself, and the world come through in the mixture of cruelty toward this alcoholic uncle on his mother's side of the family, and the judgment of the indifference toward John shown by his father.

When John finally protests that there's "[n]o need to get on your high horse," Suttree thinks he has him beaten on every count. They are both alcoholics, and they are both looked down on by Suttree's father because of the lower social status of his mother's (and John's) family. To Suttree, however, it makes a difference that he does not lie about his drinking. (Throughout the book, Suttree and the narration somehow seem to evade the possibility that he is simply an alcoholic. Perhaps this is because that possibility disturbs the existential possibilities for the hero, as it might seem to tilt the book's fundamental problems away from the importance of action and back toward the importance of "blood" to Suttree's father.) Again, more noble than John, Suttree has embraced a lower-class social space, and even chosen it, fully, in rebellion. But the striking difference between these two relatives is not so much that the older man is a fool and the younger one feels superior to him through the righteousness of honesty and a stronger intellect and education; it is that the old man who came to see about his nephew is treated by him with such cruelty.

Robert Jarrett's Lacanian reading of "Suttree's double consciousness" puts the focus on Cornelius's memory of a stillborn twin. Aware that in a kind of quantum alternative, Suttree might have instead been the twin that did not live, Suttree's twin "antiSuttree haunts him continually [. . .]." The resulting conflict is at times one of near equals, and between them, the Suttree and "antiSuttree" doppelgänger can exhibit the dual drives of a young man with unresolved conflict originating in the difference between his father and mother. Jarrett's full analysis persuasively connects McCarthy's use of the doppelgänger trope to the behavior of Cornelius Suttree, particularly in terms of class-consciousness and language. Suttree is in the first sense simply caught in a conflict between the different social strata from which his parents emerged; but in a second, deeper conflict, he is caught between the mother who would suffocate him in the Lacanian originary, and the father who demands he give up his originary needs in exchange for the sublimated symbolic satisfactions of language—the language of the courts, the marketplace, and the centers of government (Jarrett 58–59).

Although Jarrett's excellent analysis helps me appreciate the complexity of the doppelgänger trope, the novel's double business has always felt strained to me. In this grab bag of a book, the double returns, it seems, whenever the other available means of framing Suttree's behavior have run out. Put another way, for instance, Suttree's innumerable complaints against every perceivable power structure in the novel, from the heavens to the practices of Knoxville cops, can also be called disappointed male idealism.[12] Certainly, the Knoxville cops are wrong. But Suttree's regard for women, along with his constant reproach to the universe, suggest an existential crisis as only young men seem to experience it: the universe is not being nice enough to me and provides me with no meaning.[13] (And there remains the possibility that for all their complexity, the struggles in Suttree's psyche may have as much to do with the more rudimentary Manichean narcissistic habits of an alcoholic brain, as with loftier quarrels with the universe.)

Whether or not McCarthy intends it as such, coming from the main character, all the angst over a stillborn twin is mostly a red herring: Suttree's problem with his father can be explained in much simpler terms, as indeed, he does with John.

> Look, said Suttree, leaning forward. When a man marries beneath him his children are beneath him. If he thinks that way at all. If you werent a drunk he might see me with different eyes. As it is, my case was always doubtful. I was expected to turn out badly. My grandfather used to say Blood will tell. It was his favorite saying. What are you looking at? Look at me. (*S* 19)

John's response points to the real problem: "I dont know why you try and blame me for your troubles. You and your crackpot theories" (*S* 19). Why does he?

Of course, Suttree is probably right that his father looks down on his mother's family—even to the illogical point of thinking the uncle's behavior, inasmuch as it retroactively indicates some essential deficiencies in the blood he shares with his sister, has since made it clear how deficient a son Cornelius will inevitably become. For a presumably educated man of the world, this is a dog breeder's idea of human identity, but it must be granted that such absurdities around class persist, especially in a country where they were not supposed to, and especially in the South, where they have persisted in particularly problematic ways.

Of course, it may be that as we slowly evolve our understanding of the way a variety of affective disorders and social ills does run in families (such as alcoholism, or clinical depression), Suttree's father may prove troublingly apt after all. In a humorous aside, the sudden appearance of Vernon and Fernon recall Suttree's anxiety of the still-born twin (again), but also offer evidence that, however much Suttree may resist the idea, his grandfather was right in his "favorite saying," "Blood will tell" (*S* 19). (And here, if the problem really was the booze, that may have been the real locus of the falling-out.) But where I think the focus of anger comes from in Cornelius's response to this attitude is in what the father does with this knowledge. As the son carries forward the guilt of the father—of judging people by their blood, and invalidating their free will—he will commit the sin again, against a family member.

For the irony here is that Suttree has taken up the father's way of thinking—or at least pretended to do so long enough to make himself feel better by torturing this wasted old relative. Suttree's speech begins with a word to delight Lacan: "Look." When, toward the end of the main lecture, he catches John looking away, he commands him, "Look at me" (*S* 19). This assertion of authority, as well as its demand for a narcissistic satisfaction, amounts to sadism: John is the other in whose humiliation Suttree hopes to be implicated. As Beauvoir describes this confluence of sadism and masochism in Sade, "by befouling and hurting the other, the torturer befouls and hurts himself. He participates in the passivity which he discloses, and in wanting to apprehend himself as the cause of the torment he inflicts, it is as an instrument and therefore as an object that he perceives himself." As with the masochist, hoping "to be entranced by the object with which he hopes to merge," "this effort leads him back to his subjectivity" (27).

In sadistically abusing John, then, Suttree collapses the distance, the distinction even, between himself and his father. By collapsing his own subjectivity into that of John—only to return into his own, distinct, subjectivity—Suttree has it both ways: he revels in his ambivalence even as he hopes to exorcise it.

Suttree's control of John during this scene is total, as he pounces on every verbal resistance. To John's "I don't know what you're talking about" he insists that John does. Not only is Suttree right, but the difference between them cannot even be one of different views; it can only be one of who is admitting the truth (and thus a difference of power). Suttree's insistence that he knows that John knows what he is "talking about" reduces John to the lowest position he could be in: guilty of exhibiting the worst evidence of their family's bad blood, John is further guilty of refusing to acknowledge that fact. And of course, this man—an uncle and a needy alcoholic—provides an easier target than Suttree's real problem, the father. (Again, it is notable that Suttree throughout the novel often regards other people, such as John, as alcoholics. He never sees himself that way.)

Moreover, abusing John puts Suttree in the position of his father, who, knowing the truth of the world, sends it to his son in a one-way communication—the letter. Unless the son changes his mind and is willing to eclipse his own identity to join the world of the law, business, and government, he is reduced in his father's eyes to the level of "the helpless and the impotent" (*S* 14). But if, as he believes that his father already considers him a bad "case,"

(*S* 19), he admits the truth of the letter, he loses himself completely. Eclipsed by his father's identity, he furthermore has no hope of measuring up. Either way, he has no hope of what Beauvoir calls a return to his "subjectivity" (27). His situation recalls Kafka's "The Judgment," where the son can barely exist, so heavy is the burden of his father on him. As this author characterized his relationship to the father, "Not as if I could appease the father; the roots of this hostility are irradicable [. . .]" (470).[14] As with Suttree, those roots seem to have grown as much hostility in the son as in the father. What Suttree keeps and reuses from the letter, then, is cruelty.

He tells John that "my father is contemptuous of me because I'm related to you." Again, rubbing it in with his command of John's own consciousness, he adds the rhetorical, "Dont you think that's a fair statement?" The word "fair" reverberates with irony. In a gesture of physical connection that only highlights the cruelty of this scene, Suttree "reache[s] across the little space and [takes] his uncle's willowing hands" to then tell him, "I dont blame you, [. . .] I just want to tell you how some people are" (*S* 19). This pretense, that Cornelius is merely trying to help John see the truth, and accept it, foreshadows the cruelty of Anton Chigurh. Both insist that their victims acknowledge the truth that they possess, as if their function were to bestow a painless grace. We know who pulls the trigger, though.

Ultimately, however, even if Suttree suspects some truth behind his father's snobbery, Cornelius remains not only the son of his lower-class mother, but also the son of his upper-class father. John, of course, lacks that compensation of having at least half-high blood. Class anxiety therefore creates an arc of social space over Suttree's time in McAnally Flats, and continues to imbue his anxiety over his father even as he "reintegrates himself," as Jarrett puts it (61), through his vision quest in the mountains, and especially during his time on the French Broad with the Reeses. Another, less personal and more altruistically social, reason for his rebellion against the father suggests another ray of light through the prism between McCarthy's life and fiction.

Cormac McCarthy was actually born Charles Joseph McCarthy, Jr., in Rhode Island, in 1933. Even the middle name came from the father. Exactly when Charles Jr. changed his name to Cormac remains unclear, but sources close to Knoxville refer to the boy they remembered as Charlie.[15] At age four, young Charles was moved with his family to Tennessee, expressly to join the father, who had moved there two years earlier for his job with the Tennessee Valley Authority (Jarrett 1).

The break with the father may have been occasioned by the name change, but more likely, leaving behind the father's name only exacerbated an existing hostility. Leslie Garrett, a contemporary novelist and friend of McCarthy's, relayed an obvious explanation to Knoxville journalist Don Williams: what serious writer would want to be called "Charlie McCarthy" in the era of Edgar Bergen's ventriloquist act? In any case, the father seems to have been largely absent, which is unsurprising given the weight of his employment with the TVA. "The elder McCarthy was in the air so much that he was one of only four Knoxvillians in Trans World Airline's Million Mile Club at the time" (Williams).

McCarthy's father, Charles Sr., grew up in Rhode Island (where Charles Jr. and his five siblings continued to vacation with their parents during summers), and was graduated from Providence College in 1927. Graduated at the top of the 1930 class of the Yale Law School, Charles Sr. edited the *Yale Law Journal.* With the advent of the TVA in 1934, he worked as its chief general counsel ("Charles McCarthy"). If this high-profile and demanding job made Charles Sr. an absent father, he would not be the first.

Charles Sr.'s academic achievement puts his son's in stronger contrast: Charles Jr. twice dropped out of the University of Tennessee in Knoxville. As of this writing, however, he keeps a regular office at the Santa Fe Institute, where most of the researchers and fellows hold a Ph.D. As he told Richard Woodward in his second interview, "I like being around smart, interesting people, and the people who come here are among the smartest, most interesting people on the planet" (100). As any reader of Cormac McCarthy's novels knows, his polymathic knowledge needed no degree; in contrast to his father, Cormac seems to have gotten what he needed from both formal and informal education without bothering over grades. On the whole, he seems never to have cared for structured education. He quotes Flannery O'Conner's answer to the question, why are you a writer: "Because I am good at it" (Woodward 104).

In this assumption that excellence in one's vocation is what counts, the son and the father seem to hold the same value. But clearly, McCarthy keeps his own measure for success, refusing, for instance, to attend ceremonies for any of the many awards he has received.[16] Beyond reading Suttree Sr.'s letter as somehow biographical material, several friends of young Charlie confirm that he and his father "often crossed swords." In an interview, Bill Kidwell, a friend of McCarthy's during his years at the University of Knoxville and—along with many other contemporaries of McCarthy at that time—the inspiration for one of Suttree's drinking buddies, has said that McCarthy's failure to observe the family religion created tension. "I think it [Catholicism] embittered him. Because of that, he was never fully at peace with his parents. That's directly reflected in *Suttree,* the same story, essentially an autobiography" (Gibson).

McCarthy's second wife, Annie DeLisle, characterizes an interest in the downtrodden that brings us back to the letter of Suttree Sr. Perhaps the son's genuine feeling for the people fictionalized in *Suttree* did not fit with the Catholicism of the schools he attended, let alone with that of his father.

> He's a very sweet, gentle man; I don't believe he was absorbed with the morbidity of [his subject matter] in any way. [. . .] He always said 'Just because something isn't pleasant doesn't mean it doesn't exist.' He felt for those who were less blessed, and that world the rest of us would ignore, he would delve into it, see where it came from. (Gibson)

This feeling "for those who were less blessed" recalls Spencer's characterization of Buddy Suttree as both a bodhisattva and a pragmatic social worker, living among and helping many of the poor characters so vividly portrayed in the novel. Psychologically, Suttree may exhibit many of the same anxieties felt by the author, over the ultimately empty gestures of Catholicism as McCarthy experienced it, over the gap between his formal education and the country wisdom but book ignorance of many of the people he cared about, over his relatively wealthy family in comparison with the people depicted in *Suttree*—and thus over possible snobbery on the part of his father. But what is inarguable is the appearance of the large-scale social effects of McCarthy Sr.'s profession as we see them in the novel.

Whatever the private nature of the falling-out between Charles Sr. and Charles Jr., the particularity of the father's job seems to explain much of the larger tensions of social space in *Suttree*, as well as the regular exploitation of its most remarkable image: a river filled with human sewage, dead bodies of humans and animals, wasted possessions, filth of all kinds, and most notably, of images of power—both human reproductive power, and electric and other artificial forms of power—gone wrong. In his capacity as the lead attorney for the TVA, Charles Sr. oversaw the displacement and dispossession of untold numbers of poor farmers and settlers (and their dead) in the valleys that filled with water as America undertook a dam-building project as significant to the South as the Hoover and Glen Canyon dams were to the West.

HEGIRAS TO HIGHER GROUND [17]

Suttree literally overruns its banks with the abject in all its forms: from a foetus, to a suicide grapnel-hooked up from the river, the images floating by the reader commingle the dead with the detritus of civilized and technologically dependent life. Even the ragman is haunted by a future more developed yet, a "specter of mechanical proliferation and universal blight" (*S* 256). Innumerable images of decay and forestalled reproductive power in *Suttree* are linked to technological waste, or suggest some reckless power beyond that of the water alone.[18] So many scenes take place in the liminal space of water, or under bridges, or in bars that could almost be interchangeable, that the novel hardly has so much of a setting as it does an unsettled constant movement—even though the circumference of its spaces (with the exception of the mountain sojourn and the river trip with the Reeses) is relatively small.

Much of the description in the long italicized rush of images through the prologue is devoted to decrepit constraints of stone and steel, "a mongrel architecture reading back through the works of man in a brief delineation of the aberrant disordered and mad." The buildings here suggest a fallen Atlantis, with "stone walls unplumbed by weathers, lodged in the striae fossil bones, limestone scarabs rucked in the floor of this once inland sea" (*S* 3). But even these stone walls are denied the main character and most of his friends, who all live in liminal spaces: on the water, or underneath someone else's traffic.

If the city suggests decay, the creek feeding the river carries worse: "bones and dread waste, a wrack of cratewood and condoms and fruitrinds. Old tins and jars and ruined household artifacts that rear from the fecal mire of the flats like landmarks in the trackless vales of dementia praecox." One item, presumably innumerable, in this flow of waste stands out in its descriptive connection between human and material death: the "blown lightbulbs like shorn polyps semitranslucent and skullcolored bobbing blindly down" (*S* 4). These lightbulbs conflate vegetable "polyps" with human skulls, blind presumably from the power of too much light, from a power that cracks their filaments. Here a pathological psychology ("dementia praecox"), ruined plants, and already useless technology are combined into blown lightbulbs in a cityscape that itself proves to have been ill-thought and since ruined. This opening stands in stark contrast to one of the last dreams Suttree has before he leaves.

In the meantime, this novel floats its houses, graves, and even, in the trotlines and brail lines pulling fish and mussels from the river, something like underwater fences. Everything feels underwater. McCarthy had already displayed the human consequences of dams, and anxiety over his father's part in building them, throughout *The Orchard Keeper* as well. Edwin Arnold's early work on correlations between that book and the Knoxville area where McCarthy grew up noted, for example, that the likely location of the government tank that Ownby shoots corresponds with structures on TVA property ("World"). More recently, Dianne Luce locates that area as

part of the Smoky Mountains claimed by eminent domain for the creation of
a National Park ("Perspectives on the Appalachian Novels"). We begin to see,
perhaps, *why* problems with housing, burial, and fencing haunt McCarthy's
work. They point toward problems with these around the author's childhood
home. He seems to have blamed his father for many of the troubles we see in
the Knoxville of *Suttree*.

Water in itself is dangerous in this book: it drowns several people in the
river and it topples a natural wall onto Wanda Reese. But water also provides
life, through the fish Suttree catches, the turtle that Michael cooks into a
soup and shares with Suttree, and the pearls Suttree helps the Reeses harvest.
Suttree meets Wanda, herself simultaneously a lower-class white gamine and
a young river nymph, just after a flood has dislodged their houseboat. This
slow flood occurs simply because of Spring rains. Before he meets the Reeses,
Suttree sees a flood victim that foreshadows the death of not only Wanda,
but also the foetus of their unborn child: "One day a dead baby. Bloated,
pulpy rotted eyes in a bulbous skull and little rags of flesh trailing in the
water like tissuepaper" (*S* 306).[19]

Water alone simply creates victims of nature, of a purely accidental universe. Because the river seems to have killed this baby and Wanda without the
interventions of technology, and because Suttree presumably feels not just
the loss of Wanda after that accident, but also some small guilt about getting
her pregnant, these deaths point back to the psychology of Culla Holme.
Rather that suggesting any guilt on the part of a father whose power derives
from the law courts of the TVA, the river's natural destructive power returns
us to the guilt of the son as an ambivalent and failed father. But because the
dark waters of the Tennessee River in *Suttree* flow with positive, as well as
negative, images, they make the perfect means of conveying Suttree's, and
McCarthy's, ambivalence about a powerful father. As Thomas Young puts it,
"Suttree's choice of life on the river keeps the 'twinned' facts of life and death
continually before him and ensures that he enact his own mortality in the
most personalized terms" ("Imprisonment" 102–103).

Nonetheless, perhaps because of McCarthy family tensions, *Suttree*
implies only a negative view of the TVA. Despite the general turn in more
recent historical reevaluations toward the damage done by that agency, the
rural electrification project and many other programs powered by the TVA
improved life for many of the area's poor, and the popular view of the TVA
as a helpful project overall persists. Locally, this can be the case for good reasons. As Dianne Luce notes, the nearby town of "Sevierville flooded regularly
until the Little Pigeon River was widened and rechanneled in 1967 in a TVA
flood-protection program. Floods of fourteen to eighteen feet were recorded"

roughly every twenty years, and "twice in the spring of 1963 (when McCarthy himself was living in Sevierville) [. . .]" ("Cave" 172, Fox A5).

That flood-protection program had to be good, if you lived in Sevierville. In "Planning and Land Use Adjustments in Historical Perspective," Rutherford Platt argues that in addition to "its series of main-stem dams which harnessed the river for power, navigation, recreation, and flood control [. . .] the TVA also developed pioneering programs in floodplain management, soil erosion management, reforestation, economic development, and improvement of housing, medical care, schools, and recreation" (39). Even if many of us discount that last item, it is hard to argue with all of these improvements.

Unless you have two reasons to be suspicious of such governmental interventions to "improve" on nature. First, as Guillemin sees it, McCarthy's ecopastoralism "favors undomesticated nature over agricultural land," let alone over concrete dams and reservoirs. McCarthy's vision refuses "the distinction that is commonly made between" "the external wilderness of nature" and "the social wilderness of the city and the internal wilderness of the human mind" (13). But as much as *Suttree* presents us with a "wilderness" of all three of these spaces, the artificiality of the disruptions of the TVA seems to have accounted for preventable human suffering for precisely those people whom Suttree's father discounts as unimportant, the "helpless and the impotent" (*S* 14). The ragman tells him he has seen a tornado that "picked up folk's houses and set em down again in places where they'd never meant to live" (*S* 257), but Suttree's father clears the legal way for steel turbines to accomplish the same thing on a larger scale.

This brings us to the second reason for the novel's implicit, yet negative, view of the TVA. The letter from Suttree's father notably excludes human endeavor outside the city, just as it dismisses the suffering of those "in the streets" (*S* 14). It was not only the homeless of Knoxville who were negatively affected, or perhaps more accurately, ignored by the social improvement programs entailed by the TVA's dam building. Many of those homeless undoubtedly arrived in the city having been displaced from their homes outside Knoxville. Introduced to us in the novel's prologue to a "[d]ear friend," are "the homeless [. . .] washed up in the lee of walls in alleys or abandoned lots." These homeless are people who have been moved—"washed up"—by water, and then "abandoned" (*S* 3).

According to William Chandler, a researcher with the Pacific Northwest National Laboratory (within the U.S. Department of Energy), the popular image of the TVA as at least adding to the economic vitality of the areas it affected is not supported by objective evidence. Sociologist Nancy Grant goes further, and more specifically, into the negative effects of the TVA:

> The large-scale displacement of farm units and the subsequent reloca-
> tion of families caused severe economic problems for the families and
> the overpopulated area in which they were forced to resettle. The ten-
> ant and poor landowner bore the brunt of readjustment. [. . .] TVA
> compensated only those who could show a direct, measurable loss; it
> ignored those who did not have written or formal access to the lands
> and refused to acknowledge the local custom of informal use of non-
> titled land as a means for supplementing income. Land speculators
> and swindlers descended on the Tennessee Valley, involving families in
> phoney or unprofitable investments. (82)

Many simply "washed up" (*S* 3) into cities like Knoxville. Of those moved from the valley filled in with Wheeler Dam, for instance, 69% ended up settling for inferior acreage (Grant 82). Black families faced an even greater chance that a claim of eminent domain would divest them of their liveli-hood. "Overall, the black communities affected by TVA reservoir removal were not given substantial help in reordering their lives. Several regional planners with considerable power to approve or reject requests held racial views that did not allow for equal treatment of blacks" (Grant 83).

Ironically, the TVA operated from a relatively new paradigm that, as Guillemin describes McCarthy's ecopastoralism, recognizes that dis-tinctions between natural and artificial space fail to hold up. Brian Black describes the TVA's ideal as following Olmstead's mediating configurations of space, "to create a middle ground between nature and civilization. Land-scape architects proved the major conveyor of this meeting as they shaped the scenery and functionality of the 41,000 square miles of the Tennessee Valley" (160). This idea of a "middle ground" helps us see another irony in the accident that kills Wanda Reese:

> The wall of slate above the camp had toppled in the darkness, whole
> jagged edges crashing down, great plates of stone separating along the
> seams with dry shrieks and collapsing with a roar upon the ground
> below, the dull boom of it echoing across the river and back again and
> then just the sifting down of small rocks, thin slates of shale clattering
> down in the dark. (*S* 361–362)

As in Ballard's cave, the word choice here inevitably recalls elements of architecture and domesticity: "wall," "plates," and "seams." The effect of this is terrible, and described in terms that indeed collapse this scene of a natural accident into the mixed spaces of a museum, an industrial slaughter house, and a quarry: "In a raw pool of lightning an image of a baroque pieta, the woman gibbering and kneeling in the rain clutching at sheared limbs and rags of meat among the slabs of rock" (S 362). In effect, Wanda has been rendered into the Christ and a slaughtered (and thus commodified) animal, but the "pieta" really is only revealed in the figure of the mother, as her daughter's body is interleaved with "slabs of rock."

With the return to the literal reality of the scene, we recognize that this fallen wall of "rock" echoes hundreds of man-made blasts enormous in comparison. The monstrosity of this personified collapse (it collapses "with dry shrieks" and "a roar"), stands in for demolition work that McCarthy never describes, but whose effects he does.

> Suttree traced with one hand dim names beneath the table stone. Salvaged from the weathers. Whole families evicted from their graves downriver by the damming of the waters. Hegiras to higher ground, carts piled with battered cookware, mattresses, small children. The father drives the cart, the dog runs after. Strapped to the tailboard the rotting boxes stained with earth that hold the bones of the elders. Their names and dates in chalk on the wormscored wood. A dry dust sifts from the seams in the boards as they jostle up the road . . . (S 113)

These are the tombstones of the poor and their dead displaced by the TVA. Suttree's vision of them suitably shows them on the move, evaginated out from both their houses, and their graves.

The concrete evidence in these scenes from *Suttree* and "The Bear" inscribe the crimes of forbears in texts that then become foundations for the guilt of sons. Ike McCaslin's familial guilt is stirred by the written records of slaves kept by his ancestors; Suttree's is stirred by touching the tombstones that have been turned upside down into tables in a bar. As in so many other scenes in McCarthy, stones speak more directly to us than the interior consciousnesses of characters—even the loquacious interiority of Cornelius Suttree.

McCaslin's imagination, his thoughts, his memories, and his feelings, are alive and vibrating on the page, and simply become more audible when they are rung by the touching of an object, or by contact with land. By contrast, Suttree's several red herrings keep him chasing down trails leading safely askew from the father. As his drinking, his fasting, his sadomasochistic session with Mother She, and his fevered dream-quest render his thoughts even more associative than interior monologue can already be, only by direct contact with objects do we feel closer to some truth about him.

These stones speak to him, as does the physical letter from his father. Certainly, he saw nothing of the exodus in the passage above, yet his imagination of it (like his imagination of his still-born twin brother), is more particular and heightened his memory of things he has more closely experienced, such as his abandonment of his own wife and child.

Faulkner's Yoknapatawpha County landscape is especially resonant with the horrors of slavery, the civil war, and the racist violence that continued beyond the supposed end of hostilities. Comparatively, McCarthy's landscapes hardly register this past—as many whites in the new South do not. Rather, the landscapes remind us of what the characters might rather forget. This is a different sense in which the past is not even past. It lives on in our reading imagination, as we infer it from landscapes, from place names, or other markers from civilized society—markers for what that society needs to deny larger prominence.

The alternative, and most notable, problem of burial in *Suttree* comes in the water burial of Weird Leonard's father. Even though he will already have been urinated on by a black man, Suttree's awareness of the misplaced family, its tombstones and recovered dead in tow, seems to refer to a white, or at least a colorless, vision of evacuees. Of course, the family name "Callahan" (*S* 371), though much less so "Williams" (*S* 369), might be assumed to belong to white families. But when we first see Suttree feel these names beneath the table, he cannot "read" them the way that Blind Richard can. Nonetheless, his imaginative recollection never seems to think of a racial difference between whose home gets left behind for the water.

But this awareness resurfaces in the form of Leonard's father, who, wrapped up for the occasion, lies on the ground outside Leonard's trunk, "like a dead klansman" (*S* 250) and yet, simultaneously, like a victim of those clansmen, unloaded from a trunk for secret disposal in the river. Indeed, when Suttree wonders if Leonard wants to "[s]ay a few words" for this "hooded father" (*S* 251), Leonard's lack of feeling highlights both the odd space into which they are "burying" this body and the son and father anxiety in Suttree's own family. Of course, the father will rise again toward the novel's end, "[d]raggin all them chains with him," as Leonard tells Suttree. "Fathers will do that," he replies (*S* 417).

When all Suttree can offer are "Catholic" words, Leonard not only protests that "He sure wasnt no Catholic," but precedes this with the simple exclamation, "Hell fire." Whatever the paltry uses this corpse has been put to by Leonard's family (they keep him, in a ruse to collect his welfare checks), this father seems either to have been guilty enough not to warrant feeling from the son, or the son simply seems that distant from him. When Leonard protests, saying, "I aint burying him. [. . .] I'm just puttin him in the river," Suttree says "The hell you're not" (*S* 251). But instead of offering words on his own account, Suttree remains silent. His silence even extends, so that "Leonard tried him in conversation on several topics as they came back up the river but Suttree rowing said no word" (*S* 252).

This silence is mysterious: just how much does this unholy burial echo some symbolic one Suttree may imagine for his father—and indeed, in the grotesque hyperbole that would then be the hood of the "klansman," his father's crimes? We cannot know. But the next chapter opens with Suttree drunk, carefully climbing "with a drunk's meticulousness the wide stone steps of the Church of the Immaculate Conception" (*S* 253).

Suttree drinks for dissolution as an ambivalent escape from, and suicidal dive into, a river of history. Until the novel works its way through its series of vision quests, any other means of resolution between the ambivalent feelings of both rebellious rejection and guilty failure seem unavailable. Drinking in *Suttree* is always an ambivalent act, as it brings both escape from and surrender to the problem that occasions it, simultaneously rejecting the father by becoming one of his victims. The booze that provides a river of social life also gets many of Suttree's friends killed. It removes him from the decay of whatever particular place he wanders into (Suttree experiences several black-outs, and the novel never fills in much of what happens that Suttree cannot himself remember), but then it returns him penniless, poisoned, and even pissed on. This last degradation accomplishes the severest form of masochism for a guilty white son of an upper-class family whose father has been instrumental in the displacement of so many black people.

Furthermore, beyond the figurative drowning in booze, Suttree risks real death by water. The novel's opening scene of the suicide pulled from the water by a grapnel hook renders this suicide into the form of a catfish, hard to take off a trotline. One of the rescue workers is seen "kneeling over the corpse trying to pry the grapnel loose. The crowd was watching him and he was sweating and working hard at the hook. Finally he set his shoe against the dead man's skull and wrenched the hook with both hands until it came away trailing a stringy piece of blanched flesh" (*S* 9). We soon see "Suttree rubb[ing] the gently pulsing muscle in his speculative jaw" (*S* 10), and later, when the ragpicker tells Suttree that he would never commit suicide in such a manner, he asks Suttree, "Would you?" "I hope not," is all that Suttree can muster (*S* 12).

Later, Blind Richard (as the blind do in McCarthy) will help us read a new loss in the tombstones. When Suttree asks him to "read" the underside of this stone table—a gravestone converted to a quasi-domestic use of holding up beer bottles in the bar of Ab Jones—"[s]omething has passed out on the river and the shanty lifted and settled in the swells. Richard suddenly placed his hands flat on the table. Then he lifted them off again as if it were hot." He has read the same name as an acquaintance of theirs, "It says William Callahan" (*S* 370–371). This is the Red Callahan who, soon after the scene in Ab Jones's bar, is shot in the face in the Moonlite diner, with Suttree nearby. Even after the descriptions of Callahan's penchant for violence, this shooting is connected to others. "All through the town tonight are folks lie dying. Sirens in the city like the shriek of jackal birds" (*S* 376).

This roll call of those falling to violence continues later. "A season of death and epidemic violence" (*S* 416). Another acquaintance is shot, another escapes the county jail. Eventually, Harrogate is arrested and Ab Jones is beaten to death by the police. Suttree sees that Hoghead, "James Henry," has also been shot to death (*S* 403). In his fever delirium, we hear Suttree's interior monologue of deathward *ubi sunt*: "Hey Hatmaker. Tell Hoghead and Donald and Byrd and Bobby and Hugh and Conrad and all of em that they aint barred. They're dead" (*S* 456). Just as the TVA has cleared many of the living and the dead from their homes in the countryside around it, Knoxville is emptying out many of the friends and acquaintances of Suttree.[20]

As Peter Joseph points out, in a "Knoxville where *ruder forms survive* you might not ever be rude enough; or, if you are, that type of survival might well be insufficient for a man who hates, or needs to feel that he hates his father and will not be denied at least a taste of the transcendence that is his birthright—especially in a world where the shadows of a bridge might reflect more vitality than he does" ("Suttree's War," 13–14, his emphasis). Most of Suttree's friends, and many of McCarthy's, did not survive Knoxville. This emptying space, as much as his series of visions and epiphanies, seems to propel Suttree to leave. That, and a dream of a better place.

The flood of imagery in *Suttree* conflates generative power with death and decay, always falling from the first into the latter. The condoms and dead babies and nightmares of twin deaths and succubae, all point to the rejection in McCarthy novels of normal family life.[21] That rejection follows from problems between father and son, concerning the nature of social conscience, sin, and ultimately evil. *Suttree* reads, increasingly, as an apology for, rather than to, the father. In this, however, the most autobiographical novel from McCarthy stands in opposition to the great work that follows it. It is one thing to reject a father's failure of social conscience. It is another to resist a more powerful father's philosophy that explains the endlessness of human cruelty.

Suttree, however, survives by only a faint resolution of the ambivalence he feels toward the father of the law courts, business, and government. As he recovers in the hospital (for the last time in the novel), his fever momentarily lifts, and we get one of the last epiphanies—however ecumenical or even Buddhist: "I know that all souls are one and all souls lonely." Whether this includes the father or not, is unclear. When next he worsens, he yet dreams "of houses, their cellars and attics. Ultimately of this city in the sea" (*S* 459).

Thomas Young characterizes *Suttree*'s descriptions of Knoxville as "an embryonic city, something like medieval London or Jerusalem at the time of Christ, with the striations of its growth still plainly visible." Young seems to see this as the primary setting of the book (rather than the river). "This primitive structure is a living record of that elemental and highly ambiguous activity of human 'settlement' which is essentially the subject of all McCarthy's fiction" ("Imprisonment" 95). I have argued that the absence, or failure, of such settlement may run closer to a steady subject in McCarthy's work. In any case, the primitive characteristics of Knoxville are indeed regularly noted in the novel by Witek and others. A brief survey suffices here, where my focus on the son and father connects to images of strange housing.

Suttree, of course, lives in that most liminal form of housing, a house-*boat*. Even this home is taken up by the doppelgänger he finds dead in his bed toward the end of the novel, and prior to that, he seems to lease it (albeit for free) to Harrogate. When Harrogate first shows up in his move to Knoxville, Suttree plays the role of a down and out real estate agent. (Suttree's work for Harrogate, both as agent and eventual landlord, is of course pro bono.) Harrogate's place is more of a space, really, except for a "little concrete vault" that he sees as "a slick place to keep your stuff." Little does he realize that, come colder weather, he will hunker down inside this miniature mausoleum-like structure intended, apparently, to store electrical equipment ancillary to the area around the viaduct.[22]

Here again race comes into the picture, as Harrogate refuses to consider living next door to blacks, preferring the smaller space under a viaduct to the cavernous underside of the other end of the bridge that roofs the ragpicker's domicile. Even as blacks received worse treatment, on average, in relocation by the TVA, Harrogate still prefers a lesser piece of real estate than to live where "niggers lives next door" (*S* 115).

In another echo of Lester Ballard's improvised dwellings, Harrogate's place boasts a stolen mattress (*S* 117). Like Ballard, Harrogate's trajectory heads—at least for a time—downward. With his plan to rob a bank by digging into it from the sewers and caves that create under Knoxville a system of civic alimentary conduits, Harrogate mimics Ballard in attempting to achieve underground what he cannot above ground. Ballard goes underground with his victims to replicate a social space.

Harrogate, a newer form of social outcast, seems less to want the feeling and touch of social life than the fuel to move through it: money. Instead of dressing up like the woman he wants, Harrogate dresses up like the man he would like to be: "And this was Harrogate. Standing in the door of Suttree's shack with a cigar between his teeth. He had painted the black one and it was chalk white and he had grown a wispy mustache. He wore a corduroy hat a helping larger than his headsize and a black gabardine shirt with slacks to match. His shoes were black and sharply pointed, his socks were yellow" (*S* 418).

This display of success follows his aboveground crime, of course, stealing from payphones. In his earlier desperation, his tunneling toward the bank leaves him first "slavered over with a gray paste" that seems like encomium, and recalls Ballard's bloodied look when he escapes his womb-grave. When Harrogate's scheme goes wrong, of course, he ends up in a sea of excrement, a parody of both his dream of swimming in riches, and of scenes of fleeting, yet genuinely felt, oceanic feeling on the part of other McCarthy characters. But even in this scheme, Harrogate represents a less severe version of the underground man than Ballard, such as when he attempts to enlist Suttree's help in telling him where he's "at" in his underground work (*S* 260). What he learns, after the explosion, is just how low he is. Where Suttree finally picks up on his trail, "[h]e had not known how hollow the city was" (*S* 276).

Indeed, it is in the larger aspects of its architecture, and in their rougher uses, that their negative characterization links up with the depiction of the river partly controlled by the TVA—and McCarthy's father. When Suttree visits the family mansion, it has long since fallen in. Here the decrepitude seems connected to a corrupt family legacy, especially as Suttree imagines previous feasts in its fallen dining room.

This early view of the domestic and civic problem as it runs closest to Suttree's father anxiety sets us up for two mythic images that will conclude the book. One is of "dogs and starving palliards" (beggars) who "contest the scraps among the straw" (*S* 136). In the novel's ending, these dogs are followed by the much-commented on "enormous lank hound" of death "sniffing at the spot where Suttree had stood" (*S* 471). The second is the also-noted water bearer. In Suttree's imagined recall of the feast in the family manor, the waterbearer "does not come, and does not come" (*S* 136). At the novel's end, he arrives in more workaday form. But he is preceded by a different water figure that deserves more attention here, as she is connected to Suttree's dream vision of an alternative civic space.

Suttree's dream of the "city in the sea" enacts an architectural ontegenic recapitulation of phylogeny. Suttree's recovery (from fever, but also from everything else haunting him throughout the book—if not exactly from his anxiety over his father) entails the rebirth of Atlantis, a city that, rather than the fouled Knoxville with its filthy river, promises a rebirth of civic space— and of sobriety—overflowing with images of fertility and clear water:

> As we watched there reared out of the smoking brine a city of old bone coughed up from the sea's floor, pale attic bone delicate as shell and half melting, a chalken shambles coralgrown that skewed into shape of temple, column, plinth, and cornice, and across the whole a frieze of archer and warrior and marblebreasted maid all listing west [. . .] We have witnessed this thing today which prefigures for all time the way in which historic orders proceed. And some said that the girl who bathed her swollen belly in the stone pool in the garden last evening was the author of this wonder they attended. And a maid bearing water in a marble jar came down from the living frieze toward the dreamer with eyes restored black of core and iris brightly painted attic blue and she moved toward him with a smile. (*S* 459–460)

Here, the city is born out of the water, rather than sitting astride it. The water, rather than conveying a bloated foetus, or trash, bathes the pregnant belly of "the author of this wonder," no less than a young girl. And finally, instead of the detritus of modernity, Suttree gets his drink from "a marble jar" come to life from the heights of architecture—judging roughly from the description, around 2,500 years before the TVA. The solution in *Suttree*, then, whether or not "all souls are one" (*S* 459), does quite well without the father by going much farther than ever before, or since, toward a vision of sacred fecundity, of salvation through a feminine power. This feminine power seems to enact the final of many salvations of Suttree, overwhelming the novel's long run of a dangerous river corrupted by twentieth-century technological control of its power.

We have not seen such a maiden again in McCarthy since this image, and even before Suttree leaves Knoxville, she is replaced by a boy "ladling out water in a tin dipper" to the construction crew building a road out of this city far from the sea. But the next novel will bring alive that archer, that warrior, as the work lists to the west. And another shift takes place: despite the fact that I find no hint of reconciliation with the father, specifically, in

Suttree, we will see that once his "sins" are lifted to the level of the judge's philosophy, the son will lose the contest.

SINS OF THE SON IN *BLOOD MERIDIAN*

If *Suttree* details the dissolute rejection of a corrupt father by a son unable to find his way, but able to help others, *Blood Meridian* functions partly as an apology to the father for not joining battle with unambivalent zeal. Surprisingly, *Blood Meridian*'s taut thread between the judge and the kid places it directly under the rubric of anxieties about family and domesticity, even though such anxieties are easier to follow in the other novels.

   Blood Meridian seems to concern those aspects of life (wandering and war) that have least to do with domesticity.[23] The kid is so quickly established as a rough customer that we can forget how young he is, even as his name ought to remind us. Another way to see him, however, is as a "kid" wandering from his orphanage in the book's opening, to his adoptions, first by Captain White, then by Glanton's party, and eventually, by the judge.[24] For his part, the judge evades easy identification as a father figure because of his neotony. But as Rick Wallach notes, "infantile imagery pervades this novel in unexpected, unsettling ways. [. . .] many of the judge's features actually complement those of the kid, who is 'not big but he had big wrists, big hands,' [. . .]" ("Judge," 126). In the hands, at least, they even look alike. Because Holden and Glanton resemble Fedallah and Ahab, or Mephistopheles and Faust, we can miss that resemblance between Holden and the kid. On the level of psychology, however, it is the relationship of the judge to the kid that most resonates.

   In his first two adoptions, the kid is initially taken up by an intermediary. This accommodates the force of the judge's language, so that he does not immediately eclipse the kid. Yet, the narration regularly slips into the judge's word choice, suggesting a preternatural connection between the narrative hints of the plot to come, and the judge's regular assessments of the action as it unfolds. In his declaration that only war makes men more than "antic clay" (*BM* 307), therefore, the judge is providing an answer at the ending of the book to a question posed by the narrator about the kid in it's beginning: "His origins are become remote as is his destiny and not again in all the world's turning will there be terrains so wild and barbarous to try whether the stuff of creation may be shaped to man's will or whether his own heart is not another kind of clay" (*BM* 4–5). Either the kid is mere clay, however evolved—or more, as the judge would have it. The trope, however, is taken over from the narrator by the judge.[25]

In nearly every scene explicitly involving both the judge and the kid, we feel the tension of this question: will the son prove to be more than "antic clay?" Nonetheless, I have never been sure that the judge is serious in his characterization of the kid as a potential disciple, a son who might truly follow in his footsteps. To Holden, the kid serves more as a foil. We might even imagine that this narrative so biblical in tone has more than one narrator slipping in and out of the redacted version of its mythic story, and that at times the judge takes hold of the story in order to use the kid to set you, the reader, up for a final argument that swallows up potential resistance. As such, this judge is another powerful father going on about his business, only troubling himself with the son in order to point out his shortcomings, until the end, when he consumes what might have been an opposing force.

For this to be the case, the kid must move along a path of moral development, admittedly an unlikely path in *Blood Meridian*. And yet, key scenes involving the kids actions—and as often, inactions—suggest that he does just this. The problem with this direction in reading *Blood Meridian*, however, lies in the temptation to make too much of the kid's resistance, to see in him more of what we want to see than what is there. Instead, I will argue that the kid fails both to follow fully, and to fully resist, the judge's answer to the "clay" question. Edwin Arnold sees this contest between the judge and the kid in terms that are nearly Manichean: the judge is evil, and the kid's failure to resist him fully constitutes a moral failure equal to that of Culla Holme ("Naming"). But while I agree that the kid fails to be cold enough—to resist the judge in full—I think the novel demands us to give the judge his due, as horrible as that is. In that way, the kid also fails to be hot enough, to follow this dark father.

Unlike Arnold, I cannot see the judge's philosophy as pure will to power against a moral universe. His verbal play with the gang along the lines of mystery and their inability to see truth does not mean that *he* cannot. The judge's answer to the clay question embraces war as the highest form of contest, refuses moral protests to this, and dances to erase altogether a distinction between the dancer and the dance. Certainly, at the local level—which is to say, if we imagine him anywhere near us, let alone our children—he is walking evil. But in his dancing (as well as other clues) he may also represent an alternative position: destructive power, yes, but not within a binary moral system. That said, the power of his representation in this novel is such that he can still be viewed on different terms. As Arnold sees him, he is pure evil in a Christian context, and even an ahistorical devil attempting to steal our souls: He can never, indeed, die, "as the epilogue illustrates. Fences will neither hold the judge nor constrain the force he calls to in each of us. But moral choice remains; the judge can still be faced" ("Naming," 63).

In Eastern terms, however, the judge makes a more persuasive argument. Rick Wallach identifies Holden with "Shiva, who dances the dance of war and cosmic destruction." ("Judge," 128–130). We might also add that his arguments to the kid recapitulate those of Krishna to Arjuna in *The Bhagavad Gita*: join war for your fear of dying betrays you to be a slave of maya, illusion, as does your fear of killing others. You are they and they are you, so engage in that ultimate contest wherein the game of life realizes that illusion most fully. By doing so, you will simultaneously aver the larger truth, that all is one. In a unified existence, what is violence?

The judge puts this in the language of a legal contest. First, he disposes of appeals to truth outside the case, by invalidating morality as "an invention of mankind for the disenfranchisement of the powerful in favor of the weak. Historical law subverts it at every turn." This Nietzschean idea served Nietzsche as a corrective; he was looking for a balance he had decided was lost, between reason and the dance. Holden, however, refuses any distinction between the two.

> A man falling dead in a duel is not thought thereby to be proven in error as to his views. His very involvement in such a *trial* gives evidence of a new and broader view. The willingness of the principles to forgo further argument as the triviality which it in fact is and to *petition* directly the *chambers* of the historical absolute clearly indicates of how little moment are the *opinions* and of what great moment the divergences thereof. For the argument is indeed trivial, but not so the separate wills thereby made manifest. Man's [. . .] knowledge remains imperfect and howevermuch he comes to value his judgements ultimately he must submit them before *a higher court*. [. . .] Decisions of life and death, of what shall be and what shall not, beggar all question of right. In elections of these magnitudes are all lesser ones subsumed, moral, spiritual, natural. (*BM* 250, my emphasis)

I have highlighted some of the legal language, as it might now be a good place to recall the letter of Suttree's father: "the world is run by those willing to take the responsibility for the running of it. If it is life that you feel you are missing I can tell you where to find it. In the law courts, in business, in government. There is nothing occurring in the streets. Nothing but a dumbshow composed of the helpless and the impotent" (*S* 13–14).

To read both arguments after allowing for the possibility that neither is a relativist, let alone a nihilist argument—that in fact, there may be some "higher court" to which one may appeal—means allowing for the possibility that the fathers here could be right. My aim here is not to argue that, but to suggest that we might see the whole of judge Holden's argument here, in his speech on war, and indeed, throughout *Blood Meridian*, as a bloody extension of Suttree Sr.'s letter. If so, then it follows that by providing Holden with the strongest possible argument for his case, and by allowing him to win, as it were, that argument, McCarthy has followed the son's escape in *Suttree* with a reversal of that story, and just once, a complete collapse of an insufficiently powerful son into the power of his father.

How much does the kid resist this argument? The kid's rejection of the judge at first amounts to no more than a mysterious absence in the narrative description of scenes of group violence. Beyond that lack of information around the kid's behavior during the gang's attacks, we can discern a series of small rebellions. In one, the kid merely rides beside Toadvine and, by his silent presence, implies protest. Searching for the violent Gileño Apaches they have been hired to kill, the gang instead finds "a band of peaceful Tiguas [. . .] and slaughter them every soul" (*BM* 173). The men first gather about their campfire the night before and attend to their weaponry,

> as if the fate of the aborigines had been cast into shape by some other
> agency altogether. [. . .] No man stood to tender them a defense.
> Toadvine and the kid conferred together and when they rode out at
> noon the day following they trotted their horses alongside Bathcat.
> They rode in silence. Them sons of bitches aint botherin nobody, Toad-
> vine said. The Vandiemanlander [Bathcat] looked at him. He looked at
> the livid letters tattooed on his forehead and at the lank greasy hair that
> hung from his earless skull. He looked at the necklace of gold teeth at
> his chest. They rode on. (*BM* 173)

Because the narrator tells us that no one "stood to tender" these non-violent Indians any defense, we may infer that someone might have but did not. What the kid and Toadvine "confer" about is mysterious, until they both approach Bathcat. The kid's position alongside Toadvine bolsters his protest that "Them sons of bitches aint botherin nobody" (*BM* 174). As befits this gang of killers whose words are usually handled by the judge, Toadvine's protest is met with the rebuke of silence and the power of visual rhetoric over that of words. Bathcat simply looks at the man making this argument, so that Toadvine's filthy ethos undermines what he has just said. Given a common visual trope that otherwise takes up much of the energy of the gang in scenes of dialogue, it is surprising that Bathcat, confronted with this argument from this quarter, did not spit.[26] We know from previous description that Toadvine has been tattooed as a horse thief (as well as whatever "F" stands for), lost his ears in combat, and adorned himself with the teeth of his victims. Any remonstration from this man against violence, whatever the situation, becomes ridiculous immediately as his appearance reasserts itself.[27]

Toadvine's moment of doubt is overlaid, therefore, by his killer's visage, (complete with labeling for anyone unable to guess at his criminality). The word "cast" in relation to the "prefigured" destiny of the Tiguas is also ironically suggestive for Toadvine: he, too, is marked for his role. Such marking, writing, coining, and similar inscriptions of fate, are much the concern of the judge. The distinction between the gang and the "peaceful Tiguas" depends again on spatial configuration: these are not nomadic people, but "aborigines" (*BM* 173). As original occupants of a region, they are tied to the land on which they make their living—in contrast to the gang on horseback, on the move. And they are "cast"—molded—for death.

Well after this scene, as the kid sweats through the removal of a Yuma arrow from his leg by a doctor in San Diego, the judge seems to visit the kid in a dream. It is the one passage giving us clear information on Holden's title of "judge," as he is accompanied in the kid's vision by a "coldforger."[28] The man works under the judge's shadow,

> perhaps under some indictment and an exile from *men's* fires, hammering out like his own conjectural destiny all through the night of his becoming some coinage for a dawn that would not be. It is this false moneyer with his gravers and burins who seeks favor with the judge and he is at contriving from cold slag brute in the crucible a face that will pass, an image that will render this residual specie current in the markets where men barter. *Of this is the judge judge* and the night does not end. (*BM* 310, my emphasis)

This means that the judge's superhuman power rests on knowledge of a universal order—an order of whose knowledge the kid (and as the judge says, any human being) is denied. The judge's mysterious origin only bolsters this aspect of his identity: he is from nowhere.

Rather, the judge is a familiar of the moon and stars. As such, he speaks regularly of the gap between a larger order in the universe and the human inability to see any order but that false order which it imagines for its own solace. Nonetheless, as the kid sees the judge from a position of fevered convalescence in San Diego, the judge is a judge for a *false* moneyer, whose coinage is minted for a morning that cannot come. "[T]he night" that "does not end" is that night in which this moneyer coins the temptation of men to evil. Within the kid's vision, the implication is that there is yet some other order to the universe—or at least that the judge's order is at best another false one. This scene of moral counterfeit is key to many questions about the book's violent assaults on all things civilized.

Toadvine's face has been "cast" in just this manner, and it is easy to imagine that his branding has the opposite effect of that achieved by the branding of cattle or other domestic animals. Instead of belonging to someone, or to a place, Toadvine is branded so that he will be shunned—forever on the move outside civilized places. His protest before the murder of the Tiguas therefore amounts to little. Nonetheless, there seems to be something missing in the cast of Toadvine, given his ability to feel some measure of pity—however rare or meager—for some of the gang's victims.

The kid is even less firmly cast, and is furthermore not yet fully tempered. Throughout most of the book's action, he is an adolescent, a yet-formed man, however frequently the narrative describes his physical abilities in adult terms. By the time the book can finally call him an adult, and therefore draw attention to his age as no longer sixteen but now twenty-eight years old, the judge has already accused him of betraying his duty to violence. The kid's resistance to the judge's arguments for war, then, constitute the betrayal of a father by a son. The son only makes it under pressure, and fully only after he reaches maturity. Even then, he lacks resolve. This is ironic, in that the homeless, nomadic condition of the kid and the gang further undermines a normal family relationship such as that between a father and son—except in that troubled tradition of fathers training their sons away from the hearth.[29]

The kid's youth is typical of a McCarthy main character. Their age is medial in terms of space: they are too old to be at home, yet too young to settle down elsewhere. Orphans, drifters, searching and constantly moving, they belong to no place. The ultimate expression of that homeless identity is the horsed warrior who kills peaceful people in their own homes. But at this ultimate expression, even Toadvine—and arguably the kid—hesitates at least once. In so doing, they betray the judge's command of them against the ordered spaces of civilized society. For the judge, however, the kid remains a special case, a son resisting his philosophical father.

THE KID TAKES THE HIGH COUNTRY

In the kid's most notable resistance, he disobeys a direct order—albeit one that he receives by chance.[30] Having drawn a lot to stay behind with one of the wounded men and kill him, the kid reneges. At first, this might seem humane of him. To Shelby's pleas to get it over with, however, the kid replies with silence, then a reminder of who is in control, and then a yielding of that control to Shelby. "If you want me just to leave you I will. Shelby didnt answer." The kid then pushes the man to make the decision: "You'll have to say" (*BM* 207–208).

By attempting to remain silent, the kid seems as cold as Bathcat, simply looking at the man making an appeal to pity. (The kid, as if to harden his resolve against appeal, does spit.) Even this kid, who the narrator has already told us had an early "taste for mindless violence" (*BM* 3), is not eager to shoot an unarmed man simply because he is wounded and cannot travel. We may infer that the kid has thus far participated in the violence, but he somehow has no taste for the killing that would be kind: the lottery may seem cruel, but under the circumstances of the gang's flight from a brutal enemy, it amounts to euthanasia.

Euthanasia, however, is a morally difficult action, requiring a human sensitivity to long-term values (over short-term ones) that has yet to be reached at this point in *Blood Meridian*. For the gang, spending time on this probably indicates merely a warrior ethic more geared toward toughness than to mutual respect. If the kid is to reassemble an evolved morality in contradiction to the judge's celebration of death, he must get past this step, but he fails by neither shooting nor really helping Shelby.

By failing in this crucial resistance to the judge, the kid is left neither warm nor cold. Glanton, out of some rough code of behavior, leaves behind some of his good men to dispatch those who can no longer keep up on the retreat. Here it is the kid, tempted by the coinage of the judge, who is yet more primitive than Glanton: he appeals to chance—the irresistible illogical amoral power behind the evolutionary course of nature—when he reminds Shelby that it is he, the kid, who has the gun. But unlike the judge, the kid then does nothing, merely postponing Shelby's fate.

The irony here lies in this medial moment: to walk away without killing the member of your gang is deemed cowardly—inhuman. To kill the fallen, however, seems morally dangerous, as it is both the action of a human evolved enough to perform this action out of mercy, and of a human enjoined above all to celebrate death. True euthanasia is impossible without human

morality, but the judge would object that killing the fallen is anything but
euthanasia. Rather, it enacts another embrace of the ultimate human game:
when you can no longer play, you must be taken out of the game altogether,
and by another player. Otherwise, you have failed to play your part in an
ultimate contest.

The kid, however, is not tough enough to walk away and leave his
charge, the way a healthy wolf would leave a wounded one behind its pack.
Instead, we see a hint of ambivalence, growing like a moral tumor, in the
kid. Unable to "just get on with it" and kill Shelby, he nonetheless will
not own the action of leaving Shelby alive. "You'll have to say," he tells the
dying man. Shelby's appeals, now tearful, move the kid to some short-term
mercy. After pulling Shelby under some brush, he leaves some of his water
with him (this is a serious sacrifice in the desert). Then he leaves the man to
whatever fate is approaching in the form of General Elias and five hundred
Sonoran troops. All this takes time, and a delay in travel across rough country can mean death. Most importantly, it leads to the kid becoming cut off
from the gang. Shelby's pleas have worked on him, however, and the kid is
even slower in catching the fleeing scalp hunters, because he stops to help
yet another man.

This man he helps more actively, to a point. Tate's horse has pulled up
lame and he is leading it by the reins. The men are at first too suspicious of
each other to "ride and tie" (or take turns riding the kid's good horse, with
the other man following on the fading horse), as whoever is on the good
horse "might just keep ridin," and leave the unlucky man soon afoot.[31] The
kid's decision is odd, then, as he does what no animal would; yet his action,
evidence of enough human feeling for the man that he will not go on without him, at first does neither of them any good: the kid simply dismounts,
and accompanies Tate as if his own horse were faltering (*BM* 210). Again,
these acts of sympathy are weak substitutes for both the courage to enact a
full rebellion against the judge and aver the highest morality of self-sacrifice,
or the opposite courage to leave these flutterings of conscience behind for a
full return to the game.

At the kid's suggestion, he and Tate then "pull for the high country. As
long as we keep goin uphill we'll know we aint got in a circle" (*BM* 210). This
is odd, in that the weather is turning cold, and it will certainly be colder as
they gain in altitude. They also, as Tate worries aloud, "never will find Glanton." Cut off from the gang by Elias's pursuit, they will be leaving the fight.
Abandoning their fellows to an even tougher fight without them, they are
guilty of cowardice. We are tempted, however, to interpret "the high country" as a place more humane: as they climb above the snow line, they begin

to "take turns riding the good horse and leading the lame" (*BM* 211). This means that each has to trust the other; they are now willing to cooperate for their common good, despite the fact that each, in his turn, might abandon the man with the bad horse and do better for himself. It is no coincidence, then, that they are traveling at a tangent from the fleeing Glanton gang; they are climbing into the higher country of common sacrifice for the purely human construction of value we call selflessness and morality—at least for themselves, apart from their former allegiance to the murdering gang. Having begun his scene with Shelby at a more primitive moral stage than Glanton, the kid now climbs to a higher one with Tate.

Still, the two men are caught in the snow by scouts of Elias. The kid alone shoots his way to an escape. What follows is a solitary trek of about three days in a high desert, night and day, without food. In a passage reminiscent of Cornelius Suttree's mountain fast in McCarthy's preceding book, the kid nearly hallucinates. Beginning along "a rocky promontory" and "wild uplands," the kid witnesses a mocking clash of order and chance in the natural world around him. "[T]he Pleiades" and other stars burn "with a lidless fixity," juxtaposed against a "heaven" that is "a barren range of rock so enfolded in that gaudy house that stars lay awash at his feet and migratory spalls of burning matter [cross] constantly about him on their chartless reckonings" (*BM* 212–213).

From this liminal space, between the animal yet cultural struggles of men below and the chaotic clash of mountain rocks and stars above, the kid then witnesses the running battle between Elias and the gang. This "collision of armies," to the kid, who has indeed been willingly "cut off" from the gang, is now "remote and silent on the plain below." The horses below him now "little" and "dark," and the men "distant" (*BM* 211–213), the kid has climbed to the perspective of a disinterested observer.

As is usually the case when a literature takes place on a setting of higher ground, the struggles of mortal men assume a new order of importance; against the grander conflicts of order and chance in the universe, they cannot matter so much.[32] No coldforger of the judge can find the dawn beyond this moment, "mute and ordered and senseless until the warring horsemen were gone in the sudden rush of dark that fell over the desert. All that land lay cold and blue and *without definition* and the sun shone solely on the high rocks where he stood" (*BM* 213, my emphasis). This landscape lies under the high meridian between the natural universe and the artificial struggles of human beings to be more, or less, moral. It is notable that the battle witnessed from so far away by the kid is for the first time a battle with the gang fought by a governmental authority that now regards them as lawless murderers. Indeed,

as the kid later discovers when he picks up their trail in the desert, the gang
have attempted to hide the bloody specie of their trade, "the scalps taken on
the Nacozari [. . .] burned unredeemed" (*BM* 216).

The descriptive nomenclature now stretches into the wild images and
wilder language of a starved man on a vision quest.[33] The narrative bolsters a
reading of the kid's decisions as caught in the meridian between animal and
human modes of action, when the kid himself confuses wolves with men. He
sees a fire, and in front of that fire, he expects to see men. He lies down to
better catch their shadows—as if these would reveal the true nature of what
casts shadows—"but he saw nothing move. When he went on again the fire
seemed to recede before him. A troop of figures passed between him and the
light. Then again. Wolves, perhaps. He went on" (*BM* 215).

This brief scene, of the kid lying on his stomach and watching wolves,
not only echoes Plato's cave allegory, but also foreshadows the early scene in
The Crossing, when Billy Parham sneaks out of his house at night to watch
wolves. Parham does this on all fours, as if to imagine himself one of them.
Here the fire turns out not to be manmade, but "a lone tree burning on the
desert." Struck by lightning, the tree is called "heraldic." The next sentence
deepens this suggestion that some slow transformation in the kid is at work.

> The solitary pilgrim drawn up before it had traveled far to be here and
> he knelt in the hot sand and held his numbed hands out while all about
> in that circle attended companies of lesser auxiliaries routed forth into
> the inordinate day, small owls that crouched silently and stood from foot
> to foot and tarantulas and solpugas and vinegarroons and the vicious
> mygale spiders and beaded lizards with mouths black as a chowdog's,
> deadly to man [. . .] (*BM* 215)

Etcetera. This is McCarthy in his most tendentiously mystical mode, trying
the reader's patience with a bestiary not only of beasts but also of words truf-
fled up from the roots of older dictionaries, and venturing into a quagmire
of implicit metaphysical meanderings. We might dub such nodding as LSD
McCarthy.

At the end of such passages, there is always the suggestion that we have
arrived somewhere heretofore unseen. Is this an example of McCarthy falling
into what Blackmur calls "the putative mode in which, lofty as it was, Melville
himself could not long deeply believe" (131)? In the long sentence partially
quoted above, we become situated, with the kid, among a large group of the
lesser, stranger, and more dangerous accidents of evolution, until this: "like
seemly gods, silent and the same, in Jeda, in Babylon." Then these various

creatures—all of them predators—assemble into a *"constellation* of ignited eyes that edged the ring of light all bound in a precarious truce before this torch whose brightness had set back the stars in their sockets" (*BM* 215, my emphasis).

What truce does this tree *herald?* The coming coinage of killers in league with one another, of simple animal predation evolving to the next step: common enterprise for longer-term goals. By not preying on each other, however, predators create the next step of evolutionary complexity: they forego immediate gains for their own genetic perpetuity for the sake of enterprises with more symbolic reward—the reward of a game. Eventually, in human form, such killers trade coins for the sex and food that would otherwise be their immediate gains in predation. This burning tree heralds to these most primitive killers the coming of the coinage, the symbolism, the deferred reward that leads the Glanton gang to bother with contracts at all. McCarthy modeled his Glanton on the historical Glanton, whose fiancée, and thus his chance at civilized life, was stolen and killed. Yet rather than become a raging maniac, the historical Glanton took up a murderous form of animal and symbolic revenge: the taking and selling of scalps.

The kid's solitary trek in the high country reveals the tensions within him, already, between order and chaos, between killing with the reptilian hindbrain, and killing with the cerebral cortex. Drawn away from the gang by a series of ambivalent moral tests, the kid returns to them changed.[34]

What happens next remarkably suggests the first novel of the trilogy to follow: the kid tames a horse. After he finds a loose packhorse, we watch a foreshadowing of the idealistic scenes between John Grady Cole and the wild mustangs in *All the Pretty Horses.*

> [The kid] spoke to it. He could hear its deep pulmonary breathing out there and he could hear it move and when it came back he could smell it. He followed it about for the better part of an hour, talking to it, whistling, holding out his hands. When he got near enough to touch it at last he took hold of it by the mane and it went trotting as before and he ran alongside and clung to it and finally wrapped his legs about one foreleg and brought it to the ground in a heap. (*BM* 217)

The rhythm here is not new to *Blood Meridian,* but the words are: they are words of relation, of attempted communication across the gap between humans and animals. For the first time, we see the suggestion of a sublimated sexual impulse arising in the domestication of an animal; this becomes a regular theme in *All the Pretty Horses.*

This particular horse has already been trained, of course, but only to carry dead loads. After the kid's fasting trek, and that claim that the sun touched only him on the promontory, we are at the dawn of a new world. The dark conference of predators around the heraldic tree is now followed by an image of the first cooperation between man and horse. And it is this dream of primeval identification that powers John Grady Cole's dreams—those dreams that keep him going in a world whose cultural codes are too complex for him. In this sense, we may imagine another meridian: one of the blood of the horse's great "pulmonary breathing out there" brought across the space of wilderness into the trust, then the command, of a man.

After these scenes of the kid in new relationships with a universe perhaps beyond even the judge's control, he is all the more suspect in the eyes of the Glanton gang: "They looked bad. They were used up and bloody and black about the eyes [. . .] Glanton's eyes in their dark sockets were burning centroids of murder and he and his haggard riders stared balefully at the kid as if he were no part of them for all they were so like in wretchedness of circumstance" (*BM* 218). They resent having had to fight without his help.

The judge knows there is more to resent. The kid has been off on an errand of more import than he could himself realize: away from the judge, he has climbed through a shaky recapitulation of evolved human morality. The kid has thus taken a more active step that recalls Suttree's dream of the ideal city, where ontogeny recapitulates phylogeny. But even as this reconstitution of morality is too weak in the kid to bolster him beyond mere survival for another hundred pages, it nonetheless constitutes a refusal of the judge's worldview.

The difference between Toadvine's early verbal objections and the kid's sojourn is still that between words and actions: the kid has not yet aimed a gun at the judge's head. As is often noted of the book, the narrator seldom describes the kid during a group attack. For all the shocking viciousness of the kid's individual battles, we do not see him shoot women and children, or scalp anyone. Though we see him quick to violence early in the book, as soon as he joins the gang, he disappears into its attacks. We can reasonably infer, however, that the kid is complicit in the violence and more likely active in it. We can therefore depend on the judge to tell the truth when he describes the kid's ambivalence about, and perhaps half-hearted participation in, the gang's killing.

THE CONFESSION AND THE JAKES

Toward the end of *Blood Meridian*, judge Holden, the demonic figure that haunts the book's protagonist, visits "the kid" in jail. The Glanton gang has been dispersed, their leader's head split open and most of his scalp hunting followers slain by Yuma Indians or hanged by California law. The kid is picked up not long after the Yuma massacre—and the judge—has cut down most of the gang. Like Ballard, and Suttree, the kid has ranged freely without a home. His participation in violence has deranged him because this violence (against all constraints of space and time) coincided in the kid with some minute sense of decency connecting him, however tenuously, to civilized values.

We see some proof of this connection late in the book, after the kid's release from prison. He wanders for twelve years, gradually moving from occasional violence to marginal employment. At age twenty-eight, he is for the first time called by the narrator "the man," instead of "the kid" (*BM* 314). Until that moment, the pages of this wandering give repeated attention to the discrepancy between his chronological age (though unstated until page 314) and his experiential age. During this wandering, the narrator simply calls him "he," and then finally "the man," just after our protagonist witnesses a carnivalesque band of religious pilgrims crossing the wilderness. This change in the narrator's designation of the kid as a man increases the importance of the following scene.

The next day, he finds the band of pilgrims massacred: their bloody self-scourging and ritual reenactment of the passion of Christ have been exceeded in violence that is no longer symbolic, in real murder and mutilation. In a scene that suggests the most compassion we can find in McCarthy's protagonist, "the kid" (as he is called again, one last time) thinks he has found a survivor. He stoops to speak to "an old woman kneeling in a faded rebozo with her eyes cast down" (*BM* 315).

To heighten the mythic quality of the scene, the narration even places her "alone and upright in a small niche in the rocks" and she wears a "shawl" made of "the fabric and figures of stars and quartermoons and other insignia of provenance unknown to him" (*BM* 315). Indeed, such figures occur repeatedly in the descriptions of the heavens above *Blood Meridian* and in the speeches of the judge, where they always stand for some order in the universe, and even for predetermination of the actions of men. The judge has much to say on the inability of men to access that information, that knowledge in the stars and the moon. Indeed, the narrator here tells us that these "insignia of provenance" are "unknown to" the protagonist. In the figure of this woman, he has cause to believe that he has at last found a potential connection to that knowledge.

He as much as confesses to her, pitying and excusing himself, but finally making an argument that in his suffering he recognizes both her danger and the sacrifice of what he takes to be that of her companions. The scene occurs in sight of these massacred pilgrims, including "the hooded alter-christ [. . .] cut down and disemboweled" beside a knocked-over cross.

> He told her that he was an American and that he was a long way from the country of his birth *and that he had no family* and that he had traveled much and seen many things and had been at war and endured hardships. He told her that he would convey her to a safe place, some party of her countrypeople who would welcome her and that she should join them for he could not leave her in this place or she would surely die. (*BM* 315, my emphasis)

The scene, with its attempted connection between an orphaned American expatriate and a wise old native of a land that is foreign to him, foreshadows many lesser scenes with Billy Parham in *The Crossing*. The connection also reminds the reader of the homeless condition of the confessor: he is "a long way from the country of his birth," and clearly, "a safe place" is somewhere else. Even the identity of those "who would welcome" the old woman depends on place: they are "her *country*people" (my emphasis).

This confession, however, reaches only the air. In a rare scene of physical contact without violence, we seem him touch the old woman's arm. "She moved slightly, her whole body, light and rigid. She weighed nothing. She was just a dried shell and she had been dead in that place for years" (*BM* 315). This figure of mystical knowledge, then, was not a member of the tribe of penitent Christians at all. Or if she ever was Christian or penitent, her membership is now distant in time and place. It is too late for the kid—or man—to make this confession, let alone to offer some kindness to an old woman in need, as he has already taken part in too much killing of innocents. In this way, the scene stands as a bookend to that of the judge visiting the kid in prison: on both ends of a moral continuum, the kid is judged and found wanting. On one end, the kid stands in a wilderness attempting and failing at confession; on the other end, he sits in the constrained space of a jail cell, accused of wavering in his role as the judge's disciple.

The kid's position relative to this old woman in the mountains is further analogous to that between Glanton and an old woman killed years earlier. Looking for Indians to scalp, Glanton's Delaware Indian scouts and "the outrider Webster" find an "old crone, half naked [. . .] under the shawl she wore" (*BM* 97). Webster tells Glanton that she cannot walk, explaining her presence in an abandoned camp. Like the woman the kid finds years later in the niche, this "old crone" also hears nothing, yet she "bites" instead of speaking (*BM* 98). She is also alive to look up at Glanton. "Neither courage nor heartsink in [her] old eyes. He pointed with his left hand and she turned to follow his hand with her gaze and he put the pistol to her head and fired" (*BM* 98).

In a scant gesture of mercy, Glanton distracts the old woman's attention before he kills her; still, he kills her. Before we realize he will have her scalp, he kills her as he would a lame horse. After this gunshot, even McCarthy's otherwise distant narrator yields to some pity: "The explosion filled all that *sad* little park. Some of the horses shied and stepped" (*BM* 98, my emphasis). Meanwhile, the physical consequences of this violence are graphically given. "A fistsized hole erupted out of the far side of the woman's head in a great vomit of gore and she pitched over and lay slain in her blood without remedy." Glanton, ever the businessman about murder, tends to his gun and orders one of his men to "[g]et that receipt for us" (*BM* 98). The slim possibility that this was an act of euthanasia evaporates in gun smoke, as a man steps up to scalp the old woman. Her crime seems to have been that she was in the wrong place at the wrong time.

The kid, however, lacks a replacement for the judge's powers of dance, of rhetoric, and physical power because these originate in the power of the judge's philosophy. Indeed, the novel brilliantly turns high curves of rhetoric where it nearly falls off into absurdity, as we see hints of the kid's sorry lack of vocabulary and rhetorical power; he can hardly even follow the judge's metaphors and allusions. In this sense, we might take him for a stooge, if it were not arguable that in McCarthy, the unknown heart and soul of a character are assumed to exist in powers unevidenced by mere verbal prowess.[35]

McCarthy instead shows us the kid's failure sexually. The kid's inability to perform with the prostitute ("You need to get down there and get you a drink, she said. You'll be all right" *BM* 332) makes it clear that in place of the judge's dance, the kid has no alternative procreative power. In this sense, he is still "the kid" in relation to the judge as father.[36]

This sexual failure signals his reversion from procreation to death in an outhouse. Indeed, as Lester Ballard's ultimate failure comes in ambivalent imagery that conflates the generative womb of his cave with the bowels of mother earth, the kid's failure sends him to the jakes, an outhouse. Having failed both in joining the father willingly and in rejecting him actively (through killing him), the kid must be devoured by him.[37] The judge thus rapes, murders, and quite possibly consumes part of him. Given the shocked reaction of the unnamed man who next opens the jakes door (in a tough town), there may indeed be no more left of the kid than what we last saw of Kenneth Rattner and Lester Ballard—what you could scoop into a bag.

This end for the kid, being taken by his spiritual father, further echoes Boehme's claim that death swallows sorrow, and that "death and dying are the very life of the darkness" (*BM* i). When the kid opens the door to the jakes, he meets his end in several ways: "The judge was seated upon the closet. He was naked and he rose up smiling and gathered him in his arms against his immense and terrible flesh and shot the wooden barlatch home behind him" (*BM* 333). The strong suggestions of a violent assault melding anal rape, murder, and cannibalism are unavoidable.[38]

In *Blood Meridian*, McCarthy reached back a century, to incidents of such horrific violence that there can be no rational explanation for them. But what if the explanation lies beyond rationality? At the end of *Suttree*, we still have no means of accommodating the worldview of the father, and his actions seem linked to much of the suffering of the main character's friends and acquaintances. An imaginative act might momentarily reconcile the son's love of the father with his shame at the father's relatively much less serious crimes. What kind of imaginative act could accomplish this? Elevate the minor crimes of an attorney by focusing on his fundamental moral failure and translating that to the most sweeping moral outrages, in scope and in time, in American history. To treat people as inconsequential in the movement of a larger history—this can be said of both the TVA projects and the scalp hunting, buffalo hunting, and fence building that followed the Mexican-American and Civil wars.

But how could one possibly elevate the bloody history of those last endeavors? *Blood Meridian* elevates war to its most mythic power by reaching back to that time before gadgetry took the individual heroism out of skillful killing, before it became less the work of berserkers and more the work of machines. War at that point in history retained its game-like qualities. (The judge's duel analogy, along with its courtroom tropes, would seem immediately ridiculous when applied to the realities of much modern combat—even if other McCarthy arguments about violence, such as those pitting chance and free will, would not.) Still conducted at close range, one victim or combatant at a time, the gang's warring realizes their part in the age-old human game of killing one another for, often, nothing. War cannot be the aberration; it is the rule because it most fully employs the only quintessential human ability. "Men are born for games. Nothing else" (*BM* 249).

This might be Krishna talking, as much as the judge. If, as both tell us, the ordered universe we see out there is an illusion, and the reality is a dumbshow, a game, then one joins battle as heartily as one joins all things in human life—to play out our parts in full. Of the judge, we are told, "He never sleeps. He says that he will never die" (*BM* 335). If it is not madness to fully accommodate, if only for a moment, the judge's arguments (at least in order to see these as an extension of Suttree Sr.'s, and thus of McCarthy Sr.'s), then we must not make the mistake of allowing this singular character to fool us into thinking that he is, indeed, necessarily unlike other men.[39] In *The Bhagavad Gita*, Krishna tells Arjuna this of all men:

> If any man thinks he slays, and if another thinks he is slain, neither knows the ways of truth. The Eternal in man cannot kill: the Eternal in man cannot die.
>
> He is never born, and he never dies. He is in Eternity: he is for evermore. Never-born and eternal, beyond times gone or to come, he does not die when the body dies. (50)

Krishna's argument relies on the conceit that Christianity shares with Hinduism on a deep level: that this world is unreal. Regular tropes of gaming occur more often in Eastern religious thought; these run throughout *Blood Meridian*. Moral law, according to the judge, forgets the larger game in which war is merely another, albeit crucial, game. Indeed, it rigs the games of life for those unsuited to play fully, to play whether they will win or lose, live or die. In a fair game, the strong win, the weak lose (and, we should add, the lucky win and the unlucky lose). Moral law—according to the judge—spoils the game (*BM* 250).

The judge's rhetoric on war avails itself of the dynamics of the mentor and student, the erastes and eromenos (both are always male in the West, as the tropes around this dynamic arose from a homophilic culture). Judge Holden tells us that war "endures because young men love it and old men love it in them" (*BM* 249). If this is more generational than necessarily familial, it nonetheless employs the homoerotic imagery that will return in the kid's death in the jakes. It also echoes, yet reverses, the homoerotic epistemology of Plato's *Phaedrus*.[40] Unlike Plato's young eromenos, however, who would learn knowledge from his mentor by the two of them coming close to, yet ultimately avoiding, the physical realization of love, the judge's charge should learn by action. (In this sense, the informative text is again *The Bhagavad Gita*.) If the lesson is not taken up, the judge will teach it by raping and murdering his pupil. Or, if I am right in suspecting that Holden knew the kid would never take it up, he will do the same to him, by way of example to us. A sobering thought.

It is in the prison scene (when the judge cannot get his hands on the kid) that the judge most presents himself as the father of a failed son. "Let me see

you" (*BM* 306) echoes the very first lines of the novel, "See the child" (*BM* 3).
The judge's rebuke is clearest even as he reminds the kid,

> Dont you know that I'd have loved you like a son? [. . .] You came for-
> ward [. . .] to take part in a work. But you were a witness against yourself.
> You sat in judgement on your own deeds. You put your allowances before
> the judgements of history and you broke with the body of which you were
> pledged a part and poisoned it for all its enterprise. (*BM* 306-307)

The judge's rhetoric then employs another biblical allusion. "I spoke in
the desert for you *and you only* and you turned a deaf ear to me" (my emphasis).
He then proclaims his highest truth of the book in its most direct form: "If war
is not holy man is nothing but antic clay" (*BM* 307).

To the judge—and McCarthy—the gang's mandate is therefore written
far deeper than the contracts for scalps that set them about their profession.
Analogous to the coins of fate, war is stamped into human nature. McCarthy's
first interview by Richard Woodward quotes his one direct statement about violence:

> There's no such thing as life without bloodshed, [. . .] I think the notion
> that the species can be improved in some way, that everyone could live
> in harmony, is a really dangerous idea. Those who are afflicted with this
> notion are the first ones to give up their souls, their freedom. Your desire
> that it be that way will enslave you and make your life vacuous. (*BM* 31)

So says the author in interview, at least.

Whatever the strength of this conviction as an ineluctable truth, it does
not follow that McCarthy therefore celebrates slaughters. There remain in this
violent book, as I have pointed out, scenes that suggest a moral undercurrent
in this sea of a book floated by amorality and antinomian violence. There is
even a hint that the Glanton gang gives up killing and running and taking no
shelter for more than a few nights, surprisingly, because it runs out of the urge
to stay on the move. Why, otherwise, do they make the odd choice to take
over the ferry on the Colorado? That the biography of Chamberlain providing
McCarthy with a rough plot includes all this hardly matters; this is a novel and
might have turned in a thousand different directions. If, nonetheless, the gang
constitutes a primal force of violent movement through open space—as they
most certainly do throughout most of the book—what on earth are they doing
settling down?

Chapter Five
"What happens to country" in
Blood Meridian

> You wouldnt think that a man would run plumb out of country out
> here, would ye?
>
> (Toadvine, *BM* 285)

SPACE AND IDENTITY

Most of McCarthy's fifth novel describes a space devoid of law and morality, testing the reader with the severity of its violence. In the previous chapter, I explored the central problem between the judge and the kid, and therefore one of the central problems of the book: "[N]ot again in all the world's turning will there be terrains so wild and barbarous to try whether the stuff of creation may be shaped to man's will or whether his own heart is not another kind of clay" (*BM* 4–5). The answer given by Holden explains the book's violence as an answer to this: "If war is not holy man is nothing but antic clay" (*BM* 307). Holden's position, as well as the preponderance of the novel's structure and force, demands a space for unbridled war, for violence unconstrained by pity. This connects the book's psychological arc—its concern with the relative positions of a mythic son and father—with the judge's philosophy. In this chapter, I would like to add another connection between those arcs and the arc of history.[1]

One definition of the book's "meridian" might be this: the line in history before which the problem of the human heart's will was *tried* (in the sense of a mythic court, but also in Melville's sense of purification in a "Try-Works") in the fire of pure war. Beyond that line, history takes over: the possibilities of the heart are indeed become molded like clay, fired in killing, and now cracked in guilt. By "history," I mean our evolving conception of that away from the darker version referred to by Holden as "the historical absolute" (*BM* 250). I will read connections between Samuel Chamberlain's *My Confession* and *Blood Meridian*, the tension between the Glanton gang as an antinomian force and an ironically evolved group of killers headed for domesticity, the book's difficult title, and its Epilogue, all toward an appreciation of how McCarthy sketches this line in not only mythic, but also historical strokes. The Epilogue renders space into place by describing the coterminous lines of three salient events in the West: the nearly complete genocide of a people, the nearly complete extermination of an animal, and the realization (in carefully mechanical enlightenment terms) of a geographical abstraction.

McCarthy's best work cannot be reduced to the level of suasion. Along with an absence of families, nothing is so persistent in all McCarthy's books as the idea that violence is timeless. But the wistfulness and regret that color McCarthy's later novels, as well as the temptation to outright nostalgia— even as his best writing always indicates the inefficacy of that nostalgia— only heighten our sense, since *Blood Meridian*, that something has happened to country at the end of that book, and that whatever has happened is more complex than the mere loss of some better time. Widely read as an anti-nomian revel, *Blood Meridian* rather eventually describes a shift in time; though most of its story details the lawless violence of a roaming gang, the book includes the story of their inevitable constraint and defeat (with the notable exception of the judge, dancing forever). Beyond the line indicated by the book's title, something indeed happens to country: antinomian space becomes historical place. And with that shift comes the burden of memory, loss, and even sentimental longing.

That sentimentality usually remains buried in McCarthy, but it is easiest to see in two relations: one between the son and the father (and this has been usually so deeply buried, yet so acrimonious, as to seem like anything but sentiment); the other between McCarthy's heroes and their physical settings. Because the second is the most obvious, McCarthy's more widely-noted achievement is to capture that feeling for space in terms that resonate with readers beyond those caught up in mere cowboy mythology, or in narratives of male wandering that attract many young male readers. The popularity of this second relation reveals our weakness for trying to have our spaces without them turning into other people's places. We want, each of us relatively alone, to have our country as a field of movement that is nonetheless secure, our own place within unlimited possible space.

In *Blood Meridian*, the transformation of country from space to place occurs in a movement parallel to a collapse of philosophy into history. That central question about the human heart's ability to transform "the stuff of creation" cannot be fully answered in the affirmative if history is to have any say at all at the end of the experiment. And here we can include Holden's "historical absolute" beyond the forensic aspects of his oratory, especially if we see that rhetoric collapsing into deliberative persuasion of the kid. Indeed, if Holden believes his characterization of this question, it can only be answered indefinitely, and so it is that the judge has his answer in music, in dance, in eternity. Even a partial answer that yes, that heart has that power, will present itself on one level in not only the symbolic terms of myth, but also in the particular terms of history. So it is that the Epilogue demands both a mythic, and a historical, interpretation. The judge may go on dancing, but the rest of us are left to clean up the mess, mourn the dead, and tend fences.

We might also see the book's structure as beginning with twin arcs, one higher than the other, converging to a middle path. The path of the kid burns up in the judge's consumption of him, while the high point of Holden's philosophy—the dance in which he erases the distinction between its performer and its performance—arcs down to the line of history. For this reason, the Epilogue's language remains mythic, indeed even becomes more mythic than most of the novel. Simultaneously, however, the Epilogue includes references to historical details larger than those that, through Chamberlain's *My Confession*, informed McCarthy's story of the gang. The Epilogue thus becomes both a larger and a smaller story than that of the kid, the gang, and Holden.

The Epilogue insists on a mythological reading, and refers to the larger movements of history that lay behind the gang's scalping trade, but it also throws into relief the smaller, more particular, points of history. *Blood Meridian* is a larger book than one detailing even the enormous movements through space that we call Manifest Destiny. And yet the very mythic terms of its Epilogue throw into such relief the countless killings often detailed in the violence that preceded it that we are compelled, ultimately, to connect that sweep, that movement, to the particularity of individual lives—for this reader, it refers me back to Glanton's shooting of the old woman in the village square:

> The woman looked up. Neither courage nor heartsink in those old eyes. He pointed with his left hand and she turned to follow his hand with her gaze and he put the pistol to her head and fired.
>
> The explosion filled all that sad little park. Some of the horses shied and stepped. A fistsized hole erupted out of the far side of the woman's head in a great vomit of gore and she pitched over and lay slain in her blood without remedy. Glanton had already put the pistol at halfcock

and he flicked away the spent primer with his thumb and was preparing
to recharge the cylinder. McGill, he said. [. . .] Get that receipt for us.
(*BM* 98)

If by "history" we now mean to include, even to focus on, what happened to
individual people at a particular time and place, I think the Epilogue forces
us to remember both the mythic claims that open the book, and the loss of
lives that its inscriptions of space into place entailed.

Still, it must be noted that there is no one named in *Blood Meridian*
whom we or any of the characters might mourn. The preoccupation with
burial that I have discovered in all the other McCarthy books, for instance, is
entirely absent from *Blood Meridian*. This certainly does not mean the book
buries its dead. For all the shock of its killings, we are not really surprised
to see the dead in this book cast into canyons, impaled on Mesquite limbs,
hanged from trees, or simply strewn across a desert landscape—no more than
we would be surprised to see dead animals unburied in the wild. This makes
perfect sense: McCarthy is reaching back to a near past that, at least in the
troubled landscapes in which he sets his action, yet held spaces oblivious to
human attempts to make of violence and death something metaphorical, and
thus safely removed from violence and death as facts. Bones are as good as,
but no better, than stones in its twilight of wilderness, of frontier.

The book's third epigraph, a *Yuma Daily Sun* item, describes anthro-
pological evidence of scalping in what is now Ethiopia—300,000 years ago.
Nonetheless, *Blood Meridian* ends at a line in history beyond which the age-
less violence of the gang will no longer be possible on the scale at which we
find it, *where* we find it in this book.[2] Also after that line, we see the preoccupation with burial return (as it were) as McCarthy's plots return to the
twentieth century. Before that line, however, the first scalp we see taken by
the gang clarifies one of *Blood Meridian*'s central subjects in both mythic and
historical terms: the rendering of human beings into a "receipt," a symbol of
value and power belonging then to the person with the scalp. After Glanton
finishes charging that weapon, he takes "the dripping trophy from McGill
and turn[s] it in the sun the way a man might qualify the pelt of an animal
[. . .]" (*BM* 99).

How do we read this alongside what I have argued can be read as a
quarrel between a son and a father? Not easily, and yet this novel, as any
great novel, works at more than one level, and demands our focus at different
times in different ways. In many ways, the central figure of *Blood Meridian* is less the kid than Holden. When he tells the kid, "You put in your
own allowances before the judgements of history [. . .]" (*BM* 307), his

use of the word "history" is larger than mine. He means that passage of time comprehensible only at the scale of wheeling stellar bodies and his immortal dancing form. What he certainly does not acknowledge, is history as a constantly revised human attempt to agree on what happened, and why, among humans alone—let alone in the terms of a moral project.

Yet, this book also demands, as Edwin Arnold argues, a moral reading ("Naming" 44, 52, 63). Like the rest of *Blood Meridian*, then, we must read the judge, as well as even Glanton's scalping of this old woman, in simultaneously historical and ahistorical terms. I cannot agree with critics who see any mythic reading as somehow entailing a moral and political failure to acknowledge the crimes of American history, simply because I cannot see how the one reading logically prevents the other. In fact, I suggest they are connected.

That the Glanton gang actually settles down to take over a business is comically civilized of them. We might remember, from the kid's high country vision, that conference of lesser predators around the heraldic fire, and imagine them on the march, in league for a common purpose. Imagine, further, that they evolve to the point where they understand a common language (although we must imagine one of them—a four-legged Holden, as it were—much better at this than the rest), and imagine that this animal gang are then one day tempted to give up their nomadic life. Settling down to predation without hunting, imagine our band adapting the ordinary commercial transactions behind a ferry business such that a confluence of nature (the Colorado river) and culture (the doctor and his ferry, and the historical sweep of settlers from East to West) might provide our killer owls, scorpions, lizards, and snakes with home delivery. We might therefore concede some possible advantage to such a situation: if one can hunt without moving, one expends less energy.

Nature, however, often selects out the slow predator: unless you are the biggest predator around, you need to be able to move quickly when necessary. Even lions have their hyenas. The Glanton gang finds theirs. When the Glanton gang settles down in this way at the ferry, they doom themselves to collective extinction. That parade of rough civilization that should afford them an easy living will inevitably bring tougher civilization with it. But before that occurs significantly, the Yumas arrive. A wolf cannot play at being a sheep for long without suffering the fate of a sheep. So, too, the Glanton gang plays at settling down, only to become prey to another form of predator.

Before the gang steals the ferry business and, for the only part of a long novel of riding on, settle down, they necessarily civilize their appearance.

Glanton surveys the ferry and then takes some men to the Yuma camp downriver. Even the narrator calls the use the Indians have made of the clothing of white settlers "fool's regalia" (*BM* 254). One duty of a fool, however, is to mock his king by mimicking his appearance in extreme. The word "regalia" strengthens the suggestion that the chief of the Yumas is a king of a superior tribe. As Glanton mocks their appearance, however, their appearance mocks him. The transmogrification of the clothing of white civilization into what the gang would term savage use also recalls a previous conflation of identity in McCarthy's depiction of Indians.

In "Filibusters and Fundamentalists: *Blood Meridian* and the New Right," John Beck juxtaposed the book's early description of the massacre of Captain White's company, with a recollection of the Reagan era. To Beck, McCarthy's description of Indians amounts to Rambo-like xenophobia, a caricature of the racial other as having no identity beyond that of animals dressed in the garb of colonial violence. In short, Beck argues that the novel is not an ambiguous depiction of violence at all, but is instead a "fundamentalist" and "reactionary" fever dream of Reagan's America.

This reading fails to hold up against a close reading of this and other passages from the same book. Throughout *Blood Meridian*, figurations of identity defy the simplicities of ideological lenses (certainly those making the intentional fallacy in surmises on the author's politics). In fact, the Indians receive the only particularity of description in that passage, while the white invaders they kill are simply undifferentiated "men" (*BM* 53).[3] After that first massacre in the book, the careful reader would not be so dismissive of the unusual costumes of the Yumas. Like the judge, who alone among the gang "seemed to weigh them up at all" and is therefore "sober in the doing," we may see that Indians with a grotesque appropriation of the garb of Western clothing are anything but safe to sit with, but precisely because they, like their enemies, have crossed identity lines (*BM* 255). After Glanton insults the Yumas in racist English (foolishly assuming they cannot understand him), their chief simply asks them "De dónde viene?" ("Where are you from?" *BM* 255). They give no answer, and McCarthy gives us no more of this meeting, but as we see in the ensuing two chapters, the gang is no longer going anywhere.

First, Glanton becomes stuck on the idea of taking over the ferry by duping the Yumas. The idea seems to come to him when he finds out that the ferryman, a doctor with the absurdly ironic name of "Lincoln," gets a dollar from every person he takes across the Colorado river. Glanton wants the ferry as his own, and he will use the Yumas as cannon fodder to take the fortified position of the ferry crossing. He will then settle down with a steady trade of brigandage without the bother of further travel. We should remember, however, that he is thus giving up a business of killing Indians at "a hundred dollars a head" (*BM* 79), for a business of at least pretending to service settlers as they cross a river, for a "[d]ollar a head" (*BM* 253). Even with price gouging in the plan, this is a surprising change in careers.

If the change seems absurd, we might remember the earlier evidence that the trade in scalps has run out for the gang, and they have recently been pursued by an army of the very governments that originally hired them for protection against the Indians. (This is the slow, but bigger predator on their tails.) After their first series of campaigns for the city of Chihuahua, they so trouble the town with their drunken and violent celebrations that as they leave, we see scrawled all over the town, "Mejor los indios" (*BM* 171). *Better the Indians* than these brutes, is the feeling of the civilized citizens of this Mexican city. The gang is not fit for civilization, and yet civilization hired them for protection from so-called savages.

Indeed, the gang's own dress and demeanor, as well as the inclusion in the gang of various races and nationalities (even Delaware Indians), make it ridiculous to posit that they *represent* American Manifest Destiny in the form of a band of white Indian-killers. First, they are hardly all white (whatever that is). Second, they kill anyone they please, for a variety of reasons that are only provisionally connected to anything so ephemeral or quotidian as a local political agenda. Here they are, these putative representatives of American Manifest Destiny, as they first appear to the kid and Toadvine:

[And] they saw one day a pack of viciouslooking humans mounted on unshod indian ponies riding half drunk through the streets, bearded, barbarous, clad in the skins of animals stitched up with thews and armed with weapons of every description, revolvers of enormous weight and bowieknives the size of claymores and short twobarreled rifles with bores you could stick your thumbs in and the trappings of their horses fashioned out of human skin and their bridles woven up from human hair and decorated with human teeth and the riders wearing scapulars or necklaces of dried and blackened human ears and the horses rawlooking and wild in the eye and their teeth bared like feral dogs and riding also in the company a number of halfnaked savages reeling in the saddle, dangerous, filthy, brutal, the whole like a visitation from some heathen land where they and others like them fed on human flesh. (*BM* 78)

We have to be told that they are "humans," and even then, their description is folded into that of their weapons and their animals, so that the whole becomes a gang not unlike what we imagined of those animal predators around the heraldic fire.

Rather than suppose these to be the gleaming white bad guys of revisionist history, we might notice that the gang here seems to exist at the evolutionary stage of periodic change that I suggested. Turn time in a circle and these *are* the predators of the heraldic fire, only slightly evolved.

By the time they reach the ferry, however, they are no longer free to roam. They are also tempted to develop (at least in a few of their number) rude forms of decency. They exist at the ferry as at a meridian, between the last possible wide-ranging gang violence in America, and the continually violent yet state-sanctioned, or racially identifying, or ideologically driven gang violence extending beyond that meridian.

Denis Donoghue suggests that the gang is purely antinomian.[4] If so, then any law, even the law that is implicit in the verbal agreement they make with the Yumas to share the ferry after taking it, is simply their pasteboard mask. Thrust through that mask, the judge might say, and you find out the truth of violent struggle, a truth older than fictions of God, or morality, let alone the smaller fictions required of civilized life. The scene where Brown goes to San Diego for provisions has been regularly cited as a proof that the gang is purely set against any of the values—indirect, and dependant as all values are on metaphor, symbol, and deferrals of reward—of civilization.[5] Brown wants an ornate and finely-worked shotgun cut down by a farrier, an act that would erase all the cultural codes implicit in the gun's gold-plated claims to anything other than its primary purpose: killing.

Donoghue's *The Practice of Reading* provides the strongest argument for reading the entirety of *Blood Meridian* as a purely antinomian work. First, Donoghue employs Northrop Frye's generic distinctions to claim *Blood Meridian* for the romance, rather than the novel. The argument implicitly recalls Hawthorne's protests in the "Preface" to *The House of Seven Gables*, where Hawthorne makes a distinction of spatial freedom: the novel is bound, constricted, by the codes and constraints of domestic place; the romance is free to explore the open space of action without constant connection to morality or ethics or, indeed, any codes at all. In Donoghue's definition, the romance becomes freer yet than Hawthorne could have imagined: it comes closer to physics than to sociology, psychology (let alone politics), or indeed any exploration of human meaning. As Donoghue sees it:

The last thing it needs is what the novel thrives on, a settled society with a complex system of personal and social relations which the novelist negotiates as the substance and *pressure* of reality. The "historicized myth"[6] to which *Blood Meridian* refers is one in which men acquire the aura of gods or devils by sheer *force* of will and are recalled with fascination for doing so. ("Teaching *Blood Meridian*" 264, my emphasis)

The characters of such a work are not bound to reason of any kind, let alone moral considerations. Rather, their agency arises in the space of the romance, without any codes of conduct apart from that space's mute logic of chemistry and geology. The members of the Glanton gang:

are forces of nature, not of nurture; there is no common law of culture to be known, obeyed, respected. They are as innocent and as opaque as the rock. Under some dispensation each of these figures might be considered an individual, not entirely dispelled in the commonality, but here they are merely disturbances of the landscape, movements of life hardly distinguishable from the rock they may be fancied to have come from after millennia of unanswerable but pointless evolution. ("Teaching" 266)

This is persuasive on the character of the gang as a whole. And, insofar as the most important contribution that *Blood Meridian* may make is to the urge for an aesthetics unfettered by smaller concerns, it is more persuasive still. Yet there remains the final conflict in the book, which Donoghue characterizes as its "most remarkable section" ("Teaching" 269). The "last sixty pages" of this section begin with the killing of Glanton by the Yuma chief, after the gang has double-crossed the Indians and kept the ferry to themselves.

How did the book reach this crossing? The judge will later accuse the kid of having "poisoned [the entire gang] in all its enterprise" (*BM* 307). But surely, the kid has no power over Glanton's decision to stop and take over the ferry. He may poison the gang by his very presence, as we may guess (we have little evidence of it) that his ambivalence may at times have been visible to the other men. In this sense only may the judge be right; otherwise, his condemnation of the kid's failure to fully participate has more to do with his disappointment in the kid (as a father in his son) than with a real feeling that the kid doomed the gang.[7]

The "poison" charge, then, may be disingenuous. The judge (smart as he is) would know the gang was running out to the end of its line. The gang may initially be made of rock, as Donoghue has it, and move with no more than the brains of rock-think sped up to the rate of human violence. (Indeed, the numerous passages where the book describes them in an undifferentiated landscape suggest this.) Certainly, Donoghue's reading away from the quotidian concerns of a novel remains persuasive up to the Colorado crossing (if we ignore evidence of more subtle sympathies in the kid than Donoghue recognizes).

It is at this crossing, however, that the gang loses some of that stone-like quality. Instead of the book merely moving its pressure of brainless violence from the gang to the relationship between the judge and the kid, it makes a logical shift in emphasis. At that ferry, key members of the gang begin to take up a mode of existence that is more human, albeit on a notably rudimentary level.

They had already been in business, but it was an ironic business of movement against themselves. That is, if the Indians represent a force of movement against the settled citizens of the City of Chihuahua, then the gang had more in common with those Indians than it has with the Mexican citizens—"Mejor los indios" (*BM* 171). This puts these mythical figures in a position customary for cowboy characters in general: they fence themselves in, or they tame the West for the civilized life that they cannot join but which seems the inevitable destination of evolution (however pointless). Count, if you can, the dead who die at the hands of the Glanton gang, and perhaps half (if that) are Comanche or Apache raiding parties. Of the rest, many are the women and children of hunters and warriors who live on the move, caught at the moveable homes of their teepees. As many more are settled peoples, whether the "peaceful Tiguas" (*BM* 173) or the mestizo citizens of small border towns, where the gang scalps as freely as they do in Indian camps.

To use Donoghue's term, the gang is indeed a "force" or "pressure," but they are not merely a force of violence in any direction that nature would allow. If that were the case, they would avoid the negotiations, however primitive, that regularly occasion their killing (contracts for scalps, or the agreement with the Yumas). Rather, as Donoghue also points out, they are particularly directed against a form of civilization higher than themselves:

> It may appear that *Blood Meridian* is a post-Nietzschean fiction expressing what Lionel Trilling calls the "bitter line of hostility to civilization" that runs through modern literature. [. . .] Trilling claimed that "nothing is more characteristic of modern literature than its discovery and canonization of the primal, non-ethical energies." Referring to Mann's

assertion that the chief intention of modern literature is to escape from
the middle class, Trilling extended it to cover "freedom from society
itself." [. . .] [*Blood Meridian*] appears to give privilege to the primal,
nonethical energies, it virtually ignores the values of civilization and
society, and it seems to endorse Nietzsche's claim that art rather than
ethics constitutes the essential metaphysical activity of man. ("Teaching" 276–277)

Perhaps, then, the meridian of the title is that line between actions
that are pure force, and those that are "metaphysical" and yet unconstrained
by ethics, free in art. If so, the meridian of the title distinguishes between
a land of primal killing for no real reason beyond that reason that mer-
cury behaves as it does when you pour it on a rock, and another, more
advanced land*scape* of violence: one deliberately directed against civilization. It requires some mind, after all, to be mindfully against—rather than
oblivious to—mindedness.

Inside *Blood Meridian*, however, I have difficulty distinguishing between
these two types of violence. It may be that the line the meridian draws is that
between violence that is oblivious to the concerns of domesticity (whether
unconsciously or defiantly so), and a violence that is being gathered up in an
inexorable historical movement. That movement extends through the wilderness and frontier of a continent over which, in the 1840's and 1850's especially, several different national and ethnic forces fought. Across the line from
that movement is *our* landscape, so constrained by fences, highways, and now
fiber-optic cables, that even the most solitary and chaotic antinomians have a
shorter career of violence than does the Glanton gang.[8] These constraints of
The Border Trilogy may be largely absent from the bulk of *Blood Meridian*. At
the ferry, however, we begin to see those constraints on the horizon.

DEFINITIONS OF COUNTRY

After seemingly innumerable massacres, almost constantly on the move, the
violent nomadic horsemen of the Glanton Gang are indeed run to ground.
Having avoided settling down but tracked by the forces of the very governments that once hired them, they uncharacteristically take over a fort, only
to suffer a quick massacre by Yuma Indians. Those gang members that survive end up on the run, with less room to run in. It is then that a member
of the gang named Toadvine is asked where he might go, and he complains,
"You wouldnt think that a man would run plumb out of country out here,
would ye?" (*BM* 285).

A similar complaint ends McCarthy's *All the Pretty Horses.* A hundred years after the Glanton Gang runs amok, John Grady Cole returns from his own violent trip to Mexico. Though his errands are remarkably less bloody and primitive than those of the previous book, they depend no less on his assumption of an open country. Like Toadvine and the kid he might be speaking for, John Grady depends on a sense of country as possibility. When his friend Lacey Rawlins suggests that, having come back with his dreams turned into nightmares, he might stay with him in Texas and get a job on an oilrig, his reaction indicates the persistence of the myth of Western space. With that hundred years passed since the Gang's fenceless homicidal wandering, John Grady is no less possessed of that horse culture sense of limitless space in which to roam, even as he is puzzled by the limits he keeps seeing in it. His friend argues, "This is still good country." John Grady replies, "Yeah. I know it is. But it aint my country." Asked, "Where is your country?" John Grady can only reply, "I dont know [. . .] I dont know where it is. I dont know what happens to country" (*ATPH* 299).

What do Toadvine and John Grady mean by "country?" One definition particularly suits McCarthy's characters: "[a] region, territory, or large tract of land distinguishable by features of topography, biology, or culture."[9] This order is evident in these novels, though the last feature is initially marginal, at best: as Holden would have it, culture exists only as a flim flam, biology manifested in blood. To Holden, the more salient aspect of the country is a sense of space before it is rendered into "place"—before it can circumscribe what the heart might "try." It is therefore necessary that McCarthy's frequent and now famous descriptions of the country they cross indicate something apart from human comprehension, let alone human control. *Blood Meridian*'s gang traverses a mute cinder of a planet, something we hardly have language for. Even the mere "topo" in the above definition reflects our need to make spaces into places. As we see in the Epilogue, the enigmatic ending of *Blood Meridian* concerns itself with just this activity in the country.

Comparing another repetition between these fifth and sixth novels, we add to our sense of "what happens to country." Traveling across the desert in *Blood Meridian*, the kid finds human babies "hung [by Indians] from the broken stobs of a mesquite" tree (*BM* 57). A hundred years later, John Grady rides across what could be the same territory and finds birds, impaled by the wind on the thorns of "roadside cholla" (*ATPH* 73). From babies to birds: the violence is still there, but stepped down several levels. We may continue to theorize "frontera," and indeed see the continuing flux of claims and mix of cultures across the American West and Mexican North. But even given the horrors of the contemporary drug trade, and people dying of dehydration while crossing into El Norte, the contests are not so bloody there now as they had been. Country, then, means the same thing across these novels in terms of potential space rendered into limiting places. Yet, the scope of violent freedom in that country—in both "countries"—has narrowed.

So, what has happened to effect this change? John Wegner points to war; the meanderings of McCarthy's characters back and forth across the border between the United States and Mexico reveal a serious lack of historical knowledge on the part of those gringos.[10] The sheer military force of "our" country—as a nation-state—effected much change in the more general country of McCarthy's characters. (In his weaker moments, McCarthy gives us Mexican lecturers on this throughout *The Border Trilogy*.) Oddly enough, I will argue that the gang also seems strangely drawn to settle down, and that this moves them (as much as Ballard to his cave) to try on the perverted domesticity of the ferry crossing. The book's title, too, circumscribes its own space. And finally, *Blood Meridian*'s enigmatic Epilogue will deepen our understanding of "what happens to country" to include a larger plan that constrains space and the freedom of those antinomians who would continually move through it.

When the gang reaches the Colorado River, they encounter a natural boundary that has also become a line of historical demarcation. Frederick Jackson Turner's paper on "The Significance of the Frontier in American History" claims that "natural boundary lines"—of rivers, climate shifts and shifts in flora, and significant geographic formations (such as mountain ranges)—created "successive frontiers" across the American West.[11] The gang has roamed freely across the area of "arid lands, approximately the ninety-ninth meridian" and far to the West (Turner 9). They have freely crossed the then-disputed Mexican-American border at Texas (where the Rio Grande river is in most places relatively easy to swim or wade), and they have largely ignored Mexico's Northern border, which was even more disputed at that time and was about to be redrawn farther South.

Rick Wallach points to the ninety-eighth meridian, instead of Turner's ninety-ninth, in his claim that the meridian of the title is very likely the one near Nacogdoches, Texas, where the kid first meets judge Holden (*Sacred Violence* "Précis"). More likely (and as Wallach implies by the word "perhaps"), a definitive correspondence between a particular line of longitude and the meridian of the title cannot be made. At best, we may imagine the "blood" of the title to indicate a generally *latitudinal* movement westward, following both the sun (whose latitudinal meridian shifts with the seasons) and the general direction of the gang. If that, however, we must concede that such a claim of correspondence between the poetic line of the title and any abstract geopolitical demarcations of longitude or latitude is a misleading "string in a maze" (to coin a phrase from the judge): we imagine such a correspondence because it imposes a false but comforting order on the universe.

McCarthy's title draws attention to lines of demarcation that have more to do with human conceptions of, and agreements on, land and landscape, than with Turner's "natural boundaries." For now, it may be said that the gang has also ignored such distinctions as international borders. Nonetheless, the space in which the historical Glanton gang "rode on"[12] was becoming cut up into spatial abstractions: spaces cut up to become future places. The political necessity to determine a border between Mexico and the United States after the war in 1848 merely continued an American national urge to divide the lands of its frontier into separate townships, ranges, and lots according to principals based on meridian and base lines.

In this usage, a line of meridian only runs North and South, perpendicular to base lines running east and West. At this writing, I live less than two miles from a street called "Baseline" that indeed runs from the nearby Flatirons (the first foothills of the Rocky Mountain Front Range), all the way through Eastern Colorado (with only a few relatively small breaks), to become the North / South boundary between the states of Kansas and Nebraska. Such a line of demarcation (in this case a rather long street) is evidence of the historical pressure to control America's wilderness by plotting it out into abstract divisions of space. Not long after the American Revolution, "Congressman David Howell of Rhode Island complained that America's new western territories were 'the most complicated and embarrassing Subject before Congress since peace has taken place'" (Continental Congress & Constitutional Convention Broadsides). The remedy for this embarrassment (for politicians in the East) was to control the land of those "territories" with ink, well before applying gunpowder.

Beginning with the Land Ordinance of 1785, the early United States sought to control its Western frontier before its citizens ever officially settled on it. The need for public schools was also considered reason enough to divide all lands beyond the Alleghenies into parcels of thirty-six square mile ranges and six-square mile townships, with a one-square mile portion of every township allotted for a public school. This system begins with an arbitrary line (at about the 84th meridian) designated the 1st principal meridian. With a "base line" declared at the 40th Parallel (indeed, the one described above), additional base lines could then be drawn at multiples of six-mile strips (Indiana Historical Bureau; *Encyclopedia Britannica* "Land Description").[13]

What this meant for the historical Glanton gang is that an irresistible force was drawing down on them. Indeed, their contract to collect scalps for Sonoran municipalities was occasioned by the United States failure to "suppress" Indian incursions into Mexico (a requirement of the Treaty of Hidalgo) from across the new border ("Gadsden Purchase"). After their running battle with Elias, the gang could expect only less room to roam. As the United States settlement filled in those six-mile square spaces on the map, Northern Mexico (still the national space where the ferry crossing existed) was likewise becoming less tolerant of wilderness lawlessness. Of course, the area around the confluence of the Colorado and Yuma Rivers was hardly settled in the spring of 1850, when the gang takes over the ferry. Yet McCarthy's title hangs over their heads: false constructions of order such as meridians for settlement and development draw real blood. Indeed, McCarthy's Epilogue suggests that what inevitably follows the gang's traverse along a meridian of blood is a physical inscription of such lines on what was once open space.

In addition to the pressure of cultural demarcations on the landscape, the gang does have some geography with which to contend. McCarthy does not have his gang go to the Grand Canyon, yet the gang that Samuel Chamberlain rode with did reach this nearly impassable void. The real John Joel Glanton, in search of the El Dorado in which he and many men still believed, led the gang down a draw to the Grand Canyon in 1849. There, the mighty Colorado River's cut through a land raised thousands of feet above the surrounding country presented them with dangers from below and above. The gang complained about one of these on the way: traveling down a canyon, they would drown if there were a flash flood. Chamberlain, on arriving at the Canyon, imagines himself to be the first white man ever to see it from that vantage point (284). In any case, Chamberlain's view of the Canyon cuts off his Glanton gang's progress, and prevents them from realizing their leader's plan to travel down the Colorado River.

Both judge Holdens, in the novel and in Chamberlain's account, increase their discourses on geology at this point in the gang's travels. The historical Holden tells Chamberlain that he knows Glanton is headed for a dead end but that he does not care: he will get to see the Canyon. In the novel, recording nature so as to imprint his stamp over it (often to efface the thing seen and described) is of the utmost importance to the judge. According to Chamberlain, the real Glanton thinks he can get to the Pima village on the Gila River by taking this route (283).

Meanwhile, that real Glanton was looking for a literal El Dorado, the fabled city of gold. "To find this great city, to sack and plunder it, appeared to the crazed brains of Glanton a matter of easy accomplishment. All believed in the legend, and all swore to follow Glanton to the death" (Chamberlain 274). Twice more Chamberlain refers to this city of gold. First, Glanton thinks he sees its towers in the distance. "We sat in silence gazing on this realization of our hopes, when the mocking laughter of Judge Holden broke the spell. 'So, Glanton, this is El Dorado, is it? The city of gold and fair women! I wish you joy of discovery—a city of sandstone built by dame nature!'" (Chamberlain 275). Holden's amusement here is interesting, as he sees Glanton's mistake as one of taking nature for culture.

The second time Glanton declares El Dorado in sight, he is metaphorically right: it is the ferry across the Colorado. As Chamberlain describes the scene, Glanton "told us that this ferry was our 'El Dorado, our gold mine,' *the gate to California*, and he proposed to seize it, kill the Indians if they objected, capture the young girls for wives &c." (288, my emphasis).

The image of a gate here is interesting. As Turner admitted later, his frontier thesis, with its steady march Westward, was complicated by the California Gold Rush: he deemed the frontier line in the middle of his century to be the Missouri River "(omitting the California movement)" (9). This is a remarkable omission. By mid-century non-Indian and non-Mexican settlement in the arid parts of the West was still relatively sparse. That "California movement," however, in the rush for gold and a longer steady stream of emigration changed the pattern. Both Chamberlain and McCarthy note that the gang's numbers dwindle as men leave for the gold mines. The Southern "gate" to this was the ferry on the Colorado. Beyond it lay "one hundred and thirty miles, according to the Indians" of nothing but sand, with "no water to be found" (Chamberlain 287).

However freely the gang has roamed, even they could not survive an extended period of brigandage in such a place. Remaining at the ferry means trading the uncertainty of life in this remaining open space, with all its hostility, for an "El Dorado" of crime in the guise of legitimate business.

In both books, Glanton, an Ahab of the desert, is set for a settlement. It is remarkable that in McCarthy's story, too, the man sets out for a fabled gold city. Rather than looking for people to rob (of money or scalps), wherever they may be found, McCarthy's Glanton is for the first time looking for loot in a settled location.

THE GANG DOMESTICATED

What follows the taking of the ferry is the shortest chapter in the book, most of which concerns the attempted social work on James Robert Bell, the "idiot" (*BM* 233), by Sarah Borginnis (*BM* 256–258). This woman, the only named woman in the entire work, is given a grand article, "*The* Borginnis" (*BM* 258, my emphasis), as she sets about the notable work of cleaning up this man who has never risen above an animal condition. Here McCarthy is again drawing on Chamberlain, as the spelling of her name matches only Chamberlain's version of the many spellings for a woman known at the time as "The Great Western." The historical person was impressive enough, in an amusing number of ways, that she merits many accounts. "Sarah's nickname derived from her size, comparing her to the largest steamboat built to that day, the Great Western. It is said she stood six feet tall" (Sepich 51). McCarthy avoids the nickname, yet he observes the accounts of her size in all references to her. As John Sepich notes, McCarthy also "does not present" the "wanton side of Sarah" that is strongly suggested in historical accounts (53).

Instead, the novel uses her in an interesting way: she makes the only genuine gesture of domestication in the book. By attempting to treat a severely mentally handicapped man like a healthy human being, she silently insists that the lowest of men is nonetheless a man, deserving of humane treatment and capable—or so goes the plan—of civilized behavior. The plan to civilize James Robert fails, however. In a parody of Huck Finn escaping from Aunt Sally, he wriggles out of the clothes put on him by this Great Western woman and her female assistants. He returns to the water where they bathe him and, unable to distinguish between his reflection and himself, (a parody of Lacan), he falls in to drown (*BM* 256–258). Again, McCarthy presents a man as having barely crawled across some evolutionary meridian between animals and humans.

In an ironic alternative domesticating act, judge Holden rescues the man, slapping him as if he were a newborn but birthed into a lower evolutionary station (*BM* 259). Later in the novel, the judge walks in slow pursuit of Tobin and the kid with "the idiot before him on a leather lead" (*BM* 297). James Robert is thus led back over the border of his animality. The judge's odd domestication of a man more animal than human also serves as evidence against the kid's rebellion toward moral possibilities. It provides another bizarre image of civilized life, even though The Borginnis's attempt to clean up James Robert has failed. This man on a leather leash is a pet—what else? Glanton has his dog, and now the judge has his man at heel.

Glanton, for that matter, has consciously renounced some part of his humanity in order to exist in defiance of moral law—a slightly different thing than existing in ignorance of it. In a passage of free indirect discourse, Glanton seems to recall this struggle against prior civilized feeling:

> He'd long forsworn all weighing of consequence and allowing as he
> did that men's destinies are given yet he usurped to contain within
> him all that he would ever be in the world and all that the world
> would be to him and be his charter written in the urstone itself he
> claimed agency and said so and he'd drive the remorseless sun on
> to its final endarkenment as if he'd ordered it all ages since, before
> there were paths anywhere, before there were men or suns to go upon
> them. (*BM* 243)

The parallel paths of "suns" and "men" here suggest that latitudinal
meridian I mentioned. Meanwhile, Glanton seems to have been active in
his contest with that path as something predetermined. He seems to say
as much here, with the word "forsworn." This is, of course, Ahab's position. The phrase "long forsworn" suggests that at one time, Glanton was
a different man, even a man who presumably lived with the constraints of
society in mind.

This phrase "long forsworn" also recalls McCarthy's historical source.
According to Chamberlain, John Joel Glanton had "a deep *religious* feeling and a strict moral conduct" as a young man (his emphasis). This gave
way to a life of scalping Indians only after Glanton's seventeen-year-old
fiancé was abducted by a war party of Lipans, who killed her in a running battle with the pursuing Texians (268–269).[14] The historical source
(a questionable one in some details) is germane here because an important
detail—Glanton's change in character from "strict moral conduct" to professional killing—is hinted at in McCarthy's phrase "long forsworn." By
that simple phrase, the book admits of a past moral position on the part
of the gang's leader.

When the gang builds fortifications to protect themselves from the
Yumas, they call the position "Fort Defiance" (Chamberlain 288). Presumably, this is in defiance of the social order of the settlers, subverted
when the gang steals the ferry. As the action soon proves, however, the
place name they choose is ironic. It is the social order of the Yumas that
has been defied, and the Yumas will have their revenge, in both Chamberlain's account and McCarthy's fiction.

In an interesting departure from the historical account, McCarthy
adds the social setting of a meeting and agreement with the Yumas. By
doing so, he heightens our sense of the gang dealing in the language of
social codes—even as they plan to break them. By contrast, the historical gang simply shoots the Yumas to begin with, taking their women for
"wives." In McCarthy's book, the gang returns from their meeting with

the Yumas riding "upriver among the floodstained trees talking quietly among themselves like men returning late *from a social, from a wedding or a death*" (*BM* 256, my emphasis).

Well after the massacre of the gang, the judge in his prison interview with the kid interprets the claim of the civilized community, that the kid's actions are a problem of "the country" and its lack of sufficient constraint: "They wanted to know from me if you were always crazy, said the judge. They said it was the country. The country turned them out" (*BM* 306). In this scene, the judge is making a distinction between behavior that is acceptable to civilized places and the unacceptable (or "crazy") behavior of men on the loose in the surrounding space of "country."

Now what seems crazy is the conflation of horsed killers with domestic constraints that recall the very values of civilization that they have been so violently set against. The Yuma chief actually kills John Joel Glanton in his bedroom—his "chamber"—and this formerly horsed warrior Glanton dies presumably with his boots off, in bed. No one reading the book for the first time would guess that this man will die indoors:

> When they entered Glanton's chamber he lurched upright and glared wildly about him. The small clay room he occupied was *entirely filled with a brass bed* he'd appropriated from some migrating family and he sat in it *like a debauched feudal baron* while his weapons hung in a rich array from the finials. Caballo en Pelo mounted into the actual bed with him and stood there while one of the attending tribunal handed him at his right side a common axe the hickory heft of which was carved with pagan motifs and tasseled with the feathers of predatory birds. Glanton spat.
>
> Hack away you mean red nigger, he said, and the old man raised the axe and split the head of John Joel Glanton to the thrapple. (*BM* 275, my emphasis)

Ironies abound here, especially if we fail to forget that McCarthy's Glanton had "forsworn all weighing of consequences" (*BM* 243) after the historical Glanton's bride had been taken from him. Beginning his Indian killing when his bride-to-be was taken before their wedding night, Glanton's career is ended with Caballo en Pelo joining him in bed to consummate a bloodier passage. Thus, the head of a gang of rock-like half-humans, or more philosophically noble antinomians, gets his come-uppance in a parody of his own, late, reversion to domesticity. And like the kid, he is symbolically unmanned in the act of his killing.

IN SEARCH OF THE BLOOD MERIDIAN

If the country of *Blood Meridian* turns out insanity, what constraining influence, if any, does the title of the book effect around its country, and its language? As I have argued, there are many ways in which the gang is more complex than animals, even as they are animalistic; more antinomian than amoral, even as they are often that, too; and more domesticated, if perversely so, than has previously been noted. In the governing irony concerning space in McCarthy's works, even this extreme gang of roaming criminals is drawn, crazily, toward a relatively domesticated position—and that is where their putative leader dies.

What, then, is the spatial demarcation—in deeper mythological and philosophical terms—indicated by this book's title? We may return to the image, by now notable in most of McCarthy's previous books, of the fence. This structure of demarcation will return in *The Border Trilogy*, and yet it has been largely absent from *Blood Meridian*. This book's country is yet unfenced. Rather, it is the Glanton gang, as hostile as any group could be to social order, that nonetheless carries within it an invisible fence. We read that the gang is "federated with invisible wires of vigilance" (*BM* 226). The most notable fence in the novel, however, is only hinted at, although in two ways.

First, the meridian of the title constitutes a symbolic fence. There is no important sense of the sun's meridian pointing to the literal noon of day in this novel. Frequent references to the sun's meridian as an indication of noon serve the narrative rather as a structural motif: apart from semantics, the repetition gives the reader the sense that whatever the content of the novel, its narrative is proceeding under some regulation of form. This regulation provides the sense that whatever mayhem occurs on the ground, the regular movement of heavenly bodies is assured.

In a book filled with the judge's Nietzschean subversions of any order, one wonders at the problem of perspective: the sun, of course, is not actually moving around the earth; that is only its apparent motion. We know, despite our senses, that the movement we perceive actually occurs the other way around. On a striking number of occasions, McCarthy refers to the "bloodred sun." The book's secondary title is "*The Evening Redness in the West.*" Numerous references to "blood" indicate that redness, and we may remember that our perception of a single color is in itself a trick of the perceiver's selective perception of the full spectrum of light. The second title, then, points again backwards. Rather than providing us with a reliable reference point (a meridian, the sun), against which we might measure the actions of the book, we are instead thrown back on a realization that all we can do is to perceive, and in perceiving, we see something that is not objectively true.

There simply is no such thing as a "meridian," without the presence of a perceptive entity. Locating one longitudinal position in relation to the horizontal movement of the sun (and the gang) necessarily excludes all other possible longitudinal points as constitutive of what the title claims is a singular blood meridian (not "meridians"). To the observing eye, the sun appears to be directly over only one point on the earth at any given moment, and only appears so to someone standing on exactly that point at that moment. A meridian, then, is something that depends on spatial and temporal particularity. In this spatio-temporal particularity, it is a purely subjective phenomenon. Nonetheless, given its force through repetition, each variable point, under each "meridian" so named by the book, becomes a singularity.

If we read that word in terms of physics, the metaphor gains in meanings without helping us determine any one meaning: in physics, a singularity is "[a] point in space-time at which gravitational forces cause matter to have infinite density and infinitesimal volume, and space and time to become infinitely distorted" (*American Heritage*). This is a fit metaphor for a book whose wide-open spaces ultimately lead to rape, murder, and possibly cannibalism in an outhouse, a book whose presiding judicial authority prosecutes the protagonist for not fulfilling a spiritual calling to war, and a book whose dancing survivor's mortal identity expands into the immortality of the dance.

If we read this blood meridian in historical terms, we see that the title subverts the many political readings attempted in critical responses to *Blood Meridian*. A meridian only functions from a local perspective. The idea of a meridian is silly if one appeals to a global, let alone universal, point of view. (All moral claims are by necessity attempts at a universal point of view, including the multicultural value of infinite difference, as that too is assumed to be a universal value.) Indifferent to the concerns of the relative brief moment of all human history, the sun will have its movements and the earth will obey the larger body's gravity. What, from this point of view, could the death of thousands, even millions, matter? McCarthy taunts the reader with this possibility, by collapsing the imagery of an astronomical point of reference into the liquid vital not to the universe, but only to humans and other animals: blood. This is a human meridian indeed, drawn in blood.

By juxtaposing astronomical with human scales of value and points of perception, McCarthy regularly suggests that morality, ethics, historical judgments, are human things. They are appeals to order: do this, don't do that. But as appeals to order, they claim foundational stability on unstable grounds. McCarthy is no postmodernist in at least this important sense: he does not describe a world of continually relative, atomistic flux. Rather, he consistently points out—whether in his narrator's references to the sun, to stars, the moon, and their cold indifference to human activity, or through his judge's slippery philosophical discourse—that indeed there is an order to the universe. The truth of that order is, however, inaccessible to human beings.

This does not keep us from imagining that order, however. To do so, we anthropomorphize whatever we see. We demand a human relationship in a universe that refuses such silliness. The sun is "blood" red, it lies "to the west in a holocaust" (*BM* 105), even though there is no such thing as a *whole* burning within human history; rather, there are horrible burnings that are nearly total to particular groups of people: Jews, Native Americans, Armenians. McCarthy's judge is horrible to us precisely because he reminds us that the sun moves indifferently to the relative match flares in our history, however much they burn us. The judge's stars, by contrast, burn cold.

No matter how much we insist on imagining a human relationship to an order we cannot really see, our appeals bring only silence. Nature is nonmoral. McCarthy hedges his bets that we will understand this by accompanying his astronomical descriptions with descriptions of the earth itself in nonmoral terms.

In symbolic terms, *Blood Meridian*'s title creates an interpretive problem with no solution behind the deepening ineffability of its symbol. It simply describes, in the most general terms, the spatial problem that haunts all of McCarthy's books, in language suitable for his most philosophically explicit treatment of that problem.

Second, however, another meaning emerges when we confine our questions about this title to the constitutive space of McCarthy's nine novels. Then, rather than the sun's diurnal zenith, the book's primary title seems to point to another type of meridian: a demarcation that occurs but once in history. Harold Bloom may be right about the book's transcendence of the particular history of the United States and its exercise of Manifest Destiny through the American Southwest (Josyph, "Tragic Ecstasy" 14–15). But this does not mean that the book is not importantly located in that historical condition. This meridian is therefore one that does arise out of history, but one that is then most meaningful within the intratextual movement of McCarthy's language through nine novels.

The book's primary title can suggest larger concerns while still working as a point of reference for historical reading. Such historical reading only becomes the kind of false comfort subverted by the judge if it is taken as the only way to read the book. McCarthy's depiction of identity, as I have elsewhere argued, is far too complicated for the kind of simplistic reading that sometimes passes for postcolonial critical work on American literature. Nonetheless, McCarthy borrowed significant elements of the book from a source (Chamberlain's book) that recounts, however loosely, the transgression of a line in history.

Although it is unimportant to the Glanton gang, they cross the meridian of blood between lawless killing and the legal, civilized, near-holocaust carried out not only by the United States, but also by the local Mexican governments, by creating a trade in dead human beings. The rendering of scalps into scrip accomplishes a commodification of the Native American, even as it is accomplished by a gang that is ironically a multi-cultural bunch of murderers. The gang is ironically enacting civilization. Their conduct is well termed "barbarous" (*BM* 78). Like the putatively uncivilized tribes at the borders of the Roman Empire, the Glanton gang is indeed beyond the pale of civil authority even as they enact that authority. This is one reason why the kid is shown both under the conscription of a supposedly authorized command, with Captain White's force, and in league with men who at first glance seem to be operating out of no law but the natural law of mindless predation.

The judge reminds us that the ignorance on the part of the gang as to their violent function does not alter the function itself. This book couples words with violent actions. As Holden says of Sergeant Aguilar, "Words are things. The words he is in possession of he cannot be deprived of. Their authority transcends his ignorance of their meaning" (*BM* 85). Words are not only put into the air after their deeds, in the many fireside dialogues dominated by the judge's s forensic rhetoric; they are also put down on paper, in the Chihuahua City contract to hunt scalps.

Unwittingly, the gang exists at a liminal moment in history. This is particularly true of the history of the United States in its Southwestern region, but it is also true in a larger sense. The gang pass a meridian of blood, a historical moment, beyond which the function of violence will not be allowed as wide a scope in North America as it is in their passage. Beyond their blood meridian there will be fences to slow the antinomian energy of such impulses, even when (as in the case of the younger, more innocent heroes of *The Border Trilogy*, the impulse is not sanctioned by a governmental authority). The primary title *Blood Meridian* works at the highest metaphorical level even as its components point to the most literal understanding of the novel's main action: men cross a new boundary of blood, leaving it bloodier.

THE EPILOGUE'S ANSWERS

The Epilogue is only half a page of italicized text. It begins,

> *In the dawn there is a man progressing over the plain by means of holes*
> *which he is making in the ground. He uses an implement with two han-*
> *dles and he chucks it into the hole and he enkindles the stone in the hole*
> *with his steel hole by hole striking the fire out of the rock which God has*
> *put there.* (*BM* 337)

Harold Bloom reads the fire in this mysterious Epilogue as Promethean.
Prompted by Peter Josyph to consider this action as "a process of digging
holes, of setting dynamite to build a fence: the closing in of the West,"
Bloom responds:

> No, no, no, that's a very bad interpretation. That two-handed imple-
> ment is, as I say, doing one thing and one thing only: it is striking fire
> which has been put into the rock, clearly a Promethean motif, and he
> is clearly contrasted with creatures who are either goulish [sic] human
> beings, if they *are* human beings, or already are, in fact, shades, looking
> for bones for whatever nourishment that might bring about. [. . .] I
> cannot see that as any kind of allegory of anything that has happened to
> the American West. ("Tragic Ecstasy" 14–15, italics original)

But the tool must be a post-hole digger, as McCarthy, or any
reader acquainted with manual labor must recognize. And given the dual
trajectories of the philosophical question of the heart's will (particularly
given the judge's answer to it) and the historical movement that both
informs the plot and is described by it, I see no reason not to read this
passage in both mythic, and historical, terms. What Bloom is objecting
to is the hitching of this Epilogue to a political plow; he rightfully sees
that the sharpest edges of books are sullied and dulled by such treatment.
Yet, claiming a mythic meaning for a passage does not preclude one from
simultaneously, or at least alternatively, finding a historical moment that
informs that passage—especially if the cumulative weight of that moment
only adds to the larger significance of what is represented.

The first part of Bloom's interpretation derives soundly from the phrase
"*the fire out of the rock which God has put there*" (*BM* 337). That is fine,
but a reader who has wielded a post-hole digger—which is a two-handed
implement for digging holes—for more than a few minutes could not fail to

connect this description of McCarthy's with the simple act of digging holes
for fence posts, or some other placement, such as a marker. (Sensibility, that
ultimate requirement for good close reading, does not suffer from physical
experience.) We need not choose between historical and mythical readings
of McCarthy: he works in both areas, and the links between things that have
indeed "happened to the American West" and the older stories echoing in
McCarthy's imagery simply add to the power, to the fullness and scope, of
his achievement. It is regularly McCarthy's practice to build onto history stories whose meanings reach a mythic level. Until some speeches in *The Border Trilogy* hit the reader's head against their historical foundations, however,
they usually reveal themselves in sufficiently opaque language that it would
be ridiculous to rule out mythic or other symbolic readings. We may return
to the passage, then, with an eye toward both levels of meaning.

   The historical references I will find in this passage are nothing if not
Promethean, even as their evidence adds to John Wegner's regular point that
history exerts unseen forces in McCarthy's work. The activity described in
the Epilogue refers to historical aftermath, however—to the culmination of
years of violence: especially around ten years leading up to 1883 (although
the Glanton Gang will have started much of it earlier). Because of the rapid
temporal movement in the end of the main narrative, and details in the cryp-
tic Epilogue itself, we can reasonably infer that the action of the Epilogue
itself—the movement of its figures—takes place around 1883. That would
be fifty years following the birth of the kid, and fifty before the birth of
John Grady Cole. This Epilogue, then, hangs over all McCarthy's work as
a significant historical meridian. Before it, the Glanton Gang has wandered
on horseback unconstrained by fences, across a largely pre-nomian space not
even altered enough to warrant the cultural baggage of the term "wilderness."
The Gang's massacres of peaceful Tigua Indians, as well as their assaults on
small Mexican towns, certainly gives evidence of scattered forms of civilization. Indeed, in these acts the Gang performs an antinomian function. But
Judge Holden's regular arguments, quoting Nietzsche right and left, as well as
the ease with which the Gang wanders, suggests that the Gang's movements
constitute a last hurrah in this territory for blood unstaunched by even the
most primitive codes of conduct.

   Other figures follow this man across the ground. They are "*the
wanderers in search of bones and those who do not search*"—two groups
behind the man digging holes. The first group is easily identified as
gatherers of buffalo bones. The kid's (or as the book calls him this late,
"the man's") recent encounter with "bonepickers" (*BM* 317) bolsters this
identification. Indeed, Elrod, the doppelgänger whom the kid kills just

before he finds the judge (and his death) in Fort Griffin, is among these bonepickers. These "*wanderers*" (bonepickers) constitute the first group.

The second group are either running new fence lines, or surveying the landscape. If fencing, they are working with fence posts enabled by the man digging; if surveying, they are placing some similar posts as markers. Either way, they accomplish this through the work of the first figure's hole digging. (It is unnecessary to narrow our interpretation to fencing or surveying or even both; both have their evidence and both contribute to the same implications.) As for fencing, the meridian of the American West—in the sense of its division by fencing—occurred too chronologically close to the killing off of most of the American bison not to associate the two actions. As for surveying, that can enable fencing.

In any case, this second group ("*those who do not search*") has gone altogether missing in Bloom's otherwise insightful reading. This group of men:

> *move haltingly in the light like mechanisms whose movements are monitored with escapement and pallet so that they appear restrained by a prudence or reflectiveness which has no inner reality and they cross in their progress one by one that track of holes that runs to the rim of the visible ground and which seems less the pursuit of some continuance than the verification of a principle, a validation of sequence and causality as if each round and perfect hole owed its existence to the one before it there on that prairie upon which are the bones and the gatherers of bones and those who do not gather.* (BM 337)

Could these not then be surveyors? Whether or not they are leaving behind a visible demarcation across the land is debatable, though likely. A posthole digger wrings a substantial amount of sweat from a man merely putting down markers, so a fence—something permanent to show for that labor—is more likely. As should become clear in a minute, though, such fencing may be running just apace of actual land grants and deeds; certainly it would be done according to a plan (or plat) and even something more conceptually important than the mere realization of a plat: "*the verification of a principle.*"

Beneath the mythic meridian that is indeed quite compelling—of a Promethean figure stealing God's fire—lies the bloodier meridian realized through historical operations: the gathering of the bones of exterminated Buffalo, and the reckoning of the plats first imagined in the Land Ordinance of 1785, with a man now marking off the land—whether through fencing or not, space is being turned into place.

The first appearance of barbed wire in the West led to an astonishingly rapid change, not only in ranching practices, but in conflicts between large and small ranchers, ranchers and sheep herders, and ranchers and farmers (Milner, et al, 264–265).[15] Partitioning off the land certainly could take place more easily after the elimination of animals that, in fast-moving herds of incalculable numbers and unaccustomed to being constrained in their movements, might wreck such fencing. Railroads paid for buffalo killing, and the government subsidized the killing of this animal so crucial to the lives of Plains Indians. Partitioning the land, furthermore, is crucial to anyone attempting to take it from those Indians. Some hundred years earlier, the *Eastern* "West" divided into six-square mile portions of land was no longer confined to the imaginations of Eastern politicians; ranges and townships across the greatly expanded *Western* West were quickly set up along the plans imagined in the Land Ordinance of 1785.[16]

Indeed, those *"who do not gather"* proceed behind the hole-digger *"less the pursuit of some continuance than the verification of a principle, a validation of sequence and causality as if each round and perfect hole owed its existence to the one before it"* (*BM* 337). What *"validat[es]"* this *"sequence and causality?"* The regular spacing of the holes. What *"principle"* is here *"verifi[ed]?"* That the space of the American West can indeed be transformed from the "embarrassment" referred to in one resolution by the Continental Congress, into a demarcated set of places.[17]

The setting here is simply noted as *"the plain."* That is not a desert, but more likely some place in the space of grassy plains extending from Canada all the way South toward the Texas Gulf: grass all along this area, with wells dug into the Ogallala Aquifer (which runs from North Texas to South Dakota), allowed cattlemen the food and water necessary for herds, and farmers the water necessary for crops. This was the land settled most of all by fencing, and it merely extended, albeit by hundreds of miles, the "frontier" to be planned out in the principled imagination of the Land Ordinance.

The language of the Ordinance even suggests the mechanistic metaphors of McCarthy's Epilogue, with its attention to temporal and spatial order. Here is the description in 1785 of the process by which marking off the land must attempt an accord with the theoretical division of that land by meridians and base lines:

> The lines shall be measured with a chain; shall be plainly marked by chaps on the trees and exactly described on a plat; whereon shall be noted by the surveyor, at their proper distances, all mines, salt springs, salt licks and mill seats, that shall come to his knowledge, and all water

> courses, mountains and other remarkable and permanent things, over
> and near which such lines shall pass, and also the quality of the lands.
> (Indiana Historical Bureau)

In the description of the Epilogue, there are no trees to "chap," nor any
"mountains" to interrupt the progress of these workers. This would make it
all the more likely that the work of surveyors would proceed with a delicate
reckoning between sight and imagination, between the "*principle*" and the
actual holes being dug in the ground. Whether or not the holes being dug
will be filled with fence posts, the only way to mark a landscape bereft of
trees with any reliable "lines" is to put holes in it. In the most open land, little
in the way of "remarkable and permanent" variations could "come to [the]
knowledge" of a surveyor; rather, the surveyor is freer to bring his "knowledge"—his false ordering of nature—to the ground. Would not Holden be
pleased at this?

The killing of the American bison by private hunters and those contracted by the railroads resulted in their near extinction by 1883 (Milner
152).

> If a roof had been built over the southern plains in the early 1870's,
> the American zoologist William Hornaday wrote, it would have been
> "one vast charnel-house." During the fall of 1873 the corpses, stinking
> and rotting in the sun, *lay in a line* for forty miles along the north bank
> of the Arkansas River. William Blackmore, an English traveler, counted
> sixty-seven bodies in a space not covering four acres. The bodies were
> those of bison. (White 237, my emphasis)

The year before the introduction of barbed wire, a buffalo hunter named
George Reighard killed, on average, one hundred buffalo every day of his
employment with an outfit hired for this purpose. This hunting trip took
place in the Texas panhandle, in 1872: "Asked, years later, whether he felt
pity for the animals as day after day he dropped his hundred, he replied no,
he did not. 'It was a business with me. I had my money invested in that outfit . . . I killed all that I could'" (White 237).

Recording this point of view in his chronicle of the slaughter, "Animals
and Enterprise," Richard White is understandably unable to avoid impos-
ing just the kind of retrospection of regret that McCarthy generally avoids:
"Money and pity, these are the words that mark *a great divide* in the history
of the American West. Reighard stood at a point where animals were only
dollars on a hoof; those who later asked him about pity regarded animals as

being worthy of concern within a human moral universe" (237, my emphasis). White's "divide" suggests a line has been crossed, a meridian between what we like to think of as our more subtle moral order, and a more primitive one behind us.

White also reminds us that another line existed in 1872, one less temporal than spatial, between two peoples: one people to whom animals are commodities, and another people to whom animals were nearly equals. The Plains Indians, as well as the animals they depended on, were driven to near extinction within a decade of 1872. Much of the work toward this eradication was accomplished in the American Southwest well before the remains of Northwestern Lakota Sioux were rounded up into reservations such as Pine Ridge, South Dakota—the site of the Wounded Knee massacre in late 1890. The intentional large-scale killing in the Southwest had begun almost half a century earlier, with the Glanton gang notable in the enterprise.

It would be a mistake to suggest here that McCarthy's novel is intended to evoke "pity," to use Richard White's word, over these events. Yet the realization of the imagined grid organizing the frontier, the advent of barbed wire to enclose portions of that grid, and the eradication (sometimes undifferentiated in the execution and more so in the results) of both the American bison and the American Indians, are coeval, as suggested by McCarthy's language.

Joseph Farwell Glidden patented barbed wire on October 27, 1873. By 1876—only three years after its introduction—2.84 million pounds of the stuff had been produced, but by 1880, that production had been dwarfed by 80.5 million pounds. "With barbed wire *and* the railroads, the cowboy's days were numbered" (*New Encyclopedia of the American West* 80, their emphasis). Not only to cowboys still accustomed to open range ranching, but presumably more so to anyone on horseback riding in attempted disregard for the new order being set out on the land, barbed wire became known as "the Devil's Rope" (Evan 72).

Where, then, and when, do we locate the blood meridian—this singular circumscription presiding over McCarthy's book? I have attempted to position several meridians, lines both philosophical and historical, abstract and visible, as likely referents: like suspects in a line-up, they seem to me to have had suspicious contact with one another. And I have also suggested that a chronological division operates here as well, dividing McCarthy's books, and indeed significant moments in American history.

What happens to country in *Blood Meridian*? The answer echoes in the books to follow, and in this country. Roughly fifty years between the births of the kid and John Grady, one of the blood meridians in this book divides their possibilities of flight. The kid seems at first able to roam where he pleases—until the massacre of the filibusterers. From that point on, the Glanton gang rides on and on through a free arc of antinomian violence, until the external pressures of enclosing civilized authority, the natural boundaries even of the wide open west, and their own ironically persistent human tendency toward settling down lead them to "run plumb out of country" (*BM* 285). Key coeval developments in fencing, plotting, extermination, and eventual settlement (or conquest) of the Southwest cluster around the ten years leading up to 1883. What happens to country, is that history, eventually, constrains both its violence and its freedom.

The figure of a line, a meridian, between McCarthy's fifth novel and the subsequent *Border Trilogy*, leads me to mention Cole here. As the scant domestic spaces that end the trilogy are prefigured in *Blood Meridian*, then the illusory open spaces in *The Border Trilogy* echo those of *Blood Meridian*. Keeping in mind the image of John Grady Cole introducing Billy Parham to the wrecked home site (a space that is half place, and that is losing its solidity with time) that he hopes to renovate for his beloved prostitute, we can look back to the spaces of *Blood Meridian*. Then, with the image ending *Blood Meridian* establishing a last line of demarcation, fifty years between the trilogy and its precursor, we can proceed to the spaces of *The Border Trilogy*. McCarthy closes his *Blood Meridian* at a line of division between a world without pity and a world consumed in it, yet nonetheless persistently cruel. But at the end of this book, it seems premature to end with that observation. A more proper closing is less ambitious in its false orders, more poetic, and mysterious; McCarthy's image alone: "He strikes fire in the hole and draws out his steel. Then they all move on again" (*BM* 337).

Chapter Six

From Country to Houses in
The Border Trilogy

I dont know what happens to country.
(John Grady Cole, *ATPH* 299)

We got the little house lookin good, didnt we?
(John Grady Cole, *COTP* 260)

THE HOUSE TRIMMED IN BLUE [1]

We left the two protagonists of *The Border Trilogy* standing near its tragic conclusion, outside the abandoned "old adobe" house they will renovate for John Grady and his intended, Magdalena. Another in a long line of empty houses by this, McCarthy's eighth novel, it is an empty space left by lives long departed.

> The floor was of packed clay beaten and oiled and it was strewn with debris, old clothes and foodtins and curious small cones of mud that had formed from water percolating down through the mud roof and dripping through the latillas to stand about like the work of old-world termites. In the corner stood an iron bedstead with random empty beer-cans screwed into the bare springs. On the back wall a 1928 Clay Robinson and Co. calendar showing a cowboy on nightherd under a rising moon. He passed on through the long core of light where he set the motes to dancing and went through the doorless framework into the other room. (*COTP* 145)

The young man walking between these two rooms is John Grady Cole, whose ranch home at the beginning of *The Border Trilogy* lay some four hundred miles east, near San Angelo, at the geographic heart of Texas. We may note in passing that the "curious small cones of mud" suggest a cave of Ballard's. More importantly, however, many of the details above mirror, in decrepit reflection, the one room near the beginning of *All the Pretty Horses*, in which John Grady felt at home.

It was his grandfather's office. The grandfather has died, the father had already left, and so John Grady imagines himself taking up the position of power over both the place of domesticity and the space of wilderness—extending the family line in this way. As circumstances have it, however, this sixteen-year old boy is in no power to assume that position, and so he chooses to leave the maternal homestead before his mother can complete the sale of the property.

Mrs. Cole, née Grady, has divorced from John Grady's father, a troubled veteran of World War II who survived a Japanese prisoner of war camp. It is notable that throughout the *Trilogy*, her son is never referred to as "John," but rather as "John Grady." Of course, in Texas it is common for people to be referred to by both their first and middle name, but by calling his main character "John Grady," the narrator reminds us that his mother's blood runs stronger than his father's. In a patriarchal culture, John Grady's strongest heritage is matrilineal: his mother is the exception in a long line of ranching men.

> His grandfather was the oldest of eight boys and the only one to live past the age of twenty-five. They were drowned, shot, kicked by horses. They perished in fires. They seemed to fear only dying in bed. The last two were killed in Puerto Rico in eighteen ninety-eight and in that year he married and brought his bride home to the ranch and he must have walked out and stood looking at his holdings and reflected long upon the ways of God and the laws of primogeniture. (*ATPH* 7)

The woman "brought" to the ranch, presumably from some relatively safer outpost of civilization, dies in the influenza epidemic of 1918. John Grady's grandmother, as it happens, is the older sister of the dead wife—a replacement importation of the feminine into the dominion of men. Then "the boy's mother was born and that was all the borning that there was. The Grady name was buried with that old man the day the norther blew the lawnchairs over the dead cemetery grass. The boy's name was Cole. John Grady Cole" (*ATPH* 7).

The insistence on the patronymic fails: first, by its own insistence; second by the matronymic immediately pushing it farther from his given name in "John Grady Cole;" and third, repeatedly, as the patronymic is rarely recalled in the rest of the novel. The events that set John Grady on his first adventure have everything to do with family trouble. Mrs. Cole prefers life in San Antonio; with a gap in the line of primogeniture occasioned by the divorce, the feminine presence on the ranch retreats to a relative center of culture. In a relative metropolis—compared to the open countryside of the family ranch—John Grady's divorced mother is attempting to make a new life. The family lawyer tells John Grady, "Son, not everbody thinks that life on a cattle ranch in west Texas is the second best thing to dyin and goin to heaven. She dont want to live out there, that's all" (*ATPH* 17). His mother prefers a more civilized life of places, rather than "out there" on the edge of place and space. Notably, she also wants theater.

Her choice of the stage is a choice of codes and customs divorced from immediate connection to the world. Indeed, is not civilization the choice of deferral, of symbol and sign, at a farther remove from the material world? Art, culture, the niceties of domestic comfort, are simply refinements of basic needs. One vital aspect of *The Border Trilogy* arises from its development of an already existing anxiety in McCarthy regarding civilization. How much refinement can be allowed human life without losing an honest relationship with the natural world? How much distance can be allowed human beings from their natural conditions as animals? And further, how close can a man live to other people without losing his authenticity? The stoic bets hedged on these questions led, inevitably, to the cowboy existentialism of *The Border Trilogy*. The suspicion of refinement, anthropocentrism, and social spaces that collapse all too readily into the constraints of place—through nationality, class, or even gender—preceded these putative cowboy books. It simply existed in the Southern works as stoicism without the hat and boots and horses seized on by sentimental readers.

John Grady cannot understand his mother's alternative to the hardscrabble life of his matrilineal ancestors. This anxiety is most readily apparent in *The Border Trilogy*'s descriptions of houses. As I will argue, homelessness, wandering, and the difficulties of the young men in these three novels in avoiding spatial constraint, constitute primary forces in *The Border Trilogy*. A concomitant constraint on those forces resides in the power of fences, a power that also dominates these three narratives. Fencing, of course, is given to *The Border Trilogy* by the Epilogue to *Blood Meridian*.

Blood Meridian has few houses or fences, and in such bloody pages, no time for burials. Nonetheless, spatial demarcation is its most regular metaphorical subject. Given the sheer number of dead in that work, it is fitting that *All the Pretty Horses* should begin with a burial. Furthermore, that any McCarthy novel can begin with a proper burial reinforces the sense that the larger work does move to new concerns with its move to the new landscape of the American West and Mexican North. John *Grady Cole* picks up, as it were, where John *Wesley* left off, but with this proper burial of the patriarch, and other slight improvements in his situation.

Yes, John Grady has lost his grandfather, and figuratively lost his father (as Mr. Cole's time in the prisoner of war camp seems to have left him physically and, or, psychologically emasculated). But he had both to begin with, and unlike Rattner, his father's failures are not criminal at all, but rather the combination of sheer bad luck (both torture and illness have wounded him) and a vague weakness of character evidenced by his history of gambling. The father's mere presence sets us up for the slow movement toward an embrace of family life by the end of *Cities of the Plain*. And given that this is, after all, a McCarthy novel, by comparison with those of other McCarthy protagonists, the relationship between John Grady and his father suggests something psychologically tender, even as it foreshadows the mythic power of the father figure ending *No Country for Old Men*.

Nonetheless, *All the Pretty Horses* begins with the burial of John Grady's patriarch. In the Western novels the way is thus clear for character flight extending farther than any we see in the Southern work. And after the bloody historical movements of *Blood Meridian*, the way is clearer still—if only at first—for the young North Americans of *The Border Trilogy* to light out for new territory. (That way will prove more constrained than they expect, but they do ride in a partially nostalgic remembrance of a horse culture whose violence has been conveniently forgotten, but which sufficiently subdued enough resistance to their movements that, for a time, these new teenagers can ride on, too.) And on a smaller scale, the burial of John Grady's grandfather occasions a local loss of medial space between domesticity and wilderness. In response to that loss, John Grady must either move to the confining place of San Antonio (giving up wilderness and its open spaces), or become homeless.

The rest of this chapter explores apparently contradictory forces working on characters in *The Border Trilogy*, by arguing that John Grady Cole, Billy Parham, and even Billy's brother Boyd may be understood as performing various chivalric and domestic roles.[2] Charles Bailey's view of John Grady employs the generic terms of Arthurian legend, of chivalry, in an understanding of John Grady's early heroic roles.[3] Natalka Palczynski has found other evidence of chivalric roles in the Trilogy. To this idea I would add that John

Grady, in particular, is ultimately driven by a longing for the domestic—or at least a medial version of domesticity, one that holds sway over both house and landscape.

As I noted in my introductory chapter, earlier scholarship on McCarthy has attempted to explain the problems with housing in his work. Terri Witek's "Reeds and Hides: Cormac McCarthy's Domestic Spaces" notes that "[n]early all the protagonists [. . .] flee from or lose their homes" (136).[4] Going so far as to read McCarthy as a particularly anti-domestic writer, Witek claims that he is "at his most fierce and convincing when taking on [. . .] conventional images of community life as the spaces we choose to call home" (136). How can works regularly read as road novels and stories of chivalric wanderers be nonetheless concerned (ultimately, Witek seems to say) with the domestic? Is it possible to understand *The Border Trilogy* both as road stories and stories of domestic longing and loss?

The connection between the roles of homeless wanderer and those that are more housebound can be seen in generic terms similar to those employed by Bailey. We may speak of John Grady Cole, Billy Parham, and his brother Boyd, as knightly figures. John Grady also aspires to the estate of a landholder and housekeeper, or squire. Billy and Boyd Parham meanwhile exchange roles, variously, as both knights and squires.

By moving from the lost ranch house in Texas toward its replacement in Mexico, John Grady's path leads eventually only to parodic fulfillments of his desire for a medial space between domestic places and wilderness spaces. By the end of *Cities of the Plain*, he arrives at two consecutive "rigged-up dwelling[s]" (Witek 137): first, an abandoned house that he attempts, in an improvement on Lester Ballard's remodeling, to reclaim; second, when he dies in the "clubhouse made from packingcrates" (*COTP* 256).

Billy and Boyd Parham lose their home and go on similarly chivalric errands. They too live in a world where one takes to the road in part because one's house is not quite a home. The generic terms that Bailey has used for John Grady on horseback (the terms of chivalry), might have included one that translates particularly well into the unhorsed world of the domestic: the squire. In *The Border Trilogy*, the role of squire can be a knightly means to a medially domestic end. The chivalric roles found in these three novels further entail relationships along different points of a spectrum between the domesticity of the house and the landless space of the knight's errands.

Several terms are helpful in understanding McCarthy's anachronistic cowboys as (variously) both chivalric and domestic. John Grady is both knight and courtier, yet I will argue that he eventually settles for the role of husband. Billy Parham is more difficult to place within the medieval tradition of landless knights, yet he too is sometimes ambivalently drawn toward domesticity, a landed position to which one definition of the word squire refers. Boyd, on the other hand, is much like John Grady in his knightly abilities, and he is the least driven by domestic longing. Boyd, however, is a squire in a different sense. *The Oxford English Dictionary* gives several definitions for the word squire. It is (1) "one ranking next to a knight under the feudal system of military service and tenure," and close to this sense is the squire who is himself hard to tell from a knight: (8b) "squire-errant, a squire who acts like a knight errant." The term is also applicable to characters considered analogous to a medieval squire (*OED* def. 2), and thus even more applicable to McCarthy's characters.

In accord with the entitlements of a significant, if secondary, position in feudal society, a squire may also be a landholder. McCarthy employs this usage directly in reference to the murdered farmer in *Outer Dark*: the man is more than a mere landholder. We might even consider him as having a Southern version of the Southwestern position to which John Grady aspires in *All the Pretty Horses*: the Grady patriarch was both homeowner and landowner, with power over both the domestic and natural realms. This is a higher domestic position than living in a rehabilitated cabin, and it is only the reduced circumstances of *Cities of the Plain* that lead John Grady to settle for mere husbandry, rather than squiredom. Finally, a squire may also be someone who courts ladies—though not necessarily (as in Boyd's case) a courtier. Palczynski and I see both John Grady and Boyd in these roles, and other chivalric roles akin to them, in *The Border Trilogy*.

Edwin Arnold and other critics have already noticed the variety of roles played by McCarthy's characters. Of Billy Parham, Arnold writes that "[a]lthough Billy is nomadic, home and family are important to him; indeed, he has spent his entire life looking for that which he lost as a young boy when he left New Mexico to take the wolf back into the Mexican mountains" ("Last of the Trilogy" 232). Arnold also recognizes a longing for the domestic in John Grady Cole. *The Border Trilogy* therefore continues McCarthy's preoccupation with domesticity lost or unattainable. "Few successful marriages are to be found" in McCarthy's novels ("Last of the Trilogy" 235), and John Grady's desires will be frustrated:

> [I]n *Cities of the Plain* (*omitting the Epilogue*) the suggestion of childlessness, barrenness holds sway. In this world, John Grady's dreams of marriage and domesticity are, as Rawlins and Billy and

others try to tell him, unrealistic, especially given his choice of brides, both of whom are, in their own ways, unattainable. (Arnold "Last" 236, my emphasis)

EYES FOR THE SPREAD [5]

John Grady Cole is powered by a domestic drive underlying his knightly impulse to the road. In *All the Pretty Horses*, the primary surface genre of the Western (with that litany of cowboy ancestors) perhaps makes it easy to forget the particular circumstances left behind when our hero rides to Mexico. We do not, in fact, have evidence of ranching life outdoors in the beginning of the book; rather, we have something else, indoor concerns: of social relation, and of an office.

The book begins by an equation of death and loss of domesticity: once the grandfather is buried, the house will be sold. Before losing Alejandra and Magdalena, John Grady loses his last chance at love in Texas, Mary Catherine. Before losing La Purísima and a tentative future on the Cross Fours ranch, he loses the ranch of his grandfather. John Grady, no less unhoused than many other McCarthy characters, begins his "quest" not as a "youthful prank" (Jarrett 100), but in search of something he loses at the beginning of *All the Pretty Horses*: a secure domestic space. By the beginning of his second quest in *Cities of the Plain*, he is determined to recover a lesser form of that space. It is partly because of this determination that John Grady acts for a time as courtier and knight.

By "domestic," I simply mean those things having to do with the primary domestic space, the house. "House" might seem to be opposite "road;" the two impulses and their requisite aspects of space, however, are not incommensurable. Gaston Bachelard, in his *Poetics of Space*, addresses both types of space. The unconscious is "housed" (10), and Bachelard claims that "the house is one of the greatest powers of integration for the thoughts, memories and dreams of mankind" (6). Yet, Bachelard's house is significantly conceptual—if not transportable. It is the "ousted unconscious" that, as we see in McCarthy, takes to the road and its freedoms.

> The normal unconscious knows how to make itself at home everywhere, and psychoanalysis comes to the assistance of the ousted unconscious, of the unconscious that has been roughly or insidiously dislodged. But psychoanalysis sets the human being in motion, rather than at rest. It calls on him to live outside the abodes of his unconscious, to enter into life's adventures, to come out of himself. And naturally, its action

is a salutary one. Because we must also give an exterior destiny to the interior being. (Bachelard 10–11)

Here is, perhaps, another possible definition of any novel: that it is a work of art that "give[s] exterior destiny to [an] interior being." Michel de Certeau perhaps took this idea further, developing the relationship between space and narrative:

> [N]arrative structures have the status of spatial syntaxes. By means of a whole panoply of codes, ordered ways of proceeding and constraints, they regulate changes in space (or moves from one place to another) made by stories in the form of places put in linear or interlaced series: from here (Paris), one goes there (Montargis); this place (a room) includes another (a dream or memory); etc. (115)

From the desk of John Grady's grandfather (here), we will go to the Hacienda de Nuestra Señora de la Purísima Concepción (there). We may translate Certeau's phrase "put in linear or interlaced series" as the term "plot." Then Bachelard's metaphorical sense of the term "psychoanalysis" might also be substituted for plot as it pertains to John Grady. But Bachelard assumes that the actions on the ousted consciousness "are naturally salutary." Before the word "salutary" might stop us, however, Bachelard enlarges his topoanalytic range. "To accompany psychoanalysis in this salutary action, we should have to undertake a topoanalysis of all the space that has invited us to come out of ourselves" (11). Here Bachelard is including in his spatial considerations something more familiar than houses are to John Grady. In a rapturous passage on roads and paths, Bachelard quotes George Sand: "What is more beautiful than a road? [. . .] It is the symbol and the image of an active, varied life" (12).

We have had interesting explorations of John Grady as a figure of the road, thorough enough for Richard Anderson to name this role as that of the picaró,[6] and for Brian Evenson, in "McCarthy's Wanderers: Nomadology, Violence, and Open Country," to detail variations of the "nomad" in McCarthy (41). Bachelard's focus, however, suits Palczynski's view of John Grady the knight becoming what I argue becomes John Grady the would-be husband. Bachelard sees the road as part of a potential "two-fold imaginary geometrical and physical problem of extroversion and introversion." But he does "not believe that these two branches of physics"—road and house, exterior and interior—"have the same psychic weight." *The Poetics of Space* "is devoted to the domain of intimacy, to the domain in which psychic weight is dominant" (12). Interestingly, Bachelard himself cannot avoid including the road and the path, despite the fact that his focus is insistently on domestic spaces. I understand his distinction between the interior space of houses and the exterior space of road and path to correspond to the interior place of the "court" created by the ranch house, and the exterior space that creates the "range" around it.

Because John Grady's parents are divorced, he visits his father at the hotel in which the father is living, with "white wicker furniture with the window open and the thin crocheted curtains blowing into the room" (*ATPH* 11). When John Grady is at the ranch house, however, he is "back" at "the house" (*ATPH* 10). Although the mother has no desire to keep the medially domestic space created by her deceased father's ranch house, she is the reluctant guardian of domesticity. The father, however, is already living in a domestic simulacrum. His is the domesticity of the transient, with curtains blowing into the room through an open window. Hers is the domesticity of heritage, the ranch having been handed down on her side of the family, along with its domestic space, the ranch house.

I write "domestic," but more accurately, the most precious space that John Grady loses at the beginning of *All the Pretty Horses* is peculiarly intermediary. It is his grandfather's office, his by rights (as his mother does not want it) but enjoyed by him for only a moment. This office is an enclosed space from which a man (as it were) can look out over a wilderness whose wildness remains present through oral history, yet one which is contiguous with the comforts of the kitchen, and of a "she" (mother or wife) standing at the door. Compare the following description of John Grady's grandfather's room with that of his father's room in the hotel.

> He entered his grandfather's office and went to the desk and turned on the lamp and sat down in the old oak swivelchair. On the desk was a small brass calendar mounted on swivels that changed dates when you tipped it over in its stand. It still said September 13th. An ashtray. A glass paperweight. A blotter that said Palmer Feed and Supply. His mother's highschool graduation picture in a small silver frame.
>
> The room smelled of old cigarsmoke. He leaned and turned off the little brass lamp and sat in the dark. Through the front window he could see the starlit prairie falling away to the north. The black crosses of the old telegraph poles yoked across the constellations passing east to west. (*ATPH* 10–11)

The objects in this room are inert, as dead as the grandfather. Yet they once commanded through two directions both the exterior world and a more domestic interior space, where the "clock struck eleven in the front room across the hall" (*ATPH* 11). This office space has no white wicker and there is nothing "crocheted" about it. We have oak furniture and brass is the material in control of the passage of days and of artificial light. You do not even need verbs in this room, where a man can sit and know how "the Comanche" (a collective singular noun suggesting generalizing epistemological power on the part of its user) "would cut the [telegraph] wires and splice them back with horsehair."[7] Even one's daughter (or mother) is framed here, in silver. This intermediary space, as commanding as any Benthamite panopticon, occasions the most comfortable body language John Grady will exhibit through two novels. "He leaned back and crossed his boots on the desktop." What can one not know from this space? "Dry lightning to the north, forty miles distant" (*ATPH* 11).

His mother, known to him and us only as "she," briefly intrudes on this squirely realm. "What are you doing?" she says (*ATPH* 11). John Grady's reply is sufficient in a word:

"Settin."

It should be considered, then, how much weight John Grady is carrying when it comes to houses, domestic intimacy, and squiredom, as he leaves his grandfather's ranch. If we see his journey into Mexico as a quest not only for the open range required by the cowboy but for a domestic space from which to command both house and "starlit prairie" (*ATPH* 11), then we know he has a long way to go when he arrives at La Purísima. He quickly moves from bunkhouse to barn—not far from the prize stallion that is his double in the courtship with Alejandra. But he never gets much further.

It is easy to see La Purísima's resemblance to a feudal manor in the following passage found by Palczynski. In *Allegory of Love*, C. S. Lewis describes a typical setting for a courtly love romance: a Provençal court of the Middle Ages:

> We must picture a castle which is a little island of comparative leisure and luxury, and therefore at least of possible refinement, in a barbarous country-side. There are many men in it, and very few women—the lady, and her damsels. Around these throng the whole male meiny, the inferior nobles, the landless knights, the squires and the pages—haughty creatures enough in relation to the peasantry beyond the walls, but feudally inferior to the lady as to her lord—her "men" as feudal language

had it. Whatever "courtesy" is in the place flows from her: all female charm from her and her damsels. (Lewis 12)

Palczynski has made the connection between this description in Lewis's *Allegory of Love* and the introduction to La Purísima in *All the Pretty Horses*: "By dotting the land with bodies of water, La Purísima becomes an island made up of miniature islands:"

> The western sections ran into the Sierra de Anteojo to elevations of nine thousand feet but south and east the ranch occupied part of the broad barrial or basin floor of the bolsón and was well watered with natural springs and clear streams and dotted with marshes and shallow lakes and lagunas. (*ATPH* 97)

La Purísima is a place of "*comparative* leisure and luxury" (Lewis 12, Palczynski 111, her emphasis). Palczynski goes on to point out that John Grady and his friend from Texas work hard in their new surroundings, but because they were looking for this work, it become a labor of love.

> There is no necessity for John Grady to break sixteen wild horses in four days (*ATPH* 100). [. . .] John Grady accomplishes the feat to prove his unparalleled horsemanship—that he is a great cowboy [. . .] a great knight. The feat will gain him an audience with the hacendado, an interview for a more courtly position.
>
> The breaking of the sixteen horses becomes tournament-like when a peasant audience picnics outside the gate (*ATPH* 106). By the last day "there were something like a hundred people gathered, some come from the pueblo of La Vega six miles to the south, some farther" (*ATPH* 107). The "performance" of breaking the horses is similar to a medieval tournament, which served to entertain the peasantry, impress the nobility, and earn the participant a greater status at court. In *The Book of the Courtier*, Baldesar Castiglione wrote that the perfect courtier should be "an accomplished and versatile horseman" but should also put forth every effort and diligence into surpassing the rest just a little in everything. John Grady sets himself apart through his feat, "so that" (in Castiglione's words) "he may be recognized as superior" (Castiglione 62), despite the fact that he claims no distinction between himself and Lacey when he tells the hacendado "We don't have no leaders. We're just buddies" (*ATPH* 114). (Palczynski 111–112)

Only one of these "buddies," however, is invited to breakfast with the hacendado. At this breakfast, John Grady proves that his knowledge of horses extends from the natural world into the world of culture: he has read Wallace "front to back" (*ATPH* 116). This accompanying scholarship is at least a small proof of the "refinement" that Lewis argues is necessary for attendance at court. John Grady's chess is better than his pool game, but playing the most powerful man and woman at La Purísima at their respective games again proves that John Grady's refinement is sufficiently malleable: he is at home outdoors and indoors. As is often noted of the chess game with the Dueña Alfonsa, John Grady's moves figure importantly around the knight— the symbolic horse, a horse of culture, an interior horse.

Palczynski also notes the importance of sprezzatura to the courtier. This attitude is interestingly translated into the codes of the cowboy myth, particularly in descriptions of John Grady in relation to his friend, Lacey Rawlins. McCarthy draws attention to John Grady's possession of this quality by contrasting him with Lacey. John Grady breaks horses in record time, he is a passionate lover (if we draw any conclusions to his having a stall near the stallion), and, as Palczynski puts it, "he speaks reasonably and without affectation, often in fluent Spanish: all things that Lacey does not and cannot do. John Grady even rides the stallion with a graceful nonchalance: bareback and shoeless" (*ATPH* 129, Palczynski 112). These qualities help him win favor with the hacendado and help him attain his promotion, albeit still housed in a barn. This particular barn seems nonetheless closer to the main house, the "court," than does the bunkhouse with Lacey among unnamed vaqueros.

Terri Witek sees the relationship between the big house and the bunkhouse as one of uneasy dependency. "The economic vigor of that beautiful home and its family depends on the bunkhouse, which is finally too close for comfort" (138). So, too, the castle depends on the work of landless knights, none of whom is allowed to approach too closely the lady of the house. At La Purísima, unrequited love is supposed to ensure the uneasy distinction between inside and outside which all social systems require, and which feudalism maintains in a severe distinction between interior courts and exterior lists, between the space inside the castle's walls and the "barbarous country-side" outside them.

The "barbarous country-side" to which Lewis refers is the range through which John Grady and Lacey have come: the land between the lost Grady ranch and the mountains that protect La Purísima. It is a land where rough men offer to buy Blevins. It is where "the *landless* knight" described by Lewis (12, Palczynski's emphasis) roams on the range. "Again, the certain loss of the Grady ranch underscores John Grady's position as a knight from outside La Purísima. 'Landless knighthood,' Lewis explains, is 'knighthood without a place in the territorial hierarchy of feudalism'" (Lewis 11–12, Palczynski 112–113).

It is not enough to be a knight at court; one must be a courtier as well. When John Grady arrives at La Purísima, he already possesses knightly chivalry from his exterior adventures. Palczynski notes that he has yet to learn how to be "courteous," which is an interior skill of courtly and domestic spaces. Bachelard's words work interestingly for John Grady as knight: he certainly does "enter into life's adventures" and "come out of himself." But does his "exterior destiny" find at La Purísima an "interior being?" (Bachelard 10–11).

Palczynski's reading of Lewis is key to understanding this question:

> On La Purísima's island of refinement, away from the barbarous "man's" world, dwell the lady and her damsels. Only a few women exist on this island: Alejandra, her unseen mother, and the Dueña Alfonsa—which makes it easy for our knight and courtly lover to select his love object: there are few from which to choose. From the lady (Alejandra) flows "courtesy," which permeates La Purísima with a softness that is the beauty and fertility of the female body. The landscape of La Purísima is described in terms similar to those commonly used for a woman's body: soft and fertile. The "basin floor of the bolsón" is "well watered." Water signifies a feminine vitality, as it makes the land around it rich and fertile. All of La Purísima is "dotted with [. . .] shallow lakes and lagunas (*ATPH* 97)." All of it is fertile and soft and welcoming—like courtesy. (Palczynski 113)

In his new setting, our all-American cowboy lives the "idea of Quixote" as the hacendado says, until things take a brutally realistic turn and he and Rawlins are arrested (*ATPH* 146). John Grady then relies on his knightly skills to battle "evil" in prison so that he can return to his love. Bailey's description of John Grady's first knife fight reads it in medieval terms: the "homemade knives become swords and metal cafeteria trays become shields" (75). Having survived yet another test, John Grady continues to develop his courtly lover persona by dreaming and idealizing his love object. Yet it is no longer possible to imagine that he can play any role whatsoever at La Purísima. When he and Alejandra reunite it is outside the Edenic court and countryside of the Bolsón de Cuatro Ciénagas, and John Grady is ready to exchange his courtly lover status for something more domestic and permanent: marriage. She would lose La Purísima, but he tells her "they could go to live in his country and make their life there and no harm would come to them" (*ATPH* 252). Alejandra reveals the importance of her place at court when she refuses to trade it for this comparably humble domesticity.

John Grady wants to be Alejandra's husband, but Alejandra never intends to become his wife. Lewis cites two reasons why courtly love romance was denied legitimizing conclusions:

> Two things prevented the men of that age from connecting their ideal of romantic and passionate love with marriage. The first is, of course, the actual practice of feudal society. Marriages had nothing to do with love [. . .] All matches were matches of interest, and, worse still, of an interest that was continually changing [. . .] The second factor is the medieval theory of marriage—what may be called, by a convenient modern barbarism, the 'sexology' of the medieval church [. . .] According to the medieval view passionate love itself was wicked, and did not cease to be wicked if the object of it were your wife. (13–4)

Palczynski cites Lewis's first observation to explain the doomed circumstances of John Grady and Alejandra's relationship (Palczynski 114). The second factor is more relevant in *Cities of the Plain*: there the idea of passionate love or sex as wicked plays a significant role in John Grady's relationship with Magdalena. Though John Grady's wooing of Magdalena is not a courtly love romance, the "sexology" of the church—medieval or modern—introduces yet another conflict in a relationship that is already too complex to promise a happy ending.

John Grady is remarkably unsuccessful as a potential husband. In Alejandra, he chose a woman so highborn and virtuous that his relationship degraded her, and he could offer the authority of her court no enticing "interest," as Lewis would see it. Rather, the lady of the court at La Purísima loses her virginity, and at La Purísima, "a woman's reputation is all she has" (*ATPH* 136).

In Magdalena, John Grady chooses a woman so low and degraded that it is impossible to rescue her from the depths to which she so innocently and pitifully has sunk. Nothing he says or does can raise her from that lowly state and release her from the clutches of a stereotypically evil pimp. He cannot raise her up from wickedness, and his passionate love for her is itself wicked according to the medieval Church. Marriage certainly offers Magdalena no salvation. John Grady has stained the Virgin who was Alejandra, and failed to remove the stain from the Whore who is Magdalena, whom Bailey describes as "the holy whore, victimized by the church and state" (78). In contrast to Alejandra, John Grady finds in Magdalena someone whom he cannot tarnish: someone whose past is darker and more painful than his. He never again becomes a courtly lover after losing Alejandra. After losing Magdalena, he will not live to become a husband.

KNIGHTS AND SQUIRES: BILLY AND BOYD PARHAM

In *The Crossing*, the medieval setting seen by Palczynski in *All the Pretty Horses* is recalled from a lower vantage point in the feudal hierarchy, particularly in the feria scenes. As the feudal elements of the first book in the trilogy allow the reader to see John Grady in the roles of knight and courtier, the second installment displays several chivalric and knightly characteristics in Billy Parham and his brother, Boyd.

Billy and Boyd exhibit the knight and squire's relationship that was first introduced between John Grady and Lacey in *All the Pretty Horses*. This is the sense in which a squire is "one ranking next to a knight under the feudal system of military service and tenure" (*OED*). Translated into cowboy terms, this type of squire is a sidekick who, among other duties, helps to highlight the knight's superiority by serving as an example of what is average. We have already seen how Lacey works as John Grady's squire and how John Grady's excellence distinguishes him from the rest of the ranch hands at La Purísima. This relationship between knight and squire is replicated in *The Crossing* when Billy uses his status as the older brother to exercise authority over Boyd, thus assuming the superior position of knight.

Boyd's exceptional horsemanship, however, far outshines that of his brother, and it is not long before the brothers change places. As Billy falls into Boyd's shadow, he falls as much into the role of squire to Boyd's new knightly position. "Boyd advanced upon the horses where they stood leisurely cropping the roadside grass and threw his loop. The throw anticipated the Bailey horse and as he raised his head to move away he raised it into the loop. Billy sat his father's horse watching. I could do that, he told the horse. In about nine tries" (*TC* 243–4).

Billy cannot deny this inferiority to Boyd, who is (despite his small frame) an impressive spectacle on horseback. "Boyd came out of the trees at a gallop. He was bent low over Keno's neck and he was holding the bridle-reins of Billy's horse in one hand and the shotgun in the other and he carried the reins of his own horse in his teeth like a circus rider" (*TC*

210). There is a striking similarity between Boyd's "circus rider" aspect and John Grady's tournament-like performance breaking the sixteen wild horses at La Purísima. Though John Grady is relatively more understated and certainly more laconic, in key moments, both boys are exhibitionists who challenge the limits of their own talent.

The superiority that is characteristic of the knight in relation to the squire extends beyond horsemanship into the realm of romance, as a squire may be also (OED def. 4) "[a] man, esp. a young man, who attends upon, accompanies, or escorts a lady." And again, in the sense of a squire being potentially synonymous with a knight in his undertaking of quests (particularly of rescue), the squire may work as much as the knight for the heart of a damsel. It matters little that Billy is the brother who initiates the rescue of the fourteen-year-old girl; he cannot maintain the chivalry necessary to woo her properly once the rescue is affected. Boyd is slightly more "refined" than Billy (to recall Lewis's word), as we see when he admonishes his older brother for cursing in front of the girl. Boyd is a purist about this: it does not matter whether the girl speaks English or not, "That dont make it not cussin" (*TC* 212).

Palczynski notes again the influence of medieval literature here:

> The narration calls attention to the medieval nature of the chivalric tradition in which Billy, Boyd, and the girl are living. "Trekking in the starlight between the dark boundaries of the mountain ranges east and west they had the look of storybook riders conveying again to her homeland some stolen backland queen" (*TC* 213). The knight and squire on horseback delivering a queen to her homeland is a direct allusion to medieval chivalric and courtly love literature. The scene echoes Spenser's *The Faerie Queen*—with ironic translation into the harsh landscape of *The Crossing*. As much as John Grady's courtly love scenes with Alejandra, the chivalric rescue of a damsel in distress by Billy and Boyd reflects the medieval roots of the Western romantic tradition of love. (117)

COME BACK TO THE RANCH AG'IN, HUCK HONEY.

Despite the important position given women in medieval romance, Lewis notes a countervailing value. In the Middle Ages, the romantic love felt between a man and a woman was not nearly as important as the love men felt for each other. C. S. Lewis noted that "[t]he deepest of worldly emotions in this period is the love of man for man, the mutual love of warriors who die together fighting against odds, and the affection between vassal and lord" (9).Z

Similarly, in the American romantic sentimentalism that insists on cowboys falling in love with women, there is a countertendency of the homoerotic type that Leslie Fiedler has famously found embedded in many American novels outside the Western genre. This countertendency fits within a set of binaries in the trilogy: interior (feminine) domestic constraint in place vs. exterior (masculine) spatial freedom. In *The Border Trilogy* (as in many a Hollywood film today), male relationships with other males are therefore all-important.

Edwin Arnold notes this in McCarthy's trilogy when he writes that "the primary love stories in these books are between men and men" ("Last" 236). Lewis's "mutual love of warriors" is most notably exhibited among the men working on Mac's ranch in *Cities of the Plain*. The "affection between vassal and lord" is a good description of the relationship between Mac and his ranch hands. Mac serves as both a father figure and friend to all his employees. Billy also exemplifies this tradition of the love of male for male. He attaches himself to John Grady, whom he considers a replacement for Boyd (Arnold, "Last" 231–2). With John Grady, Billy receives a second chance to be a brother and a squire.

The squire's role of sidekick requires him to take care of his knight, whom he loves and is responsible for protecting. Women, however, are a threat to such a relationship's demands that the two men be free to roam the wide-open spaces:

> Women not only upset the "mutual love of warriors" by absorbing the knight's attention, they also present numerous problems that the knight is required to solve. Women attract knights into dangerous situations, making it more difficult for the squire to protect his knight. It is no surprise therefore, that the squire resents the woman with whom his knight falls in love. Lacey exhibits this resentment in *All the Pretty Horses* by trying to discourage John Grady from pursuing Alejandra: "I dont see what evidence you got that she's all that interested in you" (*ATPH* 138). When John Grady asks him immediately after their discussion of Alejandra whether he is sorry he came down to Mexico, Lacey shows both his disapproval of the romance and his worries about its future by replying, "Not yet." He is implying, of course, that if John Grady continues the relationship, he will indeed become quite sorry that he came to Mexico. (Palczynski 117–118)

Palczynski notes that Billy's resentment of women is similarly strong.

> In *The Crossing*, he resents "the girl's" intrusion on his relationship with
> Boyd. Billy tries to make Boyd feel guilty about his feelings for "the girl"
> by asking, "You aint above runnin off with her. Are you?" (*TC* 237). Billy
> is angry that Boyd would abandon his own brother for a girl. In Part III of
> *The Crossing*, Billy becomes squire-sidekick for Boyd, and so must do his
> knight's bidding. His job is now to take on the same errands as his knight;
> he therefore agrees, if reluctantly, to meet "the girl" and bring her back
> when Billy is wounded and forced to stay in bed. It is not, however, his
> own errand to run. (Palczynski 118)

"Just as Billy's story in *The Crossing* repeats in broad outline John Grady's in *All the Pretty Horses*, so does Billy's relationship to John Grady in *Cities of the Plain* bear strong resemblance to that he held with Boyd" (Arnold, "Last" 232). Billy will try to discourage John Grady from pursuing Magdalena, but eventually he again acts as the second of a man pursuing a woman—again he is squire to another man's quest. When Billy surveys John Grady's potential home, he says to John Grady, "More and more you remind me of Boyd. Only way I could ever get him to do anything was to tell him not to" (*COTP* 146). The resemblance between John Grady and Boyd becomes clearer, as John Grady becomes Billy's second chance at making things right. Billy therefore agrees to go to the White Lake and attempt to buy Magdalena from Eduardo. Billy never gets over his resentment towards Magdalena, and "blames Magdalena, not Eduardo, for his friend's death" (Arnold, "Last" 227). As he holds the dead John Grady in his arms, he does not cry out the name of the pimp who stabbed his friend, but rather exclaims, "Goddamn whores" (*COTP* 261).

Billy is unsuccessful in his role as squire to a knight. His job is to take care of his knight, yet each time he fails. He repeatedly blames himself in *The Crossing* for not having looked after Boyd properly. When Boyd has been shot and is being operated on by the doctor, Billy says to him, "I didnt take much care of you did I?" (*TC* 307). About John Grady to Mac, he says, "I should of looked after him better" (*ATPH* 263). Billy's final task as squire caretaker is to give each knight a proper burial in the country of his birth. The best he can do with Boyd is to carry his bones across the border, in another scene of improper burial in a McCarthy novel. With John Grady, at least Billy can hold the lifeless body up in a pietà, before presumably conducting his friend across the border. Having missed this second chance at saving his true love—his fellow warrior—Billy then punishes himself again with a wandering exile. After he loses John Grady, this squire's exile lasts the rest of his life.

JOHN GRADY AND BILLY'S LAST ROLES: UNHORSED AND UNHOUSED

After giving up courtesy, John Grady loses even chivalry. His chances at "settin'" in the medial realm of the squire landholder—as one whose dominion is both domestic and wild—are long lost. He says to Mac, "I want to get married and I thought for one thing if you didn't care I'd just go on and sell that horse" (*COTP* 142). This is an extraordinary thing for that character to say. This certainly is not the "all-american cowboy" (*COTP* 3), nor Alejandra's knight, talking. In a capitulation of all his previous roles, John Grady sells his horse for $300 so that he can marry the prostitute Magdalena and set up a humble house. This kind of thing makes it hard to remember that the screenplay version of *Cities of the Plain* was written before *All the Pretty Horses*.

Fighting for her while she is still alive seems out of the question to the John Grady of reduced circumstances. In several details, his situation is reversed from that at La Purísima: there is no "lady" at the Cross Fours, and so the land is "overdue" and "fixin to dry up and blow away" (*COTP* 62). As elements of the medieval setting of La Purísima are strikingly absent at both the Cross Fours and the White Lake, so, too, John Grady is ready to compromise more than ever before. In Alejandra, he had the idealized lady, but no reasonable plan for reclaiming the lost ranch that set him in her direction. In Magdalena, he has a girl who needs rescuing, but his plans for her are not so grand as to include the stewardship of a ranch. What role does he plan on with Magdalena? Husband.

The *Oxford English Dictionary* gives two definitions for "husband:" he is both a "man joined to a woman by marriage" and a "freeholder [. . .] [of] his own house." The word connotes nothing about quest and conquest, the freedom of movement given a landless knight, or even the greater station afforded the squire-landholder. These roles of the husband are diminishments, departures from those of frustrated courtly lover and horseback-nomadic knight. Instead of a lady high born to a court, John Grady as husband merely needs a wife—one who feels unworthy of him is a good choice for a life that is neither approximate to a court nor loosed upon the road.

In a scaled-down version of the Grady ranch house's intermediary office of control, John Grady sets up a domestic space in a cabin from which he must haul wheelbarrow-loads of trash (*COTP* 199). It takes him three weeks to clear the trash; he works on the cabin "all through" a "month" and more (*COTP* 177). Instead of a chapel, it will have a small clay saint. Its floors are of clay. Its location on a hill might be that of a minor castle: but we suspect it is much more modest in proportion. Both Billy (*COTP* 180) and Héctor (*COTP* 200) try to warn him that it is cold up there at night, but it clearly has a view: the sunset yields "running fire deepening to darkness over the mountains to the west" (*COTP* 180). In a striking scene of two cowboys who long ago lost their homes, Billy helps John Grady paint "windowsash." Blue. Afterwards, John Grady hears a laconic echo of Billy's own loss of a home (*COTP* 181).

John Grady has learned from his courtly failure at La Purísima the lesson his father taught him on poker, "[w]hat you won was gravy but what you lost was hard come by" (*COTP* 214). The importance of the old adobe cabin to John Grady is primary in the absence of a larger court to which he might gain entry. There is striking irony in the death of this hero in a "clubhouse made from packingcrates" (*COTP* 254): it occurs "worlds away" (*COTP* 216) from the house he trimmed in blue for his beloved (*COTP* 179).

And what of Billy's end? Configurations of domesticity are more rare in *The Crossing*, but in *Cities of the Plain*, Billy too will end up horseless, wandering for the comfort of a place to be. His trip with Troy may be seen as a type of house hunting. John Grady comments on this when he says, "We'll all be goin somewhere when the army takes [the ranch] over" (*COTP* 50). Billy's beginnings, however, were never as dependent on interior space as were John Grady's. In his own book of the trilogy, Billy Parham is not long in a house at all, much less in a family home.

The Crossing opens with the movement of "they" from one "country" to a "new country" (*TC* 3) though these are simply the adjoining counties of Grant and Hidalgo in Southwest New Mexico. The first sentence names the brother Boyd "not much more than a baby," well before we get Billy's name. We never get the names of the parents. The house, for Billy and his brother, is no more than a place to sleep. Its first mention merely serves to frame the wildness outdoors, which will be the deeper concern of these brothers: "In the new house they slept in the room off the kitchen and he would lie awake at night and listen to his brother's breathing in the dark and he would whisper half aloud to him as he slept his plans for them and the life they would have" (*TC* 3). The parents are not mentioned at all—though we assume they are among the "they" who "came south out of Grant County" (*TC* 3).

Domesticity of any kind is simply absent from most of *The Crossing*. When we do see houses or the provision of food (usually by women for men), the appearance of domesticity merely serves the wandering brothers as temporary hospitality. Even then, Billy is as likely to encounter abandoned houses as full ones. The one full house that most welcomes him he seems hasty to leave. After catching the wolf, Billy stops at the property of an unnamed man whose wife, Jane Ellen, takes pity on the wolf and has their hired hand doctor its leg. Jane Ellen has at this point fed Billy, after his arrival interrupts the family's supper. The home he lost may still haunt him, as Arnold claims ("Last" 232), yet this is a true home, something he never had. One might imagine it harder to leave—even on a quixotic quest to return a wolf to its supposed home. Billy, however, does not even stay the night, leaving instead at "all but dark" (*TC* 71). Jane Ellen sends with him most of the food he will eat until he is arrested and the wolf taken from him, as well as the winding sheet in which he will eventually wrap the wolf's dead body (*TC* 124).

Billy is like the wolves to which the hacendado's son compares him at the feria. When Billy argues that "the wolf knew nothing of boundaries," the "young don" replies that "whatever the wolf knew or did not know was irrelevant and that if the wolf had crossed that boundary it was perhaps so much the worse for the wolf but the boundary stood without regard." When Billy then says that he "had not known that he would be required to pay in order to pass through the country the hacendado [says] that then he [is] in much the same situation as the wolf" (*TC* 119). McCarthy has already shown us this, however, when he has Billy creeping through the snow on all fours—having left his bed in the middle of the night—to watch the wolves run antelope at the beginning of the book (*TC* 4). Unable himself to recognize boundaries and their potentially serious consequences, Billy crosses them into and out of the territory of others. Like the wolf, he takes food from the civilized places of others, and like the wolf, he expects no consequences of his movements.

An old man's name for him has come true before Billy realizes it: he is indeed "huérfano"—an orphan (*TC* 134). The loss of his parents, however, strikes Billy in only a single sentence. When he sees the evidence of the murder of his parents, "He looked at it all and he fell to his knees in the floor and sobbed into his hands" (*TC* 165). To be fair, we are told that he is grieving; McCarthy, however, is capable of much more effective description—even when the effect is to indicate emotion indirectly. Compared to the long suffering wolf, Billy's killing of it in mercy, and his cleansing of its body, this is less than underplayed. It isn't necessary, however, to discount Billy's emotion at the loss of his parents to argue that what is more important to him than domesticity and its ties is wildness: a wolf, his brother in the role of landless knight, and the "country" in which he happens to live—not the home. It is not so surprising, then, that Billy's particular adoption of various squirely roles does not include landholder, or gallant. Those roles are less wild and depend more on interior places, than exterior space.

The important thing for this orphan is therefore to "rescue" his brother from fosterage (that is to say from another house) and to go back across the border to find stolen horses. As in the first book of the trilogy, the theft of a horse is coupled with the loss of family as an impetus for leaving home. Unlike John Grady, however, whose father is dying, whose mother is no longer interested in the medial home of the ranch, and whose ranching grandfather has just died; Billy and Boyd come from a more modest family: they do not own the house they live in (*TC* 10).

The "indian" they meet while gathering wood is the ultimate impetus for Boyd's involuntary leaving. (He returns the offer of Parham hospitality from the boys by murdering their parents.) With exceptions, one weakness McCarthy's fiction sometimes shares with less richly ambiguous work is his depiction of Native Americans. Indians are regularly made to signify wildness in McCarthy—but so, too, are most young men in any McCarthy novel. The romantic imaginative rendering of many of his young men places them in opposition to civilization of any kind, certainly to domesticity. The Indian in *The Crossing* is simply a pure type of the wild boy— perhaps with much in common with Billy, who leaves his house in the night to walk like a wolf to see other wolves. When the Indian is offered the hospitality of the Parham house, he replies "I dont want to come to the house. I want you to bring me somethin out" (*TC* 7). The Parham house is something this wild boy cannot trust, but the Indian's reasonable fears of getting "shot" (*TC* 7) at the house cloud into something more ominous. The double wildness of wolf and Indian encountered by Billy sends Billy twice away from domestic space, and finally exiles him from any role afforded by it.

Elsewhere we see Billy reluctant to be at home wherever he finds himself. He feeds himself on horseback from the tables at the feria, walking the horse along the tables and taking the food up from the domestic into the horsed world of violence and homelessness. Before he knows it, he is lost, "[h]is home had come to seem remote and dreamlike" (*TC* 135). After saying "he had no home" (*TC* 236), he later tries to deny his role of wanderer as he had that of orphan, telling a gypsy that he is not a man of the road. "But the gypsy only smiled and waved one hand. He said that the way of the road was the rule for all upon it. He said that on the road there are no special cases" (*TC* 414).

At the end of *The Crossing*, Billy stops at a "waystation" (*TC* 423) somewhere east of "the Black Range" (*TC* 422) and the Continental Divide. He goes to sleep in one of three roofless adobe buildings—certainly no home. Because of what happens next, however, it feels as if Billy is in an abandoned house.

It is doubtful that we are to believe that the dog Billy abuses at the end of *The Crossing*, who makes "a strange moaning sound" and who howls "weirdly" and "with a terrible sound" (*TC* 424), is literally the throat-cut dog that lived through the murder of his parents. The dog's strangeness, "perhaps [. . .] a hunting dog, perhaps left for dead in the mountains or by some highwayside" remains symbolic: "Repository of ten thousand indignities and the harbinger of God knew what" (*TC* 424). Billy's weeping in the last paragraph of *The Crossing* follows his unanswered call for the dog and his witness of the first detonation of an atomic bomb. That Billy is homeless, awakened from sleep in a roofless and abandoned building, only foreshadows his condition in the epilogue of *Cities of the Plain*.

There, the final role of Billy is akin to that of John Grady: both are unhorsed, and at the end each is housed only through the hospitality of others—John Grady in the child's packingcrate playhouse, Billy in the home of Betty. McCarthy's would-be cowboys live with only a dim awareness of roles outside those clustered around chivalry. What domestic roles might be available to them they turn out to be ill-equipped for, living as they have most of their lives in exile from the domestic. Their time on the horse makes them ill suited to the house. The final scene of *Cities of the Plain* suggests strongly that the chivalric roles promised by cowboy mythology are ultimately impossible to fulfill.

The beginning of the last section of the Epilogue finds Billy still on the road again, having "slept that night in a concrete tile by the highwayside where a roadcrew had been working" (*COTP* 289). Rather than horses, lifeless construction trucks—trucks for making more highways—surround him. Billy, having long ago rejected the charge that he is a man of the road, is now surrounded by the construction of roadway that has more to do with international trade than with metaphors about homelessness. Yet homelessness is Billy's condition, and McCarthy's preoccupations with men of the road and their loss of domestic space returns in an ironic but also ambiguous ending: Billy is taken into someone else's home.

The family that take him in are at first unnamed. Billy's bed is marginal to the house, "in a shed room off the kitchen that was much like the room he'd slept in as a boy" (*COTP* 290). Reminding us of the tenuous home Billy and Boyd are traveling to in the beginning of *The Crossing*, McCarthy risks a sententious ending to his trilogy by pointing directly to the central irony behind all his cowboy heroes: they begin their books by wandering from home and tend to end them dying homeless.

The dialogue that concludes the Epilogue recalls *The Crossing*, by having a character disagree with Billy about his identity. Billy tells Betty, the woman of the house, "I'm not what you think I am. I aint nothin.[8] I dont know why you put up with me" (*COTP* 292). What is the assumption behind this statement that Billy is making about Betty's view of him? What is the something he believes that she sees in him? If it is the opposite of "nothin" (even as a double negative), is it something heroic? Billy's insistence that whatever she sees in him is false seems to rest on the assumption that she sees in him something admirable. She replies, "Well, Mr Parham, I know who you are. And I do know why" (*COTP* 292).

There are two ways to read this ending. If we read it straight, then Billy is modestly arguing against what he assumes is some form of respect for his position as a landless knight—a cowboy of the mythic type pervading American sentimental culture. His laconic stoicism, indeed his insistence that in reality he "aint nothin," could simply bolster the chivalrous identity he seems to have internalized. More than irony, however, Billy's speech is steeped in ambiguity. We cannot know where, exactly, to read this speech along a spectrum between false modesty and true (ironic) humility. The choices lie between extremes: between a straight, sentimental reading of him as a chivalric hero; and a cynical dismissal of him as a phony cowboy who ropes dogs instead of steers, is reduced to acting as an extra in a film, and who finally ends up homeless. The statement is ultimately ambiguous.

Less ambiguous, however, is Betty's reply, "I know who you are" (*COTP* 292). This might seem to be a contradiction of a disingenuous disclaimer; contrary to "I aint nothin," she could be saying I know you're an admirable man after all. But what she says next undermines the possibility of either the straight reading (in which he is indeed a chivalrous hero), or the cynical reading (which dismisses the power of his mythic identity at least as a negative example of what happens to men without homes). Betty's position is important to note, because the scene is presented to us after McCarthy has compared Billy's room to the one "he'd slept in as a boy" (*COTP* 290). Sitting beside Billy "on his bed with her hand on his shoulder" (*COTP* 291), she is filling a previously vacant position. The mother hardly mentioned at the beginning of the novel has been replaced by a surrogate who claims to "know" even more than "who" Billy is, as she continues, "And I do know why" (*COTP* 292).

This is nearly inexplicable. McCarthy everywhere refuses his readers an easy sense of "why" anything happens. His more prolix secondary characters offer plenty of theories, but they seldom convince. Betty is speaking, however, from a position usually absent from a McCarthy novel: she is the woman of the house. In an ironic submission to domestic space, Billy is now under her roof, insisting he "aint nothin." From Betty's point of view, however, Billy is a lonely man who has lost his home and his brother, with no one but a stranger and no place but a stranger's home to comfort him.

Despite the fact that domesticity, in the form of houses and homes, creates an uninhabitable place for these characters, chivalric roles depending on exterior space ultimately depend on authority within domestic places. The occasional depiction of viable domesticity, however, suggests less that McCarthy is making a wholesale critique of domestic possibilities, than that he is simply interested in characters who have bad luck with their families.

They also have problems with their fathers. But at the outset of *The Border Trilogy*, John Grady's true problem with his father is simply that he lost him. The various roles afforded McCarthy's main characters in *The Border Trilogy* proved impossible to live through. Characters who lose things are apt to pursue something to replace them: the lost houses of McCarthy's cowboys set them interestingly on horseback as knights and squires—even if their return to some substitute home proved invariably inglorious.

Chapter Seven
Fetish and Collapse in *No Country for Old Men*

> The fathers shall not be put to death for the children,
> neither shall the children be put to death for the fathers:
> every man shall be put to death for his own sin.
>
> (Deuteronomy 24:16)

> *The other thing is that I have not said much about my father*
> *and I know I have not done him justice.*
>
> (Sheriff Bell, *NCFOM* 308)

COLLAPSE

We may see many more novels yet from Cormac McCarthy. But on first reading *No Country for Old Men*, it is hard to believe so. Everything in this novel seems to have collapsed, or seems headed that way. The book's structure seems to collapse, starting with a bang into what seems to be one genre that only slides down into another. The villain, an avatar of judge Holden, even kills people by collapsing their frontal lobe with a cattle gun, which at first seems simply to dispatch them through the same damage as a bullet, except that the closeness of the killer—"He placed his hand on the man's head like a faith healer" (*NCFOM* 7)—might make us look for more than madness in this method.

The apparent protagonist is killed three quarters of the way through the novel. The true protagonist grumbles along in monologues that begin each chapter. For all his West Texas stoicism, these soliloquies begin to run on, well beyond the framing device we thought they were, into an increasingly tangled mix of memories and stoic Western conservative positions on past and present. Sheriff Bell, this true protagonist, is trapped in time. So haunted by the past that he can only see the present as a dark and confusing mourning over the dead, Bell follows his grumbles about how much worse things are with fearful prognostications about how worse will be what days may come. Structurally, his italicized monologues begin to rush in sooner after each dwindling parcel of the apparent story (which hardly resolves). Bell's confessions take longer—and again longer—until the book collapses into one of his dreams.

Given this book's screenplay antecedent, one wonders at the possibilities of shifting light: the bright sunlit desert over Moss, the antelope, and the drug deal gone bad might imperceptibly fade into the darkness of that dream. Thus *No Country for Old Men* gradually reveals itself to have begun as one book, under one reading of its title in a bright light, only to slip away into another book, eventually fulfilling the depth and darkness of the title's reference to a poem by Yeats. It begins as a (relatively) young man's book, and ends in the voice of a middle-aged man who nonetheless seems to be quite old—as old as "Sailing to Byzantium" demands.

I must confess that in one reading, this novel simply seemed a failure, a tossed-off screenplay barely redacted into a novel in a genre that does not hold much interest for me. It seemed even to fail at that, as if the author's heart was not secure in the pot he might have meant to boil. *No Country for Old Men* starts hot, but then cools, and finally mists over. I ought to know better, and yet the novel's apparent conservatism seemed so insistent that against all better judgment I began to suspect (as many reviewers have) that this indeed indicated the frightened political views of an author now twenty years older than Bell and yet speaking through him. The structure collapsed so obviously as to raise the question of waning aesthetic powers; why not (the critic in hubris wonders) a waning political sensibility as well? (As if to disagree with a few readers is to have lost marbles.)

But then I reread it.

In short, everything about this book seems one way, but then does not—thus my repetition of "seems" fits a first impression. On subsequent readings, it becomes clearer that all these apparent collapses derive from the reality that this story is told with an awareness that many things have already collapsed in the previous novels. The title works in its reference to a retreat: after we are meant to begin in one country, with one book, we are meant to end in another space and another book, the true *No Country for Old Men*. And whatever the author's politics, Bell eventually voices the fearful feelings and positions of many Americans.[1]

For this chapter, I will refer to those aspects that stand out most in the book's beginning, that do not immediately (in a first reading) likely reveal themselves as parodic, and that create those aspects of genre fiction that have led to the labels applied to it as a "crime novel," etc., as the Young Man book. This is Moss's book. The Old Man book, however, is that simultaneous novel, buried early on (at least before rereading) and apparently set up as a generically typical narrative foil for the Young Man book. This is Bell's book, initially only italicized, and it is the book that ultimately sounds deeper resonances with the title, *No Country for Old Men.*

This novel simply does not work as a direct delivery of the Young Man book, nor should it. This is one of those works whose apparent failures create unexpected difficulties which can only resolve in rereading, where the novel then resonates in quiet success. I will attempt to offer a reading that, rather than pretending to have interpreted the book in that second way (the way I read it now), will instead parallel what the novel itself accomplishes: the appearance of one book with merely two voices, until those two views compete, and finally one overtakes the other. This is the only way I can answer several questions that first struck me about *No Country for Old Men.* Why would McCarthy deliver a taut, if thin, crime novel that only collapses into jeremiad? Who, really, is the main character of this novel? And why does this novel's structure so obviously collapse?

Among the reviews of the book so far, those reviewers obviously predisposed toward the strengths of this author (such as Joyce Carol Oates) find in *No Country for Old Men* a winnowed-down version of what they liked, but also what they did not like, in previous McCarthy books. Others simply praise whatever seems likely to satisfy, and disparage what surprises, a reader acquainted only with *The Border Trilogy.* Still others give the book its due but only (as I was tempted to do) by praising the power of its initial genre, writing off apparent weaknesses either as aspects of the genre or failures to fit that genre of fiction in which McCarthy seemed suddenly to be indulging. The quickest description of that genre well fits the limited space of the synopsis for the book among the *New York Times Book Review*'s "100 Notable Books of the Year" for 2005: "Women grieve, men fight in this hard-boiled Texas noir crime novel" (33).

This genre label underestimates *No Country for Old Men* because it proves accurate only for the reader's first acquaintance with the book. The ease, however, with which we might agree with that label reminds me of Glanton underestimating Caballo en Pello. Whether the book proves to be that powerful or not will depend on whether continued rereading rewards the reader. This is not *Blood Meridian* in its initial effects. But it is not supposed to be. Neither is it ultimately a "hard-boiled Texas noir crime novel" at all. It merely starts out that way.

It ends up as a coda to *All the Pretty Horses*. And in that way, *No Country for Old Men* not only extends but also begins to resolve the son and father anxiety found in McCarthy, even if doing so means a step backward into a nostalgic evocation of mythic archetype. The image closing the book can only be arrived at, without thoroughgoing sentimentality all along the way, by opening the book in a different genre—a different country, as it were. This movement creates the structural shift I referred to already as a collapse. While *No Country for Old Men* reinforces the loss of space to place that we have already explored, it does so by answering many remaining questions about the father and son tension developed through the previous eight novels.

Granted, McCarthy is known to hold onto manuscripts (as most writers do). *No Country for Old Men* began as a screenplay and may have sat around in a drawer for some time before McCarthy turned it into a novel. But the book's ending can hardly be imagined on film, or at least cannot be imagined in anything approaching the "hard-boiled Texas noir crime" film that McCarthy may have originally envisioned. As it refuses those genre labels, the book collapses under the weight of the son and father anxiety that is only forestalled by the fetishism and violence preoccupying its opening.

FETISH

What makes readers call *No Country for Old Men* a crime novel is not the commitment of any number of crimes, nor the violence in its depiction of those crimes. Nor has this label stuck to the book because of its comparatively terse style, or rather, not for that reason alone. After all, *Blood Meridian* certainly details more crimes. And a terse prose style characterizes much work that we would never think to call "noir" or "hard-boiled" for that reason alone. The salient characteristics of the cheaper forms of the genre fiction with which McCarthy seems to be working have more to do with technological fetish.

This begins with Anton Chigurh's cattle gun. At first, the cattle gun seems merely a small hook for the screenplay that preceded this material's present form as a novel. "The pneumatic hiss and click of the plunger sounded like a door closing" (*NCFOM* 7). This attention to sound, and the fact that Chigurh wears this apparatus in a nearly cyborg fashion, recalls Frank Booth in *Blue Velvet*. It feels like a gimmick. Although the cattle gun might provide a manner of killing someone with less noise than a conventional gun, so would a knife. Given the difficulty that law enforcement has in getting across the wide spaces between this book's crime scenes, and given Chigurh's ready use of guns for close-range as well as long-range killing, its purpose is not practical.

Thus, the detail becomes truly important. By killing people with a cattle gun, Chigurh is turning them into livestock, denying their humanity. Moreover, by shooting them in the forehead with it, Chigurh simultaneously deprives them of their living sight while imprinting in them a symbolic third eye—a visual representation of the enlightenment on matters of chance and destiny that he sometimes provides in a brief pre-murder Socratic dialogue. But we must also note that Chigurh's requirement of this tool to accomplish what Holden does with his hands (*BM* 179), points to his mortality (as do his wounds from combat and the car crash).

Chigurh can extend his thin line of philosophical argument regarding free will so as to extend Holden's (and McCarthy's) larger arguments on this. On first reading, these feel like comparatively weaker forms of philosophi-cal additions to a narrative that would otherwise rest more perilously on the voice of Bell. And ultimately, Chigurh's dependence on technology (not only weaponry, but on medicines, for instance, or on a telephone bill to track his victims) increases the distance between him and Holden. Chigurh needs gadgets, technology, to get around; he could never carry his own rock to sit on in the open desert. What seemed a weakness in the novel here, however, proves necessary to the way it works. Chigurh cannot be Holden because we no longer see devils or angels in our time, and Anton Chigurh is a vil-lain of our time, and of the places created by the *Blood Meridian* Epilogue I discussed in Chapter Five. Although he kills everyone he sets out to kill, we last see him limping away, looking relatively mortal: "They watched him set off up the sidewalk, holding the twist of the bandanna against his head, limping slightly" (*NCFOM* 262). He has even had to buy this bandage from one of the boys who caused the wreck. Why doesn't he just shoot these boys and take it?

So they can see him. After all, apart from his secondary function in providing the novel with some philosophical content alternative to Bell's jeremiads and confessions and dream vision, Anton Chigurh's visual possi-bilities as a striking movie villain fit perfectly his primary role in this novel's opening. He is himself a fetish of a villain, boiled down to a few villainish characteristics. Moss notices only these: "Blue eyes. Serene. Dark hair. Some-thing about him faintly exotic" (*NCFOM* 112). Beyond this politically safe "faintly exotic" and the mix of dark hair but blue eyes, Chigurh lacks any striking physical characteristics for us to remember him by (again, unlike Holden), except for the contrast between relatively sensitive features (blue eyes, a serene countenance) and his lethality. His name even serves first to suggest the geographically indeterminate origins favorable for a post-cold war movie villain, and then second to point us on to his philosophy. In this way, Chigurh is the villain whose character resides only in what he does and says. This, too, is not only characteristic of many film villains, but also of the crime novel genre. By "crime novel" I do not mean to refer to Chandler or Himes or other deft authors, but rather to the interchangeable serial novels that rely on formula and fetish in order to satisfy the desires of young male readers.

Weaponry fetish nearly overcomes the novel's first chapters. Even before the cattle gun, Chigurh satisfies that fetishistic need of crime novels not only to describe killing, but also to describe killing and other crucial activities of the hero and villains through the use of some surprising stratagem or technological apparatus. The characters must do things that the reader might not think of, such as blow the cylinder out of a lock "with the cobalt steel plunger of the cattlegun" (*NCFOM* 80). Note the specificity of the metal: "cobalt." To pre-adolescent (and increasingly, adolescent and older) male readers still uncertain about their vulnerability and power in the world, their sexuality and its possibilities, and (compared with women at the same age, on average) their intelligence, the minutiae surrounding objects that seem to afford their user power in that world become all-important. The phallic thrust of the cattle gun is so obvious as to deserve no further comment.

Anything that can be added on to an already desirable object that will afford greater lethality, greater speed, greater vision, or more information, fills in for what young men fear they lack. True intimacy with a young woman, friendship with someone they can completely trust and confide in fully, respect (or even time—let alone emotional intimacy) with a parent, acknowledgement from teachers—whatever is possible at any age among most of these things cannot be secured until after adolescence. But within the pages of a science fiction novel, or a crime novel, or as members of a car club, etc., young men can find ready substitutes for feelings of innate power, and honest emotional connection.

The details provided in descriptions of the fetish objects in *No Country for Old Men* call on the very generic terminology that the novel ultimately shrugs off. The string of qualifiers in the phrase, "hard-boiled Texas noir crime novel" narrows and specifies whatever aesthetic space might still be granted any "novel." The definitions of "hard-boiled" as a trope are "2. Callous; unfeeling" and "3. Unsentimental and practical; tough." The stereotypes regarding the location, "Texas," are too numerous to go into, but suffice to say this aspect of *No Country for Old Men* will seem to continue in the line of stoic cowboy existentialism that made *All the Pretty Horses* so popular, but which it, and particularly *Cities of the Plain*, also called into question, even to the point of parody.[2] But it will nonetheless allow Moss to go shopping for more fetish items.

Lest we assume that this "crime novel" might work in an optimistic mode where justice prevails and the hero lives, the word "noir" signals the disappointed male idealism that would complete the shield against vulnerability that this genre requires. *No Country for Old Men* so thoroughly exploits the fetishes of its apparent genre that by the third chapter I kept expecting one of the characters to slap around an obviously effeminate gunsel. But this book would not even allow such a vulnerable man on the side of the villains. Any sign of weakness at the surface level of characters marks them for dead. Thus, Moss never even seems to consider the loss of his wife when dealing with Chigurh. And when he knows he must run from the drug dealers—on foot—"he realize[s] that he would never see his truck again. Well, he said. There's lots of things you aint goin to see again" (*NCFOM* 29). Such as his wife, which is not the first thing to occur to him as lost.

Moss's character is first seen burdened not only by gear and descriptions of gear, but by the stereotypical situation in which we find him and the body language he assumes there. To be fair, anyone hunting in that part of the country might want that gear, and sitting on volcanic rock requires—even of someone accustomed to the back country—a slightly careful pose; a volcanic ridge is not, after all, a desk chair and does not feel like one. But the attention paid to all these aspects of the scene keep the reader safely distant from any deep identification of Moss's character:

> Moss sat with the heels of his boots dug into the volcanic gravel of the ridge and glassed the desert below him with a pair of twelve power german binoculars. His hat pushed back on his head. Elbows propped on his knees. The rifle strapped over his shoulder with a harness-leather sling was a heavybarreled .270 on a '98 Mauser action with a laminated stock of maple and walnut. It carried a Unertl telescopic sight of the same power as the binoculars. (*NCFOM* 8)

Even if we need to think about whether the .270 could hit the antelope at nearly a mile's distance (one supposes in order for readers up on their gun knowledge to infer something about Moss's willingness to take chances that could result in harm to other creatures), why do we care about the material of the stock?

That is not a complaint. Rather, this brief look at a passage that precedes many more fetish descriptions makes it clear to whom the book seems to be aimed: a Young Man enamored of these details.[3] We soon see "a Canjar trigger set to nine ounces" let loose a "150 grain bullet" fall short enough to ricochet "off the pan" to hit one of the antelope in the leg (*NCFOM* 9, 10). So much for all that gear and knowledge. Even the ground has been turned into something one might possess—a "pan"—in its flatness. Nonetheless, in this scene just before Moss's world collapses around him, turning him into the prey, he simply was too far away from these antelope for even the "twelve power german binoculars" and the "Unertl telescopic sight of the same power" to make it clear to him that he was too far away. And that his impressive gun could not shoot far enough.

Here is where, on rereading, the genre fetish gives itself away as self-conscious, and either parodic, or momentarily indulged in to set up the Old Man part of the novel. Having succeeded in seeing the antelope but failing to see the impossible distance between those desired objects and the power of his gear, Llewelyn will soon have to put his knowledge to use in recognizing the gear of others. Note that these items are recognized by Moss in detail, as the narrative remains close to him. (We do not get nearly so many of these details when the narrative follows Chigurh, let alone Bell.) Moss's knowledge of their particularity and appreciation of their value stands in for the dreams and details of deep character provided John Grady, for instance. Those levels of deep character—provided not only in dreams, but also in descriptions of setting and character movement involving John Grady, and even Lester Ballard—in *No Country for Old Men* have dried up into volcanic ridges and hardpan desert. By contrast, the vulnerability of John Grady and Ballard is revealed, while Moss's is concealed by fetish. I cannot find a dream, a gesture, or a pose in an environment from which to infer anything about Moss's character except that he is tough.

Moss's discovery of the rip-off focuses on the men only after, and even then among, their gear. He notices first that their "vehicles were four wheel drive trucks or Broncos with big all-terrain tires and winches and racks of rooflights" (*NCFOM* 11). When, on his return to the rip-off site, the truck pursues him, he hears its "slow lope of the cam. Big block engine" (*NCFOM* 28). Moss, a welder, might note that this truck—as indeed any truck that could clear rocks and other variations in the "pan" of a real desert without losing its oil pan or getting stuck would have to be—has been improved on. It can go farther, and (with that cam) faster from a dead stop, and this matters if it will be chasing you. Yet, it is highly doubtful that even Moss would be thinking about these things when he has every reason instead to be concentrating on, perhaps, the particular guns they might have and how they will use them on him. But realism is not the point here (if it ever is). The point is to add the next group of items to our list of Moss's knowledge of fetish presumably important to the Young Man reader.

The guns will soon regain their importance, of course. Moss has already found "a shortbarrelled H&K machinepistol with a black nylon shoulderstrap" lying in the lap of the dying drug dealer (*NCFOM* 12–13). As in a video game, where the player picks up one after another weapon, weighing the relative accuracy and lethality of each weapon for different situations, Moss's tour of the rip-off site leads him through a small arsenal, including a shotgun modified to delight David Brown, "fitted with a pistol stock and a twenty round drum magazine" (*NCFOM* 12). The "nickel-plated government .45 automatic lying cocked in the grass" that Moss finds "between [the] legs" of the man with the money—now dead—(*NCFOM* 17), reveals the obvious connection between guns as fetish objects and male sexual power. This "cocked" pistol (of a high caliber, we might note) has done the dead man no more good than did the .270 Moss used against the antelope. We might also note that this weapon is "government" issue, and therefore use our knowledge of that to suspect that some arm of law enforcement—whether acting undercover, or illegally—was involved in this drug deal gone wrong. But this proves to be a red herring, as nothing significant along those lines ever turns up in the plot.

Characters in this genre must also do things in a particular way, either in a manner that is immediately recognizable and manneristic, such as in the *Dragnet* dialogue to come, or through some surprising novelty of detail that fills in for the lack of more standard character development. Thus, instead of writing that Moss merely looked through his binoculars, the noun for the fetish object is turned into a powerful (and new) verb: "He glassed the terrain slowly" and finds the scene of the rip-off, and then later "glassed the country to the south" to find the man with the money (*NCFOM* 10–11, 15).[4] Any strong writer knows to find strong verbs. But this one highlights the object used to enhance Moss's vision more than it does what he is looking at. Scopophilic power depends on the differential of seeing and not being seen, as we are reminded when Moss is the one on the run, emasculated in the desert sand, worrying in a suddenly not-so-macho fashion about the very realistic dangers of spiders and snakes he might be inviting up the legs of his jeans (*NCFOM* 30). Furthermore, Moss "glass[ing]" the desert floor seems to possess enough heat along with light to melt the sand that comes into his view, to turn it into glass.

His trick of hiding the money in ventilation shafts similarly provides the particularity that promises to distinguish what would otherwise be a run-of-the-mill scene of, well, hiding the money. We need to believe that the man who seems to be our troubled hero is intelligent and powerful; even when he is outnumbered and outgunned, his sheer toughness (inexplicable as a distinction when guns are involved), his disciplined refusal to become attached to women, let alone anyone else, and his cleverness are all stand-ins for those qualities desired (and therefore felt lacking) by the insecure reader of genre fiction. But the neat verb given to Moss to use with his binoculars does not help him hit his target.

And hiding the money in the ventilation shaft only fools everyone but the one man he hopes to fool, Anton Chigurh. Compare the descriptions of the two men involving ventilation ducts serving Moss as a cache. Moss goes first, having cleverly bought a shotgun (and again, recalling David Brown's visit to the farrier), "a hacksaw and a millfile," tent poles, sidecutters, and that most useful of items for ingenious men: duct tape (*NCFOM* 87).

> He untied the little nylon bag and slid the poles out. They were light-weight aluminum tubes three feet long and he assembled three of them and taped the joints with duct tape so that they wouldnt pull apart. He went to the closet and came back with three wire hangers and sat on the bed and cut the hooks off with the sidecutters and wrapped them into one hook with the tape. Then he taped them to the end of the pole and stood up and slid the pole down the ductwork. (*NCFOM* 101)

All this careful detail only stiffens the symbolism. Moss goes to much trouble first to shove the money down one vent, only to pay for a second motel room that he luckily is correct in assuming contains a vent connecting to the same trunk line of a central air conditioning system.[5] Then he must construct this single "pole" from the tent poles to create yet another extension of himself so that he can reach the money. Not only is all this activity conspicuous, but it is also time-consuming and liable to failure—in a Hitchcockian moment the hook on his pole nearly fails him in reaching the goodies. But at least it can be said that Moss, no sentimental fellow, refuses to be loyal to one air duct.

Here is Chigurh retrieving the bag after Moss has been killed by one of the many gang members looking for him:

> He pulled the little bedside table over to the wall and stood and took a screwdriver from his rear pocket and began to back the screws out of the

louvered steel cover of the airduct. He set it on the table and reached in
and pulled out the bag and stepped down and walked over to the window and looked out at the parking lot (*NCFOM* 243).

By comparison, Chigurh retrieves the bag without all the improvised phallic
extensions and cleverness of Moss, who in any case seems to have become
less consummate in his ductwork insertions by this point.

So, we note both that Moss's knowledge of and care with fetishistic objects always fails him. And we note that he is the only one so deeply
caught up in all these details of the crime novel genre. Moss's character is
indeed a parody of the hard-boiled hero for a Young Man genre novel. Moss
reveals this to a comic degree in two of his later scenes.

In the first, he goes shopping again. Granted, Moss needs clothes, as
he is in the quintessential tough-guy position of walking out of a hospital
wearing nothing but the backwards gown. Earlier, he has bought clothes at
a Wal-Mart, but in this shopping trip, he is preparing for imminent combat
and must look the part. Moss has already noted the "expensive pair of Luc-
chese crocodile boots" worn by Wells (*NCFOM* 154). Now in a clothing
store after hours, Moss receives the kind of service that might make Bell
rethink his cynicism about the loss of manners. The details here prove that
Moss is no dime store cowboy: he buys the least expensive boots and is only
particular about his jeans. When the owner asks him if "white socks" suit
him, he replies, "White socks is all I wear." In this shopping scene so typical
of Hollywood films of the last twenty years, we are forced to wait until Moss
gets everything he needs—and we even get his underwear size (*NCFOM*
190–191). The attention to details continues to boil down his character
until he seems dangerously malleable in fitting the requirements of genre
fetish.

In the second scene, Moss picks up a hitchhiker. The dialogue then
finishes out the stereotypes, with lines like "I dont know where you're at
because I dont know who you are" (*NCFOM* 225), and the hitchhiker's
question, "So are you sorry you become a outlaw?" and Moss's answer:
"Sorry I didnt start sooner" (*NCFOM* 228).

The easiest interpretation of all this is that McCarthy simply meant to
boil the pot (or rather, in this case to boil his new novel in it to a hard-boiled
consistency), and deftly managed these details to create the taught noir hard-
boiled crime novel that readers seem to be recognizing in *No Country for Old
Men*. But if so, why do all these gadgets so miserably fail their users? Usually,
when loving detail is lavished on something possessed by the hero of genre
fiction, it will save his neck. Here, the details prove meaningless as Moss is

failed by his binoculars, his scope, his rifle, his airduct stratagem, and essentially by his clothes and his dialogue. Why?

The first sentence of *No Country for Old Men* reads, "*I sent one boy to the gas chamber at Huntsville*" (*NCFOM* 3). Many readers noticed that Texas had never executed anyone in a gas chamber. Complaints from enough of those who somehow enjoy McCarthy's work and yet are sticklers for accuracy in the correspondence between novels and life, grew loud enough that McCarthy actually released a statement through his publisher: "I put it in there to see if readers were on their toes" (Garner).

Perhaps. But only if we do not make the foolish assumption that this author—who almost never comments directly on his work—means by "on their toes" that a reader should be attuned to meaningless correspondences between the details of fiction and the details of life. What difference is there, really, between a gas chamber and an electric chair, a needle and a firing squad, except in absurd quibbles over the process chosen by the state putting a man to death? These differences are either analogous to those between a "Canjar" trigger and some other type, or they are differences of symbolic import. By "on their toes," the author of *Blood Meridian* might more likely mean that a reader ought to be alert to the foolishness of falling for literal truths in a book, of falling for the fetish instead of reading for the symbol.

As an intentional "error," the gas chamber reference strengthens the first sentence for a novel that seems to be aimed at a Young Man readership, but that proves to be something else. As with the fetish details that also mislead a first reader, this first sentence makes it clear that in *No Country for Old Men* there can be no simple recognition of just what the book is about. Not with any particularity in one answer. In general, it is about movement, and thus, about space. First Moss, and then Bell, flee the spaces in which we first find them, even as the world-narrowing power of Anton Chigurh threatens to collapse that space into a coffin. When Moss is finally killed at that three-quarter mark, the collapse of the Young Man book forces readers to acknowledge the true protagonist, and to recognize an altogether different genre at work. As Bell's voice takes over, so does the new genre—even as the chapters begin to fall inward and dwindle down. In the meantime, the spaces of *No Country for Old Men* have become differently unstable for both Moss and Bell.

SMUGGLING SPACES

First, *No Country for Old Men* merely echoes the collapse of space already occurring in *Cities of the Plain* and begun with the Epilogue to *Blood*

Meridian. Allowing for numerous exceptions, we can see that throughout the novels, the general run allowed characters in flight first extends, and then contracts. With John Wesley and then Cornelius Suttree both leaving the terrain of the Southern novels, we actually find the greatest latitude of movement when *Blood Meridian* takes us back a hundred years earlier. After its meridian, we have seen the journey narratives of *The Border Trilogy* were doomed to collapse into a smaller and smaller space, like a lasso tightening around the necks of those characters. In "The Last of the Trilogy: First Thoughts on *Cities of the Plain*," Edwin Arnold commented on what many readers saw with some surprise in that novel: "adjustment to a diminished existence, illustrated by the growing number of confined spaces found throughout this novel: barn stalls, hotel and bordello rooms, long dark corridors and back alleys, hospitals and morgue labs, all leading to the packing crate in which John Grady, the all-american man of the west, meets his death" (235).

Not only the Epilogue of *Blood Meridian*, but also the kid, meeting his death in the jakes, should have prepared us for this. As David Holloway and others have observed, McCarthy's understanding of the twentieth century includes the story of increasingly unavoidable commodification: not only every activity, and every place, but every person becomes subject to the strictures of economic activity. As I have put it, space becomes places. No, John Grady and Lacey, "they" do not "expect"—or really allow—"a man to ride a horse in this country" any more (*ATPH* 31). Not, at least, across the separately owned parcels of land demarcated by those barbed wire fences these boys have to cut and mend in order to make their way across West Texas.

Space, therefore, has collapsed into smaller places well before *No Country for Old Men* begins. That Llewelyn Moss takes an ill-advised shot at too great a distance and probably fatally wounds an antelope, and that it takes him so long to walk toward it (as if he would get close enough to shoot it again), fools even this native of the area into thinking that out there in the desert, he can pick up what does not belong to him and get away with it.[6] A visit to this area confirms the ease with which Moss might feel he has all the space in the world. Indeed, despite his modern equipment, Moss fails to get close enough to the antelope for a successful shot. But this does not erase the border observed at the Rio Grande River that Moss ends up splashing into and crossing back and forth. As soon as Moss picks up the wrong prize in this *frontera* space, he is in smuggling country. There, the movement of the man with the contraband, or the money, is constrained more than he might know, while the sense of place of those, such as Bell, who are not directly involved in smuggling feels suddenly unstable. Smuggling spaces confound the usual laws of physics regarding spaces collapsing into place. Moss's hope to disappear nonetheless proves foolish.

As it happens, another disappearing act in the book involves the drugs. We might reasonably expect that a plot retailing the found-drug-money conceit in any novel might have a bit more to do with the drugs. Money has not been a direct concern in McCarthy novels. But smuggling has, in a variety of ways. And given the noir aspect of the book, we might even expect someone to use drugs: at least a secondary picaró similar to a Blevins or Harrogate might get high. But the drugs here only briefly serve the direct purpose of providing evidence (among much other evidence cited by Bell) that civilization is falling apart. Beyond that, they prove merely to be the kind of contraband that we have seen before in McCarthy, even if the black tar heroin Moss finds in the back of the dying man's truck is, compared with previous contraband, an inherently dangerous substance of no legitimate value to Moss.

Nobody does the dope in *No Country for Old Men*, although we do get head-shaking *Dragnet* dialogue about frying brains without a cattle gun. "What am I supposed to do with this?" asks the sheriff of Eagle Pass, referring not to the drugs but to the nifty transponder. Bell's Joe Friday says log it for evidence and then begins the hardboiled editorial duet taking us back to the drugs:

> Dope.
> They sell that shit to schoolkids, [the other sheriff] said.
> It's worse than that.
> How's that?
> Schoolkids buy it. (*NCFOM* 194)

For Bell, drugs merely represent a larger post-sixties slide in American moral values. He won't disagree with Moss Senior, who won't blame Vietnam but says, "Vietnam was just the icin on the cake. We didn't have nothin to give to em to take over there." That last explanation recalls the regularity with which these novels surprisingly revolve around exchange goods.[7] The elder Moss goes on, "You cant go to war like that. You cant go to war without God" (*NCFOM* 294–295). Here "God" seems to have been the missing thing to "give em to take" to Vietnam. Drugs are the substitute for God, then, in the fallen world according to Bell. By contrast, the transponder receives more attention in this novel. It tells you the location of a man who thinks he can disappear. It collapses space into place with a beep.

Drugs turn out not to be the point. The heroin here is more symbolic than realistic. In *No Country for Old Men*, the reduction of space includes one constraint doomed to failure: the control of a border and the eradication of smuggling—truly an unfulfillable dream. In the most circumscribed space of Knoxville in *The Orchard Keeper* and *Suttree*—its government buildings and their controlling reach beyond their walls—what is regarded as contraband is that which otherwise might move around uncontrolled on its own, spreading disease or preying on livestock. The government there seeks regulation of movement; where it cannot hope for that, it demands the eradication of what moves.

The government therefore attempts to tax the movement of alcohol, and eradicate raptors and bats. But in the case of the bounties, this reversal of the usual transaction little matters. The results are the same as with all commodified goods, whether organic or synthetic, alive or dead: they transport more easily when reduced to their essence—or at least the essence visible in the market that, because of some disparity or surfeit, offers a bounty for them, dead or alive. This reduction of the commodity becomes easier, though, if what the economy desires is its erasure. To erase wolves or bison, a bounty on just their hides should suffice—though perhaps also their bones, as we see before the kid reaches Fort Griffin in *Blood Meridian*. Bats and birds are small enough to move whole. If it is the erasure of a people that is desired, then for the purposes of transportation those people can be reduced even further, given their size—to nothing but their scalps, as we see in *Blood Meridian*.

Holloway examines the many objects exchanged in McCarthy:

> In a fictive realm where scalps, children, buffalo bones, ferry crossings, ornate weaponry, whisky, landscape, and life itself are all merely "things" to be bought and sold according to the laws of the marketplace, the heterogeneous diversity of the object world is reduced to a single identity, a homogenous mass of matter, a collection of things linked together by their common exchange-value, their shared status as commodities in a commodity world. (104–105)

I would argue only that *Blood Meridian* includes some uncommodified terrain, spaces not yet rendered into places. At least not until the book's Epilogue. But it, too, depends on a type of proto-smuggling.

The border fiction renders smuggling in more obvious terms. After the reinscription of any a border's power by *Blood Meridian*'s Epilogue, the illegal transport of commodified objects amounts to literal smuggling, if not to those doing the carrying. Billy Parham believes he is repatriating the she wolf. And John Grady is, in more than just the legal sense, recovering the horses in a reenactment of older border struggles. Mr. Johnson tells of a 1917 raid "to cross some stolen horses we'd recovered" (*COTP* 63). But the phrase "stolen horses" comes before "recovered" in such a way as to remind us that there can be disagreements about horse ownership. To "cross" your own horses amounts to "recover[y]," but to "cross" someone else's amounts to smuggling. In *No Country for Old Men*, we hardly see any border crossing at all. And yet, the fact of smuggling hovers over the destroyed men and trucks found by Moss.

Bell professes some knowledge of the bloody history of the area. "*That country had not had a time of peace much of any length at all that I knew of. I've read a little of the history of it since and I aint sure it ever had one*" (*NCFOM* 307). Nonetheless, that history seems lost on him. Or, as would be more typical not only of someone professing Bell's views, but also of most people professing political views that seem opposite them, he has likely read selectively; he has read only one side of a many-sided subject. In his arguments—notably all of which are appeals to emotion written by an author who, in Holden's case, has proven himself quite capable of working the corners of ethos and logos as well—Bell refers only to the "settler" side of that history. When he argues that for "*the early settlers*," watching their wives "*and children killed and scalped and gutted like fish has a tendency to make* some *people irritable*" (*NCFOM* 195, my emphasis), Bell reveals that he has forgotten about, or is ignorant of, the peoples already living in that area for centuries before those "*early settlers*," receiving the same treatment from the very real Glanton gang and their ilk.

This seems so obvious to me, and that it ought to be obvious to anyone reading this book, that *No Country for Old Men* has begun to assume an important position for me in our time of divisive, even polarized lack of genuine civic rhetoric. Bell's use of the word "*early*" echoes the empty repetition of the word "aboriginal" or "native" on the other side of this history, reducing an understanding of our collective bloody past to a sibling argument over who had dibs on a territory, or on who started the violence over it. As if either putatively white "settlers" or idealized "native americans" knew of no violence until they encountered one another and began the scalping.

Bell's fearful and therefore selective history leaves him ironically more, not less, vulnerable to the realities of the continual and inevitable violence of smuggling spaces. The seemingly sudden killing in his county (with a law enforcement response that, ineffectual as it is, leads Bell to compare the rip-off to a historic flood twenty years earlier) feels like an invasion of lawlessness previously unknown to those parts. Even if we ignore the illegal crossing of humans and horses in Bell's younger years, his willful ignorance that things were not, indeed, better in the old days *in toto* weakens his legs for standing strong wherever he finds himself.[8] Bell's sense of place falls away from under his feet, like the desert and mountains in that area when, after an inland sea dried up, heaved itself into a landscape that is more often than not sideways or upside down. We see Bell driving, more and more, across larger swaths of West Texas—but always a bit slow (unhurried enough to stop for coffee and pie) so that once he arrives, the most recent history has not only missed hurting him, but has also rendered the horror at his destination—of a drug shoot-out, a burned car, a motel shooting, a grieving father—distant to him. When these places become a single frighteningly open space to Bell—a borderland where the border keeps nothing back—he retreats.

Smuggling spaces therefore reverse the otherwise inexorable human trend toward reinforcement of boundaries and commodification of goods under cross-boundary agreements, such as NAFTA. They resist the recognition of borders agreed on in treaties, of taxes levied by governments they hardly recognize, or refuse to recognize at all. Most of the traffic on the international highways in the epilogue of *Cities of the Plain* may be sanctioned by NAFTA, but a significant proportion of it is sanctioned by underground economies trafficking in illegal narcotics and illegal aliens, both supplied on the cheap to the U.S.

The world cannot be wide enough, however, to run from Anton Chigurh. Despite the reversal of place into frightening space for Bell, Moss's actions put him under the power of the same constraints as those limiting the movements of John Grady and Billy in *Cities of the Plain*. All are endangered by the determination of space by a more powerful other. This is another reason why McCarthy chose the gas chamber for the execution visit that opens the book: the gas chamber is the only modern means of executing a man or woman that already creates a controlled space around the condemned, separating him or her from the rest of the world before death makes that separation irrevocable. (In lethal-injection—the method used at Texas's Huntsville prison—the use of intravenous tubes, rather than syringes directly injected into the condemned, along with the removal of those administering lethal injection to a separate space from the room containing the man or woman strapped to the cross-like table, are all attempts to translate this spatial distinction into our drug-obsessed and medicalized culture.) The gas chamber recalls the "hiss and click of the plunger" from Chigurh's cattle gun, sounding as it does "like a door closing" (*NCFOM* 7). As such, the closing door of the gas chamber collapses space.

FLIGHT TO JERUSALEM

Although it begins in italicized remembrance, the subject matter of that opening (Bell's visit to an execution) seems on first reading to be of a piece with the action that follows it. With all the violence in the roman type, it seems that this typographical remove for a relatively contemplative voice will serve merely to offset the violence, even to comment on it in ironic detachment—as if Bell is standing outside action that is occurring within a space safely sealed off from him. These monologues raise at least three questions.

First, how do Bell's monologues compare with previous italicized prologues for McCarthy chapters? After all, McCarthy has often used this technique. Here, contemplation alternates with the action. But not on anything like the level of the fireside chats of Holden, where philosophy asserts itself over history, between each massacre in *Blood Meridian*. Neither does the typographic switching provide the social voice of an oral history outside the action of the main character, as in *Child of God*. Whatever distance there is between Sheriff Bell's regular italicized reflections (actual thinking, or so it seems) and the action on the ground—following Llewelyn Moss and Anton Chigurh and even Carson Wells—we realize that rather than functioning within the generic expectations of the crime novel genre, these monologues begin to overwhelm that action.

Second, then, how do Bell's monologues fit the genre shift in *No Country for Old Men*? Initially by presenting that spatial separation for comment on the Young Man book, but eventually, by accomplishing the genre shift begun by that book's structural collapse. Particularly when the Young Man book later refuses to provide standard (or even cleverly modified) plot points that would have satisfied a crime novel structure, something has to fill the void. Bell's voice is there to fill in the relatively lengthening silences between gunfire. Indeed, the structure of the Young Man's book within this novel runs backwards, in comparison with the usual escalation of violence to a climactic shoot-out. Here, mayhem explodes along the border one third of the way into the book, opposite the end of a second act in a conventional three-act screenplay. We never actually see Moss die but are rather told the story third-hand, from the point of view of a deputy who got his version from a witness. Moss and his hitchhiker have simply disappeared from us, like Ophelia, with only their bodies making a reappearance to occasion a few words from the true protagonist. Bell's monologues pick up the pieces after the characters starring in the Young Man book within *No Country for Old Men* have run out of luck, time, and space.

By providing us with a character that is not so hard-boiled as is Moss to comment on the action, the narrative includes a moral center that Bell, laconic in his speech during that action, could not otherwise provide outside the tight-fitting constraints of *Dragnet* quips. In a work of film noir such as *Double Indemnity*, Leonard Neff's voice-over narration accomplishes both an ongoing confession and an ironic distance from the action that will conclude with his death. In that film, the voice-over performs Neff's confession to Barton Keyes, the "bulldog" who remains forever watchful, and yet who proves to be one step behind helping Neff by catching him. By the end of *No Country for Old Men*, Bell has similarly failed to help Moss by catching *him*. But as here the genre shift moves the weight of the novel onto those monologues, we have our last question about them.

Third, what is the deeper nature of Bell's italicized monologues? Bell has begun a very different confession from that of the central figure in a noir narrative. The book ends with Bell so defeated that he can only retreat into an image of a past that never existed, into a mythology that seems more of a defense than a viable dream. Instead of a vision of how a man might live outside the space of his dreams, Bell's dream only throws into sharper relief the losses in his life. In this sense, Bell's monologues serve as evidence that his conscious control of life has become overwhelmed by unconscious fears more than those myriad worries he cites in his earlier grumbling over the state of society. The narrative including his combat confession points to guilt over his behavior during combat. But that, too, proves to be another red herring (the circumstances of his position with the machine gun prove that his guilt over leaving that post is notably inflated). Bell's real fears lie deeper, and thus his monologues employ the comparatively dreamlike quality of italicized type to take us into those fears, in the darker space of the unconscious.

As I had first read into the new country of the Old Man book, however, the force of the genre fiction that preceded it—despite its failures, ultimately, to conform to that genre—kept me from recognizing the new genre as a total replacement of the earlier book. The new genre turns out to be, on rereading, evenly and fully realized throughout most of Bell's monologues. Until this new genre itself collapses into the unconscious, it repeats the laments of Jeremiah in the Old Testament.

In the King James Version of that book, Jeremiah's first worry is that he is insufficient to his god's purpose. God has to inform him that he is his son in a special way, that he has already "ordained" him to be "a prophet unto the nations" before his birth (1:5). Jeremiah nonetheless exclaims, "Lord GOD! behold, I cannot speak: for I am a child" (1:6). God solves this problem of insecurity in two ways. First, he tells Jeremiah simply not to say that he is a child (in other words, to grow up by pretending to be grown up). Second, God assures him that he will put his words into Jeremiah's mouth. It is a father's reassurance to a son that the son will become a man, but nevertheless that the son will always keep within him the power and truth of the father's word—that he will always be a son.

The "evil" that God is worried about first comes from another space, "out of the north" (1:15). At first, God's purpose is to empower Jeremiah to guard against this by building "a defenced city, and an iron pillar, and brasen walls against the whole land" to protect what seems to be a remarkably small space within which God is not offended and his new prophet cannot be harmed. But immediately, the evil appears to be within that space, as well. This is the jealous and vindictive God displeased with the failures of his chosen people: "And I brought you into a plentiful country, to eat the fruit thereof and the goodness thereof; but when ye entered, ye defiled my land, and made mine heritage an abomination" (2:7). A bit more will suffice:

> Hath a nation changed their gods, which are yet no gods? but my people have changed their glory for that which doth not profit. Be astonished, O ye heavens, at this, and be horribly afraid, be ye very desolate, saith the LORD. For my people have committed two evils; they have forsaken me the fountain of living waters, and hewed them out cisterns, broken cisterns, that can hold no water. (2:11–13)

Bell's complaints recapitulate these concerns of his God. First, he sees the evil as having arrived from outside his place in the form of somehow invading Indians that *"scalped and gutted like fish"* the women and children of those *"early settlers"* (*NCFOM* 195). Here, Bell's patriarchal assumption that the actual *"early settlers"* were the men, and not so directly *"their"* women and children, fits perfectly the typology of the Old Testament, as well as the archetypal unconscious idealization of masculinity for which we are headed. Second, the evil arrives from the outside in the form of drugs, run and dealt by "Mexicans." As Bell seems to assume that all of these are Mexican nationals (indeed, it is unclear if Bell regards Mexican-Americans as part of his flock), these dealers are outsiders.

But here is where the problem collapses one spatial degree, from xenophobia to the mistrust of one's own tribe, matching perfectly the collapse of God's fears in the book of Jeremiah: the second threat is that the children inside the walls of the space protected by God's prophet have not heard God, or have forgotten him, and that they will therefore adopt foreign gods and customs. Bell's *Dragnet* dialogue now assumes a biblical tone, echoing God's shift from xenophobia to a frustrated wrath against the children who have forgotten him: "It's worse than that," he tells the Sheriff who has commented on the outside threat (the drug dealers who sell to "schoolkids"). "Schoolkids buy it" (*NCFOM* 194). In other words, no one makes them use drugs; they choose them. The most heartfelt expressions of jeremiad fears in Bell's monologues concern children, whether unborn, of school age, or grown up and gone to war. He worries about Moss, and the other inhabitants of his county, with a patriarchal feeling for them as his figurative children.

Bell is a model for the god in McCarthy's philosophy: a slightly doddering figure old before his time, worried first about the evil from without the space he keeps for his people, but then secondly worried about the evil taken into that space, and ultimately worried that, quite apart from whatever evil might exist outside that space, his people have lost their way—they have forgotten to listen to him. But it is also the case that he may have forgotten how to speak to them. Thus the third, inmost worry of God and Bell is that their children have given up their acknowledgement of what is good and righteous because of some failure on the part of God or Bell; the parent ultimately owns all failures of the child.

Asked about the (apparently sudden) high crime rate in his county, Bell looks within that place: "*It starts when you begin to overlook bad manners. Any time you quit hearin Sir and Mam the end is pretty much in sight*" (*NCFOM* 304). Here again Bell's worry is centered in the children (the ones buying the drugs, rather than the ones selling them), whom he sees as having lost their sense of place, in the sense that they no longer automatically show verbal respect for people who have gone before them. The first identification of the problem, however, points to parents. Bell doesn't point right back at himself, but at the reporter with that "you." By no longer exercising sufficient authoritative control, however, the patriarch is really the origin of the sin. The trope embedded in "overlook" suggests not only a hierarchical differential of power, but also distance.

McCarthy shows us this the first time we see Bell as a character in the narrative: "Bell climbed the rear steps of the courthouse and went down the hall to his office. He swiveled his chair around and sat and looked at the telephone. Go ahead, he said. I'm here." After this grumbling—like a father who knows he is about to be bothered again with something trivial to him and yet important to his child—Bell picks up the phone and we infer the other side of the conversation from his. "Mrs Downie I believe he'll come down directly. Why dont you call me back here in a little bit. Yes mam" (*NCFOM* 41).

This cornball moment almost dropped the book from my hands. Worse than a formulaic film, this seems closer to something from a long-running television series whose best writers have all wandered off to better gigs. It introduces Bell in the perfect manner, of course, for the Young Man's book as it so perfectly fits the cliché of the beleaguered and bored country lawman about to be overwhelmed by the excitement of the plot that will engulf him. And yet, it also introduces how Bell sees himself. Surprisingly, long after one endures this scene, it echoes through the collapse of Bell's jeremiad into his dream.

First in this telephone scene, note Bell's good manners: at age fifty-seven, he uses both the honorific "Mrs" and "mam" for a woman who is probably older. The cat stuck up a tree emergency is so clichéd as to bring on the severest pain in the reader: yes, our sheriff character's office is normally a slow place. My, how Anton Chigurh will, by comparison, shake things up. Bell first resents this call. "It's money, he said. You have enough money you dont have to talk to people about cats in trees." On second thought, however, he remembers his role as the protector of people whose concerns may seem trivial to them, but for whom those concerns are important. "Well." The period suggests another pause. "Maybe you do" (*NCFOM* 41).

Maybe. But we notice Bell's ambivalence here, his understandable feeling of being put out to little purpose, and even the uncertainty permeating his reminder to himself that indeed, as sheriff in a largely empty county with a few frightened people scattered across the desert, his job does include reassuring old women about their cats. His errands quickly involve chasing after Moss (or might have involved chasing after Chigurh, which he seems assiduously to avoid). Nevertheless, his stops at the house, the pace of his dialogue, his pauses for coffee and pie, reveal that his favorite part of the job really is not in having to listen to his children, but rather in an enjoyment of the places of his office. Moving between his desk, his car, a booth in a cafe, and across somewhat frightening wide open spaces to various towns in which he is always known and recognized, give him the feeling that his children recognize in him the patriarchal figure who deserves recognition, verbal respect, freedom of movement, and pie.

But this does not mean he has been speaking to his children with regularity, much less with success. And even if he has, on what authority can he speak? His ethos seems limited to that of a reluctant counselor for the tremulous owners of wayward cats. It might also be his job to actually protect them. But he knows he is ineffectual at this (as indeed was the God of Jeremiah

worried about those people to the north): he is so outgunned and outnumbered as to make it ridiculous for him to take a stand against the drug dealers.
And they know it. *"I think for me the worst of it is knowin that probably the
only reason I'm even still alive is that they have no respect for me. And that's very
painful"* (*NCFOM* 215). Bell's only hope, as God's in the book of Jeremiah,
is that his children will again recognize righteousness, show respect for his
authority, and refuse to take up the evil customs (drugs, another religion)
from outside the place of safety within the larger wilderness.

Why would Bell's children listen to him? Bell, like many a real sheriff
in West Texas counties, and like the god regularly discussed by many McCarthy characters, is powerless to do anything about evil. Or—and this provides evidence of a more troubled theology, and one that must retain some of
the resentment of the distant father so hated by Cornelius Suttree—God is
merely preoccupied. In *Suttree*, he busies himself with floods and dams and
collapsing slate walls, oblivious to the carnage beneath his play. Like a giant
child himself, he moves things around from time to time, sometimes curious
about the progress of an individual ant—perhaps even an ant-on-sugar—but
he does not preside over a simple top-down universe in which he regularly
mediates the activity on lower levels of existence. [9]

This is why I argued at the end of Chapter Four that Holden's claims
should not be too readily discounted as inaccurate. Morality may be something conjured up, like a trick, by human beings living in a nonmoral universe. Morality may be inevitably medial, with no connection up or down.
Our feelings of connection below, to animals and the natural world, proves
to be no more than our inability to evolve out of anthropocentric habits of
epistemology. So, too, our feelings of connection above, to the larger universe: these may only be an unkillable figment of the empathic systems our
brains have evolved for our life as social creatures. Just as we are good (and
terrible) at imagining what someone else is thinking and feeling, we might
simply have the habit of projecting a god onto a universe that has none.

Bell's final dream makes it difficult to tell whether Freud, or Jung,
should be our guide on this last question. Freud, of course, derided "oceanic"
feeling as a delusion resulting from the failure to recognize "the reality principle" (11–12). Jung, on the other hand, believed that such feelings evidenced
the truth of a collective unconscious. This isn't the space to settle between
these two, but I remain curious as to how McCarthy's visions, dreams, and
descriptions of feelings of a deep connection with the universe ultimately
come out: true, or delusional?

I cannot see this resolved within the books. But either way, we are
headed down to myth and the unconscious with Bell, as his role speaking the

worries of Jeremiah wears down under the terrible weight of God's absence, and as his role as a symbolic god proves that he, too, remains too far from people to really help them. The possibility that any god might intervene on the behalf of Bell and his people seems ruled out by Bell's uncle when he asks him,

> Do you think God knows what's happenin?
> I expect he does.
> You think he can stop it?
> No. I dont. (*NCFOM* 269)

RIDING FROM JERUSALEM

Thus, even the jeremiad, the genre that so takes over *No Country for Old Men*, itself wears out, collapsing into confession and dream. The key to Bell's inability to meaningfully intervene on the behalf of his citizens goes all the way back to his departure from an absurd situation where he most certainly would have been killed and probably would not have accomplished anything but killing a few more German soldiers. And yet, this memory seems to ruin his ability to think of himself as effective in any way. Bell's war experience seems to have damaged him irrevocably; he has already fought, even bravely, and yet the hopelessness of continuing that fight emasculates him. But this obsession with a particular guilt proves to be an unreliable inflation. As such, it leads inevitably to a projection of that inflated archetype that remains outside Bell's ability to integrate the god-like power of his position into a whole personality.

Bell's concluding dream, as well as his jeremiad worries, echoes another father in McCarthy. As with the god of The Old Testament, we have only a general name for him, his family name alone: "Cole." As with so many other names in McCarthy, this one resonates with meaning. One step down the alphabet from "Cold" (and thus more remote), the name sounds the same as "Coal," that last cinder that carries within its heart the fire that must not be allowed to burn out in movements through the endless space of darkness. Perhaps only now does the insistence of the narrator about John Grady's name ring true: "The boy's name was Cole. John Grady Cole" (*ATPH* 7). Even seeing his mother with another man does not flush him from the San Antonio hotel where he spies on her. He must be sure that she is sleeping with someone other than his father before he can leave San Angelo, or at least that she has indeed renounced his father's name. By checking to see if she has used that name to register for her own room, he finds out: "No," the clerk tells him. "No Cole" (*ATPH* 22).

Like Bell, John Grady's father first appears to us as an already defeated, emasculated, and sorrowful man. He tells John Grady that "[w]hat you won was gravy but what you lost was hard come by" (*COTP* 214). This pronouncement comes as a posthumous recollection two novels after the father's admission that in one poker game he "won twenty-six thousand dollars in twenty-two hours of play," including the hand for "four thousand dollars in the last pot," "with three natural queens" (*ATPH* 12). Judging by the reduced circumstances of his domestic space in the hotel, we know that Cole Sr. has lost more money than he has ever won. The one "queen" he had in life deserted him, long before the war took away his masculinity in some other way. He tells his son that "It aint her fault. I aint the same as I was" (*ATPH* 12), even though well before Cole Sr. left for World War II, John Grady's mother abandoned them both. "She left out of here. She was gone from the time you were six months old till you were about three" (*ATPH* 25). Like many of McCarthy's young male would-be fathers, this mother headed West, to California.

The failure of Cole Sr. as a father figure originates in this, and subsequent, emasculations. He is just as ruined as Bell, and even shares the idiosyncrasy of stirring his coffee out of nervous habit—with no sugar in it (*ATPH* 24, *NCFOM* 90). Like Bell, he cannot assimilate the news, where even the domestic conflicts of movie stars echo his own private sense of failure: "How can Shirley Temple be getting divorced?" he asks his son. Then he continues, "The Good Book says that the meek shall inherit the earth and I expect that's probably the truth. I aint no freethinker, but I'll tell you what. I'm a long way from bein convinced that it's all that good a thing" (*ATPH* 13). Cole's cynicism here may seem atheistic, but no more so than Bell's ultimate inability to believe in a God who can, or will, intervene on earth.

Nonetheless, Cole Sr. gives his son a saddle as an early Christmas present (*ATPH* 14), and it is the father, rather than the son, who at least verbally pushes for some time together—riding horses—telling John Grady, "You dont have to if you dont want to" (*ATPH* 9). This remains the only scene in all of McCarthy where a father makes any gesture toward emotional connection with a main character. What follows?

First, John Grady puts off this ride. But eventually, they go out together, and we seem to see the son from the eyes of a father who appreciates him:

> The boy who rode on slightly before him sat a horse not only as if
> he'd been born to it which he was but as if were he begot by malice
> or mischance into some queer land where horses never were he would
> have found them anyway. Would have known that there was something
> missing for the world to be right or he right in it and would have set
> forth to wander wherever it was needed for as long as it took until
> he came upon one and he would have known that that was what he
> sought and it would have been. (*ATPH* 23)

The highly biblical language here ("but as if were he begot" and the finality of "and it would have been") is actually King James diction. As such,
it points us as readily to myth as to the religion that seems less powerful
for John Grady, that seems unrecognized by his father, and that has failed
Bell.

Spatially, this scene enacts a dream fulfilled as it could rarely be in
that fenced country of 1949, and as it never occurs for McCarthy's other
protagonists. These two, father and son, are moving through open spaces
without the violence of the Glanton gang and yet among ruins that suggest
the impermanence of some of the constraints on space that have appeared
here since the kid rode through. "The wreckage of an old wooden windmill
fallen among the rocks" and "[a]n ancient pickethouse" almost suggest the
decay of a pastoral. They even pass "crippled fenceposts propped among the
rocks that carried remnants of a wire not seen in that country for years."
This could be the fencing from *Blood Meridian*'s Epilogue. Indeed, after
that fallen windmill, we get the quintessential *Blood Meridian* sentence:
"They rode on" (*ATPH* 23).

John Grady knows his father is dying, however, and that he is already
powerless—was always powerless—to preserve the family's reserve of a
land where horses can still be found. As I have argued in Chapter Six, he
must ride on to replace everything he is losing outside San Angelo. But we
have now seen that not only his grandfather, but also his father will be left
behind—one buried, and the other heading for the grave.

Bell's father has also died, while Bell was still relatively young. Meanwhile, Bell's marriage has survived the loss of an only child. At his first
mention of her, he immediately says he will not talk about her. Then, later,
as the chapters collapse around his monologues, he confesses that he talks
to her. "*She would be thirty now. That's all right. I dont care how that sounds.
I like talkin to her. Call it superstition or whatever you want. I know that over
the years I have give her the heart I always wanted for myself and that's all
right. That's why I listen to her*" (*NCFOM* 285). This confession turns out

to be only an admission that the father keeps a lost child alive through his own voice.

But either this remains too private for Bell to elaborate on, and end with, or it does not ring in his heart as does the loss of his father, or even his confessed feelings of guilt over combat and as a failed father-figure for his county. Because here we have an idea, a thought, more than an image. And thinking never matches the power of image. Bell's evocation of his daughter remains at the level of sound—possibly quite powerful to him, but we cannot know for sure. "*I listen to what she says and what she says makes good sense. I with she'd say more of it. I can use all the help I can get.*" It may be moving that here the father is listening to the child, and has indeed traded places with her, taking advice from her. But we know nothing about what it is that she tells him. Bell cuts off these thoughts and we never return to them: "*Well, that's enough of that*" (*NCFOM* 285).

This is thinking. And for the first time since *Suttree*, and fundamentally in a different way, McCarthy has characters thinking all over the place in *No Country for Old Men*. Bell sometimes uses the phrase to lead up to what he is actually thinking about. But more often, a phrase such as "he thought about that" refuses to tell us more than what we could already have inferred. McCarthy also uses such phrases to collapse the space between psychology and a social tension between characters in this novel. In a parody of this, Chigurh picks up a signal from the transponder and wonders who still has it. "He could think of no reason for the transponder unit to be in the hotel. He ruled out Moss because he thought Moss was almost certainly dead. That left the police. Or some agent of the Matacumbe Petroleum Group. Who must think that he thought that they thought that he thought they were very dumb. He thought about that" (*NCFOM* 171).

This "thinking" is nothing like Suttree's interior monologues, but is rather the often meaningless expository thinking on the part of characters in genre fiction—again, filling in the spaces of their absent characters with plot machinations of no import. The inclusion of the full name of the evil corporation involved in the drug smuggling even takes us back to fetish; here the specificity of the name stands in for the much deeper complexity of the relationships between real corporations and drug smuggling. But that would take time, and Chigurh is busy thinking.

My reference to this last evidence of the genre book we have already left behind is meant to point out how much Bell, too, has been "thinking." And it does him no good. Rather, his "thoughts" revolve much less around matters of immediate responsibility and possibilities of action than do Moss's and Chigurh's. Rather, Bell is continually trying to think himself free from feelings without denying their power. Rejecting the Western assumption that all psychological phenomena are the products of each individual mind that is experiencing them, Jung argued that the contrary is the case: "Psychic existence is the only category of existence of which we have *immediate* knowledge, since nothing can be known unless it first appears as a psychic image. Only psychic existence is immediately verifiable. To the extent that the world does not assume the form of a psychic image, it is virtually non-existent" (*Portable* 486, his emphasis).

It may be that the loss of his daughter remains an important component of Bell's character. And Bell's confession about his actions in combat may also inform his sense of guilt as a failed father. By telling his uncle that story, we approach an image that occasions Bell's thoughts about it. But the description of Bell's actual use of the machine gun nearly tilts back to the gun fetish of the earlier book.

> That thing was aircooled and it was belt fed out of a metal box and I figured if I let em run up a little more on me I could operate on em out there in the open and they wouldnt call in another round cause they'd be too close. I scratched around and I dug around some more and come up with the ammo box for it and I got set up behind the section of wall there and jacked back the slide and pushed off the safety and here we went. (*NCFOM* 275)[10]

This has its merits, but they are not strongly related to Bell's guilt. In fact, this is not at all the language of a confession, but rather the deftly handled transcription of a good storyteller not at all averse to having himself imagined in a heroic act. Furthermore, there is no image here, but rather another of the good storyteller's stock in trade: expert "doing."

In place of "thinking," we have the same kind of impressive "doing" that I earlier characterized as another aspect of the crime novel genre: the things handled, and the way they are handled here, is what is important. And in another echo of Moss and his guns and truck fetishes, this is a scene of modern warfare, centering on the specificity of technology involved. It can of course be objected that any question of Bell staying in that position is absurd, as eventually a half-competent officer among the Germans would have them pull back as a shell blows this machine-gunner to pieces. Bell earned his medal by picking up the machine gun at all. Beyond that, his guilt is misplaced. Why?

Because the power of images around his father keeps that man at an impossible remove from Bell. Even as Bell confesses that he knows he is, in some ways, "*a better man*" than his father (*NCFOM* 308), it is hard to believe that Bell truly feels this way.[11] The image we have of the father includes in him an impossible power, one that Bell can never hope to assume. We might imagine this broken-down sheriff waking from his dreams, pleading as did Jeremiah, "Lord GOD! behold, I cannot speak: for I am a child" (1:6). Here is the image of the father who was not even on the battlefield with Bell that day, and yet is so assumed to possess a superior courage that this image will surpass Bell's description of fumbling for an ammo box. In Bell's words, his father would have "set there till hell froze over and then stayed a while on the ice" (*NCFOM* 279).

BELL'S DREAM

Bell's final dream includes an image familiar in Freud, but with a figure whose archetypal power can best be understood through Jungian theory. First, the fact that the father is carrying fire. In *Civilization and its Discontents*, Freud discusses a primeval scene around a fire. In a now-famous footnote, Freud ponders what might have been a first realization of the human (and particularly, and as Freud would have it, only male) capacity for control of emotions in order to control nature. In this mythic scene, Freud imagines the first person to realize that fire might be preserved, and carried forward.

> Putting out fire by micturating—a theme to which modern giants, Gulliver in Lilliput and Rabelais' Gargantua, still hark back—was [. . .] a kind of sexual act with a male, an enjoyment of sexual potency in a homosexual competition. The first person to renounce this desire and spare the fire was able to carry it off with him and subdue it to his own use. By damping down the fire of his own sexual excitation, he had tamed the natural force of fire. (37)

This imaginative idea suggests the overemphasis on constraint and repression that refers most accurately here to Moss, and the Young Man book. But we can keep this in mind as something behind Bell's dream.[12]

Second, as I have argued in my interpretation of Bell's combat confession, his father looms too large in his imagination. And the tension between image and "thought" running through Bell's monologues further calls on Jung for another interpretation of the final dream. In Jungian terms, the image precedes all of Bell's ideas, and the grotesquely heavy mythological weight of the father in his dream explains Bell's inability to work out any coherent thoughts to explain an overwhelming feeling that, in comparison to his father, he must forever remain a child. Jung insists that before the idea comes the image, tracing "idea" back to the ideal forms in Plato and before that, to "the 'primal warmth' of the Stoics" and the "ever-living fire" of Heraclitus (*Archetypes* 33). Because Bell cannot see an image of himself realizing his father potential, that potential is only available projected outside him, in the form of the archetypal father figure we recognize in his final dream.

As Jung also saw that in the presence of the image, there is a release of emotion, we can also see why this dream closes *No Country for Old Men*: the archetype in this dream is so emotion-charged that it generates more emotion than any other for Bell. Archetypes also become strongest during abandonment, or after a loss. The murders in *No Country for Old Men*, particularly the death of Moss and the hitchhiker, remind Bell of the death of his daughter. He talks about his daughter in the second monologue after he views the bodies in the morgue (*NCFOM* 240–241, 285).

Another reason to continue with Jung, more than Freud, is that Jung's acceptance of a mythological explanation for "oceanic" feeling provides us with an explanation for Bell's thoughts and visions without merely pathologizing them, as would Freud. For Jung, the telos of humanity is the recognition of godhood, and the self is the recognition of the god-like in temporal life. Instead of projecting this out into religion, Bell's recursive and obsessional thinking about the problems besetting his sense of place and his relationship with both his lost father and his lost daughter eventually move him away from his role as Jeremiah. But he cannot manage to find the god in himself, particularly as he feels that he is a failure for the citizenry he will leave behind. He therefore falls back on an archetypal image that signals his past and current failures, even as it seems to point to nostalgia.

The move to archetype for Bell become clear in his comments about the water trough:

> You could see the chisel marks in the stone. It was hewed out of solid rock and it was about six foot long and maybe a foot and a half wide and about that deep. Just chiseled out of the rock. And I got to thinkin about the man that done that. That country had not had a time of peace much of any length at all that I knew of. I've read a little of the history of it since and I aint sure it ever had one. But this man had set down with a hammer and chisel and carved out a stone water trough to last ten thousand years. Why was that? What was it that he had faith in? It wasnt that nothin would change. He had to know bettern that. [. . .] And I have to say that the only thing I can think is that there was some sort of promise in his heart.

And I dont have no intention of carvin a stone water trough. But I would
like to be able to make that kind of promise. I think that's what I would like
most of all. (NCFOM 307)

Thinking about this trough, Bell nearly advances farther than he does in
his last dream toward Jungian individuation. Of course, the creator of this
trough did have faith—in himself, but also in all those who would follow
his passing in archetypal terms. The "promise in his heart" had to be that he
would simply show up, and do this work for the sake of its own creative exercise, the skill it takes, and some sense that what he works at would indeed
endure. That promise is the promise one makes in creating something in a
bid for immortality. Three resonances we find in the trough advance all this
in Jungian terms, but also in more particular terms for McCarthy.

First, in Jungian terms, the trough represents the mythical possibilities
of taking over the power of God. One of the first complaints that God makes
to Jeremiah involves the control of water: "For my people have committed
two evils; they have forsaken me the fountain of living waters, and hewed
them out cisterns, broken cisterns, that can hold no water" (2:13). By hewing their own troughs, humans become as gods, as Jung would see it, both in
their assumption of a power previously thought by unindividuated people to
reside only in a transcendent God, and also in their exercise of an all-important creative impulse that Jung argues is crucial to individuation.

Second, in biographical terms, the trough remarked on by Bell, seen
together with the complaint of God to Jeremiah, recalls work of the TVA,
of which McCarthy's father played a crucial role. The dams hewn from the
rocky terrain around Knoxville in *Suttree*, the artificial reservoirs they created,
and the usurpation of the power supposedly held only by a transcendent god
over "the fountain of living waters"—there the Tennessee River—all point to
a powerful father figure in control of both the creative impulse and its use to
usurp the power of God.

Third, Bell's emphasis on the craft involved in a human being taking
the time to create something "to last ten thousand years" brings both the biblical and the patriarchal power derived from this object under the power of
the son of the man who worked for the TVA: Cormac McCarthy. As I have
remarked in Chapter Two, McCarthy's regular valuation of skilled manual
labor remains central to his vision.[13] Despite some ambiguity embedded in
both the language concerning this water trough, and in the language regarding the cistern in Jeremiah, it is possible to imagine that in Bell's admiration
for the durability of the trough, we might have a metaphorical recognition
of the work McCarthy Sr. helped accomplish (good, as well as bad, for the

people in that area) with the TVA. Perhaps. But the enormity of the TVA project, and the lack of individual skilled artisanship in building a cistern more likely comparable to the one that angers God in Jeremiah, seem all to make that unlikely in any direct way. Nonetheless, it might be possible that the metaphor, although perhaps not intentional (or conscious, as Jung would have it), still arises from feelings on the part of the son to make peace with the father—perhaps.

Jung's famous dream of moving a candle through darkness was interpreted by him to mean that we must guard the light of reason and consciousness from the dark storms of the unconscious. The brighter the candle, the deeper the surrounding darkness (*Memories* 87–90). But unlike Freud, Jung acknowledged that the demands of the unconscious cannot be overcome. Hard necessity—such as running from Anton Chigurh—can relieve you from the burden of demands arising from the unconscious. But Bell avoids hard necessity. Indeed, he lives a relatively slow life, which for Jung opens him up to the neurotic obsessions we hear in his ruminations on evil threatening his community from without, evil being purchased from within his community, and evil being adopted by his community's children as they live lives of increasing leisure.

In this last worry, Bell actually doesn't go far enough: it is not in the lack of "Sir" and "Mam" that children run astray, but in an almost total lack of hard necessity in the lives of even many underprivileged children. If Bell wanted to make a difference there, he would open a horse riding camp and get them all busy from an early age. He might learn, and then teach these children, the craft of hewing stone. He would in this sense realize the father archetype that is still outside him, figured only in his dreams of his literal father leading the way. Despite having lost a child, he would become an active father in his community.

But this is not that story. And indeed, Bell's severe limitations—he has no creative outlet, no craft nor art, and he seems amazed even at the idea of working on something "maybe just a hour or two after supper"—confound him. Whatever the assorted overlaps may be between Bell's politics and McCarthy's, this sheriff is in no resonant way the writer, whose devotion to craft and creativity is continually established on his pages, and whose habits with every hobby he could find have been remarked on in interviews with him and with Knoxville residents and what family will speak to an interviewer.

Bell's limitations here leave him projecting all his potential power for creative and procreative power onto his dead father, until that father disappears behind an inflated archetype. Bell cannot achieve a dialogue with such an archetype, particularly as this one, in the form of Bell's laconic father, remains silent in the dream: he *"never said nothin"* (*NCFOM* 309). Rather than recognize all the various elements of his identity, Bell struggles among them, at times fracturing, such as when he veers wildly from one complaint to another seemingly unrelated one. This means, however, that the power of the silent figure riding before Bell in his dream carries with him more than one element of Bell's desperately various projections.

The father archetype in the dream furthermore resists interpretation into a single identity, for two reasons. First, this father represents not only Bell's father, but all fathers. As a symbol from both Bell's individual unconscious, and as Jung would have it, a collective unconscious as well, the dream's father figure cannot be reduced to an actual figure at all. The situation itself, particularly in the primeval aspect in which Freudian theory would interpret this carrying of a sacred fire, in Jungian terms reaches beyond a literal historical moment, as much as beyond Bell's individual psychology. The scene recalls Jung's,

> *archetypes of transformation.* They are not personalities, but are typical situations, places, ways and means, that symbolize the kind of transformation in question. [. . .] They are genuine symbols precisely because they are ambiguous, full of half-glimpsed meanings, and in the last resort inexhaustible. [. . .] The discriminating intellect naturally keeps on trying to establish their singleness of meaning and thus misses the essential point; for what we can above all establish as the one thing consistent with their nature is their *manifold meaning,* their almost limitless wealth of reference, which makes any unilateral formulation impossible. (*Archetypes* 38, his emphasis)

Bell's obsessions survey a variety of possibilities, unable to settle on a single problem that might explain his general sense of a world gone wrong. Things missing, that he somehow assumes were always there before, worry him: a lack of manners, a lack of discipline in schools, a lack of religion. Meanwhile he continues to fear evil as something that will be smuggled in from the outside, and eagerly adopted by his community's children. *"These old people I talk to, if you could of told em that there would be people on the streets of our Texas towns with green hair and bones in their noses speakin a language they couldn't even understand, well, they just flat out wouldnt of believed you"* (*NCFOM* 295).

This neurotic fixation on the details that somehow indicate to Bell a lack of social codes (rather than an alternative set of them) of course echoes

Blood Meridian: there *were* such people in *their* Texas towns, and they were scalped and killed or run off. But here Bell's fixations also point back to the inflation of the father archetype: unable to follow his father (feeling guilt for the loss of his child, the abandonment of fellow soldiers, and his departure from his job as sheriff), he is caught between two extremes: the heathen pollutions of his community's children, and the impossible power of the father image that he cannot integrate into himself and thus which he all too easily imagines in ideal terms.

This nostalgic final image of *No Country for Old Men* follows Bell's father, carrying fire in a horn, riding into the darkness of the past. The image returns us to the title. Yeats wrote "Sailing to Byzantium" in 1927 and it appeared in *The Dark Tower* in 1928, three years after he received the Nobel Prize for Literature, but three years after the Free State. "The memory of terrible struggles was fiercely alive [. . .]," as M. L. Rosenthal recounts. The poems of *The Tower* "report the hopes and disillusionments of those years, and Yeats's feeling of inadequacy for the physical side of the struggle" (xxv). Rosenthal's proof of this is most obvious in "The Road at My Door," and indeed, that title might work as well for McCarthy's novel.

> An affable Irregular,
> A heavily-built Falstaffian man,
> Comes cracking jokes of civil war
> As though to die by gunshot were
> The finest play under the sun.
> [. . .]
> I count those feathered balls of soot
> The moor-hen guides upon the stream,
> to silence the envy in my thought;
> And turn towards my chamber, caught
> In the cold snows of a dream.
> (113)

Bell ends with a dream, just as McCarthy's narrator did in the enigmatic epilogue to *Cities of the Plain*. This dream follows yet another confession, beginning in the tacked-on phrasing of a guilty afterthought that the speaker cannot allow himself to leave unremarked on. This book knows it has struggled, that indeed many of the previous books have struggled, with something it often refused to directly address: *"The other thing is that I have not said much about my father and I know I have not done him justice"* (*NCFOM* 308). Our West Texas *Hamlet* then ends in two dreams.

The first is the child's dream, quotidian, faint, about money given and lost—exchange value and the power of the father in nearly literal terms. The second is the grown child's inflation of the father to an archetype:

> *like we was both back in older times and I was on horseback goin through the mountains of a night. Goin through this pass in the mountains. It was cold and there was snow on the ground and he rode past me and kept on goin. Never said nothin. He just rode on past and he had this blanket wrapped around him and he had his head down and when he rode past I seen he was carryin fire in a horn the way people used to do and I could see the horn from the light inside of it. About the color of the moon.* (*NCFOM* 309)

This could be Jung himself in *Memories, Dreams, Reflections*. Jung's transformative dream of a candle surrounded by darkness was interpreted by him as the place of consciousness moving forward through the never-ending space of an unconscious too dark to be held away beyond that small sphere of light. "It was night in some unknown place, and I was making slow and painful headway against a mighty wind. Dense fog was flying along everywhere. I had my hands cupped around a tiny light which threatened to go out at any moment. Everything depended on my keeping this little light alive." But Jung sees himself carrying this light, and when he looks back, the "gigantic black figure following" him proves to be a threatening "*vita peracta*"—the life already accomplished, lived, and perhaps ended. Here, the leading figure is the dreamer, breaking free with every difficult step from that dark figure that would negate its progress.

> The storm pushing against me was time, ceaselessly flowing into the past, [. . .] It exerts a mighty suction which greedily draws everything living into itself; we can only escape from it—for a while—by pressing forward. The past is terribly real and present, and it catches everyone who cannot save his skin with a satisfactory answer. (*Memories* 88)

In Bell's dream, the dreamer has no answers, and is already turning backwards to follow the vita peracta—in his case, a father archetype moving backwards—through an already sterile landscape (*through this pass in the mountains. It was cold and there was snow on the ground and he rode past me and kept on goin*). Bell has no satisfactory answers to the challenges of life, and the dark figures of his failings are indistinguishable—despite what he claims—from the dark future he sees in the soulless eyes of Chigurh, or the man he visits before his execution. Bell can only register that fear that swallows up the self and erases all distinctions between inside and outside, past, present, and future. Beyond melancholia, Bell grasps at the words of Jeremiah, of his disappointed, jealous, and ineffectual God, of a grumpy old man's conservative politics, of a Lord Jim somehow carrying a burden of guilt under his medal, of a father who's only child has died. These problems overwhelm him, but they are the manifestations of deeper anxieties with which his conscious mind can grapple while his dreams ride off into the dark following someone else's light.

Bell has yielded his failed father's position to become again the son. And the distant father leads him in a way that Bell's father seems not to have done in life. In Bell's own implicit understanding of the dream, locating it as he does as a dream specific to his father and himself, the longing here is strongly conservative, even reactionary, with a pull backward in time to a selective moment when one might, presumably, with nothing but horse and fire in a horn, start over. Of course, one still has to wonder how far these two would get by riding human hopes along like that with no woman I sight. The father alone seems to be the answer here, with some promise of realigning values and practices toward a pure direction that can only be indicated by him. And the nostalgia here hangs on the dreamer's hope that through that pass in the mountains he will find just the right earlier time—not so early as to get scalped, but before the fences might hem this father and son into the narrowing spaces of the West after *Blood Meridian*.

The initial conflicts powering *No Country for Old Men*, then—conflicts of genre and structure—resolve themselves only by falling out of the way of a new (older) generational conflict that itself falls away to older fears yet. Bell's dream insists on its interpretation, however much we might go beyond it, that Bell is finally, in this vision, paying some attention to his father, doing "*him justice*" (*NCFOM* 308). We should return to this level of interpretation because it both extends and reverses McCarthy's ending of *The Border Trilogy*.

With the death of John Grady, we had the slightly older brother figure Billy acting as something of a patriarch. But *No Country for Old Men*'s father wins the book's arguments so overwhelmingly and insistently that many readers will want to throw the thing away, rejecting it as an unredeemable conservative jeremiad. Even if one rejects the hazy but implied politics of Bell's monologues, it would be a mistake to reject out of hand the force of emotion that occasions them. Bell's rants may sound like those of a grumpy old man, but their frustrations center on nostalgia for a world of impossible safety—especially for young people. Behind his regular accusations against the younger generations that, to Bell, have lost their way, his loss of innocence in World War II (deepened with the losses in Vietnam), and the unbearably personal loss of his daughter, Bell's relationship to his father seems to lie deepest toward the root of his individual psychology.[14]

The reactionary call of Bell's dream to follow only the father also stands in contrast to the motherly function of Betty at the end of *Cities of the Plain*, which was to console and forgive. Where Betty essentially tells Billy that he is too hard on himself, the silent father in Bell's dream as much as says *yes, you are right; the world has gone awry. Follow me, as I carry the proper fire of truth into a better future.*

But of course, this dream stretches and strains, as do all conservative visions, to get back to a past where the possibilities remain sufficiently uncorrupted by the chaos of change. In Jungian terms, we can also see that the image of Bell's father presents us with Bell's projection: where he feels he cannot travel, he imagines his father to lead the way—backwards. The paradoxes here suit the solution of *No Country for Old Men*, as the father's solutions to the problems of the son are inevitably conflicted between setting him out to a future incomprehensible to the father, and recalling him to the values already lost in time to the father. Bell's dream says to us *do not go a further step forward.* That's a harsher generational shift to the past than the blind man's mysterious talk with Culla Holme.

But ultimately, to put my original conceit to work in reverse, the fact that the collapse of the jeremiad into Bell's unresolved Jungian vision is not up to starting the novel, but must rather slip into its form when the crime genre collapses, ought to remind us that *No Country for Old Men* says more to us than Bell's dream. It tells us two stories—one hard-boiled and one worn down—and thus eventually it tells us a third story, about the inadequacy of both responses to a world of male violence. After the struggles of several sons (and a few fathers) in eight McCarthy novels, the ninth ends with a vision of the father's most reactionary solution: the older generation wins only in retreat, while Anton Chigurh limps away to future evil.

Chapter Eight
No Place for Home

The universe is no narrow thing and the order within it is not constrained
by any latitude in its conception to repeat what exists in one part in any
other part.

(Holden, *BM* 245)

For each fire is all fires, the first fire and the last ever to be.

(*BM* 244)

ARCS WITHIN THE ARC

McCarthy's spaces have proven various, demanding a variety of means to
explore them. From compromised houses, broken fences, and strange graves,
the reader can now look up—into larger, and more conceptual, spaces—as
much as down, into the ambivalent psychological space constrained by the
skulls and rib cages of the main characters. To a surprising degree, more feeling can then be found in these protagonists—or felt, as it were, by even a cautious reader, as we read down through those fissures in domestic and social
constraints. Reading with a skeptical eye on possible biographical connections between McCarthy and his creations, we attended to the many angry
and orphaned sons, and those rarer yet notably reluctant fathers. Working
upward, we have also seen from the inmost spaces of McCarthian psychology the social, historical, and philosophical spaces in his work. Reasonable
inferences ultimately reveal verticality implicated in this novelist's cosmology. Much is made here, and in other criticism, of the horizontal qualities of
McCarthy's novels. It is now time to explore the relation of these interior and
exterior spaces, and to find an image from within the work that suggests the
verticality of that relation.

In my opening chapter, I noted the emergence of discernible rules underlying McCarthy's descriptions of space. After reading these nine novels, now something more definite, more architectonic, emerges. In this concluding chapter I will borrow from McCarthy an image that might extend our understanding of McCarthian spaces in two directions. First, we can imagine it as an ordering vertical structure within which the various spaces discussed here can be understood in relation to one another. Second, we can still recall that these novels enact their horizontal power by propelling their protagonists through space. Movement, flight, and escape, after all, still characterize McCarthy's fiction as much as do his spaces. What I have attempted, moving through the previous chapters, and now in this conclusion, is to arrive at some understanding of the relation of those flights to the variety of spaces from, to, and through which McCarthy's young men run.

In appreciation of the psychological interiors inferred through the preceding chapters, we have seen the variety of related forces behind those flights. Restlessness, disappointed male idealism, antinomianism, and a deep urge to violence move these characters, but they also run for the fulfillment of unattainable desires. They run from ambivalent feelings for fathers usually distant or dead, and a few run from fatherhood. They run from broken domestic spaces, or try—as did Lester Ballard, in this sense the most poignant of the characters—to recapture even some mediated squalor already lost in their descent toward death. They run from authority, from the social constraint of a powerful father, or his drunken negligence, from the state's constraints of taxation (of liquor in *The Orchard Keeper*, a family farm in *Child of God*, or the seizure by eminent domain of a ranch in *Cities of the Plain*), from the narrowing possibilities of societies moving ever away from work in the natural world, or from the severest reach of emergent anarcho-capitalism (the hired armies, gangs, and contract assassins of both *Blood Meridian* and *No Country for Old Men*).

And what is most missing that McCarthy, and therefore this book, has nearly avoided indicating at all? Motherhood. These young men run from mothers more frequently dead or absent than even their fathers. After the death of John Wesley's mother late in his book, mothers disappear either before the opening of a novel or soon thereafter. Rinthy's search for her "chap" creates a single, heart-rending exception to this, when *Outer Dark*, having followed the most reluctant of McCarthy's fathers, grants the child and Rinthy the following "frail agony of grace." The reunion of Rinthy with her child in death—a decadent union, as I will describe such proximity between sons and fathers—is described as if to spare Rinthy full knowledge of this. "She went among this charnel [of her dead child's "chalk bones"] curiously. She did not know what to make of it" (*OD* 237). And our last view of her includes that other mediated grace allowed McCarthy's old men, as "after a while little sister was sleeping" (*OD* 238). This novel centering on the most reluctant father enacts a prosopopoeia of the mother that in the other books is either dead or absent; *Outer Dark* even charges that mother with a relentless drive to find and reclaim her stolen child.

That mothers of the characters disappear after the death of John Wesley's only deepens the son and father anxiety I have examined thus far. The resulting chasm of domestic failure, its threat of collapse and death at home, propels sons through the mountainous forests and barren deserts of McCarthy's books. Unable to confront the disavowal of motherhood (a more painful realization than the father's indifference, let alone his wrath) these sons do their best to forget the mother altogether, as most of the novels simply kill her off so early as if to obviate any conscious resentment. Guilt over that resentment's unconscious persistence surfaces oddly; the kid is implicated in his own mother's death as she gave birth to "the creature who would carry her off" (*BM* 3). John Grady's mother runs to the theatre, but this is merely a more nuanced escape from the world of real blood and horses that is her odd inheritance; before her son reached a year of life, she had run from raising him (*ATPH* 25).[1] Only *The Orchard Keeper* and *All the Pretty Horses* include the indifference of an uninvolved mother; only John Grady is seen to feel the pain of that neglect.[2]

Although we may glance healthier lives, even families, in the periphery of these novels, the downward trend of McCarthy's young men cannot be fit into a sociological complaint; these are not novels that bemoan better possibilities for young men any more than they are glorifications—as the hastiest critics and some particularly innocent fans declare—of a life on the run. To think so is to miss the higher reaches of that verticality I will later explore: McCarthy's philosophy is always expressed through flight, but never only through a world of atoms, of disconnected (or neutered) austerity.[3] In the glance provided by McCarthy's most photographic passages, we do glimpse a world given no distinction, no anthropocentric resonance. And indeed, McCarthy regularly warns us away from anthropocentric consolations, or a passage evoking oceanic feeling proves to be reserved for a protagonist who will soon blink such mystical scales from his eyes.

And yet, resonance returns, even if it sometimes reaches beyond human epistemological limits. Moments of apparent dissociation (not only psychological, but physical—chemical at the sub-molecular level of ions), followed by an overweening theoretical reading of his paratactic sentences, can offer the reader eager to find in McCarthy one thing after another and no order

beyond that of accident a delusional, if nobly cold, ironic comfort. This critical error may be less common than that of reading into McCarthy meanings
that are not there, or believing an apparent metaphysical ascension is more
than one character's delusion, but that makes it no less an error. Gaze into
the depths, and the heavens, of these novels and you find a pervasive eschatology that itself reaches up to an entropic chill that pervades more than the
flat desert below. Among the characters, nonetheless, I have argued that one
finds feeling. Much of that feeling, however, centers on loss and death. In
human terms, but also beyond the larger biological world, all is dying. At
both human and cosmological levels, then, that eschatological force assumes
orders of magnitude and relations of complexity beyond atomistic drift.

Edwin Arnold, whose "Mosaic of McCarthy's Fiction" provides my
attempts to trace deep connections through these books an admirable model,
notes the novelist's refusal of anthropocentric consolation in "'Go to Sleep:'
Dreams and Visions in the Border Trilogy." There Arnold concentrates on
McCarthy's method of relating moments of insight often denied his protagonists, focusing on the way dreams allow us the kind of access to character
interiority that I have argued is also available through the descriptions of
setting. A key passage discerns the "realization that the balance and beauty of
the world exist beyond any rational, anthropocentric sense of 'equity' that is
given to both John Grady and Billy Parham" (57). At the center of that realization is death. That does not, however, mean that McCarthy can be read
fully as a fundamentally nihilistic author, and indeed, Arnold looks beyond
this challenging darkness and finds faith. I do not, and yet I find a different,
if less comforting, consolation. Death is the central fact of all nine novels,
yet even in the darkest of these books death is situated against complementary orders of structure that, however difficult to grasp, grant the deathward
direction of these fictions their greater force by contrast. Initially, the humorous distance between ordering structures and the characters provides readers,
if not the characters themselves, some relief. But I will argue that this relief
fades away in the last three novels, leaving nothing but a stoic existential
drive that itself begins to fall away in *No Country for Old Men.*

In Beckett, a sense of humor outruns even those bleakest moments
that cannot be endured by the most heroic existentialism. In McCarthy,
Suttree alone among the protagonists possesses a sense of humor sufficient
to help him endure the limits of his existential reach. Sylder displays a sense
of humor, but he is arguably not a main character. Because Suttree is the only
obviously autobiographical character in the novels, he alone is given a sense
of humor (and education) sufficient to achieve any ironic consciousness of his
situation. His are the only thoughts to which we are allowed some intimate

access. Bell's monologue remains at the distance of speech—we hear his voice as if spoken (the italicized text lacks any suggestions of the self-consciousness of writing, but rather features several marks of spoken language).

It would therefore seem that, especially as we only find a regular sense of humor in antagonists and secondary or tertiary characters (such as Harrogate, innocent as he otherwise remains), McCarthy is more interested in the naïveté of young men so innocent—if not ignorant—as to lack an ironic distance, a sense of humor, or indeed very much self-consciousness at all. Writing through decades when his contemporaries have so fruitfully and extensively explored well-educated navel-gazing self-referential sarcasm that many novels now collapse under such self-consciousness, we may consider McCarthy's exceptional habit here a gift to the variety of literature in our time.

Instead of laughing their way on, McCarthy's protagonists press on in ignorance; they outrun death as long as they do, only by dint of their dreams, desires, and delusions, or in the case of Billy, a stoic perpetual motion. In this sense, McCarthy's books reveal a birth astride a grave but with little awareness of this on the part of the characters.[4] For all the death in the novels, knowledge of death usually comes slowly to any discernible level of character consciousness. Except for Billy (and we will return to his case in the end), the fact of death stands against their forward motion, bending their line of flight into recursive wandering. Ballard persists through a dynamic, if incredibly perverse, force of imaginative life. (He speaks to his dead, imagining them engaged with him in the normal life he cannot attain.) John Grady's first education in the evil of the world fails to keep him from pursuing another unattainable ideal, in his second appearance; we might say that in *Cities of the Plain* that knowledge better equips him to pursue an even less attainable, and more death-directed, ideal. Even the kid, after becoming "the man," denies the power of death in judge Holden's arguments. These characters all exhibit some positive force. Yet the final word of the novels remains clear: their end is death.

If not optimism, a vitiated drive away from death does recur in the main characters. Arthur Ownby first exhibits that drive. Some success in running from death is then found by John Wesley. Only Suttree escapes as well as John Wesley. Hope for the future returns when Suttree's visions finally lead him toward the better city of his dreams—notwithstanding that final vision's dependence on mythic imagery that we, and McCarthy, know to be undependable. We glimpse this drive in the kid as a nascent, if insufficient, force as he becomes the man. Although this man fails to successfully oppose the judge, he nonetheless refuses active union with him, even as that means becoming another one of his victims. John Grady and Billy and Boyd Parham become the most heroic of McCarthy characters, even as the two younger charges of Billy cannot be saved by him. Indeed, in the web of failed rescues that creates the plots of *The Border Trilogy*, we may say that heroic failure weaves the central thread: John Grady cannot save Jimmy Blevins or Magdalena any more than can Billy Parham save the wolf, his brother Boyd, or in the end, John Grady. After so many failed errands, it is fitting that in *No Country for Old Men* we feel that twilight has fallen on such heroism. Death returns, the inevitable fact. It becomes clearer—so much so that Bell proclaims it—that death succeeds most when one has lost the child, failing to displace the father by becoming him.[5]

Throughout, deaths in McCarthy novels are those violent ones that call our attention to theodicy. (One can no better explain the death of Wanda in a universe controlled by some god than one can explain thousands washed away by an ocean.) But this novelist does not stop at depicting the occasional complaint to god, as in Bell's darker moments, or Billy's curse as he carries away John Grady. McCarthy goes further, reminding us in passages from the judge or Anton Chigurh (passages we would prefer to explain away as madness, or some antagonistic anti-philosophy meant to stir our moral urges, or some capitulation to anarchy or aporia or agnostic abandon), that our evolved systems of morality may be accidental. They exist precariously situated above an animal world aligned more closely to the mute sensibilities of rocks and stones and trees than to our sufferings. Above such morality, the stars wheel indifferent, in a universe that some god (or goddess) may have given a spin, but which will not be adjusted any more. And always, at least in the universe we can only ever infer, time is running out.

But that does not mean that morality in McCarthy's worldview never existed, any more than the inevitable failure of dreams to be realized means that their force did not create life against that inevitable darkness. It is simply the case that such force remains the imaginative provenance of humans, and that it cannot be confirmed by the natural world, or some god, or by chance. It can only be confirmed in the imaginative attempt that will inevitably fail. When I return to this upper level of McCarthy's philosophy, then, it will help to remember that the eschatological course in that philosophy outruns Christianity, with its figuration of the death of all humans. Ultimately, this author goes beyond such a "worldview" and reaches a cosmology. In that cosmology, however, the precarious order of all things is also running out of time.

The image I will borrow from McCarthy for understanding both the horizontal flights and the vertical relation of space in his works is of the arc,

in the senses of that word as both a particular movement and its subsequent
trajectory—a line of flight as well as the space through which that flight rises
and falls. Arcs recur throughout the novels, but my point of departure begins
with a very small one from *Cities of the Plain*: "Billy flipped the butt of the
cigarette out across the yard. It was already dark enough that it made an arc
in the fading light. Arcs within the arc" (*COTP* 147).

This odd passage can take us further if we allow that nothing here
reaches beyond a sketch. After all, if it sufficed to assemble an argument for
an unassailable architectonic structure governing all of McCarthy's work, we
would have found him writing philosophy, instead of (surprisingly) philosophical novels. This is one reason why this particular image is arguably more
suitable than many: its expression does not entail what Frank Kermode calls
in Yeats a "myth." The "system," rather, that Yeats developed proved useful;
only when that system becomes congealed into myth does it create problems.
"Now and again [Yeats] believed some of it, but in so far as his true commitment was to poetry he recognized his fictions as heuristic and dispensable,
'consciously false.' 'They give me metaphors for poetry,' he noted. The dolls
and the amulets, the swords and the systems, were the tools of an operationalist" (104). To extend too far McCarthy's metaphor of a matrix, of the
judge's coining or his thread in the maze, of the dreams of Billy's several mystical encounters, of Chigurh's coin toss, or even these less systematic arcs, is
to risk submerging one's comprehension irretrievably into a heuristic. So, the
arcs within the arc suggest the possibilities of relation in a "system" without
the interpretive baggage of a full "myth."

It remains arguable that the accoutrements of the Western, as well as
what I called in the preceding chapter the "fetish" of the crime novel—altogether the whole store of horses and wolves and guns and boots and trucks—
similarly constitute, albeit in material form, merely another metaphorical set
of "tools" for McCarthy's role as "operationalist." Furthermore, his mixture
of both realistic and self-conscious (even humorously parodic) treatments of
the generic details of this system has grown through *The Border Trilogy* and
No Country for Old Men. Rather than undermining the power of McCarthy's
vision, that mixture allows us (as in Yeats) to break free from taking what
Kermode calls "nonsense" so seriously that we miss the serious imaginative
possibilities extending from, and well beyond, those metaphorical "systems."

> Yeats [. . .] said that the System enabled him to hold together reality
> and justice in a single thought. Reality is, in this expression, the sense
> we have of a world irreducible to human plot and human desire for
> order; justice is the human order we find or impose upon it. The System

is in fact all Justice; in combination with a sense of reality which has
nothing whatever to do with it, it became a constituent of poems. The
System is a plot, a purely human projection, though not more human
than its apparent antithesis, reality, which is a human imagining of the
inhuman. For a moment, Yeats saw himself as an emperor dispensing
equity, transcending both the fact and the pattern; it is what poets do.
Only rarely did he forget that whatever devotes itself to justice at the
expense of reality, is finally self-destructive. (Kermode 105)

Bearing these caveats in mind, McCarthy's image retains its power, provides us with a symbol, and only now might be properly employed even in
a guarded system of our own, suggesting those relations between horizontal
flights and vertical levels of space. If this seems a cautious path to what might
simply be declared, I mean it to be: McCarthy's cosmology includes such
provisions as allow us to imagine "both the fact and the pattern," and so we
ought to remember before employing that pattern in reading that its "reality"
is just that—provisional, heuristic.

Arcs within the arc. This is how I understand the pattern of McCarthy's novels: one arc still reaching through fading light contains within the
reach of its rising and falling trajectory so far nine novels. Within their paths,
we have traced nearly innumerable images of character flight, within which
we may trace motives unspoken or unconscious. Above those flights, arcs
of familial entropy fade over the flights of sons and fathers. Higher up, the
arcs of history throw even dimmer light over the fears, hopes, and desires
of these characters. Above that human history, we find the indifferent sun,
always "bloodred" only to the eyes of those squinting at it through a dusty
horizon, through a passage of blood. Highest of all, we see the echo of stars
that may already have died out, arcing their way so removed from human
concerns as to provide the ultimate effect achieved in these novels: all human
feeling—which in McCarthy means human suffering tempered by a little
hope—occurs at an ironic distance from the structures of the universe. As
the judge describes it, we may follow a string through the maze of the universe, but that string is the one that we have put there (*BM* 245).[6]

The place of human arcs, absurdly small and faint under the arcs of
stars and galaxies, explains McCarthy's avoidance of direct psychology more
than do my surmises (in Chapter Four) of the author's sensitivities about
his family.[7] Among readers fearful of reading more emotion out of his pages
than cautious inference warrants, McCarthy seems to some a cold fish. But
that again confuses the author with his narrators. In my opening chapter I
called this narrator's view the Hitchcockian God's eye. What McCarthy has

achieved reaches higher than mere autobiographical venting of spleen. However much we can find likely connections between the psychological drives in his characters and McCarthy's life, their confession amounts to more than the self-serving exploitation of life fueling memoirs, or the grumblings of an irascible politics that so frightened most critics of *No Country for Old Men*. The arcs of his characters amount to more than politics—though as David Holloway and others have shown, their flights cannot be fully understood without a consideration of the forces of markets and a larger economy. Their killings and retreats, scalping and running, are indeed part of what makes history. But even that word does not suffice to explain the larger structures of the work as a whole. To read McCarthy in full is to maintain in your consciousness some image that, if only provisionally, might find the imaginative reach of his works. One such image, of the many within the one, is that of arcs within the arc.

First, we have "an arc in the fading light." This single arc is small, particularized in the unlikely form of a cigarette butt "flipped" away by Billy Parham. This tiny bit of littering hardly registers against the river of trash in *Suttree*. Its light cannot compare with the false sun of the first atomic blast that wakes Billy at the end of *The Crossing* (*TC* 425)—a sun so artificial that it appears and extinguishes itself without any apparent movement within a larger system. And again, there are numerous "arcs" so described elsewhere in McCarthy. But this one's smallness suits us as a departure point, even as its complexity suggests the architectonic relation of McCarthy's spaces. That the complexity comes in a fragment further conceals that fragment's possibilities; its isolation first drew my attention. It seemed wholly unnecessary, even gratuitous, a description merely meant to bring to life the scene in which it occurs; yet it does not appear in one of McCarthy's rolling extended sentences, where we might understand it as an expression of pure rhythm, or sound, without semantic significance. It therefore seemed immediately to point to a higher level of reading not only this passage but all of McCarthy. Furthermore, hiding such a passage, as it were, suits a writer who so regularly trades in metaphors of weaving, mazes, coinage, and other tropes invoking both a revealed lack of order and a concealed order. Stitching such a trope in such an apparently insignificant place in his narrative fabric points both to intention and accident, to pattern and reality.

"Arcs within the arc" is more complicated, however, than some of the other spatial tropes that tease us in our search for McCarthy's philosophy. By presenting us both with the image of the many within the one, and an entropic fall, this image resonates with those otherwise incommensurable levels of space—psychological, social, historical, and philosophical—while nonetheless preserving the overall eschatology, and eventually the entropic cosmology, of these works. The consequence entailed by this image, a gravitational constraint, prevents our imaginations from escaping the downward trend of these novels. The impulse to delight in escape comes naturally to any but the most moralistic readers. And its theoretical possibilities have already tempted those encountering the force of that horizontal drive in American literature through the kind of rhetorical flights that only theoretical reading affords.

Gilles Deleuze and Claire Parnet may have argued that Anglo-American literature finds its expression through a "line of flight," but their enthusiasms over this resemble the hyperbole often characteristic of selected French views of America. Between hailing Melville, and later on Fitzgerald and Kerouac, as American proponents of flight as an "active" "deterritorialization," something horizontally heroic, they include George Jackson: "'It may be that I am fleeing, but throughout my flight, I am searching for a weapon'" (36). Deleuze and Parnet refuse to make any distinction between this imprisoned Black Panther leader and the characters of novels in their literary heroes of flight, or to mention Jackson's violent death, along with three prison guards and two other prisoners.[8] Whatever happened with Jackson, his line of flight—as at least Ahab's and Gatsby's in two of the writers above—arcs down to death. Enthusiasms for freedom of movement notwithstanding, lines of flight in McCarthy similarly trend toward death. The gravity, as it were, that pulls down the paths of McCarthy characters will be important to the larger vision we must work up to from their individual arcs.

RECURSIONS HOME:
PSYCHOLOGICAL, SOCIAL, AND HISTORICAL ARCS

Most immediately, the single little arc of Billy's cigarette seems to reach back to the preceding books of *The Border Trilogy* (which, after all, were written after the screenplay version of *Cities of the Plain*), and can be traced all the way back to *The Orchard Keeper*. We can first read up from this image of the many within the one the symbolic recurrence of son and father tension in these books. In other words, within each of the levels of spatial constraint in McCarthy there are the individual arcs; arcs within the arc that is itself one of many other arcs within a larger arc.

In the scene around our image, Billy has just told John Grady, "More and more you remind me of Boyd. Only reason I could ever get him to do anything was to tell him not to" (*COTP* 146). Billy's association of John Grady with his dead brother of course foreshadows the end of the trilogy. Billy's attempts to help Boyd occur after the death of the she-wolf (a symbolic mother) sends him home from Mexico, only to find both his parents murdered. The relation between Billy and Boyd that we first saw in the book's opening—"He carried Boyd before him in the bow of the saddle and named to him features of the landscape"—is regenerated and augmented by the death of their parents (*TC* 3).[9] Billy assumes a parental role, then, in even trying to "get him to do anything." A father's authority is difficult enough to wield; a brother's can prove to be practically, if sadly, useless. Billy is therefore not so much an older brother figure as a father figure, first to Boyd and then to John Grady.

The preoccupation with orphanage that is expressed at its highest pitch in *The Border Trilogy*'s ending is heightened already in several passages in *Cities of the Plain*, as I argued in Chapter Six. The adopted puppies of exploded mother dogs sets up, but in ironic opposition, the blame Billy will later heap on mothers and would-be wives, because Billy and John Grady have orphaned the puppies they then adopt. Billy's curse of "Goddamn whores" enacts a reproach against John Grady's reduced bid for domesticity, but also against John Grady's mother—indeed all mothers—as well. And his reproach includes God, as he calls out "Do you see? Do you see?" (*COTP* 261). Billy, who never himself undertakes emotional involvement with women, carries home the body of his friend who did. Along the way he encounters something from Yeats (again foreshadowing *No Country for Old Men*): schoolchildren, suddenly stopped by the woman leading them, as one would pull over a car to allow a funeral procession to pass. We see through their eyes the quickly aging Billy in a walking pietà:

> The dead *boy* in his arms hung with his head back and those partly opened eyes beheld nothing at all out of that passing landscape of street or wall or paling sky or the figures of the children who stood blessing themselves in the gray light. This *man* and his burden passed on forever out of that nameless crossroads and the woman stepped once more into the street and the children followed and all continued on to their appointed places which as some believe were chosen long ago even to the beginning of the world. (*COTP* 261–262, my emphasis)

Cities of the Plain does not in fact close with this loss of domestic possibility, however, but goes on, following orphaned Billy, the failed father, through a landscape so devoid of quotidian and domestic values that it becomes a waking dream. In a foreshadowing of the formal collapse that ends *No Country for Old Men*, Billy is finally sent by the narrative to yet another country: a country of disillusioned men still looking for their parents.

But the scene of Billy carrying John Grady's body, of a symbolic father with his dead child, presents us with a decadent union. It will be reversed at the end of *No Country for Old Men*, where Bell's dream enacts a prosopopoeia bringing Bell's father back to lead him—backwards, into a mythic past. Both endings repeat a decadent closure in which the father and son figures carry forward both life and death. The most grotesque version of this union of the father with the son, of course, occurs in the jakes at the end of *Blood Meridian*. What I mean to suggest is that already, at the level of psychological space at which I have tried to explore the father and son tension propelling McCarthy's young men with such powerful, if unconscious, force, we can glimpse the eschatology that we will find throughout higher arcs.

Indications of this decadent relation appear throughout the novels. Within the ultimate space of the universe, human arcs remain absurdly insignificant, yet to other people, our actions may create some important relation. Son and father relations have already proven not only central to the psychological space of these novels, but constitutive of social space as well. A brief overview now reveals the connection of psychological ambivalence and social tension to be regularly decadent—death-haunted, and in that darkest sense of decadence, emblematic of what we will find in the philosophical arc of McCarthy's work to be first eschatological, and finally cosmologically removed beyond human perceptions of time and space.

In *The Orchard Keeper*, the dead Rattner's child John Wesley first takes to his road after his father's charred bones are discovered, bagged, and interred. It remains notable that John Wesley only really takes that road West, departing Red Branch for good, with the death of his mother. This fact only reinforces our inference that the recursion to scenes of father and son conflict (and unity only in a decadent tableau in which one of them is dead) displaces the deeper arc of the mother's departure (here in a cemetery, in *All the Pretty Horses* in a theatre) and its effect on the son. The decadence of *The Orchard Keeper* is commingled with its biblical flood, and its plethora of images of a dead and dying world. And the ironic proximity of the dead father to the living, even growing, son looses the arc toward death in McCarthy's first published novel. Simultaneously, the social—more accurately, political—pressures to end Ownby's cyclical way of life, connected as it is to weather and seasons, and to replace it with the governmental regulation that also traps Sylder, reveal a deathward direction of that union between humans and the natural world. As I argued in Chapter Two, we may see this in Carolyn Merchant's terms as a *Death of Nature*. I call this a deathward social arc because it indicates how the society of Red Bank is losing its connection with a living, organic world that already exhibits more death than life.

The father and son tensions in the next books arc notably through social space, particularly in the tensions of taboo and scapegoating that characterize *Outer Dark* and *Child of God*. No understanding of Lester Ballard's grotesque approximations of domesticity is possible without attention to his brain, as much as his mind; that meant adding an appreciation of the neurological, as well as the psychological, damage Ballard suffers early in the book. This damage is directly linked to the father's death (if not also the living father's treatment of the child). But it is both the cause and effect of Lester's deepening deviance that he is denied a normal domestic life after the suicide of his father. That deviance arcs up from the family farm and through the woods around the community that has rejected him, ultimately falling to, and below, the earth. As I argued in Chapter Three, Ballard's psychological and neurological problems are social in origin, and social in their final decadent enclosure beyond the walls, as it were, of the community that rejected him.

This third novel extends the decadent moment of the dead father and the surviving son from a moment that precedes—as in no other McCarthy novel—the first page of the narrative. Indeed, we first meet Lester standing where he would have found his suicide father hanging from the barn rafters. Much, understandably, has been made of Ballard's appropriation of a dead woman and then his murdering replacements of her, as if he were also replacing his mother as well as acquiring the partner denied him in his deviant and outcast condition. But the ending of the novel makes it clear that he also eventually kills and communes with men. His appropriation of women's clothing suggests some possibilities here. But if Lester Ballard has also been replacing his mother, might he not also have been replacing his father? Surrounding himself with a substitute community of the dead, Ballard presents us with a horrific extension of the son and father decadence only later outdone in the jakes of *Blood Meridian*.

The ultimate vision in *Child of God* reveals Ballard's bones as an intermediary space that might house lesser organisms, simultaneously decorating the cave that then threatens to collapse into his womb-grave, "his ribs curling slender and whitely like a bone flower in the dark stone bowl" (*COG* 189). Simultaneously, the problem that Ballard poses to the community that has rejected him can only be solved by his treatment as a scapegoat. These spatial solutions necessarily conflate Ballard's psychological collapse with that of both the substitute society of the dead assembled by him, and the living community that sets in motion and reinforces his descent: every space in *Child of God* narrows to a tomb. This of course provides the novel's ultimate horror, as there is no ascent into sunlight without the reminder of our complicity in

Ballard's decadence. The bodies are compared to "hams" covered with "a pale gray *cheesy* mold" (*COG* 196–197, my emphasis), implicating any reader who may have managed an appetite while reading this novel. Our own deathward direction, as it were, pauses only as young medical students operate on and then dissect Ballard (*COG* 194), before they inevitably work on us.

As in *The Orchard Keeper*, we see there the deviance of a criminal bagged up in death, like so much trash. But we know the flimsiness of the boundaries we keep between us and what remains of Ballard in that bag. Particularly at the point of force conflating these spaces in *Child of God*, it becomes impossible to consider the psychological spaces of these books without attending to their larger, social spaces of domestic and communal constraint. Social spaces further narrow the constraints of Ballard's consciousness as we follow him through his cave. Social spaces, already evident in the first novel in the tensions between Sylder and the mansion-protecting Gifford, between Ownby and the government tank, further suggest political conflicts.

In Chapter Four, I explored how in *Outer Dark*, *Suttree*, and *Blood Meridian*, the decadent space of an ambivalent psychological relation between sons and fathers becomes most evident where these relatives most actively contest one another. Culla Holme's witness of the throat slitting of his own incestuously conceived child sets him forever circling through a wasteland. As well as in *Suttree* (and to some surprise, *Blood Meridian*), *Outer Dark* particularizes that space of ambivalence in which sons and fathers struggle away from one another, to the point that it may refract something from McCarthy's life. This psychological space grows most transparent through the actions of Culla Holme and the author's wordplay around that name in *Outer Dark*.

In *Suttree*, some likely reasons for the regularity of son and father tension in McCarthy's novels arise: some of these seem private—psychological—involving McCarthy's rejection of Catholicism, and some prolonged tension with McCarthy Sr. that we may never fully understand. By *Suttree*, however, the juncture of a father's occupation and the psychology of his son's resistance to him is located precisely in the outcast social spaces of the novel's deviant characters. Along with some disagreements about religion (and possibly the behavior of McCarthy as a young man), the occupation of Charles Sr. and its apparent effects on the son mirror those of Suttree Sr. and Cornelius. The father's highly political occupation rankles Suttree's Christian and Buddhist feeling for the downtrodden characters among which Cornelius "Buddy" Sutra—or Cornelius "Bodhisattva"—ministers and mourns.[10] *Suttree*'s anxieties over the power of not only the Tennessee River but the TVA that has attempted to wrest control of it connect the most biographical resentments and disappointments in this most psychological of all McCarthy's novels to the social space of the book, where the class differences within Suttree's family become messily worked out through his slumming in McAnally Flats.[11] This novel's regular reliance on scenes of grotesque decadence reinforces the deathward trend of both social and psychological arcs.

The spaces of *Blood Meridian*, as I noted in my opening chapter, first suggested that my original focus on houses, fences, and graves would prove to be too limited. By following the kid's departure from, and thanatotic return to, a father-figure judge, I explored in Chapter Four the psychological space that, after *Suttree*, is relatively buried in *Blood Meridian*. With both the fourth and fifth books, McCarthy then more fully traces the arcs of history also glimpsed early on, even as *Suttree* seems to have cleaved more deeply into the author's emotions, and thus more deeply into psychological space, than any other of the novels. *Suttree*'s reproach to the father so overwhelms that book with cloacal effluvia that it suggests McCarthy's resentment and guilt over his father's work in the TVA. Holden's role as a provisional Krishna, reproaching a figurative son unable to fulfill his destiny and avoid the fate of mere "antic clay" (*BM* 307), therefore reverses the triumph Suttree accomplished through his rejection of a literal and mortal father's smaller-scale crimes against society.

Much of McCarthy's cosmology may have been in place—albeit embedded vaguely in symbol, and most powerfully in image—as early as the remarkably honed aesthetic practices we see already in the first novel and extending into his most recent work. But only with *Suttree* do we begin to glimpse a fuller cosmology: at the level of personal redemption, that book struggles through varying worldviews toward some means by which Suttree can escape death. As many have noted, *Suttree* probably proposes more philosophy than it can dispose of or sort through, such that we must make our way with Suttree through numerous peripeteia that are more psychological and philosophical than social—more internal and, by Suttree's imaginative and mystical extensions, external, than the more traditionally social reversals of fortune that we call peripeteia. That Suttree indeed does seem to escape—as only John Wesley did before him, and no protagonist has since—seems to require these numerous internal reverses. In Kermode's language for the evolution of subtlety in eschatological preoccupations, such a reliance on proliferating reversals, particularly of an increasingly internal quality, enacts a necessary "disconfirmation" of "apocalypse" (30).

The fullest expression of a McCarthian cosmology becomes more evident—if nonetheless complicated—through *Blood Meridian* and the last four novels. As we saw in Chapter Four, *Blood Meridian* includes a surprising expression of the son and father tension that is more obvious in the other

books. As much as we are limited to reasonable inferences, we can come closer
to the kid's psychological space than has often been supposed, as Arnold and
a few others have noted. Still, the emphasis on historical and philosophical
space in *Blood Meridian* required another reading of that book, in Chapter
Five, where I argued that along with the philosophical arc we have yet to
fully trace, arcs of history help us explore the complex space turned into
place in the Epilogue. Holden's speeches reinforce, for the first time in such
a degree of expression, the narrator's hints throughout the novels of a more
fully realized, if elusive, cosmology.

The Border Trilogy now seems to clarify more easily the various arcs
at once, and in relation to one another. In particular, *All the Pretty Horses*
has yielded the most diverse levels of critical reading, from psychology to
philosophy, with readings of historical space, as well as of gender, class, and
economic spaces (all social spaces) between. As I argued in Chapter Six, John
Grady Cole's impetus toward Mexico lay partly in the admiration and loss of
his dead grandfather, and his rejection of an impotent and otherwise emasculated father. The closest John Grady comes to the death he will later find
with Eduardo is here conterminous with his literal father's death. John Grady
is then reborn in the prison infirmary, that place so redolent of death that it
echoes his father's cell in the prisoner of war camp—where the novel strongly
suggests Cole Sr. lost his manhood. This means that even in the novel whose
end he outlives, John Grady, too, can be found in decadent union with his
father.

> He lay there three days. [. . .] He thought of his father in Goshee.
> He knew that terrible things had been done to him there and he had
> always believed that he did not want to know about it but he did want
> to know. He lay in the dark thinking of all the things he did not know
> about his father and he realized that the father he knew was all the
> father he would ever know. [. . .] He slept and when he woke he'd
> dreamt of the dead standing about in their bones and the dark sockets
> of their eyes that were indeed without speculation bottomed in the void
> wherein lay a terrible intelligence common to all but of which none
> would speak. When he woke he knew that men had died in that room.
> (*ATPH* 204–205)

It is later that John Grady realizes what has already happened: as he
has healed, his father has worsened. After he shoots a doe in his journey
back toward the border, he wakes up and "realize[s] that he knew his father
was dead" (*ATPH* 282). Still, only after he crosses the border into Texas, a

movement across the international boundary and thus from one national—historical—space into another, can he grieve. It is another rebirth, this one finding John Grady already healed and relatively healthy, naked to keep his clothes dry, cleansed both by the river and "a softly falling rain," yet slightly, if perhaps only temporarily, changed: "He rode up onto Texas soil pale and shivering and he sat the horse briefly and looked out over the plain to the north [. . .] and he thought about his father who was dead in that country and he sat the horse naked in the falling rain and wept" (*ATPH* 286).

This is the closest we come to the full rebirth of the son with the passing of the father, and as we know, it only delays John Grady's inevitable arc down to death. Billy, at the death of his father, is only partly reborn as a father figure to Boyd—at which he fails. And Bell will be haunted by the father whose death he has outlived without rebirth, following him in dreams forever. These psychological arcs of decadent union and fall with the death of the father themselves arc down through *The Border Trilogy* and *No Country for Old Men*, as the father's death becomes increasingly important to the actions (and inactions) of the son, and the violence around the son and his inability to combat it becomes more severe. Billy, always the skeptical, even cynical father figure unable to intervene in the deaths of his figurative sons, is thus more death-haunted than John Grady.

As much as John Grady is the most heroic character McCarthy has created, he necessarily remains one of the most deluded. His early dreams lead him on paths through spatial constraints well beyond his comprehension. Socially, he seems to have no idea what he is riding into with Alejandra, and when the Dueña Alfonsa attempts to explain that those societal constraints on the behavior of her charge are written thickly in the blood of history, all John Grady can do is appeal to an ahistorical sense of morality.[12] Worse, despite the revelation we will examine later on, John Grady remains impervious to knowledge on any but the most physical level until he is literally penetrated to death in a second failed errand, in *Cities of the Plain*. We might therefore understand John Grady's death in the terms of traditional tragedy: his beliefs lead him inexorably forward toward the realization of impossibly idealistic dreams, and they entail hubris. His simultaneous willful ignorance of the funneling constraints of history, and the social strictures that history in turn constrains, dooms him to an increasingly narrow set of possibilities. His is the most tragic, in the classical sense, of all the character arcs. John Grady's arc reaches so high as to scrape the limits of those arcs of society and history—but then he must fall.

As we return to Billy carrying the fallen John Grady, in front of the schoolchildren, we see again that his "partly opened eyes beheld nothing at all out of that passing landscape of street or wall or paling sky or the figures of the children who stood blessing themselves in the gray light" (*COTP* 261). In the Epilogue ending *Cities of the Plain*, an enigmatic stranger rambles through half-coherent Borgesian trickery with Billy about dreams. "A dream within a dream makes other claims than what a man might suppose," he says. Billy's reply hints at the earnestness of what the narrative is trying to get at: "A dream inside a dream night not be a dream" (*COTP* 273).

That description of a "landscape" that John Grady can no longer see seems now to haunt *No Country for Old Men*'s lack of lengthy descriptions of setting. And the "appointed places" (*COTP* 262) to which the schoolchildren proceed foreshadows the latest book's gestures at destiny, fate, chance, and the slivers of existential possibility dwindled down by jeremiad so much that such possibility only persists within Bell's dream. *No Country for Old Men* ends by both extending and reversing the relation of Billy as a surviving father figure to a fallen son, just as the attention to unseen landscape is reversed. Similarly, Bell's dream seems so much a dream within an already dream-like extension of monologue that it feels more real than many of Bell's other stories. This occurs as well through the extension of a spoken vision again reaching beyond narrative action: rather than presenting us with the type of Socratic Epilogue ending *Cities of the Plain*, *No Country for Old Men*'s main action dissolves into the spoken visions of Bell's monologues. Bell so tests our patience with those monologues that they entirely displace any formal solution through plot (with Chigurh last seen limping away from a car wreck—more whimper than bang).

The stability of proportion between straight narration with dialogue, and the italicized monologues by Bell, shifts as early as the novel's Chapter XI, which begins as usual in Bell's italicized direct address. This is soon taken over by a scene with a speech by Bell's interlocutor. The speech is long enough that the choice to place all this within the format of Bell's monologue heightens our sense that we are being removed from the main narrative's supposedly more objective view of the world, to a more restricted space. We retreat from action—especially as Bell decides to avoid taking any—into the psychological space of voice; we retreat from the fictive world into a fictive vision further removed from that world. The pattern of the book's structure, which in my preceding chapter I read in generic terms, and as "collapse," can also be read as a falling arc. The monologues run longer as the scenes of action, given in roman type, become so short that they ultimately disappear. McCarthy's Chapter XIII opens with the usual italics, but the book ends there, in Bell's dreams. We have risen through actions at times discussed by Bell in the terms of religion, history, politics, and social values. But we fall back to Bell's dream, after several admissions that he has lost his faith in any of those larger arcs of possibility.

In McCarthy's Chapter XI, who is the man holding forth with Bell on Viet Nam—and even tossing in the entirely apocryphal (but unkillable) urban legend of the spit-on returning veteran to heap the social fault on anyone but Llewelyn? Llewelyn's father. The sheer weight of jeremiad squeezes the very typeface of *No Country for Old Men* into the emphasis, the implicit privacy, and the earnestness of italics. Moss Sr.'s, and Bell's, recriminations against a society gone wrong can make the reader wince as we see the unusually direct expression of loss overtake the stylistic abilities to speak to the heart without the distractions of a hyperbolic detail amidst structural and typographical collapse. But another way to see this is that McCarthy has handed over the narrator's duties to a particular character, and that character is more death-haunted than even Billy Parham.

As expressed by Llewelyn's father to Bell, himself the father of a dead daughter (and only child) and the figurative father to everyone in his county, the text of Moss Sr. strains into the indulgence of a myth that cursory research would reveal as false.[13] Moss Sr.'s speech further strains the typography as those italics encompass *his* voice as well—the voice of the father that Bell could never be. The spitting myth fits the larger view of Moss Sr. and Bell so well that its lack of correspondence in historical fact may have been known by McCarthy and deliberately ignored. Just as McCarthy (an author famous for his research) may have known that no gas chamber has been used in a Texas execution, he could as easily known that no verifiable account of spitting on a Vietnam vet can be found. But these are relatively paltry distinctions between the facts of the world and myths of characters, and odd distinctions on which to base a critical dismissal of a novel. Critics of *No Country for Old Men* were easily (and thus reprehensibly) led astray by gullible assumptions relating the author and the monologues of one of his characters.[14] What begins to be the salient contribution of *No Country for Old Men* to McCarthy's psychological spaces only reinforces the otherwise apparently unconnected philosophical arc we see continued in that novel: the eschatological tone itself gives way to myths of orders insupportable on a human level of reality.

The eschatological tone of Bell's monologues is reinforced by the reactionary quality of his dream. This arc flies beneath the larger philosophical problem of free will posed by Chigurh, and this relation, between psychology and philosophy, has also been set up by the Epilogue of *Cities of the Plain*. Psychologically, the extension of the McCarthian orphan's complaint has become the father's, and Billy Parham's orphan regard for the lost parents is then reversed: where Billy encounters first the trickster ghost father and then is put to bed by the foster mother Betty, Bell instead indicates early on the importance of a marriage in which his wife functions (as many women do for older men) as a mother replacement. It only remains, in *No Country for Old Men*'s final confession, to turn then to the father—first in a confession and reckoning, and then, with the ghost again laid to rest, in dreams.

To do "*justice*" to the father that Bell thinks he has not spoken of enough, we get a few more details about that character. One such detail, about a horse trader encountered by Bell père, curiously recalls Chigurh's habit of telling people what he is about to do to them. The trader tells Bell's young father "*Son, I'm goin to trade with you like you didnt even have a horse. Point bein some people will actually tell you what it is they aim to do to you and whenever they do you might want to listen.*" Bell qualifies his respect of his father, but does so respectfully: "*As the world might look at it I suppose I was a better man. Bad as that sounds to say. Bad as that is to say. That has got to of been hard to live with*" (308). To Bell the son or Bell the father? The condition on the father's failure is his own father's failure, as becomes apparent in the next phrase, a fragment qualifying that confession: "*Let alone his daddy.*" This phrase makes it clear that it is the father, after all, who had to live with the son's greater ethical standing (whether or not Bell believes that standing). More importantly, it simultaneously claims that any man's failures can be laid back on a previous father.

In McCarthy's novels, recursions home that reunite the son and the father without blood can be accomplished only in such dreams, and after the father's death. In life, Charles McCarthy Sr. died shortly after the publication of *The Crossing*.[15] We cannot know if Bell's prosopopoeia, his attempt to recall, to recover, the father he says he has not done "justice" to echoes anything from the author's life. But the directness of Bell's dream might, for understandable reasons, make us wonder.

THE LINE TO HEAVEN

McCarthy's global, even universal questions, such as those surrounding teleology, chance, and predestination, orbit outside still sizable questions on a more human scale: of epistemology, existential struggle, perception, and (at least below the level of the judge's arguments) moral and ethical philosophy, particularly as these last two give rise to the problem of theodicy. In these highest human arcs of philosophy, the apprehension allowed McCarthy's characters generally remains well below the level of consciousness allowed the narration. Indications of these arcs are instead provided by his narrators, by avatars possessing superhuman knowledge (such as the judge, or Anton Chigurh), or by what J. Douglas Canfield called "vatic soothsayers" (259). The latter usually provide us with no more than glimpses of a full philosophy through their parables, warnings, sermons, histories, and sometimes temporarily indecipherable prognostications. Between *Blood Meridian* and *No Country for Old Men*, *The Border Trilogy* is at times overrun with innumerable wise men, wise women, and a general circus of soothsayers and other proprietors of significantly greater knowledge than their protagonist interlocutors. This habit, reaching back to Ownby, teases and tortures the protagonists of these novels, letting us in on more knowledge than they can ever comprehend.[16]

This fact sits near the central irony in McCarthy's tracing of character arcs through their various spaces: we know where those characters really travel, better than they do, if only at the level of dread we know they ought to be feeling. John Grady Cole lives through romantic delusions as much as Billy Parham lives out romantic disillusionment. The kid becomes the man enough to begin carrying a bible, but "no word of which could he read" (*BM* 312), and the judge's rhetoric fails to move his fallen figurative son anywhere but upstairs with a "dwarf" prostitute, where "the man" fails at the procreative power that would oppose Holden (*BM* 332), and then back down to the jakes in a passive path to death and assimilation into the judge's dance (*BM* 335).[17] In the man's rise and fall, we see another arc into death.

The refusal of knowledge regularly constrains these characters in whatever path they might take: they simply see less than we are allowed. The books meanwhile refuse them any of the succors of art. McCarthy's own power of artifice, so notably effective for his readers, seems to be worthless as anything but a false palliative for his characters, if that. John Grady Cole looks at the "oilpainting of horses" and sees nothing to correspond with the horses known to him. His small knowledge of the discrepancy between reality and our systems for comprehension of it came from his grandfather, who, as he recalls, looked "up from his plate as if he'd never seen" this painting, and finally dismissed it by saying, "those are picturebook horses" before he "went on eating" (*ATPH* 15–16). This uselessness of art stands in ironic contrast to the pleasure of word craft that readers find in McCarthy's pages. So, too, the aesthetic visual power, particularly in McCarthy's ability to depict a scene of nature absolutely indifferent to human presence, within the pages of his novels grants McCarthy's readers a pleasure that no one in his stories can themselves enjoy—except within the dangerous constraints of foolish delusion. The disappearance of many of the pleasures of language in *No Country for Old Men* reinforces the downward arc of that work: it is as if the author has finally refused to sustain an incommensurable and thus supposed hypocritical discrepancy between the ugliness of the world he portrays and the beauty of the language with which he portrays it.

This placement of McCarthy characters, at a remove below the larger concerns often tackled by the novels, is matched by their removal above any conscious understanding of their more intimate problems. It is doubtful that John Wesley ever achieves any deep consciousness of his father's importance, or even of his mother's function in keeping him from lighting out for the territory. That Culla Holme may be acting out another such mythic and archetypal Oedipal drama seems as lost on him as the possibility that his sins run parallel and meaningfully connected to the actions of the triune. Ballard regularly voices outrage, and ironically, this most deranged of all McCarthy's main characters may have the greatest access to intimate knowledge of his problem: he is so homeless that he is entirely outcast by the surrounding community. But despite his cries of outrage, he reveals no psychological understanding of the reasons for his descent into necrophilia.

Suttree, the best educated and most self-reflective of all the protagonists (and the only one obviously modeled on McCarthy), insists in his repeated interior monologues that what most ails him is the loss of a twin brother who died in childbirth: "He in the limbo of the Christless righteous, I in a terrestrial hell" (*S* 14). But this hardly convinces, as I argue in reading the signs of other anxieties floating down the Tennessee River. And by the time we reach Billy's encounter with the stranger at the end of *Cities of the Plain*, it has become clear—lest we forgot the judge's last arguments to the "man"—that indulging in a personal hell, and even lamenting one's own situation as at all unique and untethered to the histories and fates of others, is a sign of foolish ignorance. Even the least sophisticated of McCarthy's protagonists are provided arguments, particularly in the last five novels, for fate as an irresistible force in their lives, but these arguments come from outside, and they seem never to convince them.

One of the ways in which fate manifests itself within the particular arc of a single character's life is in relation to the father. Here, a term McCarthy uses in the judge's last arguments becomes especially revealing. As the judge tells the man of "any man" in the bar in Fort Griffin,

> Can he believe that the wreckage of his existence is *unentailed?* No
> liens, no creditors? That *gods of vengeance and of compassion alike* lie
> sleeping in their crypt and whether our cries are for an accounting or
> for the destruction of the ledgers altogether they must evoke only the

same silence and that it is this silence which will prevail? (*BM* 330, my
emphasis)

François Hirsch, in the process of translating *Blood Meridian* into French,
contacted McCarthy about the word "unentailed," and received this
response:

> In other words this man could not believe that his condition was an
> accident or just bad luck. There has to be some malign force set against
> him. . . . I think that the definition of entail that is most useful is the
> one that implies a burden, as to be burdened with, but especially with
> the suggestion of an assured continuing transmission. If I am entailed
> with some quality (good or ill) I have it fastened upon me and cannot
> get rid of it nor avoid passing it to my heirs . . . (McCarthy, in Hirsch
> 210)[18]

McCarthy's explanation strongly recalls the biblical connections, and at
times conflations, of fathers and sons in arcs of guilt that I discussed in Chapter Four. In my explorations of the psychological and social tensions between
sons and fathers in this novel, as well as *Outer Dark* and *Suttree*, I stopped
short of what becomes unavoidable in this passage from *Blood Meridian*. Fate
may be written in blood, such that the sins of the father are borne by the
son. But this means more than genetic predisposition, or a legacy handed
down through psychology; McCarthy's word "fastened," in the letter quoted
above, suggests some agency. This teleological assumption itself assumes that
"gods of vengeance and of compassion alike," as the judge taunts, are not at
all "sleeping in their crypt" (*BM* 330). This second passage suggests three
ramifications for McCarthy's cosmology.

First, Holden refers to two gods: one "of vengeance" and one "of compassion." Notably, the malignant god is mentioned first in the pair. Second,
the singular word "crypt" describes only one space: were these gods to "lie
sleeping," they would actually lie together, in a single "crypt." Third, both
gods are awake, roaming the earth, and active in "fasten[ing]" upon people
their fates, including those qualities that are "entailed" by "creditors."

McCarthy's cosmology here recalls the quotation from Jacob Boehme
in the book's epigraphs: "It is not to be thought that the life of darkness is
sunk in misery and lost as if in sorrowing. There is no sorrowing. For sorrow
is a thing that is swallowed up in death, and death and dying are the very
life of the darkness" (*BM* i). This quotation comes from Boehme's last of *Six
Theosophic Points*, part 13. McCarthy has elided some of the passage, and

that elision now recalls more from Boehme's work: what did McCarthy leave out, and why?

In the original, Boehme's larger context places what in *Blood Meridian's* epigraph is often taken as a celebration of death and decadence within a vertical construction; there, by contrast, Holden would encounter obvious limits that in the novel remain subtly implicit. Boehme's original also begins by correcting a natural assumption that "the life of darkness therefore sinks down into misery." My edition also gives "There is no sorrowing." McCarthy leaves out, however, whatever his translator provided as an alternative to the following passage: "but what with us on earth is sorrowing according to this property, is in the darkness power and joy according to the property of the darkness." Then my version comes back into accord with McCarthy's here: "For sorrowfullness is a thing swalllowed [sic] up in death" (Boehme 102).

What is left out in the *Blood Meridian* quotation makes it clear that Boehme sees the life of darkness as something other, something opposed to our natural station. To be sure, it complements the life of light in Boehme's cosmology. But Boehme never assumes that we would dwell in darkness without light; he is rather describing the condition within the darkness that only a devil would inhabit. McCarthy's elision makes clear that the space of *Blood Meridian* is firmly constrained by that darkness. It does not follow, however, that McCarthy, any more than Boehme, assumes we should embrace that darkness. *Blood Meridian* simply makes it difficult for us to find our way up out of that space, while the judge provides us with several arguments (particularly in his redactions of Nietzsche) that we can only realize a fate beyond that of "antic clay" (*BM* 4–5, 307) by enjoying ourselves on the book's killing grounds.

Boehme's Part 14, immediately following the passage McCarthy quotes from Part 13, suggests vertical limits on even Holden's power of the "suzerain" (*BM* 198). Holden's claims, after all, extend more horizontally than vertically. As high as Holden reaches, he could not claim the power of God except in his acts of violence and erasure on earth. His dancing immortality—a horizontal denial of death, after all—enacts a horizontal freedom, but not a vertical one. "The freedom of the birds is an insult to me. I'd have them all in zoos" (*BM* 199). But why doesn't he? "I'd" elides but includes the conditional "I would:" he would—if he could. Holden's joy remains grounded in a life of darkness that may include knowledge of a higher light, but he cannot reach high enough to challenge that light. He can reach no higher than to direct bats in flight.

Thus he warns away his interlocutors from hopes of any metaphysical salvation. In this Holden may prove irrefutable, but he more regularly focuses his refusal of morality on the human history out of which that morality has evolved; instead of sin, he speaks of morality as a wholly fictive enterprise (as does Nietzsche). He therefore makes his most potent claims where his hands can reach them. "The judge placed his hands on the ground. He looked at his inquisitor. This is my claim, he said. And yet everywhere upon it are pockets of autonomous life. Autonomous. In order for it to be mine nothing must be permitted to occur upon it save by my dispensation" (*BM* 199). This is not only a claim, but also a complaint. And here Holden is admitting that there is work to be done even in the horizontal space of his darkness.

Here is Boehme's characterization, as it were, of this energy in him: "We cannot, then, say of the devil that he sits in dejection, as if he were faint-hearted. There is no faint-heartedness in him, but a constant will [. . .] that his fierceness may become greater. [. . .] He would be a mighty lord [. . .] for it is the strong and great life" (102). The judge—not "the devil" and yet certainly the strongest avatar of him McCarthy has yet given us—cannot become suzerain of anything beyond the earth, and his "would" reminds us that even his powers here are limited. By what? In Boehme, "the light is his misery and dread; that checks his bravery. He is terrified at the light; for it is his true poison, which torments him. Because he abandoned it, it now resists him. Of which he is ashamed, that he is thus a deformed angel in a strange image" (102).

Boehme's cosmology varies, but what seems to interest McCarthy is one half of Boehme's idea of a universe in which both good and evil are "mixed." Both originate in God, but evil has grown through post-lapsarian individuation as fast as the growth of goodness, its complement. Humans "are budding forth out of the animal image with a human image that belongs to God's kingdom, and who would fain live and grow in the human image, in the right man." In Boehme's address to his ideal reader, he clearly assumes that humans can aspire to "the holy life." But despite this optimistic aim, and his insistence that what he intends to impart is not, after all, "impossible to discern," Boehme's cosmology throughout *Six Theosophic Points* remains dualistic: one may aspire to a life that is finally not "mixed," but in the meantime, evil and good spring from the same earth. Evil is never wholly other (5).

The difference between this cosmology, and the more flattering one for the judge that I outlined in Chapter Five (in which Holden appears a Krishna to the kid's Arjuna), is one of time. The judge would represent a cyclical time that refuses evolution beyond that point at which humans might, in his footsteps, claim suzerainty over the earth—become gods on earth. But this course is wholly destructive; in that sense, and in his dancing, Holden indeed might represent cyclical time and regeneration through destruction. Of course, the cosmology containing Krishna is itself based on cyclical time. Our understanding of the arc of history in *Blood Meridian*, however (and the Epilogue reminds us of history), suggests a nightmare of progress, a progression up to power but back down into destruction and death. History in this book proves to be an arc after all—not a circle—and the possibilities of rebirth in violence are a temptation proffered us by the judge only disingenuously: he aims to move forward, inexorably through the darkness in which he maintains his sway.

Holden never, as does Milton's Satan, promises the possibility of vertical flight. In Boehme's cosmology, Holden might rise upward, but his challenge would presumably end in that fire of the light that is the only thing he fears. The affinities of McCarthy's and Boehme's cosmologies may or may not include belief in a God whose light so successfully constrains evil, but McCarthy seems to have adopted Boehme's incorporation of that strongest sense of linear time: an eschatological line. In Boehme, this line maintains (recapitulated in several texts) a beginning, a middle, and an end; Boehme's eschatology provides a line that leads—whatever its diversions through Apocalypse—to heaven. But McCarthy's cosmology is expressed in our time, not Boehme's, and McCarthy's eschatological expression, suitably more sophisticated, falls downward; less certain of heaven, it remains as certain of apocalypse.

McCarthy's eschatological line therefore falls, a proper arc, to a less literal apocalypse. In *The Sense of an Ending*, Frank Kermode outlines the progression of eschatology to just the type of nuanced and symbolic form that we now find in McCarthy. I have argued in the previous chapter that Bell progresses through jeremiad only to pass on to a mythic recursion in his final dream of decadent prosopopoeia. So, too, we trace the upper arc of McCarthy's overall philosophy and find it passes through three phases. The first commingles mystical, theosophical, and gnostic eschatology; the second becomes a system of scientific hypotheses on chaos, complexity theory, and constraints of fate and chance on free will; and the third finally recedes from these possibilities—these systems of imagination, after all—to find an ultimate expression of final aesthetic possibilities available only through an imagination driven less by these systems than by the power of story.

A full exploration of any one of these is beyond the scope of this chapter. But it should be possible to indicate some relation between them, insofar as we might understand at least that sketch of the general philosophical arc toward which I have worked here. If what we have found in our view of arcs sketched over arcs is a set of heroic rising and decadent falling into death, then how do we explain the reason for this? Vereen Bell's early answer was nihilism. Edwin Arnold seems to find faith, albeit a faith to which one must leap, out of existential dread. For Arnold, however, the novels contain morals that persist. How can these two critical possibilities (nihilism and morality) continue to be as convincing as they are (and in other critics, as well), without canceling each other out? It would be too easy to evade the problem one faces when neither of these possibilities seems to answer all our questions about these character flights through these dark spaces. In psychology we call that "ambivalence," and try not to notice that such a condition is often regarded, after all, as over-determined. That answer still convinces at the lowest level of, say, Ballard: his conflation of eros and thanatos well explains his arc. But how so the larger falling trends throughout McCarthy's novels?

The biblical imagery of failure overwhelms the generative possibilities of love, let alone grace, in those novels. Billy's stranger may suggest to him some Christ-like path ("That man who is all men and who stands in the dock for us until our own time come and we must stand for him. Do you love him, that man? will you honor the path he has taken?"), but the great bulk of the stranger's tale is only that dark side of the "tale" of "that man" (*COTP* 288–289). The book's title remains *Cities of the Plain*: a typological reference to cities fallen from God's favor, and thus destroyed—which is itself a typological presage of the vision of Apocalypse provided John in Revelation.

In the Epilogue of *Cities of the Plain*, the stranger's dream of a bloody altar remains stronger in our memory than "that man." The alter echoes in the "tile" in which Billy (like the traveler in the stranger's dream) also sleeps "rolled [. . .] in his blanket" after a vision of figures, robed and mysterious, recalls the unholy sacrifices of the stranger's dream (*COTP* 289). It may be that ultimately, we are to work hard enough to see in Billy—and even in Ballard—men for whom Christ stood in the dock. But that runs beyond the proportion and force of imagery in these novels, just as we must go outside *Blood Meridian* to find a cosmological limit in one of McCarthy's sources for its life of darkness. Within these novels, death outpaces any resurrections. Holden outdances any power we can find within his book. Why?

Death provides the ultimate narrative focus. Kermode notes this in his exploration of the power eschatology holds over us all in a culture of inviolably linear temporality. Notwithstanding postmodern assertions of some return to cyclical time in the West, our awareness of our eventual death inscribes an arc falling through our lives; lack of conviction that anything can happen to "me" after that death does no good to alter that linearity. Our adjustments to this fact echo those of eschatology. As Kermode describes those adjustments, chiliasm first asserts itself in a "naïve" form. But it isn't long before adjustments have to be made: "disconfirmation"—the reality that strikes you when you wake up on Wednesday and the world did not end, as you thought it would, on Tuesday—"is thwarted by typology, arithmology, and perhaps by the buoyancy of chiliasts in general." After all, "you can of course arrange for the End to occur at pretty well any desired date" (9). Eventually, however, the more perceptive realize that as much as the end may not be found on the calendar, the power of eschatology refuses to disappear for even the irreligious. We agnostics and atheists need our beginnings, middles, and ends as well. Even if we maintain too much intellectual reserve to fall for millennialism, we speak of the "end" of the day and of the week. And, as McCarthy points out in his second interview, death and dying remain the facts of human life.

"It used to be if you grew up in a family you saw everybody die. They died in their bed at home with everyone gathered around. Death is the major issue in the world. For you, for me, for all of us. It just is. To not be able to talk about it is very odd" (Woodward 103–104). Talk about it he does in these novels. But it is not surprising that the sheer pressure of death suggests comparisons with other authors misread as nihilists, such as Beckett. As I noted earlier, in Beckett, the humor saves us; it sometimes saves even his characters. Humor helps in McCarthy, but it has disappeared in the last three novels. Why?

I see an arc toward eschatology that has conterminously extinguished the light of humor. Humor, too, has risen through the early novels before its recent death. We first laughed at Sylder's sarcasm, a little. We laughed a little more at a stampede of hogs, but only a little more (*OD* 217–218). For all his horrors, we laughed more at Ballard's "Do what?" and at the dumpkeeper's daughters, "Urethra," "Cerebella," and "Hernia Sue" (*COG* 74, 26). We laughed uncontrollably at Harrogate and his melons, pigeons, someone else's shoat, his boat and bats, and his aborted Stygian bank heist as he becomes a living turd of humanity in a river of literal shit (*S* 31–35, 117, 168–142, 207–219, 269–270). The darkness of humor seemed only to enrich the laughter rising up to its zenith in *Suttree*.

Even the judge had his humor, and we laughed at his con job on the Reverend Green and the piss-gunpowder slaughter from the volcano (*BM* 5–8, 131–133). These last comic set pieces, however, directly involved human victims, and thus evinced more serious matters leavened only by this dark avatar's gusto in the work, his arms elbow deep in bat guano and piss all for stirring up killing fuel. The comic in *Blood Meridian* remains dark and uneasy, beyond richness.

We laughed long at the lightening soliloquy of Blevins (*ATPH* 67–69). But here, too, the humor in that soliloquy signaled an important shift: it is the language of the characters, more than their actions or predicaments, that is funny in *All the Pretty Horses*. Even those actions we find somewhat humorous are not laugh-out-loud funny so much as uneasily humorous. Like Rawlins, we know that "Somethin bad is goin to happen" soon (*ATPH* 77), and indeed, even Blevins's mad patter about the familial fate of being "double bred for death by fire" precedes real trouble after which this boy will eventually be shot to death (*ATPH* 68, 178). Harrogate's fate is unpleasant, but it does not entail death; as much as the deaths of McCarthy's friends and acquaintances seems to have inspired those of Suttree, this does not lead to killing off Cornelius.[19] Blevins, however, will be left dead in the desert, killed just as thoroughly by gunfire as he feared he would be by lightening. The difference, of getting killed through a metal button and getting killed by a lead bullet, proves grim and insubstantial: the death of Blevins is entailed in him from before he was born.

The Crossing's evenly serious tone then deepens the biblical sense of an end of days falling over the last three novels. McCarthy's own version of typology begins to show through more and more, as Billy becomes the representative echo of every McCarthy orphan, and then his 78-year-old orphan self (worn out by his multiple failed rescues) is echoed again in Bell. Finally, Chigurh, as a lesser avatar of evil, is Holden without gusto. Without humor, Chigurh is all business, as if his job ran on a consultant's short contract; when the end is nigh, even the devil's familiar works his assassination and recovery contracts like a corporation temp.

Instead of claiming suzerainty over as much of the earth as possible, Chigurh's project seems to be a mission of enlightening people as he kills them one by one. The seal on the forehead in Revelation is not only given by the Beast, to those fallen from God. It is first given (though unspecified, presumably in a different form than the mark of the Beast) to the twelve tribes of Israel—to God's chosen: "Hurt not the earth, neither the sea, nor the trees, till we have sealed the servants of our God in their foreheads" (7; 3). They then receive this blessing: "For the Lamb which is in the midst of the throne shall feed them, and shall lead them unto living fountains of waters: *and God shall wipe away all tears from their eyes*" (Rev. 7; 17, my emphasis). Only then is the seventh seal of Apocalypse opened, which much later brings the Beast, and his sign of 666, etc. Chigurh's insistence that people look at him as he kills them, and his disturbing, yet compelling, insistence that they recognize their entailment, their fate, but also their small actions of free will that led to this moment of their death, complicates him. Whose seal is he delivering?

We cannot be sure, but he proffers us no dance in which we might imagine the world, even through violence, reborn. He simply limps away, like one of the many exits of the Beast, the Red Dragon, and other baddies in Revelation.

Through the last three novels, humor is no longer the point even in moments, as the end is nigh. And this is conterminous with the darkening worldview. For all the arguments (and I have made some) that McCarthy may have "softened" beyond *Blood Meridian*, there is more life in the darkness of that book than in the books that follow. True, the violence of *The Border Trilogy* is less egregious, but it is more focused. Blevins bore not only a name, but a character strikingly drawn, beyond his echoes of Huck Finn. Simultaneously, the expectations of the protagonists brighten, particularly through all three boys in *All the Pretty Horses*, through Billy and Boyd in turn, and again through John Grady. Throughout *The Border Trilogy* we came to expect some struggling against the dying of the light, even as that becomes more and more futile.

This is true even when we recall the darkness of *Child of God* or *Outer Dark*. Nothing in the endings of those books feels quite like the End of Time. Truly, *Outer Dark* does suggest a world irretrievably fallen into gloom, but its indeterminate spatial and temporal qualities round it like a dream more even than those qualities often suggest a dream space in McCarthy. For all its gloom, Culla Holme's behavior seems to have called it forth. We feel for Rinthy, but even the murder of her child, in its nameless anonymity, compares oddly with the death of Blevins. And as in *Blood Meridian*, we are allowed some distance of history. These novels take place outside time, and yet in historical moments discrete enough to provide the reader with some consolation (however frail) that such times are past. And in these dark books we did find those little laughs, especially through which we were able to distance ourselves from Ballard, and from Holme.

By comparison, *The Border Trilogy*, despite its anachronistic cowboy systems, feels closer to our time. Certainly we easily feel closer to its protagonists, which is another fact leading to the relative popularity of those books. Blevins and John Grady (and Boyd, and Magdalena) die nonetheless, leaving Billy a shell of a man, haunted by death. And the collapsing structure, genre shifts, lack of rich detail beyond fetish, and the final retreat to dream that I examined in Chapter Seven argued that in general, the land of *No Country for Old Men* has dried up. Bell leaves us in despair at lost worlds, and Chigurh remains on the loose.

This is not a complaint, but an observation—and not of aesthetics, although that too can be said, but of tone: there is a larger arc to the novels, and it has risen to its zenith already, and it is falling. It may be that McCarthy produces more novels (whether wholly new or reshaped earlier drafts), and that in these books to come he may take new directions. But even if the grim deathward fall, the lack of humor, the drying of the language, were to somehow be reversed, the falling arc of the last third of these nine novels will remain.

Although McCarthy is known to hold manuscripts sometimes for years before release, it is still clear that he decides the order in which they appear (Woodward 104). And whatever order in which major drafts and revisions are written, McCarthy has every opportunity to stitch his thread through a final draft with an eye on order of publication, and he seems to do so: as Arnold and others find, and as I have argued here, the reappearance of types and figures runs beyond chance. The few main characters that live are aging longer before we leave them, but the surrounding world is darkening. *The Crossing*'s ending with an atomic explosion (*TC* 425), and Billy much later mistaking plastic bags caught on a fence for ancient sacrificial pilgrims (*COTP* 289), point to a world darkened by technological innovation. And the fuss made over Bell's reference to a gas chamber (*NCFOM* 3) instead of the lethal injection table that Jim Willett describes so well in *Warden: Prison Life and Death from the Inside Out*, or "Ol' Sparky," the chair that preceded it (219), provides depressing evidence for the death of humor in McCarthy. What, finally, is the difference between these methods of execution?

"No longer imminent, the End is immanent," Kermode tells us,

> So that it is not merely the remnant of time that has eschatological import; the whole of history, and the progress of individual life, have it also, as a benefaction from the End, now immanent. History and eschatology, as Collingwood observed, are then the same thing. Butterfield calls 'every instant . . . eschatological'; Bultmann says that 'in every moment slumbers the possibility of being the eschatological moment. You must wake it.' (25)

We feel this with Bell, and perhaps the severity of critics with *No Country for Old Men* wells up not only from the relatively recent wounds felt by many a political progressive in this country, but by fears that reach deeper even than our feelings about ongoing wars, threats to reproductive rights and other personal freedoms, or the displacement in schools of science by pseudoscience. Some of us may disagree with Bell's politics, but his sense that night is falling is with us, too. This is true without one literally expecting apocalypse. Kermode notes that the crucial position of apocalypse in

Boehme's cosmology comes from the unkillable "Joachite speculation" of 1250 (13), and that version of "transition"—the time which we feel precedes apocalypse—

> is the historical ancestor of modern crisis; in so far as we claim to
> live now in a period of perpetual transition we have merely elevated
> the interstitial period into an 'age' or *saeculum* in its own right, and
> the age of perpetual transition in technological and artistic matters is
> understandably an age of perpetual crisis in morals and politics (28).

Bell's fears, whether assumed to be the opposite of a particular reviewer's or not, run parallel to them. Anachronisms in the technology of *No Country for Old Men* (several reviewers complained about the size of a cell phone) prove equally absurd quibbles: it doesn't matter what particular type of gun kills you, or what particular type of tracking or communications devices enable the man who will hunt you down; the point is that he has more than Glanton's Delawares to track you, rearrange his contract, and eventually seal the deal. You will be as dead as the Tiguas in *Blood Meridian*, but more fully commodified.

The deals behind *Cities of the Plain* and *No Country for Old Men* match the dwindling spaces in those books. Business has indeed taken over in McCarthy. And although I am not the right critic to properly assess the economy we find in *No Country for Old Men*, I wonder if rather than "late capitalism" it is not something closer to anarcho-capitalism. The tropes of creditors, liens, ledgers, and contracts have built up steadily, already heavy in *Blood Meridian*, and they outrun any hierarchical system, depending instead on the fungibility of everything between any two or more people. By *Cities of the Plain* the army threatens to acquire the ranch by eminent domain, but they will pay for it (*COTP* 62). Contracts, rather than larger markets, even, seem to determine the bloody economics of these books. Magdalena is not for sale by her own pimp's decision (though he rents her readily), and yet a full purchase is the means by which John Grady plans on rescuing her. Money, so notable in *No Country for Old Men*, but also contract labor, is now more evident when rereading *Cities of the Plain*. John Grady claims the land and the abandoned house he intends to make into a home by mixing his labor with it. But any peaceful practice of revocable contracts that anarcho-capitalism might promise him proves as elusive as do perfectly-planned conspiracies developed by the petroleum corporation in *No Country for Old Men*, or sanctions of filibustering by the U.S. government and of scalp-hunting by Mexican city-states in *Blood Meridian*.

As Eduardo reminds us, such deals—whether attempted by individuals, businesses, or countries—are rigged, inevitably, and inherently violent. The army can take the land at any price, and Eduardo doesn't have to sell Magdalena. Trading land and women is more complicated than trading horses. In any case, Mr. Johnson reminds us not to get our hopes up: "Don't be fooled by the good rains we've had. This country is fixin to dry up and blow away" (*COTP* 62). Inevitably, both the contracts of humans with each other, and those imagined with nature, are written over null with blood, superseded by murder and war. So much for an anarcho-capitalist utopia free from violence.[20]

Obvious apocalyptic imagery would be unnecessary to convey this eschatological trend. The closest McCarthy comes, with Chigurh's cattle gun delivering its deep seals, at least carries some ambiguities in its application. The peculiarities of McCarthy's fictional moments are as adjusted for as are the forms of disconfirmation described by Kermode: "[C]hanged by our special pressures, subdued by our skepticism, the paradigms of apocalypse continue to lie under our ways of making sense of the world" (28). McCarthy's art is not so obvious as to fall for a naïve system, and "the more learned" the "novelist, the 'higher' the kind he practises, the more subtly are [the] types [of apocalypse] overlaid" (Kermode 29–30). One of these features of subtlety is the proliferation of peripeteia. This throws another light on the shift in *No Country for Old Men* that I described in Chapter Seven, of a noir crime novel, to jeremiad, to a compromised and regressive version of a Jungian dream.

Peripeteia in *No Country for Old Men* occurs not only through several "reversals" of what we expect to happen, but also by having nothing at all happen. Our surprise at the killing of Moss may not be particularly strong, but it occurs early, and not to have Chigurh find and accomplish that killing notably breaks what would be the more obvious narrative choice. Then we are prepared for a confrontation between Bell and Chigurh, but that, too, never occurs. Finally, the manner in which Chigurh is again wounded—a seemingly random traffic accident—recalls his arguments about chance, but not in any way that we might easily make sense of in this scene. That the boys in the car that hits Chigurh's truck had been "smokin dope" creates too obvious an ironic reversal for this enforcer for hire by drug lords (*NCFOM* 287). The last we see of Chigurh, he is walking away, his head bleeding and one arm broken in two places, "holding the twist of [a] bandana against his head, limping slightly" (*NCFOM* 262). Our last surprise from this novel might be to see how different a film version of it will be: what Hollywood film can allow its villain (with no revelation of his true identity) to limp away? But Chigurh must limp away with his broken arm, as this stark contrast with the judge—"light and nimble," "dancing and fiddling at once" (*BM* 335)—reminds us again of apocalypse; one beast departs only to return again, or to be replaced by another, as Revelation runs on and on.

Kermode explains that, "the End itself, in modern literary plotting loses its downbeat, tonic-and-dominant finality, and we think of it, as the theologians think of Apocalypse, as immanent rather than imminent." We then must "make much of subtle disconfirmation and elaborate peripeteia. And we concern ourselves with the conflict between the *deterministic pattern* any plot suggests, and the *freedom of persons within that plot to choose and so alter the structure*, the relations of beginning, middle, and end" (30, my emphasis). We may read this conflict, between "deterministic pattern" and "freedom of plot," as analogous to the distinction Kermode makes between "fact" or "reality"—that world that Yeats and Stevens must register only through creating fictions that cannot fully correspond with it—and the "pattern" as "system" that is that fiction. The artist has this power at his or her disposal because "the imagination is always at the end of an era" (31).

What is McCarthy's "system?" How does he balance the opposing fact—as we must call it if we are to entertain its possibility—of determinism, of fate, of what entailments are fastened upon us, against the fiction of free will? Very recent work on *No Country for Old Men* finds at least two possibilities for what I have called this second phase beyond mystical eschatology. Earlier in this chapter I claimed that although death remains the central fact of all nine novels, even in the darkest of these books death is situated against complementary forces that grant that deathward direction a greater force by contrast. I then suggested that Boehme's cosmology, with its ultimate limitations on even an avatar of the devil so powerful as the judge, confines his murderous arcs well below that of God in a first phase of McCarthy's cosmology. Now, there are possibilities that lead to McCarthy's interest in the problem outside theological answers. First, there is the philosophical problem as Anton Chigurh presents it to his victims. Second, we can put Chigurh into newer theories than Boehme's conception of a system closed in God, but within which the epistemological privilege claimed by both Chigurh and judge Holden nonetheless finds constraints: they become scale-dependent.

THE STRING IN THE MAZE: FATE AND COMPLEXITY

Another reason for choosing McCarthy's image of arcs within the arc as a means of reconciling the vertical, as well as the horizontal spaces in the novels comes from the affinity this image bears with ideas McCarthy has shown significant interest in for some years. Linda Woodson and Meredith Farmer have extended our understanding of how McCarthy's work at the Santa Fe Institute, a multidisciplinary think tank for the study of complexity science, informs his latter novels. Without being able to do justice to their full arguments, we can briefly examine both Woodson's exploration of fate and chance, and Farmer's of complexity theory, for what they have in common, and for the sense we have in these ideas that McCarthy indeed poses systems in contrast to the deathward arc of philosophy that ultimately remains the salient feature of his work.

Both the philosophical work on determinism and free will outlined by Woodson, and the threads of complexity theory that Farmer finds running through the speeches and actions of judge Holden and Anton Chigurh, entail scale dependence and imply subsumptive hierarchy. Scale dependence means that events occurring on one scale, or order of magnitude, can behave differently than those on another scale. As Holden puts it, "the universe is no narrow thing and the order within it is not constrained by any latitude in its conception to repeat what exists in one part in any other part" (*BM* 245). But this does not mean, as many have understood this passage, that the universe is an unmappable space of absolute indeterminacy. After all, the frequent allusions to fate throughout McCarthy's novels (such as the judge's use of the word "entail" that I discussed earlier) must somehow fit within this system of which Holden rightly observes, things behave differently at different orders of magnitude. Woodson and Farmer have found different systems for understanding this same interdependency of repetition, order, fate, and determinacy at a higher order of magnitude, and of variation, disorder, free will, and indeterminacy at a lower order of magnitude.

Holden warns us that the limits of human epistemology are such that we can never actually determine the ultimate truths of the universe: "the order in creation which you see is that which you have put there, *like a string in a maze*, so that you shall not lose your way" (*BM* 245, my emphasis). Nevertheless, he demands that we try:

> The man who believes that the secrets of the world are forever hidden lives in mystery and fear. Superstition will drag him down. The rain will erode the deeds of his life. But that man who sets himself the task of *singling out the thread of order* from the tapestry will by the decision alone have taken charge of the world and it is only by such taking charge that he will effect a way to dictate the terms of his own fate. (*BM* 199, my emphasis)

So we must single out a "thread of order" that is bound to be no more than the "string in a maze" that we "have put there?"

This apparent contradiction may be resolved, at least in part, by relatively recent work in complexity theory and philosophy of epistemology and determinacy. But as a heroic enjoinment to grasp whatever free will one might find, if only to find the limits of that free will, this contradiction runs all the way back to *Oedipus Rex.* Doomed by the fate entailed upon him by the gods, Oedipus nonetheless "dictate[s] the terms of his own fate" as his speeches, his demands for the truth, lead him inexorably to his own literal blindness and figurative revelation.

Woodson provides us with models that incorporate the otherwise incommensurable elements of chance and free will in McCarthy. In "'you are the battleground': Materiality, Moral Responsibility, and Determinism in *No Country for Old Men,*" Woodson finds McCarthy attempting to answer the question of whether we can see our actions in the light of moral responsibility "even if determinism were true? Or as the Dueña Alfonsa asks in *All the Pretty Horses*: 'If fate is the law then is fate also subject to that law? At some point we cannot escape naming responsibility. It's in our nature'" (*ATPH* 241, Woodson 2).

Materiality in *The Border Trilogy* may remain true on "a different plane of reference" (7) than that at which Anton Chigurh chooses to act "outside of moral responsibility" and yet true to his word (11). Woodson sees Chigurh's position as sociopathic (as indeed, anyone must in day to day life), and therefore incommensurable with a position requiring moral responsibility. Citing John Martin Fischer and Mark Ravizza, she interprets McCarthy's last novel as a call for responsibility, despite the possibility of a determined universe. Woodson uses Fischer and Ravizza's definition for the particular form of "*causal determinism*" to understand McCarthy's depiction of what I have been calling "fate:" "for any given time, a complete statement of the facts about that time, together with a complete statement of the laws of nature, entails every truth as to what happens after that time" (Fischer and Ravizza 14, in Woodson 3, her emphasis). If true, this model of determinism (among many, as she notes) threatens to invalidate moral responsibility because it obviates control on the part of any individual within this system of "the laws of nature:"

> Control is traditionally thought of as being necessary for moral responsibility; that is, a person has alternative possibilities and follows one path when another is fully in his power [. . .] (Fischer and Ravizza 20). To give up a belief in this sort of control, one would have to abandon

behavior that represents our understanding of human life. (Fischer and Ravizza 25, Woodson 14)

However, Woodson then notes that Fischer and Ravizza's theory does not necessitate that type of control; moral responsibility remains possible because there are "two kinds of control: regulative control and guidance control" (31, Woodson 14):

> Regulative control requires the ability to perform freely both an action and an alternative action. The kind of control that they argue for, instead, guidance control, need not involve alternatives (33). This sort of control involves an agent freely performing an action, whether the power to do something else exists or not. It is in this kind of control that moral responsibility is grounded. (Woodson 14)

Woodson then uses the following example: if you are driving a car with two sets of controls, you may come to a corner and turn your wheel, and see the car turn in what seems to be your direction. Unbeknownst to you, your driving teacher was going to make this turn whether you did or not. In moral terms, your choice to make that turn remains real, even as it had no consequence. "Thus, agents "can be morally responsible, even though they are not free to do otherwise" (Fischer and Ravizza 59, Woodson 14–15).

Fischer and Ravizza's arguments entail scale dependence: the heroism of the protagonists in *The Border Trilogy*, and in a much more measured sense, Sheriff Bell's refusal to let himself off the hook at the end of *No Country for Old Men*, resides precisely in the local ignorance with which they act—in their inability or refusal to recognize a lack of true free will. It is precisely "outside," as Woodson puts it (11), of the human realm of responsibility and caring for other people, that Chigurh locates his frightening ethics. Or it is at least Chigurh's awareness of an ultimate lack of real free will that enforces his ethic among lesser humans: the only free will allowed any of his victims is the ability to acknowledge the truth that they have none, or at least that their previous actions led inexorably to their appointment with him, and with death.

In that sense, Chigurh remains ironically imprisoned within his knowledge that some combination of chance and fate create an interstitial epistemological web that allows for no "regulative control." As McCarthy described this character in his interview coinciding with the release of *No Country for Old Men*, Chigurh is "pretty much pure evil" (Woodward 103). This otherwise seemingly simplistic characterization was already complicated by Chigurh's regular insistence on the importance of chance—or apparent chance—in his killings. We may also recall the limitations we found in Boehme that are entailed in the interdependency of good and evil that nonetheless constrained the judge's potential for vertical flight. Finally, Woodson helps us see that Chigurh himself, aware as he is (and as Holden is, too) of the true limits of free will, has less of it than his human, and therefore ineluctably naïve, victims. Perhaps the final abuse committed by Holden and Chigurh remains the verbal trickery whereby they tempt their interlocutors with a sense of imparted knowledge, while they are nonetheless loading their arguments toward the obviation of free will. Even so, Holden's enjoinment to take up that thread remains; with his humor, it adds to his appeal in comparison to his latter counterpart in the role of superhuman avatar of "pure evil."

Woodson carefully situates her exploration of this mediated morality with dutiful notes on the disagreements among philosophers and physicists on whether or not distinctions in time are "illusory" (15) and whether or not determinism "exists" (3). But Meredith Farmer has traced likely answers to these questions, at least as they appear to be answered in McCarthy. Farmer noticed that theories of simplicity and complexity have interested McCarthy since before he met their key theorist, physicist Murray Gell-Mann, through the MacArthur Foundation that awarded McCarthy with one of its "genius" fellowships (1n). Briefly, Farmer's definition of complexity "holds that in many natural systems, order emerges from the bottom-up, which is just to say that a collection of agents follow different rules, and from their interactions, a system with no central control emerges" (2).

This provides another means of understanding the apparent free will, or "guidance control," described by Woodson. At a local level (meaning a lower level of a complex, and thus subsumptive hierarchical system in which order obtains only as an emergent phenomenon), free will seems more possible than it might actually be. This means that one's actions may be predetermined by the system's larger history, not from a top-down authority. The persistence of guidance control—of thinking you are free—combined with the possibility that you might actually make some choices that are not wholly determined by that system's emergent order, entails moral choices even though those choices may have no direct relation to outcomes. Meanwhile, because the controlling authority of the system arises within itself as eventually retrodictable, but not predictable, we have two possible gods for a McCarthian cosmology.

One god, that connected intelligence of the entire system of the universe, may know nothing of its own futurity, but rather exists only as the sum total of all its parts at any given moment. This is the pantheistic but timeless god suggested by many of Suttree's dream visions. Another god, however, arises in an all-knowing intelligence that, because it exists only in futurity, can retrodict the past evolution of the universe, and thus knows the exact location of everything at every moment—but can do nothing about it, and did nothing to create it. This is the knowledgeable but distant, transcendent god to whom the heretic of Carborca appeals, and who Bell's uncle believes cannot do anything to change the world.

Farmer makes the connection between the name for McCarthy's "pretty much pure evil" baddie and the predictability of numerous simple organisms within a system of complexity far greater than that exhibited by any single constituent member of that system, when she notes the wordplay in his name: Anton Chigurh is "Ant-on Sugar." Or as he tells Carla Jean when she protests that he "wouldnt of let me off noway:" "I had no say in the matter. Every moment in your life is a turning and every one a choosing. Somewhere you made a choice. All followed to this. The accounting is scrupulous. The shape is drawn. *No line can be erased*" (*NCFOM* 259, my emphasis). Here, I see Chigurh as claiming no more free will than his victims, but his evil arises in his attempt to deprive them of that illusory sense of free will that enacts at least guidance control. His use of the coin replicates the judge's prestidigitation even as it refuses the heroic enjoinment to the small accomplishment of "dictat[ing] the terms" of our "fate" (*BM* 199).

Complexity theory argues that some systems evince complex behavior at the global level after depending on simple behavior on the local level. Chigurh's redaction of this distinguishes him from Holden as I have read the judge's less cautionary speeches. As Farmer describes Chigurh, he has let go of any mantle of superhuman ability:

> [H]e gives up any kind of godlike, soul-selected agency, and it is clear that he believes that he is guided by some kind of elusive principles or rules that lead him to be where he is. Of course, they are not easy to see, because complex patterns never are. Nonetheless, they exist, and we can find strands of them. For example, Chigurh is ruled by the contract formed by his word. When he finds Carla Jean, she tells him (and hopes), "you've got no cause to hurt me" (255). His reply is, "I know. But I gave my word" (255). That never changes. It becomes his refrain, opposed to her pleas. He does not see it as a choice. (Farmer 11)

But, as Woodson helps us see the possibility of guidance control, it becomes clear that Chigurh has made an immoral choice; he is, after all, "pretty much pure evil" (Woodward 103).

As Farmer has noted, perhaps Murray Gell-Mann has influenced what I will now begin to call McCarthy's "system" as much as any other *contemporary* thinker. It remains to be seen here just how much McCarthy may trust that system. But for now, it should be instructive to look further into Gell-Mann's own redaction of some more lengthy statements in "What is Complexity:"

> It now seems likely that the fundamental law governing the behavior of all matter in the universe—the unified quantum field theory of all the elementary particles and their interactions—is quite simple. [. . .] It also appears that the boundary condition specifying the initial condition of the universe around the beginning of its expansion may be simple as well. If both of these propositions are true, does that mean that there is hardly any effective complexity in the universe? Not at all, because of the relentless operation of chance.
>
> Given the basic law and the initial condition, the history of the universe is by no means determined, because the law is quantum-mechanical, thus yielding only probabilities for alternative histories. [. . .] We can think of the alternative possible [. . .] histories of the universe as forming a branching tree, with probabilities at each branching. [. . .] Any entity in the world around us, such as an individual human being, owes its existence not only to the simple fundamental law of physics and the boundary condition on the early universe but also to the outcomes of an inconceivably long sequence of probabilistic events, each of which could have turned out differently.

Chigurh's coin tosses, but also Holden's tricks, and the tarot reading in *Blood Meridian*, suggest that these characters (including the gypsies) have access to a future knowledge of how the complex order of events will run. This again elevates their position to something at least relatively superhuman, as a complex system cannot be predicted, but can sometimes be retrodicted (Farmer 3).

The presence of chance events in the system creates what Gell-Mann calls "accidents," a rich word for *No Country for Old Men*, which sends Chigurh packing after a car wreck. Accidents, like small measures of actual free will (if any exist beyond guidance control) may or may not alter the future. "Sometimes, however, an accident can have widespread consequences for the future, although those are typically restricted to particular regions of space and time." Gell-Mann calls these "frozen accidents" and notes that they produce a connective tissue of information. As chance events "accumulate," so do that portion of them that alter the future. The results are a pile of complexity: a subsumptive hierarchical system in which simple predictable events and chance events pile up together, generating a system of such complexity that nothing can adequately describe it. Rather than writing out a formula for such a system, you have to run all its accumulated events to watch them weave together. The linear (though complicated) direction of such a system, its reliance on events (some of which alter its course, others which do not) recalls many a cogent description of narrative.

The present condition of the universe depends significantly more on the outcome of chance events, accidents, and "frozen accidents" than on merely realizing the outcomes of predetermined directions embedded in "the basic law and the initial condition" that obtained at its origin. But it depends on those as well. As a whole, the universe exhibits both repetition and variation, and may, for a time, generate an increasing number of individual situations (or moments) of sufficient complexity that we may call them original, or individual—much as a character's actions recall those of countless similar characters, and yet, in the best fiction, nonetheless may manage to invent something wholly new within the constraints of their pattern. For some time, this works to foster innovation.

Bell's sense that the children have lost their way may seem at first (especially when taken on simplistic political terms) to express fears about the adoption of outside behaviors and neglect of local custom, combined with a refusal to recognize the sense of repeating traditional behaviors, such as manners: "*It starts when you begin to overlook bad manners. Any time you quit hearin Sir and Mam the end is pretty much in sight*" (NCFOM 304). His worries, it turns out, fit not only those of the book of Jeremiah, but also the bewildering array of differentiation entailed by an evolving complex system. It becomes inevitable that "*there would be people on the streets of our Texas towns with green hair and bones in their noses speakin a language [older people] couldn't even understand* [. . .]" (NCFOM 295). This event, disturbing as it is to the older residents of Bell's community, is inevitable. Complexity cannot increase without generating greater differentiation. The game can run down, however, albeit not in the manner expected by Bell. Indeed, his complaints about the present and worry for the future mask a larger worry that time is running out altogether: in general terms, what worries Bell is disorder, including the ascendance of an economic force that commodifies everything and therefore ensures the continuing value of nothing.

Gell-Mann's complex universe includes not only the generation of greater complexity, but also perhaps a shield against such deterioration in overall order. "The second law of thermodynamics, which requires average entropy (or disorder) to increase, does not in any way forbid local order from arising through various mechanisms of self-organization [. . .]" But while self-organization provides for the possibility of local recoveries of relatively robust complexity, it proves to be no guarantee against entropy. "The era may not last forever in which more and more complex forms appear as time goes on." It remains possible that "in the very distant future" entropy will have its way with the fabric of the universe, essentially wearing away its energy to hold together, unraveling its complexity, and finally breaking the parts into parts of parts. If this happens, "*then the era characterized by fairly well-defined individual objects may draw to an end, while self-organization becomes rare and the envelope of complexity begins to shrink*" ("What is Complexity?" my emphasis). The return of eschatology in McCarthy here finds its confirmation in Gell-Mann's own description.

Gell-mann's model for complexity is one of subsumptive hierarchy, wherein lower orders of magnitude reveal less complexity, and higher orders of magnitude can reveal incredible complexity. Holden clearly describes the privilege achieved at higher orders of complexity. "All progressions from a higher to a lower order are marked by ruins and mystery and a residue of nameless rage." He goes on to make this distinction architectural. "For whoever makes a shelter of reeds and hides has joined his spirit to the common destiny of creatures and he will subside back into the primal mud with scarcely a cry. But who builds in stone seeks to alter the structure of the universe [. . .]" (*BM* 146). The judge's spatial metaphor reinforces his claims of anthropocentrism and more: a will to power that only humans might achieve. "The way of the world is to bloom and to flower and die but in the affairs of men there is no waning and the noon of his expression signals the onset of night. His spirit is exhausted at the peak of its achievement. His *meridian* is at once his darkening and the evening of his day" (*BM* 146–147, my emphasis). This is where McCarthy imputes a dramatic struggle to the model. Subsumptive hierarchy entails climbing as high as one can.

Anton Chigurh's role in such a subsumptive hierarchy is lower than that of judge Holden, for instance. It is unclear whether Chigurh knows the outcome of his coin tosses, whether he has been given (or already decided on) how the outcome of the toss will translate into the killing, or the pardon, of any of his victims. He seems merely an agent helping to create, if unable to access, a higher order of magnitude where more complexity—more differentiation—might arise; it doesn't even matter if he is privy to the level of knowledge readily declaimed by Holden, because he is not an agent of action at that level. Where Holden's argument to the kid may have begun with the possibility that he would convert him, however, it ends the same as the arguments delivered in Chigurh's much more workaday delivery of existential last rites: whatever your fate, do not question it by holding your hand in front of your face.

Within larger orders of magnitude oblivious to human will, such as a predetermined universe (not predictable, and yet retrodictable), it is possible to contain a smaller scale of reality in which free will exists. This can be true even if that free will amounts to nothing more than the illusional assertion of a will that may not, indeed, be connected to any outcome beyond the epistemological limits of the assertion. Below the order of magnitude that infers (or in the judge's case, sees) a complex play of both predetermination and chance that is beyond human epistemological limits, it is possible nonetheless to hold someone to an ethical standard of action. Even if it is in some way impossible for Culla Holme not to abandon his own son in the woods, and in any case then impossible for him to save the child, it remains his duty, at least, to name him. But he does not.

The order in the heavens, above the constraints and flights on the ground and present in every McCarthy novel, seemingly so remote, remains tethered to the human struggle of slaughter and flight below. But even this possibility, of finding relation between various interpretive levels in McCarthy, seems existential at best, in works that continue to refer to the ironic gap between what humans can know and what order there may be in the universe. And the role of God remains in doubt in these works. In *No Country for Old Men*, Sheriff Bell's collapse into jeremiad is unrelieved by anything but a reference to a cold center of knowledge unable, or unwilling, to intervene. When Bell asks his uncle, "Do you think God knows what's happenin?" the answer is "I expect he does." God may retrodict the branching fork of direction taken a million times by chance events, but this does not mean that "he" has any top-down control over that direction. So when Bell asks, "You think he can stop it?" the answer is "No. I dont" (*NCFOM* 269). This answer, however, even as it suggests predetermination, does nothing to assuage Bell's guilt. It is the price Bell pays for not having lost his faith in free will, and for not having the good, and very bad, luck of meeting Anton Chigurh face to gun.

McCarthy's interest in complexity and simplicity appears in his earliest work, where we see a world that at times can be understood as repetitions in nature, for instance, such as the seven-year cycles of flood in *The Orchard Keeper*, but that at times cannot. From the beginning, however, it is easy to note that the most reliable occurrence with which any of the characters comes to some recognition is death. Indeed, the weight of death, the regularity of it, and the degree to which McCarthy lavishes his most exquisite prose, led

Vereen Bell to his view that McCarthy's work is ultimately nihilistic. Since Bell's excellent readings, however, we have found increasing evidence to complicate (as it were) that view. Edwin Arnold's regular tracings of Christian morality in the novels, even where we would least expect to find it, provide one example. Nihilism and Christianity: how can these coexist?

One explanation comes from tracing those hints of alternative or non-canonical Christian cosmologies (such as Gnosticism), or of those from Eastern philosophy. This direction allows a more complex reading of characters and actions we might otherwise see in simplistic terms, such as Holden and the action of *Blood Meridian*. We might also now think of complexity theory as a means of situating a moral imperative to exercise guidance control. This may not differ radically from that form of free will imagined by much Christian thought, where God already knows what you will do. Such a mediated free will nonetheless provides the only force against eschatology and entropy. This line, too, arcs down, following the darker, more pessimistic strain of Christian thought that finds increasing evidence of impending apocalypse. Sheriff Bell suggests this when he points to "signs and wonders" (*NCFOM* 295).

The systems of complexity theory and of mediated guidance control, with their models of compromised free will, require McCarthy's characters to act morally, even as their ability to do so meaningfully remains severely limited. The influence of these ideas on the novels provides them with their frequent indications of order, predetermination, matrix, metaphors of the universe as a continually woven tapestry, and the actions of humans as coined and otherwise constrained. And the possibility for emergent order, as well as evolving progression to greater complexity, suggests something brighter than a wholly deathward eschatology. Yet, nonetheless, the freedoms of his characters to move, let alone to change anything in the future, proves to have been compromised by new systems for understanding the place of humans in a complex universe.

In moving from the cathedral of his youth to the halls of the Santa Fe Institute, McCarthy may have escaped one enormous system of constraint, only to find new outlines, however intellectually compelling, that provide even less room to run. The ultimate effect of these influences may have been, ironically, to strengthen the importance of story. Ironically, as much as McCarthy has avoided intellectual pursuits directly involving literature, his pursuit of truth in practically every other field of human thought seems to have led him back to his own pages, and to the importance of art. But if it has, it remains unclear whether he realizes this or not. As we follow the last arcs of his work thus far, it would seem his interest in everything but literature has only strengthened his distrust of narrative, of art.

MCCARTHY'S SENSE OF ENDING

Despite his apparent mistrust of most art as providing any power to ameliorate the suffering of his characters, McCarthy remains, obviously, committed to the power of the imagination. As even Holden urged, one must try the limits of human knowledge, assuming "the task of singling out the thread of order from the tapestry" of the world—or indeed, as we have seen, the universe (*BM* 199). Holden's "singling" means that yes, there is an order to that universe, if only in one thread among many. And he assumes we will succeed only through our imaginative power, as he later makes clear. "[T]he order in creation which you see is that which you have put there, like a string in a maze" can mean that our thread of order is wholly imaginary, corresponding to no reality beyond that reality which we also can only imagine (*BM* 245). And yet the judge's shift in metaphor, from the optimistic suggestion of the tapestry containing one "thread of order," to the less optimistic "string in a maze" (wherein we could be lost), suggests that even when our imagination provides us with a false means of direction, we my nonetheless find our way through our own predicaments. The maze, he implies, is also something wholly imagined: "for existence has its own order and that no man's mind can compass, that mind itself being but a fact among others" (*BM* 245).

The difference between the metaphor of the tapestry and that of the maze, however, points to the power of imagination as a saving grace in McCarthy. Indeed, unlike O'Connor, whose characters are struck with grace from God, McCarthy's may be left to no more than imagining their own redemption from a disordered and death-directed world. Here again, only a few of the main characters seem to move under that force with any success.

John Wesley, however conscious or unconscious of that force, may be moved by it. The image of the world turning through death seems not to be free indirect discourse for him, and yet the narrator's words suggest that he leaves behind a dying culture, even a dying world: "The dead sheathed in the earth's crust and turning the slow diurnal of the earth's wheel, *at peace with eclipse, asteroid, the dusty novae*" go on to union with not only the dead heroes of myth ("with Tut and Agamemnon"), but also with "the seed and the unborn" (*TOK* 244–245, my emphasis). That last phrase suggests the circularity of time that ultimately refuses meaningful distinctions between being an "unborn" "seed" and a "dead" human being. The "gap in the fence" leads John Wesley to a "western road" beyond that organic world identified, in my second chapter, with Carolyn Merchant's history of its demise in *The Death of Nature*. The "peace" of the dead belongs to another world from that in *Blood Meridian*, let alone *No Country for Old Men*, as from that great middle book we have traced the arc of small optimism downward.

This is not to say that the early books provided any more optimistic force than the most recent work. One might even say that McCarthy has more or less alternated his endings, between imaginative departures Westward, and entropic collapses of deathward recursion. Not until Suttree do we find another potential for escape, and then again with John Grady, as he "[p]assed and paled" conjoined with his horse through their single shadow, "into the darkening land, the world to come" (*ATPH* 302). That ending already commingles more of death with life than did the endings of *The Orchard Keeper* or *Suttree*. It hints that John Grady's "world to come" will be the "darkening" land already seen (on our calendar) by Billy Parham after the emergence of the false atomic sun (*TC* 425). But however tainted by darkness are the roads and the trail traveled by John Wesley, Suttree, and John Grady, their endings are linear: they point Westward, following a setting sun.

In the last two novels such progress becomes frustrated by story: as Billy Parham's journey leads him back to a bed in a shed-like room recalling that of his boyhood, the stranger implicates him in such a straining story that the efforts of the dream, and the dream within the dream, call up several protests by Billy. He actually interrupts the stranger's story constantly, not only for clarifications toward understanding, but out of frustration and suspicion. "You've told this dream before," he guesses. He interrupts with caution that could concern a dramatic problem, a problem of veracity, a narrative problem, or all of the above: "I think I'm beginnin to see several problems." He asks, "You sure you aint makin all this up." And he protests that, "I think you got a habit of makin things a bit more complicated than what they need to be" (*COTP* 270, 274, 277, 278). This last comment may even be read as McCarthy's guilty admission that his interest in complexity theory, and other means of furthering the tropes and twists of his philosophy through the last several books, indeed might impede the power of his storytelling. I think it does, and yet that power persists.

Neither Billy, nor we, can give up. Billy tells the traveler, frequently after he has just interrupted the dream, "Ándale," or "Go ahead," or "Carry on," etc., no less than twenty times (*CTOP* 270–282). At first he uses only the stranger's native Spanish, but perhaps indicating growing frustration with the involuted story of the dream (and the dream within it), he spits before the ninth "Ándale." The stranger, responding to Billy's complaint of complication, points out that Billy "is the one with the questions" that interrupt him, so then Billy says,

"Ándale *pues*," and then "Just get on with it" (*COTP* 277–278). After that, Billy's entreaties to keep the story moving imply his own need to move through the story, eventually to escape from this dream and what it entails: "Go ahead," and "Go on" (*COTP* 280–282). Finally, when the stranger finishes the dream and answers two questions, Billy's only response is, "I got to get on" (*COTP* 288).

We never see evidence that Billy has gleaned anything from the stranger's dream, except that his telling of it seems to compel the listener. It is another instance of mystical wisdom lost on a character while imparted to us. But the meaning of this dream remains notably opaque, and we now see that the fact of its telling seems as important as the dream; indeed, McCarthy here breaks the surface of the "dream" at least twenty times—and by "dream" we must refer also to story, fiction, and that world of the imagination given to us both in simulation of reality, and as an aesthetic extension beyond that reality. The price paid here is that the reader (and Billy, it would seem) are denied the direct pleasures of deep involvement in the imagination that the dream might have imbued, all for the cost of the point made (heavily) that storytelling itself is important.

McCarthy reinforces this last idea with the "Dedication" that, after Billy has fallen asleep under the care of Betty, truly ends *Cities of the Plain*, and thus, *The Border Trilogy*. This poem speaks to us more directly, and intimately, than the author had ever before spoken in his books. It is a daring poem precisely in its naïve qualities—it fails out of context, and barely succeeds at the end of its book. But, given the arcs behind it, it surpasses its individual qualities and suggests several of the preoccupations I've tried to address in this chapter. To best appreciate it as a statement in the larger arc of McCarthy's work, it helps to remember a previous, contrasting address by the author (or at least a notably personal narrator). First, the voice of the "Dedication" does not envelop us in language, as did the opening voice of *Suttree*. That earlier voice called us to see his places, rather than him: "*Dear friend now in the dusty clockless hours of the town when the streets lie black and steaming* [. . .]." Furthermore, once leading us into that time, those places, the voice opening *Suttree* leaves us to continue alone: "*no soul shall walk save you*" (*S* 3). By contrast, the "Dedication" speaks of relation:

> *I will be your child to hold*
> *And you be me when I am old*
> *The world grows cold*
> *The heathen rage*
> *The story's told*
> *Turn the page.*
> (*COTP* 293)

This poem's voice arrives entirely outside narration, and it cannot be Billy, Betty, or the stranger. Indeed, the word "Dedication" clearly suggests this is the author, Cormac McCarthy, in his most direct address. The simplicity of expression (the rhyme scheme and its solidity) and the surprising intimacy are completely new in McCarthy. All but one of the words is a single syllable. Only "*heathen*" suggests anything of ancient language. The rhymes are exact down to the last three letters, with only the initial consonant varying—or dropping out before "*old*."

In a reverse rhopalic, the poem begins with a promise that surprises both in its direct reference to a parent's relation with a child, and in the reversal of that relation. We might not be so surprised to see this domestic connection, as we have just seen Betty reassuring Billy that she knows who he is, "and why," and tells him to "go to sleep. I'll see you in the morning" (*COTP* 282). But the speaker in the poem is making the kind of promise that a child usually makes to a parent, not the other way around. It could be a promise made to a father—given the thickness of that arc through the preceding eight novels—or to a mother, given the surprising presence of the mother figure in Betty. Then the second line achieves remarkable complexity for such simple language: now the speaker moves to an imperative, a demand as a child might make it: "*you be me*." But the line ends wisely, "*when I am old*." Only a child whose maturity has reached that moment when his or her parents revert back to a child-like state of dependence can anticipate this reversal; the child becomes the parent of the parent, now become as a child. The speaker first promises, then, not to run from the parent: "*I will be your child* to hold," (my emphasis). This promise entails the hope that the intimacy of that relation will not disappear: when I am old, you must be the "*me*" that I am now—the child, dependent, trusting, and not running from that intimacy.

But these first two lines also achieve the decadent union I explored earlier, here bringing the parent and child so close as to conflate them. It is easy to read these lines and not maintain in one's mind exactly what the relation of the speaker is to whomever this poem addresses. I followed the reasoning that this is a child speaking to a parent, but it also works to read it as a parent speaking to a child. A year after the publication of *Cities of the Plain* (perhaps a little earlier or later), McCarthy's second son, John, was born.[21] Whether or not the author had in mind a future child of his own, the poem unites parent and child as in no other passage in McCarthy—until we arrive in Bell's final dream. Something else is accomplished here, too, that shifts the usual decadence attending such unions in McCarthy outside the relation of the child and parent. Indeed, here the first two lines maintain, even with the approach of individual death in "*when I am old,*" a relative comfort implicit in the promise and the demand.

Outside, however, "*The world grows cold.*" According to Gell-mann, "various mechanisms of self-organization" can generate "local order" of both simple and complex systems, creating nothing less than a countervailing force to the second law of thermodynamics. While "*the world*" may arc towards heat death, the promise and demand between one parent and one child may create within that space some small home. Such is always the conservative hope—and by that I do not mean "conservative" in political terms. This position, rather, resembles that in *Candide*: the world may be drowned in suffering, and we may have reason at hand for explanations, "mais il faut cultiver notre jardin" (236). Certainly, any interpretation of the word "*heathen*" suggests those outside belief. As the poem's "*heathen rage*" after the line describing a world losing its order and force to entropy, this line does suggest a religious sense—however we might imagine that particularized—that out there in the space of the "*world*" the unbelieving commit their violence. This stands in contrast to the tenderness of the small space of connection between the parent and child in the opening lines.

As Kermode reminds us, the end is always "immanent rather than imminent" (30). And even Gell-mann's theory includes a dying of the light through entropy: "The era may not last forever in which more and more complex forms appear as time goes on. [. . .] [T]he era characterized by fairly well-defined individual objects may draw to an end, while self-organization becomes rare and the envelope of complexity begins to shrink." That "end" may come, as Gell-mann hypothesizes, "in the very distant future," but its shadow reaches McCarthy: he has not found a "system," as Kermode called such fictions in Yeats and Stevens, that does not entail an end of days. In other words, as much as McCarthy may continue to find order and hope in his studies of complexity theory and other systems of understanding the universe, he remains a writer, and thus an artist acutely aware of the story's eventual end. It is a fact, after all, that Billy Parham's constant interruptions of the stranger's dream story work in generative tension with his regular enjoinments to "go on," with the result that the stranger's story is prolonged (*COTP* 280,281). Like a child afraid of the dark, the disappearance of the parent at bedtime, and what nightmares may arise in the darkness of sleep, Billy ironically keeps the stranger's story going, actually delaying Billy from "get[ting] on," as he claims he must (*COTP* 288).

All we have left, then, is story, and its arc, too, is already encompassed within a larger fate; its time transpires through that small rip in the fabric of what has already been determined. Story, therefore, creates time and space out of what has already collapsed. Always aware of its imminent end, its immanence demands constant renewal. Even as "*the story's* [already] *been told,*" of *The Border Trilogy*, and of the union of the parent and child, a new vision of that same union must be created. The speaker enjoins the reader— the father? the child? us?—to "*Turn the page*" to the next variation. Nonetheless, to "*Turn the page*" at the end of *Cities of the Plain* is to close the book, to accept an ending.

Chigurh twice asks Carla Jean if she understands why she is about to die: "Do you see?" Her response is telling, a plea that seems at once to begin to see Chigurh as a divine agent and to appeal to some other, opposing and benign, power absent from the room. First, she says "Oh God. [. . .] Oh God." Then she looks "at him a final time. You dont have to, she said. You dont. You dont." Chigurh tries one last time:

> Do you understand? When I came into your life your life was over. It had a beginning, a middle, and an end. This is the end. You can say that things could have turned out differently. That they could have been some other way. But what does that mean? They are not some other way. They are this way. You're asking that I second say the world. (*NCFOM* 260)

This refusal to alter the ending of a story that Chigurh insists has already been written by the past recalls Revelation.

The book of Revelation surprises a reader acquainted only with the distillations and redactions beloved by both the fanatically religious, and the cynically secular that use whatever bits and pieces of it suit their own narratives. The full book runs on and on, through more peripeteia than the worst Hollywood action film; it would exhaust special effects experts and whole teams of video game programmers generating baddies for a first-person shooter. The span of time recounted to John, even symbolically translated, far outruns any narrative of human scale—which is probably part of the book's purpose. Revelation regularly emphasizes the frame narrative (as it were) in which John is told, and shown (by both texts, and visions) what will happen. But the time span of the revelation itself, as opposed to the events described within it, extends no further than might a prolonged dream. One can read this story of Apocalypse that takes lifetimes to play out, all within an hour.

What this means for eschatology is that the sense of immanent, rather than imminent, apocalypse is not only inevitable, but also necessary. In other words, Revelation itself presents collapsed time: for all its regenerating peripeteia that shift the force of victory back and forth from heaven to hell, the entire story has already been written, as it were, and is only being provided as a vision to John. It turns out that only in simplistic readings of Revelation can Apocalypse ever be reckoned on a naïve calendar. That book's force finally resides in its narrative power—even as it strains through its prolongation of its own ending. The true end of Revelation reads like an author's worry against editorial redactions, deletions and additions:

> For I testify unto every man that heareth the words of the prophecy of this book, If any man shall add unto these things, God shall add unto him the plagues that are written in this book: And if any man shall take away from the words of the book of this prophecy, God shall take away his part out of the book of life, and out of the holy city, and from the things which are written in this book. (22:18,19)

Carla Jean's plea to Chigurh is a plea to rewrite what has already been written. After his third attempt to enlighten her, she realizes that she was attempting to "add unto," or at least "take away from" what has already been written. He has already explained that chance events removed any guilt from her particular situation, but those events had sufficiently "frozen" her fate such that it seems either way her coin lands, he must kill her—as each branching fork in her life still grew from her marriage to Moss. Chigurh even tells her, "None of it was your fault. [. . .] You didnt do anything. It was bad luck" (*NCFOM* 257). But that earlier bad luck cannot be undone by the coin toss. The seal he will deliver to her is both revelatory and cruel: "Yet even though I could have told you how all of this would end I thought it not too much to ask that you have a final glimpse of hope in the world to lift your heart before the shroud drops, the darkness. Do you see?" (*NCFOM* 259).

This question ironically reverses Billy Parham's challenge to God as he carries the dead body of John Grady, "Do you see? Do you see?" (*COTP* 261). This is the closest to grace we come in McCarthy. Her eventual acceptance that her fate had been already entailed upon her by the past, does provide her with one glimpse of truth that this dark novel suggests she could never otherwise "see." That she should "see" this truth is important to Chigurh, and he asks her a third—and final—time, "Do you see? Yes, she said, sobbing, I do. I do. Good, he said. That's good. Then he shot her" (*NCFOM* 260).

"Things separate from their stories have no meaning. They are only shapes," Billy is told by the heretic. This is after the heretic admits that he thought he understood God, and his characterization is echoed in Bell's loss of faith in a God that is involved in human life. "I thought that men had not inquired sufficiently into miracles of destruction. Into disasters of certain magnitude" (*TC* 142). But that is only one view of a many-sided reality. To forestall the End, the heretic also has to proliferate variations in the bird's song. "The task of the narrator is not an easy one, he said. He appears to be required to choose his tale from among the many that are possible. But of course that is not the case. The case is rather to make many of the one" (*TC* 155). The stranger puts this another way to Billy, "It is the narrative that is the life of the dream while the events themselves are often interchangeable. The events of the waking world on the other hand are forced upon us and the narrative is the unguessed axis along which they must be strung" (*COTP* 283).

This again recalls the distinctions Kermode makes for imaginative power: we imaginatively extend a fiction (a dream life) to approximate and transcend that reality that we have already only imagined. We follow the thread we put in the maze we imagined. What remains is to keep moving, to develop new songs for the bird, new "events" to string upon the "unguessed axis." As the stranger tells Billy, the dreamer saw that, "a man's life was little more than an instant and that as time was eternal therefore every man was always and eternally in the middle of his journey, whatever be his years or whatever distance he had come" (*COTP* 282).

This Zeno's paradox of time and space increases the need for narrative to enable constant forward motion. But we are constantly constrained. The heretic of Caborca, we are told, finally understood that, "we long for something of substance to oppose us. Something to contain us or to stay our hand. Otherwise there were no boundaries to our own being and we too must extend our claim until we lose all definition. Until we must be swallowed up at last by the very void to which we wished to stand opposed" (*TC* 153). This is Melville's pasteboard mask of God—whether or not we find anything behind the mask. It is another reason why, even if we find in another book by McCarthy that he has resolved and unified sons and fathers, something will have to break again, someone will have to run. To live in the middest is to live always in "perpetual transition" and this powers character flight. "Since we move from transition to transition, we may suppose that we exist in no intelligible relation to the past, and no predictable relation to the future" (Kermode 28, 102). This is how character flight looks like an exercise of escape, of freedom from time. Anton Chigurh can remind us how much we are entailed by the past, if need be.

But to keep his stories moving on, McCarthy cannot place his emphasis on that corrective power too much. *No Country for Old Men* narrowly manages an escape from that total collapse. After all, does not the killing of Carla

Jean suggest that McCarthy could easily have accomplished a much stronger sense of an ending by arranging Chirgurh to kill Bell? Such an ending would run darker than the book we have; it would realize more closely the narrative proof for the philosophical system McCarthy has appropriated and developed. Such an ending, however, would reveal that McCarthy's imaginative impulse had finally been outrun by his intellectual and philosophical system. By ending with Bell's dream, he avoids that danger.

McCarthy still seems to avow the power of fiction over that of philosophy, or religion, or science, to grant human beings some "final glimpse of hope in the world to lift" the heart "before the shroud drops, the darkness" (*NCFOM* 259). An apparent growing mistrust of art, however, at least in his past power to create beautiful, if violent, fictions, threatens to slow the flights of his characters until they must sit and be told of the larger forces that constrain them, and be handed false hopes in the form of pure chance tossed against the terrible dictates of fate. That "glimpse of hope in the world" once required flight, movement, even arcing toward death, before the moment of revelation. It remains an open question, how McCarthy may continue to find new arcs within his arc. It would seem that the force for movement in his characters has begun to give in to the dwindling space around them. New books will require them to move again, if only in dreams. But whatever we find in future fictions, there is no place for home, in deserts or dreams, when one must keep moving.

Notes

NOTES TO CHAPTER ONE

1. In the "Preface to the First Edition" of *Counter-Statement* (x).
2. See J. Douglas Canfield's "Crossing from the Wasteland into the Exotic in McCarthy's Border Trilogy" for a full exploration of vatic characters through an existentialist reading.
3. For a richer discussion of dreams in McCarthy, see Edwin Arnold's "'Go to sleep:' Dreams and Visions in the Border Trilogy."
4. See especially Guillemin's Chapter Two, as well as Holloway from 158 to the end of *The Late Modernism of Cormac McCarthy*.
5. Luce's "Suttree's Knoxville / McCarthy's Knoxville: A Slide Presentation," Arnold's "The World of *The Orchard Keeper*," and Morgan's "Suttree's Dead Acquaintances and McCarthy's Dead Friends," respectively.
6. See Robert Jarrett (78–83) and Vereen Bell (124) for fuller investigations of the judge as a parodic Enlightenment figure.
7. See also Stephen Tatum's "Topographies of Transition in Western American Literature," which includes a discussion of McCarthy's habit of presenting key moments of narrative import in scenes of transition, in his *Continuum Contemporaries: Cormac McCarthy's* All the Pretty Horses: *A Reader's Guide*.
8. Suttree seems to provide one example, and yet apart from his departure from Knoxville, the only thing that suggests he has experienced any inward change is the fact that the novel ends; claims of a magical reworking toward Suttree over the anti-Suttree are too numerous to enumerate, bur only the fact that he quits drinking suggests a real transformation.
9. *The Orchard Keeper* is a Bildungsroman at least as far as it focuses on John Wesley, *Suttree* is in the tradition of the novel of emergence from alcoholic dissolution, *Blood Meridian* is a dark example of coming of age under the tutelage of a Nietzschean criminal so extraordinary as also to recall *Faust*, and the first two books of *The Border Trilogy* are obvious—although

ultimately ironic—examples of the genre. For more extensive investigation of genre in McCarthy, see Gail Moore Morrison (176), as well as Robert Jarrett throughout.

10. When Captain White's party of filibusterers attempts a shortcut to Sonora, they do so by crossing the Rio Grande "del Norte" (*BM* 42) into some of the most inhospitable Mexican mountains near today's Texas border, a "howling wilderness" (*BM* 42) that rapidly dwindles their numbers. They are little better off than the Donner Party in trying to take a shortcut without roads to guide them.

11. Robert Jarrett places this book's chronology "within a relatively brief historical period that is impossible to date authoritatively but seems placed in the late nineteenth century during or immediately following Reconstruction" (25). While this is possible, neither the resonances of Reconstruction nor the lack of particularly twentieth-century elements (such as automated farm equipment, or telephones, etc.,) prevent the story from taking place well into the twentieth century. But although my reading of *Outer Dark* does not depend on locating its particular chronological setting, the possiblity that this particularly open book—with most of its scenes taking place at a much greater remove from "home" than the other Southern novels—might be set as Jarrett sees it makes it possible to connect its absence of barbed wire fences, for instance, to *Blood Meridian* as a nineteenth-century forerunner of more constrained spaces in the novels certainly set in the twentieth century.

12. To the editor's credit, these lines did not survive the extensive cutting required by the studio. Many McCarthy scholars believe that the film might have achieved notable artistic success without such cutting. Whether the full vision of Thornton and the rest of that production would have succeeded, or simply become a *longer* bad movie remains a mystery.

NOTES TO CHAPTER TWO

1. "Dream Work," but also "Teaching *Blood Meridian*" (260).

2. See also Carol Myers-Scotton's Introduction to the volume *Codes and Consequences*, in which Kreml's more specialized linguistics essay on McCarthy goes interestingly farther into that field than the essay in Hall and Wallach's collection specific to McCarthy, *Sacred Violence*. Myers-Scotton interestingly uses a qualified version of the term "intentionality" for what is to be interpreted in characters through attention to style.

3. I am particularizing my consideration of "setting" as the novel's "landscape," for reasons that should become clear through the argument.

4. (*TOK* 245, italics and capitalization mine). This follows the tombstone inscription given for Mildred Rattner and continues "[. . .] in these

three short years already a gray and timeless aspect, glazed with lichens and nets of small brown runners, the ring of rusted wire leaning awry against it with its stained and crumpled rags of foliage."

5. Edwin Arnold not only notes that the dismantling of this fence allows for the narrative of *The Orchard Keeper* to occur, but he also sketches in one of the first and most promisingly comprehensive arguments on the "intertextuality" of all McCarthy's novels ("The Mosaic of McCarthy's Fiction" 17). Matthew Horton's "'Hallucinated Recollections:' Narrative as Spatialized Perception of History in *The Orchard Keeper*" performs an interesting, if wholly different, reading of the prologue than I offer here.

6. David Paul Ragan, in "Values and Structure in *The Orchard Keeper*," claims that McCarthy's technique of "structural juxtaposition" lends the book clear moral values. Whether that is the case or not, Ragan's article is helpful in understanding some formal characteristics of the book.

7. This cat, of whatever type, remains mysterious. Beatrice Trotignon agrees in her dissertation, "Ecriture de L'Exces dans les romans de Cormac McCarthy," with Arthur Ownby's suggestion that it is the transmigrated form of Kenneth Rattner: "Figures de la culpabilité dans une littérature où l'ombre d'Edgar Allan Poe plane encore, les chats noirs hantent les nuits de Ownby (p. 59). Aussi cette superstition quant à la réincarnation des âmes en peine explique-t-elle rétrospectivement le rituel qu'il instaure autour du cadavre de Kenneth Rattner" (Trotignon, Chapt. III 25). Ownby tells John Wesley and Warn, "Lots of times that happens, a body dies and their soul takes up in a cat for a spell" (McCarthy 227). To my reading, *The Orchard Keeper* remains more uncertain than Ownby on this point. For now, I will simply call it a "cat."

8. Of course, this is a telling omission, as much as the omission of many women from McCarthy's novels as a whole. In *The Orchard Keeper*, though, this might also be read as a telling omission within the narration, inasmuch as the rules for when names are used seem to be written by the characters as much as by the narrator. As is often the case, distinctions between the *depiction* of a sexist and (in this case) particularly androcentric world, and the realistic portrayal of that world from a mostly male androcentric view are perhaps impossible to make.

9. If not, as Beatrice Trotignon believes may be suggested by the text, the murderer of his wife ("Ecriture de L'Exces dans les romans de Cormac McCarthy" Chapt. III 27).

10. The *OED* gives this for "constable:" "The chief officer of the household, court, administration, or military forces of a ruler." A likely etymology is also noted: Latin *comes stabuli*, or "count or officer of the stable." In the rural South, a constable is an officer whose jurisdiction overlaps that of the sheriff in the town and the game warden in the woods. Gifford's over-

lap is between the law of the town and its extension into the wilderness: he stalks Sylder, trying to arrest him for driving unrevenued liquor from one domestic space to another—on rural roads surrounded by wilderness.

11. It is also interesting that Sylder's second language—Spanish—is the one more likely for the McCarthy characters of the later, Southwestern novels.

12. The dialogue is given with the italics as Sylder *thinking away*, as it were, two men who stop to help him and nearly discover the body of Kenneth Rattner just after their struggle (*TOK* 43).

13. In the Vintage edition, this is a period, with the next line of type beginning with the lower-case "f" of "following." I take this as a typo and have substituted the comma here.

14. The much-noticed "optical democracy" passage in *Blood Meridian* is exemplary of this, and in addition to Beck, James Lilley makes similar connections in "Representing Cormac McCarthy's 'Desert Absolute': Edward Weston, Ansel Adams, and the Dynamics of Vision."

15. Frank's development of this as a chapter in *The Widening Gyre* quotes Wilhelm Worringer (in *Abstraction and Empathy* 38): "It is precisely space [. . .] which, filled with atmospheric air, linking things together and destroying their individual closed-ness, gives things their temporal value and draws them into the cosmic interplay of phenomena" (Frank 56).

16. See also Trotignon's linkage of "[p]arataxis and verbless clauses" with photographic detail (74, 75, 91, 92, 218, 286, 366 "Detailing the Wor(l)d").

17. The very significant exception to this is *Blood Meridian*, where McCarthy locates (and names in his title) that point in the arc of human interaction with landscape beyond which it is no longer possible (for anyone but judge Holden, who is superhuman) to live outside of time.

18. I use *prosopopoeia* here for a sense that the landscapes presented in McCarthy are lost to us—they are as importantly psychological presences on the page, as they are depictions of historical places. Their maps are, at least on even a careful first reading, unreal.

19. *The Orchard Keeper*'s first sentence: "The tree was down and cut to lengths, the sections spread and jumbled over the grass" (*TOK* 3, italics and capitalization in the subhead are mine).

20. I use "manmade" here and elsewhere only because the assumption that men do such work is a reliable, if problematic for some, feature of the novels.

21. Interestingly, Marxist readings of McCarthy (such as David Holloway's) pay as much attention to depictions of the fractured reality of late capitalism than to workaday study of what a character such as Sylder does for a living.

22. The passage also allows a metafictional level at which we may read this passage as a fence standing against critics—or rather to critics who have not tried their hands at writing fiction.

23. The experience of trying to pass carelessly between the lines of a barbed wire fence and remain unharmed serves as better evidence for this claim than any text. One may refute it "thus" but would be advised to do so gently.

24. "wood-dust" is an exceptional hyphenate because of the double "d" resisting the customary McCarthy Saxon neologism. The detail of the "palings" being iron, rather than common deadfall palings used with barbed wire, serves to heighten the sense of the fence as pure metal (without wooden palings) against the tree as purely natural.

25. (*TOK* 246, italics and capitalization mine).

26. Looking far ahead, I will argue that the implement in the Epilogue of *Blood Meridian* is a posthole digger.

27. And in the world of *The Orchard Keeper* women, when they are present at all, occupy a position more akin to animals than human beings—worse, when Sylder gets a good laugh at June's half description of coitus in the shithouse with the woman between him and the pit below the seat. Perhaps the most prominent "she" apart from John Wesley's mother is the cat, who may be her husband Kenneth reincarnated with a switch in both his gender and his species—who receives regular attention in close-stance narration (*TOK* 174–176) and her own brief chapter (*TOK* 216–217). This "she" is last clung to by the "faint musty odor . . . of the outhouse where she had slept all day" (*TOK* 216). From one pit to another, as it were.

NOTES TO CHAPTER THREE

1. The *American Heritage* gives "deranged" the following three definitions: "1. To disturb the order or arrangement of. 2. To upset the normal condition or functioning of. 3. To disturb mentally; make insane." While it is doubtful that Ballard ever had a "normal condition of function," he did presumably have some kind of "order or arrangement" before the auction. While it is hinted that his mental capacity may be insufficient before the auction, blows to his head do not help his condition.

2. Edwin Arnold notes that "McCarthy spends over a third of the book [. . .] setting up the *reasons* for Lester's otherwise unimaginable actions, creating a world in which such actions have a cause" ("Naming, Knowing and Nothingness," 53, his emphasis).

3. This, like most of the novels, has its main plot points based in the facts of the real world; the case was a local one in McCarthy's corner of Tennessee.

4. The name "Lester" comes from the surname for someone from the city of Leicester; Lester's name thus marks him as being from somewhere else. The name "Buster" is a nickname for someone who breaks things.

5. This makes a second significant plot point related to taxes in McCarthy's Southern novels: Marion Sylder's arrest for running bootleg alcohol is for

transporting untaxed liquor over roads that were built and maintained by county taxes.

6. The technique is regularly but sparsely employed in most of the novels, such as in the opening of *Blood Meridian*. *Suttree*, of course, nearly reverses the rule.

7. This, at least, may be laid against the charge of racism in McCarthy's works: he does tell the sad truth that some whites among the lowest of the socio-economic low console themselves that they are still white. Wherever McCarthy's characters fall back on this, it reads to me as a sorry self-consolation in a moment of shame, defeat, or extreme moral turpitude. More difficult problems are suggested by the use of the word "nigger" by McCarthy's narrator, when there is no reason to read the word as free indirect discourse.

8. The focus in these last details, on automotive and domestic constraint and Ballard's approximation of the domestic in the uncanny house underground, is mine.

9. Again, it is McCarthy's narrator—who is not at this point a member of the community but the omniscient narrator of the entire novel—who uses the word "nigger" rather than the word "black," which is more regularly used by that same narrator (*COG* 53).

10. "I learned—at least—what Home could be—" Emily Dickinson, Johnson number 944.

11. My argument on *Outer Dark* will venture farther than is appropriate here. There I argue that McCarthy—at least in his role as narrator—is at best ambivalent about children in most of his novels.

12. Again, I must point to the exception of babies, however, who are the true outcasts from the sympathetic realm of McCarthy's works—until the very latest novel.

13. Part of the definition for *Saint* 1a.

14. Luce sees the cave as central to the novel: "Lester's early life prefigures his cave life, and indeed the earthly cave of oblivion is Lester's environment throughout; his imprisonment in the cave after he eludes his persecutors is a parable of his whole life [. . .] and his release from the underground cavern is a 'rebirth' into the cave of this world" ("Cave" 191).

15. "Inasmuch as ye have done it unto one of the least of these my brethren, ye have done it unto me" (*King James Bible*, Matt. 25.40).

16. The criminal Rattner is also denied normal burial. Instead, his remains are simply "pass[ed] on to" a nameless "him who placed them in a clean bag of white canvas" (*TOK* 234).

NOTES TO CHAPTER FOUR

1. Jarrett argues that with the exception of the squire's black liveryman, *Outer Dark*'s setting lacks the deep legacy of slavery that particularly

haunts the "larger South" of Faulkner's novels. Despite significant racism, the Appalachian South of *Outer Dark* hardly saw the extensive system of plantations and widespread slavery that powered the larger antebellum Southern economy. Luce's "Hog Drives, River Ferries, and Local Squires" supplied the historical background of the squire in *Outer Dark*.

2. Rick Wallach, Edwin Arnold, and several others have noted similarities between the patriarch of *Outer Dark*'s triune and judge Holden in *Blood Meridian*.

3. Guillemin also cites Jerry Leath Mills as noting that the spoiled orchard kept by Arthur Ownby suggests "a fallen Eden" (289, Guillemin 20).

4. The word "scapegoat" fits these siblings as much as it did Ballard, though it may require us to assume that Culla and Rinthy once lived with regular social interaction in at least a less remote space than the novel finds them in. I referred to Jonathan Culler's explanation of that term in my previous chapter: "[t]he *pharmakos* is cast out as the representative of the evil that afflicts the city: cast out so as to make evil return to the outside from which it comes and to assert the importance of the distinction between inside and outside" (143).

5. Donne's lines from "A Hymn to God the Father," "But swear by Thyself that at my death Thy Son / Shall shine as He shines now and heretofore:" serve as one example.

6. Originally presented in a paper at the 2002 Cormac McCarthy Conference in Tucson, Arizona, my observations on possible connections between *Outer Dark* and McCarthy's life preceded this second Woodward interview.

7. See also Gary Ciuba's "McCarthy's Enfant Terrible: Mimetic Desire and Sacred Violence in *Child of God*."

8. This of course recalls Culla waking from a dream quite similar to this story, "hollerin" enough to wake Rinthy (*OD* 5). The wordplay in Culla's last name also returns with more obvious force in this phrase.

9. I am grateful to Damian Doyle for noting this conflation of the blind man and Culla.

10. Edwin Arnold puts this well in "Naming, Knowing and Nothingness: McCarthy's Moral Parables," when he argues that Ballard "faces his guilt with a courage not shown by Culla Holme" (55).

11. If one imagines a third novel continuing in this line, the father would have to be once again in advertising, or at least some more media-related profession that, in our time, is arguably closer to the "running" of life than the law courts, business, or government.

12. Of course, Lacan provides a powerful theoretical apparatus for understanding what I'm simply calling "disappointed male idealism;" that phrase can even be understood as a gross shorthand of Lacanian terminology. But I also mean to suggest that the differences between men

and women in the world may equally derive from social, economic, and political—and indeed, also physical—accidents of difference. Put bluntly, only a young man of certain means and education and physicality finds the opportunity to complain against the universe that it does not meet his needs. (Emily Dickinson, for example, knows the situation is too complex to limit her complaints to the scapegoating of other people, or even to her quarrels with God.) The one need that does seem not to have been met in the fiction of disappointed male idealism is the love of a mother and father. Lacan notwithstanding, it may actually be possible to at least alleviate a great deal of young male angst by simply changing the ways that mothers raise—and that fathers in many cases might begin to raise—their boys.

13. Nell Sullivan's "Boys Will Be Boys and Girls Will Be Gone," and her other writings on McCarthy, regularly make a similar point.

14. Nahum Glatzer, editor of *The Complete Stories*, appears to have been the translator of this excerpt from the letters in *Briefe an Milena*, Willy Haas, ed. NY: Schocken, 1952.

15. See Morgan's "McCarthy's High School Years," as well as numerous items in the *Knoxville News-Sentinel* on McCarthy.

16. Many critics and authors, although probably fewer general readers, have found McCarthy's work up to *The Border Trilogy* superior to those three books (Williams, et al.)—and so far, it seems, to the recent *No Country for Old Men*. With the death of Erskine Caldwell, McCarthy's editor through *Blood Meridian* (and Faulkner's), McCarthy seems to have moved toward more sympathetic characters. Certainly, *The Border Trilogy*, edited by Gary Fisketjon, has found a much larger audience for McCarthy's novels. But to the tempting idea that McCarthy's work has somehow become easier, three objections might be raised. First, the propensity for readers to "like" the young men in *The Border Trilogy* probably says more about the affective fallacy and widespread nostalgia among readers than it does about those characters. Second, McCarthy holds back more on violence in the *Trilogy*, rather than really providing us with more sympathetic characters. Third, it might be objected that in exchange for the relative darkness of the first five novels, McCarthy's development of a more extensive philosophical background for his novels—particularly in allusions to complexity theory, for instance—have added depth to stories that, at a glance, go by a little easier than the necrophilia and more regular violence of the first five books. In any case, given the stuctural shift I will analyze in *No Country for Old Men*, even the likely popular material in the opening of that book doesn't seem to have prevented McCarthy from taking that novel in an inevitably unpopular direction. Whatever the critical equivocation on the recent books, McCarthy does not seem to be looking for popular acclaim any more than before.

17. (*S* 113, italics and capitalization are mine)

18. In a conference paper, William Prather has also connected the descriptions of failure and waste in the Tennessee River to the realities of the TVA project divesting thousands of poor Tennesseans of their homesteads ("The River in *Suttree*"). In a note to his "Absurd Reasoning in an Existential World: A Consideration of Cormac McCarthy's *Suttree*," Prather also raised the earliest question I could find about a possibly direct connection between the fathers of Suttree and McCarthy, hinting that McCarthy Sr.'s work with the TVA may be important to an understanding of the book's focus on the river (114n). By extending that analysis, I am arguing that McCarthy's anxiety about this project has everything to do with the son and father trouble in the novel, and that the TVA's transformation of space in the Tennessee River Valley accomplished the most governmentally controlled displacement of people from their homes, and graves, in all McCarthy's work. Not even in *Blood Meridian*, where the forces of war preceded, and extended beyond—even as they included—the official codification of Manifest Destiny, is there the careful intentionality of the TVA, a project that absolutely required the vision and planning of an American government at its height of centralized power and with abilities of communication and management far beyond those evident in most of *Blood Meridian*.

19. This image recalls Suttree's guilt as a father himself. In one waking reverie this dual identity, of both troubled son and troubled father, surfaces in a momentary conflation of the two. He remembers a dream in which he sees his father and tries to pass him, but cannot. "Yet it was not my father but my son who accosted me with such rancorless intent" (*S* 28). So, too, does the "gross and blueblack foetus clopping along in brogues and toga" (*S* 288), a description whose neotony (this not-even-born infant wears a man's business shoes, and a patriarch's "toga") conflates both father and son.

20. Wesley Morgan has traced most of these and many other names to people McCarthy knew in Knoxville, in "Suttree's Dead Acquaintances and McCarthy's Dead Friends."

21. In brief answer to critics of culture quick to reject this phrase, I would simply point out that we need not accept the repressive definitions of "normal family life" coming from the fundamentalist right in order to imagine some spectrum for which this phrase might be suitable. Say, at least, a situation in which fathers do not abandon their babies in the woods, or devour their sons in outhouses.

22. On a brief visit to this same area under the viaduct in Knoxville, I noted that this concrete structure really does resemble a rather squat crypt. It appeared to house wires that ran out from its small door down the sloping ground and away in various directions, until these proved to be vines that seemed to wait until they had reached a sufficient distance away from

it before springing leaves. Perhaps too many readers of *Suttree* have made similar visits and attempted to crawl inside Harrogate's warming hut, as the area around it is now restricted by a chain-link fence.

23. For this reason, Chapter Five is fully devoted to larger, historical and philosophical, spaces.

24. Neil Campbell has also noted the judge's function as a surrogate father for the kid.

25. Arnold sees this question as the "thematic center of the novel" ("Naming," 60).

26. See Peter Josyph on the "forty-four" instances where spitting displaces speech in moments of dialogue, in "Blood Music" (173).

27. Toadvine has already objected more strongly to the judge, after the killing and scalping of the Apache boy (that Holden almost certainly also molests). He even puts his gun to the judge's head, cursing him to hell. But the judge seems to completely ignore this act of mutiny as soon as Toadvine's nerves fail him (*BM* 164). Of course, it is Toadvine's ethos that fails him first.

28. See Leo Daugherty's excellent commentary on the figure of the graver, in his "*Blood Meridian* as Gnostic Tragedy."

29. Robert Jarrett sees this continuing enactment of "the death, absence, or denial of the father" as a distinguishing characteristic between McCarthy and Faulkner (21).

30. At least, on a surface reading. Although Glanton holds the quiver of arrow shafts, the kid clearly suspects that Holden has somehow rigged the lots. This scene foreshadows the questions about chance and the coin tosses in *No Country for Old Men*: it is less a matter of whether Holden and Chigurh manipulate the lots or the outcome of a coin toss, than how the other party responds to its outcome.

31. A horse in trouble will follow another horse more readily than it can be goaded on by its rider. In a pinch, herd (or pack instincts) trump habits of domestication.

32. Indeed, granting his characters in battle a regular recognition of this is a favorite trick of Tolstoy's and Crane's. Only Hemingway, most notably, seems to take the lack of meaning behind the battle as a personal betrayal.

33. The *Suttree* version (286–291) reaches the deepest levels of dictionary diving in all of McCarthy, straining against the sheer bulk of the narrative surrounding it to insist on some transformative experience for Suttree. Yet, after the last of the Boschean nightmares has receded, we can discern no real change in Suttree. Perhaps unlike the kid, his quest resolves nothing. As I am arguing here, the change in the kid's actions is subtle. In both instances, instead of providing catharsis, these passages dissolve away like an acid trip: the vision quest momentarily renders beautiful sense out of the chaotic universe, but leaves the tripper with little more than a hangover.

34. I would suggest that here, as in *Suttree*, McCarthy makes the common move of late twentieth-century American literature of avoiding obvious structures of climax and falling action, as well as obvious moral solutions to his spare plots. When we read *Suttree*, as well as *Blood Meridian*, something important to the plot seems to happen in these mountain trials of hunger and hallucination. Yet McCarthy avoids epiphanies that are followed by a character changing his behavior too soon. As in real life, McCarthy's characters have transformative experiences that take longer to work a change in actions than we are accustomed to in less complex narratives, such as Hollywood films.

35. This is a characteristic McCarthy shares with Faulkner only by half: he grants the most simple-minded characters nobility of *feeling* and a nobility of thought in its earliest origination that is all presumably pre-linguistic. Faulkner then goes around high curves risking embarrassing crashes by granting those characters the language to directly reveal recondite thought. McCarthy usually maintains more caution.

36. Interestingly, the narration here avoids again calling him "the man" and finishes with "he" and "him."

37. Arnold writes that "he finally runs out of time" and is killed by the judge ("Naming," 63). He seems to me, however, to have had all the time in the world, but lacked the will—an ironic deficiency given the nature of the clay question.

38. Patrick Shaw oddly calls the likelihood of rape "a fate worse than death" (103) but otherwise establishes this reading through several connections to previous descriptions of the judge, as well as in close reading of this scene. Shaw's is the first full published exploration of this passage.

39. As these arguments revolve so closely around war, and other forms of violence that have so much been the specialty of men, it seems silly to use any but this gender-specific collective noun here.

40. "But when a soul fails to follow and misses the vision, and as the result of some mishap sinks beneath its burden of forgetfulness and wrong-doing, so that it loses its wings and falls to earth the law is this. In its first incarnation no soul is born in the likeness of a beast; the soul that has seen the most enters into a human infant who is destined to become a seeker after wisdom or beauty or a follower of the Muses and a lover; *the next most persuasive is born* as a law-abiding monarch or *as a warrior and commander* [. . .]" (Plato 54, emphasis mine). The judge, of course, turns this upside down.

NOTES TO CHAPTER FIVE

1. See also Jarrett, and Wegner ("'Wars and rumors of war,'" and *Overcoming the Regional Burden*), et al., on history and *Blood Meridian*.

2. Whether space outside the U.S. has been rendered into place such that wholesale violence on the level depicted by *Blood Meridian* does not still occur is

generally less certain. Most readers might agree that in equatorial Africa that meridian has yet to be definitively crossed. About the Middle East, we might find more debate.

3. I make this argument with more detail in "Identity across *Blood Meridians*."

4. Donoghue makes this claim, however, alongside a list of other possible "traditions" that ultimately excludes only "those of the Enlightenment and Christianity" ("Teaching *Blood Meridian*" 277).

5. Vereen Bell was first in print with this point: "Brown prevails because he is without scruples and because he is oblivious to nuance, to fine ethical discriminations, to social niceties. His authority is a power of nature" (117).

6. (Frye 586).

7. In Chamberlain he confesses that his absence during the attack was intentional. In the novel, this is not at all made clear. In any case, in the novel, the judge seems to accuse the kid of more than a literal desertion.

8. If we would imagine something like the drug gangs in *No Country for Old Men* as contemporary versions of the Glanton gang, we must note that even as they threaten anyone in their way, they serve (albeit through the sale of dangerous drugs) anyone who will buy from them. From their killings, they gain nothing comparable to the gang's scalps for exchange value. Chigurh, unlike Holden, seems to be encumbered by the gang-members he only provisionally works with.

9. *American Heritage*.

10. See both "Whose Story Is It?: History and Fiction in Cormac McCarthy's All the Pretty Horses" and the dissertation, *Overcoming the Regional Burden: History, Tradition, and Myth in the Novels of Cormac McCarthy*.

11. See Neil Campbell's "Beyond Reckoning" for a fuller discussion of the intersections of the Turner myth with *Blood Meridian*.

12. On *BM* 90, this describes Glanton, and occurs in nearly innumerable instances referring to the gang.

13. The resulting discrepancies between someone's conjecture about where a place was, and where it actually was (as one could argue now with a satellite, for instance) created odd conflicts. For forty years after the Compromise of 1850, a strip of land 34 ½ miles deep and 157 miles wide at the top of the Texas panhandle seemed to belong to no one. Eventually, Oklahoma appropriated this area now known as its panhandle. Often referred to before then as "No Man's Land," the strip was for a time home to Plains Indians avoiding reservations. "The Strip had its claim jumpers, horse thieves, and other bad elements, but the 'old settlers' often emphasized in later years that the Strip had relatively few outlaws compared to other regions, due as much to the uniformly shared poverty as to vigilante severity" ("No Man's Land").

14. In accounts too numerous to mention, Anglo and Mexican residents of the area called themselves this at that time.

15. See also Henry D. McCallum's *The Wire that Fenced the West*, and of course, Walter Prescott Webb's *The Great Plains*.

16. The Land Ordinance of 1785 was signed into law eleven years later, by George Washington, as the Land Act of 1796. As Rod Squires argues,

    [t]he Ordinance of 1785 has, rightly, been given importance as the first piece of legislation that addressed the question of how should a nation proceed to subdivide the land surface. But the provisions of the Ordinance were very limited, in terms of the area it affected and in terms of many of the characteristics so familiar to land surveyors. When a new government was established the Ordinance had no legal effect. The public land surveys were continued only after Congress enacted a Land Act in 1796, legislation that should be accorded more attention.

    In the spirit of abstraction that caused those insisting on "ideal lines" no "embarrassment," I will nonetheless refer to the original Ordinance. My point is that geometry ruled the geography. As McCarthy's practice also sets up striking chronological divisions, it seems fitting—because ironic—that by merely fudging eleven years, I can here point to the Land Ordinance as preceding McCarthy's Epilogue by roughly a century.

17. While the revolution was still in progress, wrangling over western lands persisted, as states that had extensive grants from Great Britain wanted to keep them, while states such as Maryland lacked such grants and therefore wanted a more equitable division through the new Federal government. Maryland's reluctance to sign the Articles of Confederation led the Continental Congress to a resolution urging these states to remove the "embarrassment respecting the western country" (September 6, 1780 resolution quoted in Goble.) That "embarrassment" has everything to do with the move in 1785, and more forcefully in 1796, away from the vicissitudes of land ownership according to precedents and grants arising without a larger organizing feature: divide things up neatly ahead of time and you might expect less wrangling over the spoils.

NOTES TO CHAPTER SIX

1. (*COTP* 179, italics and capitalization are mine).

2. An early draft of this chapter drew from a collaboration with Natalka Palczynski, a student in one of my literature classes at New York University. The paper was given at the 1999 International Conference of the Cormac McCarthy Society, in San Antonio, Texas. We since published an extended version of the article as "Horses, Houses, and the Gravy to Win: Chivalric and Domestic Roles in *The Border Trilogy*" (*Sacred Violence: Volume 2: Cormac McCarthy's Western Novels*). I have made every effort here to note contributions made exclusively by Palczynski that appear in this chapter. In general, wherever the argument

puts the trilogy into comparison with the codes of medieval romance and courtship literature, Ms. Palczynski deserves credit—as well as for helpful editing of the original paper. Except for the important addition of C. S. Lewis and Castiglione to our argument, the scholarship is mine; the original paper having been focused on *All the Pretty Horses*, nearly all of the remaining argument on the rest of the trilogy is my own.

3. See also Gail Moore Morrison: John Grady's "journey portrays him not solely as a modern day horse-taming cowboy [. . .] but as an unlikely knight errant, displaced and dispossessed, heroically tested and stubbornly faithful to a chivalric code whose power is severely circumscribed by the inevitable evil in a hostile world" (176). We differ here only with what circumscribes that power.

4. Witek's article preceded *The Crossing, Cities of the Plain*, and *No Country for Old Men*.

5. (*ATPH* 138, italics and capitalization mine)

6. "All the Pretty Horses and The Crossing as Picaresque Novels."

7. If one remembers the Epilogue to *Blood Meridian*, one gets another idea about those holes across the plain. Here, the poles move "east to west," perhaps pulled under the meridian of a bloodred sun.

8. The kid's accusation of the judge at the end of *Blood Meridian* echoes here with irony, as does Culla's of the bearded man in *Outer Dark*: here we are meant to protest this self-effacement, alongside Betty.

NOTES TO CHAPTER SEVEN

1. Whatever the politics of *No Country for Old Men* (which are not only more discernible, but more relevant to us, than those of the author), Bell's worries surprised me with their eventual ability to alter my thoughts. Noting the desperation behind Bell's sentiments reminds me how pain of loss and fear of uncertainty is, after all, a universal condition, reaching beyond binary arguments on whether Bell's particular pains and fears are accurately located by him, or what to do about them. As much as my politics might differ from *this character's*, I must recognize the validity of feelings prompting even those ideas I might find objectionable. Furthermore, this is where aesthetics returns as an important part of reading even a politically-charged novel: to expand on thought and feeling without particular requirements on how that happens, or on what thoughts and feelings are added, seems to me a crucial part of any aesthetic experience, and an authentic value in novels—whatever their more quotidian exchange value.

2. John Grady's self-conscious smoking in the theatre lobby draws the attention of the other patrons to this boy who "rolled a cigarette and stood smoking it with one boot jacked back against the wall behind," dropping his ashes into the jeans he has cuffed for this purpose (*ATPH* 23). The waitress at the first

cafe he goes into there assumes he must be in town for the rodeo (*ATPH* 20). In San Antonio, at least, he is a walking anachronism in 1949.

3. Compare this description, for instance, with the one of John Grady "settin" in his grandfather's office (*ATPH* 11), to see how important the masculine quality of wood and metal and leather and stone are to a young man's sense of strength, of family identity, and ultimately of security within a medial position that controls both domestic space and those wilderness spaces outside the young man's immediate surroundings.

4. Wallis Sanborn, and other hunters familiar with that area of Texas, had never heard this word used as a verb.

5. If I were falling for all this without seeing the underlying intent, I could grouse that cheap motel in that part of Texas would have central air conditioning for innumerable reasons, not the least would be the cost of cooling all rooms somewhat equally, let alone obviating the possibility of any one room having much control over its temperature. But again, realism is beside the point.

6. I am indebted to Wallis Sanborn for confirming this suspicion that despite Llewelyn's experience as a sniper in Vietnam (*NCFOM* 293), Moss is too far from his prey. His shot at the antelope takes an unreasonable risk that he will indeed wound but not kill one of them.

7. Holloway's discussion of the "utopian wish object" (20) might be extended here to argue that narcotics are the ultimate object that has no value except in their ability to fool a user into feeling that he or she has escaped a world of material exchange. If so, then mind-altering drugs become contraband closest to money in their almost purely symbolic value. This makes them different than other exchange goods. I do not believe that John Grady's idealization of horses means he has no meaningful relationship with Redbo. Drugs, by contrast, have no similar value beyond the same degree as money.

8. It might also be argued that in Bell, McCarthy has created a deeply sympathetic portrait of a man preternaturally weak in the knees, who—like most of us, outside of our dreams—simply finds rhetorical justifications of old fears and desires, without the possibility of recognizing how he is thus manipulated away from free will by his—and most of our—simple, non-heroic nature as human beings. Here again it seems ironic to me the combination of sly indulgence and vitriolic condemnation that Bell has received in the majority of the reviews of *No Country for Old Men*. Lester Ballard found more tolerance than this frightened man so old before his time—as if the neighbor who does not vote the way you do poses more of a threat than a murdering necrophiliac.

9. I am indebted to two conference papers here: to Stacey Peebles's "Bean, Bell, and the Efficacy of Texas Lawmen" for historical information on West Texas Sheriffs, and to Meredith Farmer's "Coining a new standard for judgment:

Cormac McCarthy's use of Complexity Theory" for seeing the undeniable "ant-on-sugar = Anton Chigurh" connection I could not see. I will return to Farmer's larger argument, which also partially informs this paragraph's sense of subsumptive hierarchy, in my concluding chapter.

10. This scene, between Bell and his uncle, is given in roman type, in the place heretofore reserved for action. This makes some sense inasmuch as this placement provides the uncle with the space of a character; we see him outside, as it were, the stricter confines of Bell's consciousness in the monologues. But the fact that this scene takes up a significant portion of Chapter IX signals the degree to which Bell must take over the book after Moss is killed and the generic elements of the crime novel have dwindled down.

11. Not to conflate Bell with McCarthy, but simply to again examine one connection between the author's life and his creation of a character, we might place this claim of Bell's again McCarthy's in the second interview with Woodward, that McCarthy's six-year-old son is "the best person I know, far better than I am" (104).

12. It must be mentioned that Freud goes on to restrict "woman" with the domestic sphere, as "guardian of the fire which was held captive on the domestic hearth, because her anatomy made it impossible for her to yield to the temptation of this desire." In case it isn't obvious, I find much of Freud's explanation simply bizarre: as often happens, it seems to be the case here that again we have someone thinking about a situation in which they have never been: standing in the cold dark around a communal fire that provides the only warmth and light was not a common pastime in fin-de-siècle Vienna. Freud may have found among his upper-middle class patients "how regularly analytic experience testifies to the connection between ambition, fire, and urethral eroticism" (37). But to put it bluntly, even among the toughest group of homophobic (and thus aggressively homosocial) men on a back-country backpacking trip, the first man to put out a fire if the matches are lost would not be allowed to think he has won some contest. I regard the irrational sexism (as much as the more outlandish and unlikely imaginative explanations) in both Freud and Jung as weaknesses—even sometimes fundamentally damning weaknesses—in their theories as justifications for the domination of women for nothing but accidental evolutionary reasons that become as oppressive as they do only through their reinforcement in culture. I use both of them here because it seems obvious that McCarthy, through Yeats, is playing with the same material as they were.

13. "They listened with great attention as John Grady answered their questions and they nodded solemnly and they were careful of their demeanor that they not be thought to have opinions on what they heard for like most men skilled at their work they were scornful of any least suggestion of knowing anything not learned at first hand" (*ATPH* 95–96).

14. It is even curious that McCarthy has made Bell's lost child a daughter. This fits with the shift in which Bell insists that his wife is better than him, the best thing to happen to him, etc. But everything we have as evidence of this remains in Bell simply telling us so—with one exception. Bell returns home from Eagle Pass to his wife Loretta, who has cooked dinner and "put on music, a violin concerto." Outside it is snowing, and Loretta reminds him of "the last time it snowed" there. When Bell finally retrieves the memory, he says, "That's nice," but he means that "music. Supper. Bein home" (*NCFOM* 136–137). The memory recalled by snow remains private: her smile seems not to point to the loss of the daughter but to some moment of intimacy between them. But the snow outside will be reflected in Bell's dream, where, no matter how "nice" it is "[b]ein home," he will ride off behind his father, two men without women. And the connection of snow and memory, especially as the memory's quality (sad or happy) remains mixed to the reader, suggests infertility and death, and recalls Joyce's "The Dead." I am indebted to Dianne Luce for this last point.

NOTES TO CHAPTER EIGHT

1. John Grady's father tells him, as if for the first time, that, "She left out of here. She was gone from the time you were six months old till you were about three. I know you know somethin about that and it was a mistake not to of told you. *We* separated. She was in California" (*ATPH* 25, my emphasis). Here, the father indicates some guilt in two ways: first, he did not tell his son what his son seems inevitably to have already learned "somethin about," and second, the separation of the "[w]e"—the parents—is said to have led to the child's abandonment by his mother.

2. I am grateful to Dieter Boxmann for a closer reading of this son and mother tension, particularly in the levels of Lacanian theory that could be brought to bear on a clinical understanding of that tension. Considering the absent mothers in McCarthy, Boxmann observes, "separation anxiety, violent counter-dependency, attachment disorder; it makes me realize no psychological theory has a conceptualization of the disavowal of the mothering function."

3. It should become apparent why, by "philosophy," we cannot hope to mean a rounded cosmology, but rather a set of regularly visited questions to which the answers will be so various as to seem provisional, and thus arguable. It may be possible—I will attempt—to adequately sketch a structure wherein several ideas and influences maintain productive relation with one another. But ultimately, I will argue that the imaginative force of McCarthy's art runs beyond any system we may find him entertaining.

4. In Act II of Beckett's *Waiting for Godot*, Pozzo explains his aversion to distinctions in time: "They give birth astride of a grave, the light gleams an

instant, then it's night once more." Pozzo then jerks the rope with which he leads Lucky, and shouts, "On!"

5. In this sense, Suttree's loss of his child with Wanda further mitigates his escape (*S* 361–363). He may brave the hounds of death by leaving them behind with a dismissive challenge—"Fly them" (*S* 471)—but it is already too late for his two children by two different mothers.

6. In case it has not already become clear through my arguments concerning every other type of "space" in McCarthy, I should simply state that despite my interest in human evolution and even culturally evolved morality (such as what we find in the kid's high country sojourn), I see no evidence in McCarthy that even the most woodsy characters are not irredeemably removed from the "natural world" in their consciousness, their unavoidable reliance on myths (at worst) and imagination (at best). McCarthy expresses a moving, and persuasive, sense that the loss of skills such as trapping, hunting, riding, and skilled manual labor in general signal a loss of important human potential for connection with, if through dominance of, the natural world. But he never allows us to forget the dividing line between humans and the natural world from which we have evolved: John Grady is never, even in dreams, a horse; Billy is not a wolf (despite his going on all fours to see them); these young men merely know how to act like them well enough to master them. Even Ownby is nearly killed by lightening—as vulnerable in the woods as are animals on the roads. For this reason, I see no "natural" arc important to McCarthy; the "system" of arcs I see in these works is suspended, as it were, between the arc of the most basic churning of geological shift, and the arc of the galaxy imagined as the limits beyond which human imagination loses all power. For a much richer investigation of the problem of the uneasy relation of humans and nature in the novels, see Georg Guillemin's *The Pastoral Vision of Cormac McCarthy*.

7. It may also be the case, of course, that McCarthy has consciously avoided the failure Eliot sees inherent in any art that fails to move beyond the artist's personal emotions.

8. Accounts of the death of Jackson vary notably, but this much is agreed on along the spectrum from the official account to most conspiracy theories. See *The Rise and Fall of California's Radical Prison Movement*, by Eric Cummins.

9. As the heretic of Caborca (the first one, who survives the earthquake) rides from Bavispe to Batopite with his doomed son, "[t]he boy rides in the bow of the saddle before him" (*TC* 144).

10. William Spencer first explored Suttree's character traits as suggestive of a social worker in "Suttree as Social Nexus," and as a bodhisattva in "Suttree's Unknowable Self."

11. William Prather has noted particular connections between the TVA legacy and McCarthy's descriptions of the Tennessee River ("The River in *Suttree*").

12. For a proper understanding of the extent to which John Grady and Billy move through a Mexico whose history they remain ignorant of, see Wegner. Holloway provides the most thorough understanding of John Grady's failure to accept the reality of economic forces that we might also consider part of the arc of history. With the exception of adding some work on the TVA to Prather's in Chapter Four, and my arguments on *Blood Meridian*'s Epilogue in Chapter Five, I have seen fit to leave this historical arc sketched in less detail than the other arcs; others have already provided clear views of the arc of history.

13. See Jerry Lembcke's *Spitting Image: Myth, Memory, and the Legacy of Vietnam.*

14. What critics might worry about, less than the politics of individual fiction writers, is the declining ability of readers to enter any fictional realm that does not, under the interview lights, dissolve properly into memoir, preferably one turned to suasion.

15. See the obituary, "Charles McCarthy, 87, Former TVA Counsel."

16. See Canfield's "Crossing from the Wasteland into the Exotic in McCarthy's Border Trilogy" for a remarkably full exploration of "vatic soothsayers" as existential figures throughout those books.

17. Several details in the brief scene between the "dark little dwarf of a whore" and the man insinuate impotence. First, they are handed a candle along with a towel by the "old Mexican woman" before they go upstairs. Whatever happens (or fails to happen) must occur in the space between that sentence and the beginning of the next paragraph, where the man already lies "in the little cubicle with his trousers about his knees" watching the prostitute. First, we're told that "he watched her," then that "[h]e watched her take up her clothes and don them," and then that "he watched her hold the candle to the mirror and study her face there." There is no indication of him doing anything more in the first incident of "watch[ing] her" than in the second and third. The candle—handed out with a towel and presumably therefore no longer than they would need for business (not long enough to leave in the room for another customer)—retains enough wick to contrast the man's body language. Finally, any assumption that he hasn't failed to perform fades in the defensiveness of his dialogue with her. When she tells him, "Let's go [. . .] I got to go," he attempts to remain inert: "Go on." When she protests, "You cant lay there. Come on. I got to go," he slowly gets up, and picks his hat up from the floor. "You need to get down there and get you a drink, she said. You'll be all right," suggests that he is not, and perhaps has not been, "all right." His reply, "I'm all right now," can be read in a number of ways, any one of which suggests that he has not been (*BM* 332).

18. Hirsch puts quotations from McCarthy's return correspondence in all capital letters, but as all quotations from *Blood Meridian* are also given capitals, I assumed that McCarthy was not writing his letters in this manner and

therefore I have restored lower case letters. Hirsch also omitted brackets for ellipses, so we should assume that these elisions indicate that this is the translator's selected redaction of McCarthy's full wording.

19. "Suttree's Dead Acquaintances and McCarthy's Dead Friends," by Wes Morgan, traced these connections.

20. For a critique of the inability of anarcho-capitalism (as defined by Murray Rothbard) to enact its nonagression principle—which does seem to me to inform McCarthy's characterization of interactions between city-states and scalp-hunters, as well as drug and oil cartels—see Frank Van Dun's "Against Libertarian Legalism: A Comment on Kinsella and Block."

21. John McCarthy, the son of Cormac McCarthy and Jennifer Winkley, is described as "a six-year-old" by Woodward's second interview article. This piece appeared in the August, 2005 issue of *Vanity Fair* but includes a photo of the author taken at one of the interview sites and captioned "photographed near the Santa Fe Institute [. . .] on April 28, 2005" (Woodward 98). *Cities of the Plain* was available to critics in page proof form, including the "Dedication," in April, 1998 (the book was released in May of that year). The "Dedication" therefore could not have been written with John, specifically, in mind. But it certainly is possible that the author already planned on having another child. In any event, the imaginative possibilities of the poem outrun simple correspondences.

Bibliography

PRIMARY WORKS

McCarthy, Cormac. *The Orchard Keeper*. NY: Vintage, 1993. [First Edition Random House, 1965.]
———. *Outer Dark*. NY: Vintage, 1993. [First Edition Random House, 1968.]
———. *Child of God*. NY: Vintage, 1993. [First Edition Random House, 1973.]
———. *Suttree*. NY: Vintage, 1992. [First Edition Random House, 1979.]
———. *Blood Meridian, or, The Evening Redness in the West*. NY: Random House, 1992. [First Edition Random House, 1985.]
———. *All the Pretty Horses: Volume One, "The Border Trilogy."* NY: Knopf, 1992.
———. *The Crossing: Volume Two, "The Border Trilogy."* NY: Knopf, 1994.
———. *Cities of the Plain: Volume Three, "The Border Trilogy."* NY: Knopf, 1998.
———. *No Country for Old Men*. NY: Knopf, 2005.

SECONDARY WORKS

Bibliography

Luce, Dianne C. "Cormac McCarthy: A Bibliography." *Southern Quarterly* 30 (Summer 1992): 143–51.
———. "Cormac McCarthy: A Bibliography." July 2004 Update. Online. Internet. Available http://www.mid.tec.sc.us/edu/ed/eng/biblio.htm. Accessed 17 November 2005.

Selected References on McCarthy

Anderson, Richard. "*All the Pretty Horses* and *The Crossing* as Picaresque Novels." *3rd Annual Conference of Emerging Literature of the Southwest. Special Session on Cormac McCarthy*. Camino Real Hotel, El Paso, Texas. 8 Nov. 1997.

Arnold, Edwin T. "Blood & Grace: The Fiction of Cormac McCarthy." *Common-weal*. Vol. 121, 4 Nov. 1994. 11–16.

———. "Creating McCarthy." Slide Program. *The Cormac McCarthy Society 2000 Annual Conference*. Austin, Texas. 10 Nov. 2000.

———. "'Go to sleep:' Dreams and Visions in the Border Trilogy." *A Cormac McCarthy Companion: The Border Trilogy*. Edwin Arnold and Dianne Luce, Ed. Jackson: UP of Mississippi, 2001.

———. "The Last of the Trilogy: First Thoughts on *Cities of the Plain*." *Perspectives on Cormac McCarthy*. Revised ed. Jackson, Mississippi: UP of Mississippi, 1999. 221–247.

———. "The Mosaic of McCarthy's Fiction." *Sacred Violence: A Reader's Companion to Cormac McCarthy*. 1st ed. Wade Hall and Rick Wallach, ed. El Paso: Texas Western P, 1995. 17–23.

———. "Naming, Knowing and Nothingness: McCarthy's Moral Parables." *Perspectives on Cormac McCarthy*. Revised ed. Edwin Arnold and Dianne Luce, Ed. Jackson: UP of Mississippi, 1993.

———. "The World of *The Orchard Keeper*." *Proceedings of the First European Conference on Cormac McCarthy*. Berlin. David Holloway, ed. Miami: The Cormac McCarthy Society, June 1998. (1–5).

Bailey, Charles. "The Last Stage of the Hero's Evolution: Cormac McCarthy's *Cities of the Plain*." *Southwestern American Literature*. Vol. 25, No. 1, Fall 1998. 74–82.

Beck, John. "'A Certain but Fugitive Testimony:' Witnessing the Light of Time in Cormac McCarthy's Southwestern Fiction." *Southwestern American Literature*. 25.1 (Fall 1999): 124–132.

———. "Filibusters and Fundamentalists: *Blood Meridian* and the New Right." *The Second European Conference on Cormac McCarthy*. Manchester: U of Manchester, England. 23 June 2000.

Bell, Vereen M. *The Achievement of Cormac McCarthy*. Southern Literary Studies, Louis D. Rubin, ed. Baton Rouge: Louisiana State UP, 1988.

Campbell, Neil. "Beyond Reckoning: Cormac McCarthy's Version of the West in *Blood Meridian, or, The Evening Redness in the West*." *Critique* Vol. 39, Issue 1, Fall 1997. 55–65.

Canfield, J. Douglas. "Crossing from the Wasteland into the Exotic in McCarthy's Border Trilogy." *A Cormac McCarthy Companion: The Border Trilogy*. Edwin Arnold and Dianne Luce, Ed. Jackson: U of Mississippi P, 2001.

"Charles McCarthy, 87, Former TVA Counsel." *Washington Times*. 17 Feb. 1995: C11.

Daugherty, Leo. "*Blood Meridian* as Gnostic Tragedy." *Perspectives on Cormac McCarthy*. Revised ed. Edwin Arnold and Dianne Luce, ed. Jackson: UP of Mississippi, 1993. 159–174.

Donoghue, Denis. "Dream Work." *New York Review of Books*. Vol. 40, 24 June 1993. 5–10.

———. "Teaching Blood Meridian." *The Practice of Reading.* New Haven: Yale UP, 1998. 258–277.

Ellis, Jay. "Identity across Blood Meridians." *Rhetorical Democracy: Discursive Practices of Civic Engagement.* Gerard Hauser and Amy Grim, eds. Mahwah, New Jersey: Erlbaum, 2004.

———. and Natalka Palczynski. "Horses, Houses, and the Gravy to Win: Chivalric and Domestic Roles in *The Border Trilogy.*" *Sacred Violence: Volume 2: Cormac McCarthy's Western Novels.* 2nd ed. Wade Hall and Rick Wallach, eds. University of Texas at El Paso: Texas Western Press, 2002.

Evenson, Brian. "McCarthy's Wanderers: Nomadology, Violence, and Open Country." *Sacred Violence: A Reader's Companion to Cormac McCarthy.* 1st ed. Wade Hall and Rick Wallach, eds. El Paso: Texas Western P, 1995. 41–48.

Garner, Dwight. "Inside the List." *The New York Times Book Review.* Aug. 7, 2005. Online. http://www.nytimes.com.

Gibson, Mike. "'He felt at home in this place': Knoxville Gave Cormac McCarthy the Raw Material of his Art. And He Gave it Back." *Metro Pulse.* Knoxville, TN. 1 Mar. 2001: 10–14, 16. 11 Dec. 2005 <http://www.metropulse.com/dir_zine/dir_2001/1109/t_cover.html>.

Guillemin, Georg. *The Pastoral Vision of Cormac McCarthy.* College Station: Texas A&M P, 2004.

Hirsch, François. "I find it very hard to talk about translations and about translating." *Cormac McCarthy: Uncharted Territories / Territoires Inconnus.* Christine Chollier, ed. Reims: Presses Universitaires de Reims, 2003.

Holloway, David. "Cormac McCarthy and the Search for Cognitive Agency." *Proceedings of the 3rd Annual International Conference on the Emerging Literature of the Southwest Culture* (privately distributed). El Paso: U of Texas at El Paso, 1997. 376–79.

———. *The Late Modernism of Cormac McCarthy.* London: Greenwood Press, 2002.

Horton, Matthew R. "'Hallucinated Recollections:' Narrative as Spatialized Perception of History in *The Orchard Keeper.*" *Cormac McCarthy: New Directions.* James D. Lilley, ed. Albuquerque: U of New Mexico P, 2002. 285–312.

Jarrett, Robert L. *Cormac McCarthy.* NY: Twayne, 1997.

Josyph, Peter. "Blood Music: Reading *Blood Meridian.*" *Sacred Violence: A Reader's Companion to Cormac McCarthy.* 1st ed. Wade Hall and Rick Wallach, eds. El Paso: Texas Western P, 1995. 61–68.

———. "Suttree's War of the Worlds: High Noon in Knoxville." *Suttree Come Home: A Cormac McCarthy Society Conference.* Knoxville, Oct. 2004.

———. "Tragic Ecstasy: A Conversation with Harold Bloom about Cormac McCarthy's *Blood Meridian.*" *Southwestern American Literature.* Vol. 26, No. 1, Fall 2000. 7–20.

Kreml, Nancy. "Stylistic Variation and Cognitive Constraint in *All the Pretty Horses.*" 1st ed. *Sacred Violence: A Reader's Companion to Cormac McCarthy.* Wade Hall and Rick Wallach, eds. El Paso: Texas Western P, 1995. 137–148.

————. "Implicatures of Styleswitching in the Narrative Voice of Cormac McCarthy's *All the Pretty Horses*." *Codes and Consequences: Choosing Linguistic Varieties*. Carol Myers-Scotton, ed. NY.: Oxford UP, 1998. 41–61.

Lang, John. "Lester Ballard: McCarthy's Challenge to the Reader's Compassion." 1ˢᵗ ed. *Sacred Violence: A Reader's Companion to Cormac McCarthy*. Wade Hall and Rick Wallach. El Paso: Texas Western P, 1995. 87–94.

Lilley, James D. "Representing Cormac McCarthy's 'Desert Absolute': Edward Weston, Ansel Adams, and the Dynamics of Vision." *Proceedings of the 2nd Annual International Conference on the Emerging Literature of the Southwest Culture* (privately distributed). El Paso: U of Texas at El Paso, 1996. 162–66.

Luce, Dianne C. "The Cave of Oblivion: Platonic Mythology in *Child of God*." *Cormac McCarthy: New Directions*. James D. Lilley, ed. Albuquerque: U of New Mexico P, 2002. 171–198.

————. "Hog Drives, River Ferries, and Local Squires: East Tennessee Culture in the Dreamscapes of *Outer Dark*." *The Cormac McCarthy Society 7th Annual Conference*. El Paso, Oct. 2001.

————. "Perspectives on the Appalachian Novels: Arthur Ownby in Smoky Mountain Context." *The Cormac McCarthy Society 2005 Conference*. Houston, Oct. 2005.

————. "Suttree's Knoxville / McCarthy's Knoxville: A Slide Presentation." *Proceedings of the First European Conference on Cormac McCarthy*. 1999. David Holloway, ed. Miami: The Cormac McCarthy Society, June 1998.

Mills, Jerry Leath. "Cormac McCarthy (1933—)." *Contemporary Fiction Writers of the South*. Joseph M. Flora and Robert Bain, ed. Westport, Connecticutt: Greenwood, 1993.

Morgan, Wesley. "McCarthy's High School Years." *The Cormac McCarthy Journal Online*. 11 Dec. 2005. <http://www.cormacmccarthy.com/journal/Default.htm>.

————. "Suttree's Dead Acquaintances and McCarthy's Dead Friends." *The Cormac McCarthy Society 2005 Conference*. Houston, Oct. 2005.

Morrison, Gail Moore. "*All the Pretty Horses*: John Grady Cole's Expulsion from Paradise." *Perspectives on Cormac McCarthy*. Revised ed. Jackson, Mississippi: UP of Mississippi, 1999. 173–193.

Oates, Joyce Carol. "The Treasure of Comanche County." Review of *No Country for Old Men*. *The New York Review of Books*. Vol. 52, No. 16, Oct. 20, 2005.

Prather, William. "Absurd Reasoning in an Existential World: A Consideration of Cormac McCarthy's *Suttree*." *Sacred Violence: A Reader's Companion to Cormac McCarthy*. 1ˢᵗ ed. Wade Hall and Rick Wallach, eds. El Paso: Texas Western P, 1995. 103–114.

————. "The River in *Suttree*." *Suttree Come Home: A Cormac McCarthy Society Conference*. Knoxville, Oct. 2004.

Ragan, David Paul. "Values and Structure in *The Orchard Keeper*." *Perspectives on Cormac McCarthy*. Revised ed. Edwin T. Arnold and Dianne C. Luce, ed. Jackson: UP of Mississippi, 1999.

Sepich, John. *Notes on "Blood Meridian."* Louisville: Bellarmine College P, 1983.

Shaw, Patrick W. "The Kid's Fate, the Judge's Guilt: Ramifications of Closure in Cormac McCarthy's *Blood Meridian*." *Southern Literary Journal*. Vol. 30, No. 1, Fall 1997. 102–119.

Spencer, William C. "Suttree as Social Nexus." *The Cormac McCarthy Society 7th Annual Conference*. El Paso, Oct. 2001.

———. "Suttree's Unknowable Self." *Suttree Come Home: A Cormac McCarthy Society Conference*. Knoxville, Oct. 2004.

Sullivan, Nell. "Boys Will Be Boys and Girls Will Be Gone: The Circuit of Male Desire in Cormac McCarthy's Border Trilogy." *The Southern Quarterly*. Vol. 38, No. 3, Spring 2000. 167–185.

———. "The evolution of the dead girlfriend motif in *Outer Dark* and *Child of God*." *Myth, legend, dust: Critical responses to Cormac McCarthy*. Rick Wallach, eds. Manchester University Press / St. Martin's Press, 2000. 68–77.

———. "In the Barroom: Masculine Space and Homosocial Bonds/Desire in McCarthy's Fiction." *The Cormac McCarthy Society 2005 Conference*. Houston, Oct. 2005.

Tatum, Stephen. "Topographies of Transition in Western American Literature." *Western American Literature* 32.4 (Wtr. 1998): 310–52.

Trotignon, Beatrice. *Ecriture de L'Exces dans les romans de Cormac McCarthy*. Diss. L'Université Paris 7, 1999.

———. "Detailing the Wor(l)d." *Proceedings of the First European Conference on Cormac McCarthy*. David Holloway, ed. Miami: The Cormac McCarthy Society, June 1998.

Wallach, Rick. "Introduction: The McCarthy Canon Reconsidered." *Sacred Violence: A Reader's Companion to Cormac McCarthy*. 1st ed. Ed. Wade Hall and Rick Wallach. El Paso: Texas Western P, 1995. xv-xx.

———. *Blood Meridian*: Online Precis, 1996. Marty Priola. *Cormac McCarthy Society Pages:* Blood Meridian. 12 Nov. 2002. <http://www.cormacmccarthy.com/works/>.

———. "Prefiguring Cormac McCarthy: the early short stories." *Myth, legend, dust Critical responses to Cormac McCarthy*. Ed. Rick Wallach. Manchester University Press / St. Martin's Press, 2000. 15–20.

Wegner, John. "'Wars and rumors of wars' in Cormac McCarthy's Border Trilogy." *The Southern Quarterly*. Vol. 38, No. 3, Spring 2000. 59–71.

———. "Whose Story Is It?: History and Fiction in Cormac McCarthy's *All the Pretty Horses*." *Southern Quarterly*. Vol. 36, No. 2, Winter 1998. 103–110.

———. *Overcoming the Regional Burden: History, Tradition, and Myth in the Novels of Cormac McCarthy*. Diss. U of North Texas, 1998.

Williams, Don. "Cormac McCarthy Crosses the Great Divide." *New Millenium Writings*. 2004–5 Issue 14. 12 Dec. 2005. < http://www.newmillenniumwritings.com/>.

Witek, Terri. "Reeds and Hides: Cormac McCarthy's Domestic Spaces." *Southern Review*. Vol. 30, No. 1, Jan. 1994. 136–42.

Woodson, Linda. "you are the battleground": Materiality, Moral Responsibility, and Determinism in *No Country for Old Men*." *The Cormac McCarthy Society 2005 Conference*. Houston, Oct. 2005.

Woodward, Richard B. "Cormac McCarthy's Venemous Fiction." *The New York Times Magazine*. 19 Apr. 1992. 28–31.

———. "Cormac Country." *Vanity Fair*. Aug. 2005. 98–104.

Young, Thomas D., Jr. *Cormac McCarthy and the Geology of Being*. Diss. Miami U, 1990. Ann Arbor: UMI, 1998. 9029392.

———. "The Imprisonment of Sensibility: *Suttree*." *Perspectives on Cormac McCarthy*. Revised ed. Jackson, Mississippi: UP of Mississippi, 1999. 97–122.

TERTIARY WORKS FOR THIS STUDY

Bachelard, Gaston. *The Poetics of Space*. Maria Jolas, trans. Boston: Beacon, 1994.

Barthes, Roland. Camera Lucida: Reflections on Photography. Richard Howard, trans. NY: Hill and Wang, 1981.

Beauvoir, Simone de. "Must We Burn Sade?" Annette Michelson, trans. In the Marguis de Sade's *The 120 Days of Sodom and Other Writings*. Austryn Wainhouse and Richard Seaver, ed. and trans. NY: Grove, 1966.

Beckett, Samuel. *Waiting for Godot; with a Revised Text*. Donald McMillan and James Knowlson, ed. NY: Grove, 1994.

Black, Brian. "Organic Planning: The Intersection of Nature and Economic Planning in the Early Tennessee Valley Authority." *Journal of Environmental Policy and Planning*. Vol. 4, No. 2, June 2002. 157–168. <www.interscience.wiley.com>.

Blackmur, R. P. "The Craft of Herman Melville: A Putative Statement." *The Lion and the Honeycomb: Essays in Solicitude and Critique*. NY: Harcourt, Brace and Co., 1955. 124–144.

Blue Velvet. Dir. David Lynch. Perf. Dennis Hopper. De Laurentis, 1986.

Boxmann, Dieter. E-mail to the author. 26 Feb. 2006.

Burke, Kenneth. *Counter-Statement*. 2nd ed. Berkeley: U of California P, 1968.

Castiglione, Baldesar. *The Book of the Courtier*. Trans. George Bull. London: Penguin, 1967.

Certeau, Michel de. *The Practice of Everyday Life*. Trans. Stephen Rendall. Berkeley: U of California P, 1988.

Chamberlain, Samuel. *My Confession*. NY: Harper and Bros., 1957.

Chandler, William U. *The Myth of the TVA: Conservation and Development in the Tennessee Valley, 1933–80*. Cambridge, MA: Ballinger, 1984.

"Charles McCarthy, 87, former TVA counsel." *The Washington Times*. Obituaries, 17 Feb. 1995.

Clemens, Samuel Langhorne. *Adventures of Huckleberry Finn: a Norton Critical Edition*. 2nd ed. NY: Norton 1977.

"Constable." *The Oxford English Dictionary*. 1st ed. 1982.

Culler, Jonathan. *On Deconstruction: Theory and Criticism after Structuralism*. Ithaca, NY: Cornell UP, 1982.

Cummins, Eric. *The Rise and Fall of California's Radical Prison Movement*. Stanford, CA: Stanford UP, 1994.

Deleuze, Gilles and Claire Parnet. "On the Superiority of Anglo-American Literature." *Dialogues*. Trans. Hugh Tomlinson and Barbara Habberjam. NY: Columbia, 1987. 36–76.

"Deranged." *The American Heritage Dictionary*. 3rd ed. 1994.

Dickinson, Emily. *The Complete Poems of Emily Dickinson*. Thomas Johnson, ed. Boston: Little, Brown and Co., 1960.

Donne, John. *The Divine Poems of John Donne*. Helen Gardner, ed., 2nd ed. NY: Oxford UP, 1978.

Double Indemnity. Dir. Billy Wilder. Paramount, 1944. Perf. Fred MacMurray, Barbara Stanwyck, Edward G. Robinson.

Eliot, T. S. "Tradition and the Individual Talent." *The Sacred Wood: Essays on Poetry and Criticism*. London: Methuen, 1934.

———. "T. S. Eliot." Interview by Donald Hall. *Poets at Work:* The Paris Review *Interviews*. Plimpton, ed. NY: Penguin, 1989. 27–45.

Evan, Charlotte. "Time was when the Wild West Danced to the 'Devil's Rope.'" *Smithsonian*. Vol. 22, No. 4, July 1991. 72–83.

Fiedler, Leslie. *Love and Death in the American Novel*. Revised ed., New York: Stein and Day, 1966.

Foucault, Michel. "Panopticism." *Discipline and Punish: The Birth of the Prison*. Alan Sheridan, trans. NY: Pantheon, 1977. 195–228.

Fox, John. "March 26, 1965: Sevierville's Last Great Flood." *Mountain Press*, Sevier County, 26 Mar. 1984. A5.

Frank, Joseph. "Spatial Form in Modern Literature." *The Widening Gyre: Crisis and Mastery in Modern Literature*. New Brunswick: Rutgers UP, 1963. 3–62.

Frazer, James George, Sir. *The Golden Bough: A Study in Magic and Religion*. 2nd Ed. London, Macmillan, 1900.

Freud, Sigmund. *Civilization and its Discontents*. James Strachey, trans. and ed. NY: Norton, 1961.

Frye, Northrop. "The Four Forms of Prose Fiction." *Hudson Review 2*, Winter 1950. 586.

"Gadsden Purchase." *Encyclopedia Britanica*. 1962 ed.

Gell-Mann, Murray. "What is Complexity?" *Complexity*, Vol. 1, No. 1, 1995.

———. "What is Complexity?" 2 Feb. 2006. <http://www.santafe.edu/sfi/People/mgm/complexity.html>.

Goble, Dale D. *The Myth of a Classic Property Clause Doctrine*. 31 Aug. 2005. <http://www.law.uidaho.edu/default.aspx?pid=80391>.

"Gramarye." *The American Heritage Dictionary*. 3rd ed. 1994.

Grant, Nancy. *TVA and Black Americans: Planning for the Status Quo*. Philadelphia: Temple UP, 1990.

"Hard-boiled." *The American Heritage Dictionary*. 3rd ed. 1994.

Hardy, Thomas. *Tess of the D'Urbervilles: Norton Critical Edition*. 3rd ed. Scott Elledge, ed. NY: Norton, 1991.

"Haruspice." *The American Heritage Dictionary*. 3rd ed. 1994.

Hawthorne, Nathaniel. *The Scarlet Letter*. Boston: Houghton Mifflin, 1960.

———. *The House of the Seven Gables*. Seymour Gross, ed. NY: Norton, 1967.

Hendin, Josephine. *Vulnerable People: A View of American Fiction since 1945*. NY: Oxford UP, 1979.

"Holler." *The American Heritage Dictionary*. 3rd ed. 1994.

"Hölle." *Langenscheidt's German-English, English-German Dictionary*. Berlin: Langenscheidt, 1952.

"Husband." *The Oxford English Dictionary*. 1st ed. 1971.

"Implicature." *The American Heritage Dictionary*. 3rd ed. 1994.

"Inculpate." *The American Heritage Dictionary*. 3rd ed. 1994.

Indiana Historical Bureau. *Land Ordinance of 1785*. 5 Nov. 2002. <http://www.statelib.lib.in.us/www/ihb/resources/docldord.html>.

Joyce, James. *Ulysses*. NY: Vintage, 1961

Jung, Carl. *The Archetypes and the Collective Unconscious: Bollingen Series XX*. R. F. C. Hull, Trans. Princeton: Princeton UP, 1990.

———. *Memories, Dreams, Reflections*. Aniela Jaffé, rec. and ed. Richard and Clara Winston, trans. NY: Pantheon, 1973.

———. *The Portable Jung*. Joseph Campbell, ed., R. F. C. Hull, trans., NY: Penguin, 1971.

Kafka, Franz. *The Complete Stories*. Nahum N. Glatzer, ed., NY: Schoken, 1946. 470.

Kermode, Frank. *'Notes Toward a Supreme Fiction': A Commentary*. Napoli: Annali Dell'Istituto Universitario Orientale, 1961.

———. *The Sense of an Ending: Studies in the Theory of Fiction*. London: Oxford UP, 1967.

King James Version of the Bible. 18 Feb. 1997. New Centre for the Oxford English Dictionary (Waterloo). University of Michigan Humanities Text Initiative. 24 July 2002 < http://www.hti.umich.edu/k/kjv/index.html>.

Kleinschmitt, Sandra. "Holle." *Encyclopedia Mythica*. 10 Dec. 2005 < http://www.pantheon.org/articles/h/holle.html>.

Knobloch, Frieda. *The Culture of Wilderness: Agriculture as Colonization in the American West*. Chapel Hill: UNC P, 1996.

"Land Description." *Encyclopedia Britanica*. 1962 ed.

Leach, William. *Country of Exiles: Destruction of Place in American Life*. NY: Pantheon, 1999.

Lembcke, Jerry. *The Spitting Image: Myth, Memory, and the Legacy of Vietnam.* NY: NYU P, 1998.

Lewis, C. S. *Allegory of Love.* New York: Oxford UP, 1958.

Library of Congress. *Continental Congress & Constitutional Convention Broadsides: Incorporating the Western Territories.* 2 Nov. 2002. <http://memory.loc.gov/ammem/bdsds/territ.html>.

Limerick, Patricia Nelson. *Something in the Soil: Legacies and Reckonings in the New West.* NY: Norton, 2000.

———. "What on Earth is the New Western History?" *Trails: Toward a New Western History.* Limerick, Patricia Nelson, Clyde A. Milner II, and Charles E. Rankin, ed. Lawrence, Kausas: UP of Kansas, 1991. 81-88.

London, Jack. *When God Laughs, and Other Stories.* NY: Macmillan, 1911.

"Man." *Langenscheidt's German-English, English-German Dictionary.* Berlin: Langenscheidt, 1952.

McCallum, Henry D. *The Wire that Fenced the West.* Norman: U of Oklahoma P, 1965.

Merchant, Carolyn. *The Death of Nature: Women, Ecology, and the Scientific Revolution.* New York: Harper & Row, 1980.

"Meridian." *The Oxford English Dictionary.* 1st ed. 1982.

Milner II, Clyde A. "Expansion." *The Oxford History of the American West.* Clyde A. Milner II, Carol A. O'Connor, Martha A. Sandweiss, ed. NY: Oxford UP, 1994. 151–153.

Milton, John. *Paradise Lost: A Norton Critical Edition.* 2nd ed. Scott Elledge, ed. NY: Norton, 1993.

The New Encyclopedia of the American West. Howard R. Lamar, ed. New Haven: Yale UP, 1998.

Nietzsche, Friedrich. *Beyond Good and Evil.* Trans. Walter Kaufmann. NY: Vintage, 1966.

———. *The Birth of Tragedy* and *The Case of Wagner.* Trans. Walter Kaufmann. New York: Vintage. 1967.

———. *Thus Spoke Zarathustra.* Trans. R. J. Hollingdale. New York: Penguin. 1982.

"No Man's Land." *Oklahoma Historical Society.* By Kenneth R. Turner. 5 Nov. 2002. < http://www.ok-history.mus.ok.us/enc/nomansland.htm>.

No Traveller Remains Untouched: Journeys and Transformations in the American Southwest. CD-ROM. San Marcos, Texas: Southwest Texas State University, 1999.

O'Connor, Flannery. *Mystery and Manners: Occasional Prose.* Sally and Robert Fitzgerald, ed. New York: Noonday P, 1990.

"100 Notable Books of the Year." *The New York Times Book Review.* Dec. 4, 2005.

Platt, Rutherford H. "Planning and Land Use Adjustments in Historical Perspective." *Cooperating with Nature: Confronting Natural Hazards with Land-Use Planning for Sustainable Communities.* Raymond J. Burby, ed. Washington: Josyph Henry P, 1998. 29–56.

Plato. *Phaedrus and Letters VII and VIII*. Walter Hamilton, trans. NY: Penguin, 1973.

Poirier, Richard. *A World Elsewhere: The Place of Style in American Literature*. NY: Oxford, 1966.

"Proprioceptor." *The American Heritage Dictionary*. 3rd ed. 1994.

Rosenthal, M. L. "Introduction: The Poetry of Yeats." *William Butler Yeats: Selected Poems and Three Plays*. 3rd ed. M. L. Rosenthal, ed. and intro. NY: Collier, 1986.

"Saint." *The American Heritage Dictionary*. 3rd ed. 1994.

"Singularity." *The American Heritage Dictionary*. 3rd ed. 1994.

Sophocles. *The Three Theban Plays: Antigone, Oedipus the King, Oedipus at Colonus*. Robert Fagles, trans. NY: Penguin, 1982.

"Spavined." *The Oxford English Dictionary*. 1st ed. 1971.

Spenser, Edmund. *The Faerie Queene*. P.C. Bayley, ed. London: Oxford VP, 1966

"Squire." *The Oxford English Dictionary*. 1st ed. 1971.

Squires, Rod. *The Public Land Surveys and the Land Act of 1796 (1 Stat. 464)*. 31 Aug. 2005. <http://www.geog.umn.edu/faculty/squires/research/RealProp/survey/MNSurveyor/Land_Act_1796.html>.

Tuan, Yi Fu. *Space and Place: The Perspective of Experience*. Minneapolis: U of Minnesota P, 1977.

Tuttleton, James W. "Emasculating Papa: Hemingway at Bay." *Vital Signs: Essays on American Literature and Criticism*. Chicago: Ivan R. Dee, 1996.

Turner, Frederick Jackson. *The Frontier in American History*. NY: Henry Holt, 1921.

Van Dun, Frank. "Against Libertarian Legalism: A Comment on Kinsella and Block." *Journal of Libertarian Studies*. Vol. 17, No. 3, Summer 2003. 63–90.

Voltaire. *Candide; ou, L'Optimisme*. André Morize, ed. Paris: Hachette, 1913.

Webb, Walter Prescott. *The Great Plains*. Lincoln: U of Nebraska P, 1981, c1959.

White, Richard. "Animals and Enterprise." *The Oxford History of the American West*. Clyde A. Milner II, Carol A. O'Connor, Martha A. Sandweiss, ed. NY: Oxford UP, 1994. 151–173, 237.

Willett, Jim and Ron Rozelle. *Warden: Prison Life and Death from the Inside Out*. Albany, Texas: Bright Sky P, 2004.

Yeats, William Butler. *William Butler Yeats: Selected Poems and Three Plays*. 3rd ed. M. L. Rosenthal, ed. and intro. NY: Collier, 1986.

Index

Made in the USA
Middletown, DE
26 July 2023